HUMAN GROWTH & DEVELOPMENT

4TH EDITION

Chris Beckett &
Hilary Taylor

SAGE

Los Angeles | London | New Delhi
Singapore | Washington DC | Melbourne

Los Angeles | London | New Delhi
Singapore | Washington DC | Melbourne

SAGE Publications Ltd
1 Oliver's Yard
55 City Road
London EC1Y 1SP

SAGE Publications Inc.
2455 Teller Road
Thousand Oaks, California 91320

SAGE Publications India Pvt Ltd
B 1/I 1 Mohan Cooperative Industrial Area
Mathura Road
New Delhi 110 044

SAGE Publications Asia-Pacific Pte Ltd
3 Church Street
#10-04 Samsung Hub
Singapore 049483

Editor: Kate Keers
Assistant editor: Talulah Hall
Assistant editor, digital: Chloe Statham
Production editor: Martin Fox
Copyeditor: Mary Dalton
Proofreader: Derek Markham
Indexer: Gary Kirby
Marketing manager: Samantha Glorioso
Cover design: Wendy Scott
Typeset by: C&M Digitals (P) Ltd, Chennai, India
Printed in the UK

Library of Congress Control Number: 2018954282

British Library Cataloguing in Publication data

A catalogue record for this book is available from the British Library

ISBN 978-1-5264-3647-4
ISBN 978-1-5264-3648-1 (pbk)

HUMAN GROWTH & DEVELOPMENT

Sara Miller McCune founded SAGE Publishing in 1965 to support the dissemination of usable knowledge and educate a global community. SAGE publishes more than 1000 journals and over 800 new books each year, spanning a wide range of subject areas. Our growing selection of library products includes archives, data, case studies and video. SAGE remains majority owned by our founder and after her lifetime will become owned by a charitable trust that secures the company's continued independence.

Los Angeles | London | New Delhi | Singapore | Washington DC | Melbourne

CONTENTS

LIST OF FIGURES AND TABLES

FIGURES

TABLES

ABOUT THE AUTHORS

Chris Beckett studied Psychology at Bristol University and qualified as a social worker at Bangor, North Wales, in 1980, going on to work for eighteen years as a social worker and social work manager, and then for fifteen years as a social work lecturer. He has had a parallel career for some time as a writer of fiction and is now a full-time writer. His novel, *Dark Eden* was the winner of the Arthur C. Clarke award for 2012.

Hilary Taylor trained as a social worker after studying English at Oxford University, qualifying in 1973. At the beginning of her career she worked with all service user groups, and later in adult social care, mental health, group therapy and family mediation. She then moved into social work training and education, teaching at Anglia Ruskin University and also working as an independent practice teacher. She also trained as a psychoanalytic psychotherapist, and now has a private counselling and psychotherapy practice.

Other SAGE books written by Chris Beckett

- Chris Beckett and Nigel Horner, *Essential Theory for Social Work Practice*, Second Edition, 2016
- Chris Beckett, Andrew Maynard and Peter Jordan, *Values and Ethics in Social Work*, Third Edition, 2017
- Chris Beckett, *Assessment & Intervention in Social Work: Preparing for Practice*, First Edition, 2010
- Chris Beckett, *Child Protection: An Introduction*, Second Edition, 2007

PREFACE TO THE FOURTH EDITION

All the chapters in this fourth edition of *Human Growth and Development* have been updated and revised, however, the major change since the third edition is a completely new element in the form of the linked online resource we have called Tangled Webs, consisting of a series of case studies, linked to one another and to the book itself. This increases by nearly 50 per cent the amount of written material that this book makes available to the reader. The Introduction provides details of the new material, how it links to the rest of the book, and how it can be used.

INTRODUCTION

Human Growth and Development has two parts. One part is a textbook of twelve chapters, which we will henceforth refer to simply as 'the book'. The second part is an online resource entitled Tangled Webs, consisting of extended case studies which have been written to give the reader the opportunity of exploring the issues discussed in the book, and applying some of the ideas.

Both parts together are an introduction to human development designed specifically for people studying for careers in the helping professions, such as nurses, social workers, occupational therapists, teachers and counsellors. We should be clear from the outset that this is *not* a guide to intervention. Inevitably, possible professional interventions are sometimes mentioned, but students will need to turn to their own disciplines for extended discussion of the interventions appropriate to their professions. The aim of *Human Growth and Development* is to help students develop the skills and knowledge they will need to gain some sort of understanding of the lives of patients, pupils, clients or service users, at different ages and stages of life and with a vast range of different backgrounds and circumstances.

So, while not a guide to intervention, *Human Growth and Development* is about the kind of thinking that needs to precede interventions into the lives of others.

THE BOOK

The book very loosely follows the shape of a human life, beginning with a birth and ending with a death, but many of the chapters deal with ideas and topics that are relevant at many different stages of life, such as bereavement, attachment and learning. Its focus throughout is on psychosocial development – or, specifically, psychological development within a social context – rather than physical development, though it is impossible to talk about the former without some mention of the latter.

The book does not aim to be an exhaustive summary of cutting edge research in the field but rather a collection of ideas about human growth which in our experience are useful for people whose job requires them to think about human development, not as an academic subject, but as a practical matter: 'What might A be struggling with at the moment?' 'Why does B always behave in this way?' 'How might C's childhood experiences affect the way she sees the world now?'

There is no exact science to answer these questions. In practice we have to rely to a considerable extent on imagination and experience, but there is a body of knowledge that can enrich and deepen our thinking, and we try to give some sense of it here.

Interspersed in the text are 'activities' which invite readers to pause and consider the topic under discussion in relation to hypothetical situations, or in relation to their own lives.

TANGLED WEBS

The additional online material – collectively entitled Tangled Webs – is a collection of extended case studies, cross-referenced with material in the main book, and with one another. These case studies and the discussion that comes with them, are intended to provide the reader with an opportunity to explore how the kinds of ideas in this book could be used to help them deepen their understanding of real-life situations. The book will refer to them from time to time, and the discussion of the case studies will in turn refer back to sections of the book. A more detailed explanation follows below of the thinking behind Tangled Webs and how this material might be used.

TANGLED WEBS: A USER'S GUIDE

 You can access Tangled Webs by visiting **https://study.sagepub.com/tangledwebs**
The following are some thoughts about how to use the materials.

OVERVIEW

Tangled Webs is a series of interlinked and extended fictional case studies about people who live or work in the fictional London Borough of Bexford. Unlike the short case examples in the various chapters of the book, which are intended to illustrate particular points in the discussion, the case studies in Tangled Webs are deliberately written to give a sense of real lives which do not fit tidily into any one theoretical frame. So these case studies are not designed to illustrate any particular model or theory, but it is hoped that they will provide an opportunity for readers to explore complex situations, much as they might do as practitioners in their working lives, and consider what ideas about human growth and development might help their thinking.

LIMITED PERSPECTIVES

One thing to notice about these case studies is that they are all told from a particular perspective or perspectives. When you read about the Veloso family, for instance, you will see that you are told about them by a social worker called Tracey and a nurse called Deanna (who have quite radically different ideas about the family's strengths and weaknesses). We think it's important to make the point that, when it comes to human situations, there is no such thing as a completely objective outside observer.

You will find that the people who tell the stories in Tangled Webs notice some things and fail to notice others, and you will notice that their perceptions are shaped by their own experiences and preoccupations, and sometimes also by their prejudices. We are not expecting you to agree with, or approve of, everything they say, or to take what they say completely at face value. Nor should you assume that the views they express are necessarily the views of the authors.

PROFESSIONALS ARE ALSO HUMAN

In particular we have tried to avoid depicting a world neatly divided into professionals on the one hand, and the people they work with on the other. So Tracey and Deanna give their perspectives on the Veloso family, but you will see that there are also case studies about their own situations. We've called the collection Tangled Webs because the cases are all connected together.

We invite you to think about how the professionals' own experiences and circumstances may influence the way they view the lives of others. You may like to consider how your own life experience may also shape your perceptions. We do not believe that, in the human services, there is such a thing as a completely objective position. Professionals are human beings interacting with other human beings.

MISSING VOICES

You may notice that there are many missing voices: people whose perspectives are not described in the case study material. For instance in the case of Derek Harrow, you will hear from one of the support workers (Rob) in the hostel where he used to live, but not from other support workers who (by Rob's own account) take a rather different view. (What would they say, if they were given a chance?) Even more importantly, there is also no material written from the perspective of Derek himself. Similarly, in the Veloso case, while you hear the views of two professionals *about* Xenia and her mother Estrela, there is no material written from the point of view of either Xenia or Estrela themselves. This mirrors the fact that in real-life scenarios, professionals often act on the basis of reports and assessments prepared by other professionals, and also the fact that professionals cannot see inside the heads of those they work with.

But it's very important to be aware of the missing voices. What might they say about what the professionals think about them? What might they have said about their own situations if given a chance? What might they want to mention which the professionals have not noticed?

WHERE TO START?

So, you have a book, and a set of fictional case studies called Tangled Webs. Where should you start? You have a number of alternatives:

1) Starting from the book

If you are the sort of person who likes to start with an idea and then think about how to apply that idea in practice, you may prefer to start with the book.

At the end of each chapter, we highlight two or three cases from Tangled Webs which we think are particularly relevant to the subject of that chapter, though you may well find other cases relevant too.

2) Starting from Tangled Webs

If you are the sort of person who likes to start with a practical example and use that as a basis for thinking about ideas, you may prefer to start with Tangled Webs itself.

When you go into Tangled Webs, you'll find are offered (a) a list of cases and (b) a list of topics (both of these lists are also reproduced here in the book in Appendices 1 and 2 (pp. 246 and 249)). So you could, if you like, simply pick a case and see where it takes you, or you could pick a topic, see which cases are particularly relevant to that topic, and then pick a case from there.

When you have read through a particular case online in Tangled Webs, you will see that, after the case material, there are five buttons, three of which are:

- **Questions**: This is simply a short list of questions you might like to consider. It's important to remember that this is not an exhaustive list. You may well be able to think of better questions than we have done. (You may even want to question our questions.) But we do suggest you go through the questions before reading further.
- **Emerging themes**: These are our thoughts about some of the main themes and issues. Again, this doesn't necessarily cover all the themes to be found in the case, or even necessarily the most important ones. They are simply the themes that struck us, and we have our own preoccupations and blind spots the same as anyone else. But you can use them as a starting point for thinking about the case if that is helpful.
- **Concepts of Human Growth and Development**: This suggests ideas and theories from the book, which we think are relevant to the case study. This is a way back into the book because we give page references. (We will also occasionally point you in the direction of other sources of information.) Of course you may feel that there are concepts which we have not mentioned, in which case you could use the index of the book to see what, if anything, we have to say about them.

So one way of using Tangled Webs is to start with cases and use them to introduce you to ideas in the book, and then follow them up in the book itself.

Hopping from case to case

As well as including references to the book and other literature, the cases also include links to one another, so another thing you can do with Tangled Webs is to jump sideways between cases, exploring connections, differences and common themes.

THEORY/PRACTICE

What Tangled Webs is really trying to do is to let you practise the skill of linking theory and practice. We do emphasise, though, that these are imaginary cases, and, while we have tried to give some sense of the complexity of real-life situations, they are not real life, and real life is something else again.

THE BIRTH OF A HUMAN BEING

WHAT MAKES US WHO WE ARE?

CONTENTS

TANGLED WEBS

If you'd like to look at some cases before reading this chapter, two cases you could look at are: **Derek Harrow (Case B: Rob Thomas and Derek Harrow)** and **the Veloso Family (Case I)**. But you could pick almost any one of the Tangled Web cases and ask yourself 'What has made this person how they are?' Or in the case of children, you could ask, 'How will the experiences they are having now, affect the way they grow up?'

 You can access Tangled Webs by visiting **https://study.sagepub.com/tangledwebs**

In a delivery room in a maternity hospital, a mother is about to give birth after an eight-hour labour. There are four people present: the mother herself, the baby's father, a midwife and a doctor. Everyone is trying to encourage the exhausted mother ('Keep pushing!', 'You're almost there!', 'Don't forget your breathing!').

Then the father shouts out excitedly, 'I can see its head!'

Suddenly, a fifth human being is in the room, a stranger, a new being that no one has ever seen before (though across the world four new babies are born every second).

'It's a girl!' says the midwife.

It's about the only thing they can tell about her at this stage (a fact that many people these days know before the baby is even born). But soon they will weigh her and then there will be another fact to tell the relatives over the phone. If she had some obvious physical abnormality – a missing limb, a harelip, a spinal deformity – that would of course be another thing that they could see, and something that might drastically alter their initial response (see Chapter 8). But apart from that, what else can they know about her?

Even her future appearance can't really be discerned from the wizened ancient-looking little face (however much they may tell themselves she has her father's eyes, her mother's chin), let alone her future personality, her future abilities, her future life story.

What will she become? Will she be the prime minister or an office cleaner? Will she be happy? Will she be healthy? Will she be loved? Will she win honours or commit crimes? Will she one day be in a place like this bringing her own baby into the world?

It is impossible to tell.

What is it that determines what sort of person we become? Is a child's future personality already determined at birth, or is a newborn baby like a blank sheet, waiting to be written on by life? Or do we choose for ourselves who we are, create ourselves out of nothing? These are important questions, not only from an academic point of view, but also from a very practical one, because our views on these questions radically affect the way we see the world and our attitudes to other people.

In this chapter we will provide an overview of the sorts of questions that we will be exploring in this book. To begin with, we will ask you to look at your own ideas and assumptions about what makes people who they are, as it is really those ideas and assumptions which will either be validated or called into question by what you read here. We will also offer a 'health warning' about theories. Fortunately or unfortunately, no theory about human life can ever be completely objective or value free. Trying to see ourselves completely objectively is a bit like trying to catch a glimpse of your mirror image when it's not looking at you.

We will then look at two very old questions. The first of these can be summed up as 'nature or nurture'. To what extent is who we are determined at birth and to what extent are we shaped by the environment we live in? Under this heading we will discuss the factors, both inherited and environmental, that contribute to human development, and consider how these factors interact.

The second question has been debated by philosophers for thousands of years: the question of 'free will' versus 'predetermination'. To what extent are we free to choose our own lives, and to what extent are our apparent choices dictated by our previous histories?

Finally, we will mention the events that typically mark the turning points in our lives, the transitions that we all have to go through as we adjust to new circumstances and new life stages, and we will touch on the concept of personal resilience.

IDEAS, THEORIES AND PREJUDICES

It isn't only psychologists and philosophers who like to come up with theories about what makes people who they are. All of us have been studying other people all our lives, for we need to understand other people in order to work out how best to deal with them. How to make friends, how to bring up our children, how to get others to cooperate with us, how to get over painful experiences – all of these everyday questions, and many more, require us to have ideas about 'what makes people tick'. And most of us find this a fascinating question anyway. Why else do we watch and talk about reality shows on TV? Why do we spend so much time discussing the people we know, and the characters in novels and films? But our ideas about 'what makes people tick' don't emerge out of nothing and they are not really our own original thoughts. All our lives we are exposed to the ideas of others and to the 'accepted wisdom' of the society in which we live, and of the various subgroups to which we belong. So we all have an enormous store of ideas, theories, information and, undoubtedly, misinformation in our heads about what makes people what they are.

The following activity is intended to highlight some of your own personal ideas and assumptions about what shapes people's lives.

Activity 1.1

The following are some types of dangerous or antisocial behaviour which you might encounter, either directly, or in the news. Why do people behave in these ways? Jot down a few thoughts for each:

- two parents spend almost all the family income on heroin, leaving hardly any money for food or clothes for the children
- a woman violently assaults her husband
- a 12-year-old boy gets hold of a gun and goes on a shooting spree at school with the intention of killing as many of his fellow-pupils as he can
- an adult breaks the arm of a toddler in an outburst of rage
- a young man becomes a suicide bomber and kills himself and 20 others in a railway station
- a group of men rob a bank at gunpoint, seriously injuring a bank employee
- an adult deliberately torments a child by threatening him with humiliation and violence

(Continued)

(Continued)

- a man violently assaults his wife
- an elderly woman steals from a shop
- a politician accepts a bribe
- a child sets a cat on fire
- a soldier has himself photographed with his foot on the head of a naked prisoner of war
- an adult sexually abuses a child.

Comments on Activity 1.1

If you look at your answers, you may find that they fall into a number of different categories. In some cases, your answer may constitute a moral judgement: 'greed', 'selfishness' and so on. (A lot of people might describe corrupt politicians as greedy, for example, and regard that as sufficient explanation for their behaviour.) In other cases, you may have explained the behaviour in quasi-medical terms, without any moral judgement. (You might describe the boy who goes on a shooting spree as being emotionally disturbed or having some kind of mental illness, or the drug-abusing parents as having their thinking distorted by addiction.) Or, in some cases, you may have used past events to account for behaviour. (Perhaps you thought that a child who torments animals has probably been mistreated in some way herself, or that the woman who assaulted her husband may be responding to cruelty or mistreatment on his part.)

In short, in some cases, you will have been inclined to say that there is a reason which accounts for the behaviour and to some extent 'excuses' it, whereas in other cases you will have been more inclined to say that the behaviour is simply 'bad'. And you may or may not have taken into account the wider social and cultural context of the behaviour. For example, the ease with which the 12-year old can obtain the gun for his enterprise will depend on the gun control policies of the country in which he lives. The soldier and the suicide bomber may be influenced by prevailing cultural norms that demonise the enemy in the conflict, seeing them as less than human, and the suicide bomber may also be acting in the sincere belief that he is furthering a political or religious cause.

Actually which behaviour we choose to view in purely moral terms, and which behaviour we choose to understand in terms of external or internal causes, is probably quite an arbitrary distinction which is as much to do with our own personal circumstances as anything else. If you are a smoker, or if you use or have used illegal drugs, you may find drug addiction relatively easy to understand. Whether you are a man or a woman may well affect your attitude to several of the behaviours described. Parents are often more understanding than non-parents, of people who injure their children in a rage, because most parents have experienced such rages, even if they have not acted on them.

Most of us are more tolerant of 'crimes of passion' than of premeditated crimes, such as sexually abusing children or accepting bribes. And yet if we have experience of compulsive behaviour of some sort (even if it is only, say, a compulsion to buy cigarettes or play computer games), we may have personal experience that tells us that a person who appears to act coldly and rationally may in fact be driven in some way. A corrupt politician who accepts bribes is greedy, yes, but why are some greedy in that way and others not at all? If it is sufficient explanation to describe the corrupt politician as 'greedy', why is it not sufficient explanation to describe the child who torments animals as simply 'wicked'? Our personal theories and ideas about why people are as they are and behave as they behave, are often quite inconsistent and arbitrary, based on our own experience and on our own needs.

A 'health warning' about theories

Our own personal position influences the way we see the world. For instance, we are more likely to explain our own behaviour in terms of circumstances, but more likely to explain the behaviour of others in terms of their own personal qualities. (If we make a mistake at work we may see it as being due to the amount of pressure we are under, but if someone else makes a mistake, we will be more inclined to view this as evidence that they are lazy, or bad at their job, or inefficient.) This is a well-known phenomenon which psychologists call the 'fundamental attribution error' (Fiske and Taylor, 2017: 175; Reber, 2004: 155).

No theory about human beings, whether it is a homespun one we made up ourselves or one that is in a textbook, can be completely free of such biases. Things look different depending on our perspective, and on the dominant ideology of the society in which we live.

What is a theory?

A theory is an organised, coherent set of ideas that offers an explanation for something we observe or experience. In science, a theory can be tested against evidence to see if the explanation it offers is an adequate one. Some theories are easier to test against evidence than others, and the nature of evidence is itself a complex question. What constitutes evidence? Who is collecting it? What assumptions do they bring with them? How is it collected? What is the context? A theory is useful because it offers a map, a way of making sense of something. But the map is not the same as the territory. Consider the London Underground map, which has helped generations of Londoners and visitors to navigate their way around the capital since it was designed by Harry Beck in 1931. It is a classic of graphic design and clarity, but in order to achieve this it simplifies and distorts the actual geography of London. If one wants to really get to know London, as opposed to passing through it easily, one needs to walk its streets. Theory is a helpful guide and an orientation to the newcomer, but it cannot be mapped directly onto practice. We also need to learn through experience.

In this book we will look at theories which offer explanations of different aspects of human development. Research and thinking in this area is ongoing, especially in neuroscience and genetics. We do not claim to be able to cover all the newest developments. But we will examine classic theories which have proved useful and influential in the past, and encourage you to think critically about what they can teach us today.

All the ideas and theories we are going to discuss in this book contain assumptions which can be challenged. Among the assumptions you will notice and may wish to question, you will find:

- assumptions about the roles of men and women
- assumptions that take heterosexuality as the norm and do not recognise that there are many different ways in which sexuality can be expressed (these can be termed 'heteronormative' assumptions)
- assumptions that North American/European society is somehow the norm for the whole world (these are called 'Eurocentric' assumptions)
- assumptions that ideas derived from the study of prosperous middle-class people are necessarily relevant to people from different backgrounds.

As authors we try to avoid biases of this kind – or at least to acknowledge them – but we are doubtless guilty of them all the same. We offer a male and a female perspective, but we are both white, middle-class, and in our sixties (which, depending on your perspective, you might call 'old').

Many ideas have been widely accepted in the past, which we now would regard as obviously untrue. For instance, well into the twentieth century, there was a wide consensus among men in Britain, America and many other countries that women should not be allowed to choose the government of their own country. Sexism is still with us in many forms, of course, but there are very few people in any of those countries now who would seriously argue that women should not have the vote. Yet, less than a century ago, this was seen by many as a perfectly sensible and reasonable position to take.

So an idea can become generally accepted and even regarded as 'common sense', when it suits vested interests in society to accept that idea as 'true':

> Each society has its regime of truth, its 'general politics' of truth: that is, the types of discourse which it accepts and makes function as true; the mechanisms and instances which enable one to distinguish true and false statements … the status of those who are charged with saying what counts as true. (Foucault, 1980: 131)

It is naïve to think that everything people thought in the past was mistaken while what we think now is simply 'the unvarnished truth', for doubtless many of the things we think of today as being self-evidently true will also seem quite obviously untrue from a future perspective. And even at a single point in time, there is not one generally accepted truth, but many different ones. What seems self-evident in one cultural context does not necessarily seem so in another. *Any* idea serves a purpose and we should always consider what that purpose might be – and whose purpose it is. This applies to ordinary and everyday ideas, including your own, as well as to the more systematic organisation of ideas that we call a theory, and to the big ideological systems which constitute political, religious or moral philosophies.

The so-called 'nature or nurture' question, which we will now consider, demonstrates very well how ideas can be used to serve such purposes – and it provides some examples of how different ideas have been used for political ends, as well as of how ideas may be used by individuals on a day-to-day basis to justify their own position.

NATURE AND NURTURE

What determines who we are and what we become? Biological inheritance ('nature')? Or the environment we grow up in ('nurture')? As soon as we begin to think about this question, it becomes obvious that it is a crudely oversimplified one, and we cannot answer it by coming down either on one side or the other. But there is, all the same, a long-running argument about the relative importance of inheritance and environment. As well as being a philosophical and scientific question since classical times, this is also a *highly* political question. 'Nature' or 'nurture' theories can both be used by vested interests – at the level of society at large and at the individual level – to justify their position or their actions.

But before we go on, here is an exercise to explore where you yourself stand on the nature–nurture question.

--- **Activity 1.2** ---

At the beginning of this chapter we described the birth of a (fictional) child, and wondered what kind of person she would become: prime minister or office cleaner?

1   Suppose her parents were Mr and Mrs Smith. One was an office cleaner, and the other was long-term unemployed. Neither has any educational qualifications. What does that make you think about her chances of becoming prime minister?
2   Suppose her parents were Mr and Mrs Jones. Both came from distinguished, wealthy families. One is a world-famous economist, the other a TV personality. How likely is it that she will become an office cleaner?
3   Suppose her parents were Mr and Mrs Smith, but both died in a tragic accident straight after her birth – and she was then adopted and brought up as their own by Mr and Mrs Jones. How do you see her future prospects?

Comments on Activity 1.2

You will probably agree that – at least in the world as it now exists – that the child of Mr and Mrs Smith is likely, on average, to have rather more modest career prospects than the child of Mr and Mrs Jones. There are many exceptions of course but, by and large, successful people are the children of other successful people, while poor people are the children of other poor people. But why is this? Is it because successful people are born with above-average abilities – and pass these abilities on to their children through their genes? (That would be a 'nature' theory.) Or is it just because successful people are

(Continued)

(Continued)

able to provide their children with a better education, a more stimulating environment, better contacts and so on? (That would be a 'nurture' theory.)

Where you stand on these questions will be indicated by your answer to question 3. Do you think that the child of Mr and Mrs Smith, if adopted by Mr and Mrs Jones, will perform just as well, in terms of career achievements, as a natural child of Mr and Mrs Jones would do? (If so, you take a 'nurture' view on the question of career success: you think it's mainly about upbringing and social circumstances.) Or do you think that the child of Mr and Mrs Smith, even if exposed to all the advantages that Mr and Mrs Jones can offer, will still probably not be a high-flyer, because it is likely that her natural parents were not of especially high ability and she is likely to have inherited their abilities? (If so, you lean towards a 'nature' view on this question: you think it's mainly about genes.)

Of course career success is only one of a vast number of things that distinguish one person from another. Some of the differences between us are quite obviously the products of genetic inheritance, while others are undoubtedly the products of environment. Few would dispute that hair colour is the result of genetic inheritance, or that the ability to speak Slovenian is a product of environment. No one is born with the ability to speak Slovenian. The ability is acquired either by growing up in a Slovenian-speaking environment, or by being taught Slovenian by someone else who speaks it. (On the other hand, the ability to acquire language as such *would* seem to be the product of genetic inheritance, since no other species is known to be able to acquire language, whatever the environment: although some chimpanzees have been trained to use a relatively small vocabulary, they do not acquire language in the human sense.)

But when we come to discuss things such as personality traits, moral character, intelligence and abilities, then the argument becomes more difficult – and often more heated.

The 'nature' viewpoint

Although few of us have any difficulty with the idea that our genetic inheritance determines our basic physical characteristics, to many it seems far-fetched – and perhaps also distasteful – to think of genes determining our personality and behaviour as well. There are, however, countless examples in the animal kingdom of very complex and specific behaviours which are inherited rather than learnt. Spiders build intricate webs without being taught. Cuckoos, which are not even raised by their own parents, still know how to lay their eggs in the nests of other birds, just as their parents did. It seems clear that at least some behaviour patterns are encoded in the genes just as are physical characteristics, which means that, like physical characteristics, they will have evolved over time through the process of natural selection.

Studies of twins are one way in which researchers have explored the influence of genetic inheritance on personality and other individual characteristics. There are two kinds of twins. So-called 'fraternal' twins are conceived at about the same time and grow together in their mother's womb, but are no more closely related than any other pair of siblings (that is to say that they share, on average, about 50 per cent of the same genes). Fraternal twins do not necessarily look alike and may not be of the same gender. 'Identical' twins, on the other hand, result when a single fertilised egg divides and the two resulting parts start growing into separate individuals. Such twins are not always *absolutely* identical because environmental factors – in the womb, at birth, or subsequently – may result in some differences. But they are *genetically* identical: they both have exactly the same set of genes. By looking at the degree of variability between identical twins, and comparing it with the degree of variability between fraternal twins, researchers have tried to tease out the part played by genetic inheritance, as opposed to environmental factors, in a variety of psychological traits, since both types of twin are usually brought in the same environment. As Guang Guo writes:

> Twin studies show that when one twin in an identical pair suffers from schizophrenia, the chance that the other twin will be schizophrenic is about one in two; it is only one in six for fraternal twins. This gap is evidence for the existence of a genetic tendency toward schizophrenia. Similar evidence suggests that genes influence such traits and behaviors as height, weight, manic-depressive psychosis, alcoholism, cognitive development, reading skills, parenting style, rate of accident occurrence in childhood, television-viewing habits, peer-group selection, timing of first sexual intercourse, marital disruption, and educational and economic attainment. (2005: 43)

There can be no doubt that genetics play an important role in making us who we are, and research has brought, and continues to bring, new insights into how this operates. The Human Genome Project, completed in 2003, mapped and sequenced all the genes of human beings for the first time, and as this material became available to researchers it opened the door to new understandings of the causes of human diseases, conditions and behaviour.

'Nature' ideas in everyday life

In common parlance the idea of the importance of inheritance is encapsulated in phrases such as 'blood will out', 'the apple doesn't fall far from the tree' and 'the leopard can't change its spots'. The following exercise illustrates how 'nature' theories about human behaviour can crop up in a very direct way.

━━━━━━━ **Activity 1.3** ━━━━━━━

Matthew

You're a school teacher visiting a lone-parent family, to discuss the problem of the son's poor attendance at school, and his poor work when he is there. The boy – Matthew, aged 13 – is getting in increasing trouble with the law as well as missing most of his schooling and he is staying out at nights. Matthew's father left the family home when Matthew was just a year old, and now has no contact with him at all.

(Continued)

(Continued)

Matthew's mother says his father was violent towards her and constantly in trouble with the police. She says, 'Matthew takes after his father. There's nothing I can do about it.'

What is your reaction to this comment?

Comments on Activity 1.3

Matthew's behaviour may be similar to his father's in some respects, but, as you may have observed, this doesn't necessarily mean that this is some sort of unavoidable fate carried in the genes. There are all kinds of environmental reasons why Matthew might behave in the same sorts of ways as his father. For example, both Matthew and his father may have grown up in a community where there was a strong cultural expectation for boys to be tough and 'hard' and where a low value was placed on schooling. There may be a long family history of fathers abandoning their families and for sons feeling hurt and angry as a result, so that they find it difficult in turn to stay in a stable family relationship when they grow up. You may well have thought of other reasons.

But one can see how it may be easier for Matthew's mother to take a 'nature' view of this by blaming his problems on his father's genes than to face her own part in causing them. Her anger with Matthew's father is being transferred onto his (and her) son as he grows up and reminds her more and more of his father. This makes it difficult for her to engage constructively with the problems that he is facing.

'Nature' ideas in the political arena

A 'nature' viewpoint can result in a rather fatalistic attitude – 'That's the way things are and there's nothing we can do about it!' – and it can have the attraction that it lets people off the hook. We suggested earlier that it's important to think carefully about why ideas become current and whose purposes they serve. You can see that 'nature' theories can be attractive not only to people like Matthew's mother in the above activity, but also to those in positions of privilege and power, because they can be used to argue that the status quo is inevitable and seem to justify inequality. Racist ideas are 'nature' theories, as are sexist ones. And if those in positions of power can tell themselves that the poor are poor because they are 'by nature' incapable of earning a good living, or that criminals are criminals because they have criminal genes, then they can feel that they are absolved of responsibility.

But this is not to say that 'nature' theories have no validity. It can hardly be disputed that many of our characteristics are inherited: and there is certainly good evidence that genetics plays an important role in intelligence, personality and predisposition to some mental illnesses as well as to physical ones. Nor is it right to say that 'nurture' theories are necessarily less oppressive, as we will see below.

The 'nurture' viewpoint

The word 'nurture' refers in particular to the care received by a child from her parents. Nurture in this sense is one important part of the environment in which human growth takes place and few would argue that nurture in this sense does not make a difference to the kind of person we become. But when we speak of 'nurture' in the context of the nature–nurture debate, we are talking more generally about *any* kind of environmental influence, which may include anything from events before, during and after birth, to factors as diverse as cultural expectations, nutrition, education, political circumstances and so on. In short, for the purposes of this discussion, the word 'nurture' will cover all the factors other than biological inheritance which might make a difference to who we are and what we become.

In Chapter 5 we will look at the ideas of *behaviourists* (or 'learning theorists'), starting with Pavlov and his famous dogs. As we will see, this strand within psychology accumulated impressive evidence that the environment shapes behaviour according to certain predictable rules.

Marxism, hugely influential on the history of the twentieth century, sees human thought and consciousness as being shaped by the society in which it took place. In particular, Karl Marx proposed that societies, including the roles that people play in them, their beliefs and their value systems, are the product of *economic* forces. The 'means of production' – the way that the economy is organised – was the determining factor, so that a certain set of values, ideas and behaviours would prevail in, say, feudal society, and another set in capitalist society: 'Consciousness is, therefore, from the very beginning a social product, and remains so as long as men exist at all' (Marx, 1986 [1845]: 176). You will find similar assertions in the writings of many who look at human life from a sociological perspective (see Chapter 10), whether they are inside or outside the Marxist tradition.

In the next chapter we will look at psychodynamic theories, originating with the ideas of Sigmund Freud. In some respects, Freud's ideas could also be described as 'nurture' theories, both in the wide and the narrow sense of the word 'nurture'. They place a great deal of emphasis on early childhood experience, including very basic things like toilet training, as a determining factor on how human beings grow and develop (although Freud also placed a huge emphasis on instinctive drives which he saw as biological, inherited and present from birth).

'Nurture' theories in everyday life

Just as you find 'nature' theories not only in academic texts, but also in everyday life, so also do you find 'nurture' theories. The following activity gives one example:

━━━━━━━━━━ **Activity 1.4** ━━━━━━━━━━

Liz

You are a probation officer and you are meeting a new client, Liz, aged 19, to talk to her about a pre-sentence report which you've been asked to write (in which you will comment on the reasons

(Continued)

(Continued)

for her offending and the likelihood of her offending again). Liz is charged with a series of violent assaults, using knives and other weapons, on other young women.

When you ask Liz about the reasons for her offending, she shrugs:

> I can't help myself. I just see red and then my mind goes a blank. I was beaten myself as a child, you see. My dad used to beat me and then my stepdad. My mum pretended she didn't know it was going on. I was taken into care when I was 6 and my stepdad was sent to jail for assaulting me, but my mum got back together with him again when he came out. So I suppose that was it. It's just what was put into my head when I was a child and I can't help it.

What might your response be to Liz and what could you put in your report?

Comments on Activity 1.4

It may have struck you that if Liz doesn't take some more responsibility for her own actions, she is going to have difficulty persuading a court to be lenient with her. More seriously, she is going to have difficulty in changing her behaviour or progressing with her life if she doesn't see herself as having any kind of control over it.

There can be little doubt that violent and unhappy relationships in childhood can predispose people to crime and other deviant behaviour in adult life (in Chapter 3, we will consider some reasons why this is), so Liz is not wrong in seeing her childhood abuse as a major contributing factor in her present problems. But in the long run it is not going to help her if she insists on seeing her

problems in such a fatalistic way, even though in the short run it may seem easier to 'let herself off the hook' by blaming her unhappy childhood.

('Nurture' as well as 'nature' can be used to let ourselves off the hook, particularly for those, like Liz, who are genuinely the victims of mistreatment.)

But you could also argue that if it is possible to learn violent behaviour, then it must also be possible to learn another way of acting!

You could even argue that Liz's fatalism is in itself a learnt behaviour, which could likewise be unlearnt. (See the discussion on 'Learned helplessness', in Chapter 5.)

'Nurture' ideas in the political arena

Historically, 'nature' theories have been used as the rationale for oppression of various kinds, as we've noted above, and they tend to be associated with the political right. The idea that human beings are shaped by their environment, on the other hand, has always been attractive to the political left, which sees the poor as being poor not because of their innate qualities, but because they have not been given access to the advantages enjoyed by the rich.

However, the idea that human beings are entirely the product of their environment has also been used in extremely oppressive ways by the political left. The infamous Pol Pot regime in Cambodia in 1975, for example, justified the horrors of its notorious Year Zero, with its death toll of around 2 million, with the idea that it was possible to change people by totally wiping out the influence of the past, liquidating those individuals seen as responsible for transmitting that influence, and retraining an entire population to start again.

Much closer to home, parents of schizophrenia sufferers, or of children with autism, might well complain about 'nurture' theories, fashionable in the 1960s and 1970s, that blamed them for their children's problems. For instance, it was suggested that parents could make their children schizophrenic by putting them in 'double binds', giving them contradictory messages (Bateson, 1973: 201 ff). From the perspective of a parent, such theories must feel much more oppressive than theories which propose a genetic origin for these problems.

Beyond nature and nurture

It is too simplistic to reduce the various factors that make people what they are to 'nature' and 'nurture', and no one would seriously suggest that it is all one or all the other. In reality a whole range of different factors contributes to making us what we are, and genetic and environmental factors do not operate in isolation but interact with one another in complex ways:

> Counterpoising genetics and environmental influences is somewhat misleading, despite the partisan claims of people on each side. Many human traits and behaviors result from both genetic and environmental factors. Moreover, genetic and environmental influences on a trait are not simply additive. Genes "interact" with the environment. That is, genes provide the potential for a trait, but environmental conditions determine whether that potential will be realized. The same genetic codes may be expressed at different levels in different environments. (Guo, 2005: 46)

Thus it is more helpful to see nature and nurture as acting together, 'nature via nurture' (Ridley, 2004). The study of the mechanisms by which the environment acts on genes is known as *epigenetics*, a new discipline that is 'finally starting to unravel the missing link between nature and nurture; how our environment talks to us and alters us, sometimes forever' (Carey, 2012: 7). In Chapter 3, when we look at attachment, we will see how neuroscience is helping us to understand how brain development is critically affected by the kind of nurture a child receives in the early years. And it is not just in the early years that environmental influences can shape the brain. Research into neuroplasticity (the ability of the brain to change) is showing that brain development can continue throughout life. For example, scans of musicians' brains show that clear differences emerge with time and practice compared to the brains of non-musicians. For string players, the area controlling the left hand expands significantly, and in trumpeters the neurons that respond to 'brassy' sounds enlarge (Elbert et al., 1995; Pantev et al., 2001, cited in Doidge, 2007: 289).

So a complex interplay between inherited and environmental factors is at work. Some of these factors are:

- genetic inheritance
- other physical factors such as nutrition, health, physical injury, not only after birth, but from conception onwards – for example, a baby's growth may be inhibited if a mother drinks or smokes during pregnancy, and serious brain damage can be caused by complications during the birth itself

- upbringing, early relationships, position in the family (older children have a different experience from middle and youngest children, for example), traumatic and/or positive experiences
- cultural factors - nationality, social class, geography (whether one grows up in the country or a town, for example), ethnic background, time in history
- random life events (car accidents, lottery wins, chance meetings ...).

One could think of many more. But the important thing to note here is how all these factors interact with one another (see Figure 1.1). What sex we are, for example, *is* a matter of genetic inheritance and it has (of course) many purely physical implications: women can give birth and breastfeed, men can't; boys are more likely to suffer from certain inherited conditions (hae-mophilia, colour-blindness); men and women have different hormones in their bloodstream – and so on. But the way in which the sexes are viewed, the expectations of them, the roles and behaviour which are considered appropriate and inappropriate, will depend on cultural factors. (There is a further discussion on gender roles in Chapter 5.)

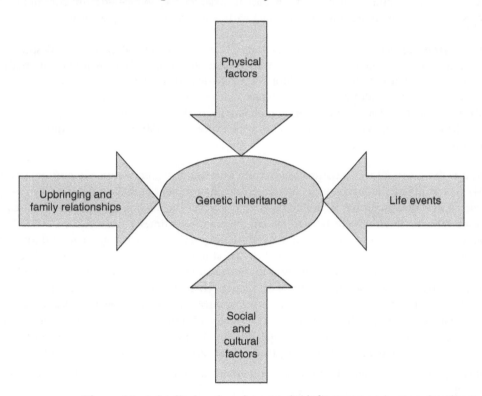

Figure 1.1 Inherited and environmental influences on human development

To give another example: physical appearance might seem a purely inherited feature at first glance, but in fact a whole range of environmental factors can affect physical appearance. In rare cases a child's physical growth can be affected not only by malnutrition but by emotional abuse and rejection ('psychosocial short stature': see Iwaniec, 2004: 52). And the *significance* attached to physical appearance will depend very much on culture, as can be seen from the fact that plumpness and white skin have been regarded as beautiful and desirable in some societies at some stages in European history, while thinness and sun-tanned skin have been the ideal at others.

Existential questions

We would suggest too that, in addition to the interacting influences of nature and nurture, our thoughts and beliefs are shaped by the fact that life poses certain unavoidable questions – 'existential' questions – which would be faced by any thinking being, even, hypothetically, an alien from another planet or a sentient machine.

For example, there is the fact of *death* (see Chapter 12). Our lives are finite. Even for an extra-terrestrial alien or a robot, the possibility of non-existence would be an inevitable corollary of existence. And there is the fact too of *individuality*. The fact that we exist as individuals means that there are other things in existence which are separate from us. So, as well as being limited in time, our lives are also necessarily located in space. (The way that we come to terms with the concept of 'self' and 'others' is something that is of particular interest to the object relations theorists whom we will discuss in the next chapter and in Chapter 3, and to theories of cognitive development, which are the subject of Chapter 4.)

Another existential aspect of being a conscious being, and not merely an automaton, is that we feel ourselves to be making *choices*. This is something we'll now discuss further.

FREE WILL VERSUS PREDETERMINATION

As human beings, we don't feel ourselves to be the passive passengers of bodies which simply respond to our genes or our environment. We feel as if we are constantly making decisions, and often difficult and painful ones. As old, or older, than the nature–nurture question, and even more fundamental is the question of whether or not we have free will. Here it is, for instance, in Chaucer's *Canterbury Tales*, written in the fourteenth century:

> But I kan nat bulte it to the bren ...
>
> Whether that Goddes worthy forwiting
>
> Streyneth me nedeley for to doon a thyng ...
>
> Or elles, if free choys be graunted me
>
> To do that same thyng, or do it noght. (Crawley (ed.), 1992: 470)
>
> (Rough translation: 'But I can't sift the grain from the chaff ... [as to] whether God's worthy foreknowledge constrains me necessarily to do a thing ... or else, if free choice is granted me to do that same thing or not do it.')

All the writers we have quoted so far in this chapter assume that there are *causes* for human behaviour, whether those causes are genetic or otherwise. Yet most of us also believe that there is such a thing as choice and personal responsibility. The French existentialist Jean-Paul Sartre wrote: 'I am condemned to be free … we are not free to cease being free' (2001 [1943]: 184). When people like Liz (in Activity 1.4) blame their behaviour on external factors outside their control, Sartre would say that they were acting in 'bad faith' by denying the existence of their own capacity to choose. Most of the world's religions see human beings as making choices between good and evil and ultimately taking the consequences of those choices.

Here is one more activity, based on a real-life case, for you to consider where you stand on this issue:

Activity 1.5

In England in 1993, Jon Venables and Robert Thompson, then both aged 10, were found guilty of the murder of a toddler, James Bulger, whom they had picked up in a shopping mall, taken to a railway line and beaten to death by hitting him with bricks. Many have said that these boys committed this appalling act because they were 'evil', while others have suggested that there must have been distressing events in their previous childhood that caused them to act in this way. What is your own view about why they might have done this and how they should be seen?

Comments on Activity 1.5

If you incline to the view that these boys were indeed evil (and few would dispute that evil is an appropriate word for what they did), you need to ask yourself precisely what you mean by that. Are you saying that they were born with a propensity to do bad things (a nature theory)? If so, how can they be blamed for what they did any more than a person born blind can be blamed for not being able to see?

Or are you saying that we all make choices between good and evil, and these boys chose evil of their own free will? If so, we'd have to ask you whether, at 10 years old, you were ever tempted to kidnap and murder a small child, and had to resist that temptation? If not, clearly this was not just a matter of choice.

Or are you saying that these boys became evil as a result of something in their upbringing? If so, you are really agreeing with those who say that their behaviour must have been the result of environmental factors (a nurture theory). The obvious question then is why do other children, from similar or worse environments, not commit such crimes? One answer might be that no two environments are exactly alike and we can never know all the subtle influences that might tip a person one way or the other. Another might be that no two individuals are born exactly alike, so the environment never affects any two people in exactly the same way.

Clearly, whether we believe in free will or not can have huge implications for how we act and how we view other people. In fact, as we noted earlier, people tend to make moral judgements in some cases and look for causes in others – and don't necessarily do so in a very consistent way. But we are not here going to attempt any sort of resolution of this question that has troubled great thinkers for several millennia, beyond offering a pragmatic compromise.

We don't wish to dissuade anyone from believing that they make real choices in their lives. We also believe that the idea of personal responsibility is necessary for society to function. But if you look at the things that you think of as free choices, and consider why other people make different choices from yours, it is hard to avoid noticing that there is a pattern. As we've discussed, evidence exists that people with the same genes are more likely to make the same choices. We also know that people can be trained to act differently by rewarding or punishing different behaviours – and that people with the same childhood experiences often have the same kinds of problems in later life.

We may not be automatons, but we are *shaped*, if not controlled, by our history and by the world around us. We suggest that this requires us to try not to judge other people in a moral sense, and to try to understand the reasons why people act as they do. And yet at the same time we cannot function without taking some responsibility for our own actions, and expecting others to take responsibility for theirs.

EVENTS, TRANSITIONS, RESILIENCE

If you think of your own life history and what has made you who you are, you will probably notice the significance of *events* of different kinds: births, deaths, moves, the beginnings and endings of relationships, leaving school, changes of job, retirement, accidents, windfalls ... Some of these events might seem to you to have been freely chosen (you choose to get married, to change your job, to go to college). Some of them may have been unexpected (a lottery win, a bereavement, an unplanned pregnancy). Some of them may have been outside of your control, but nevertheless expected (going to secondary school, leaving school, becoming an adult, growing old). Some of them may have been expected but not inevitable (you become a parent, you enter the world of work, you get a home of your own). Human growth can be understood as a complex interlocking web of such events, some of which we choose, and some of which we have to adjust to whether we like them or not. We have to change within ourselves in order to get to places that we want to reach, or even just to cope with the places in which we find ourselves.

In this book we will often come back to this theme, when we discuss the transitions which life requires us to make (becoming an adult, growing old ...) and the challenges which life faces us with (bereavement, the birth of a child, disability ...). One interesting question is how it is that people cope so differently with these things. Some are ground down by adversity, and find even small changes difficult to handle. Some seem to be much more resilient, manage change much better, and move on much more easily from painful experiences. Resilience too, a big question in the study of human growth, is another topic we will be coming back to later in Chapter 6.

CHAPTER SUMMARY

- The chapter began with an account of the birth of a child and looked at some ideas about what will shape her as she grows and develops. But ideas themselves are not fixed, so we began by giving a warning about ideas and theories. They are not neutral. People use them for their own ends.
- In particular, we looked at the debate about the extent to which our identity is determined by our genes and by environmental factors (the 'nature and nurture' debate). We looked at the way this debate has very practical implications, both in daily life and in politics, and we proposed that we need to see human growth as being the product of a number of interacting factors, of which genetic inheritance is one.
- We considered another very ancient subject of debate – between free will and predetermination – and looked at the issues this raises.
- Finally, we discussed the way our growth and development over our lives is marked by a series of events, some chosen, some not, some expected, some completely unexpected, some welcome, some not welcome at all. We looked at the transitions that we have to go through in the course of a lifespan, and at the fact that some people are much better at coping with changes than others: some are more resilient.

In the next chapter, we will look at the ideas of Freud, who saw human personality developing as the result of our having to try to strike a balance, from the moment of birth onwards, between instinctive drives, the external environment and previous learning.

Tangled Webs

Most of the cases in Tangled Webs could raise questions of the kinds touched on in this chapter. We suggested the following:

Derek Harrow (Case B: Rob Thomas and Derek Harrow). Derek comes from a family where criminality is the norm, and is himself involved in criminal behaviour. Does this suggest that 'criminal tendencies' are genetically inherited? Or does it simply show that children learn what is acceptable behaviour from their parents? There's some suggestion that Derek would like not to go down the same path as his father. To what extent does he have a free choice here? Does he have exactly the same choices as someone his age without that background?

The Veloso family (Case I). Xenia's mother, Estrela, has mental health problems. How likely is it that Xenia will herself become depressed? How much of a genetic component is there to depression? How will the environmental factors in the home (including the expectations placed upon her, the amount of attention and stimulation she receives etc.) affect Xenia's development? To what degree, do you think, in later life will Xenia be free to set aside the effects of her early upbringing?

 You can access Tangled Webs by visiting **https://study.sagepub.com/tangledwebs**

━━━━━━━ **Further reading** ━━━━━━━

Doidge, Norman (2007) *The Brain That Changes Itself*. London: Penguin.

And for a brief overview of recent developments in genetic research and their implications for child development policy and practice, see National Scientific Council on the Developing Child (2010).

THE BALANCING ACT

PSYCHODYNAMIC INSIGHTS

TANGLED WEBS

If you would like to look at some cases before reading this chapter, you might look at **Zak Renton (Case K)** or **Deanna Whitworth** and **Zoe Scott (Case L)**. Questions to ask yourself are: 'How have this person's early childhood experiences shaped the way they relate to others in adult life?' and 'What does their childhood experience help them to see, and what does it perhaps prevent them from seeing?'

 You can access Tangled Webs by visiting **https://study.sagepub.com/tangledwebs**

In the last chapter we discussed various factors – some innate, some environmental – that might play a part in human development. We want to look now at a view of the human mind that sees human development as the product of a dynamic process incorporating both innate and environmental forces. From this psychodynamic viewpoint, we are shaped by our experience as infants as we seek to get our basic needs met when we are completely dependent for survival on our carers. Through these earliest experiences, we begin to learn about the world outside ourselves and how it meets, or doesn't meet, our urgently felt innate needs. We develop psychological strategies, both conscious and unconscious, to deal with situations in which our needs go unmet – a lifelong balancing act between our inner world and the world outside. Strategies adopted in childhood are carried into adult life, where they may sometimes be maladaptive, and cause problems for the individual concerned, unless she can get help in unravelling the patterns laid down in the past.

Although this theoretical model has been developed, modified and expanded in many different directions, and although it had historical antecedents, Sigmund Freud is certainly its most well-known exponent. Freud, who was born in Austria in 1856 and died in London in 1939, remains a controversial figure. Like Marx and Darwin, he played a pivotal role in the history of ideas, changing the way in which we see the world, and the terms on which we debate fundamental issues. Many criticisms can be levelled against him – and we will discuss some of them later – but he has left an important legacy which we now almost take for granted. Many of his ideas, in fact, have entered the language and we use them without thinking about their origin. In particular, the Freudian tradition has offered the possibility of new insights into the way that apparently irrational things – madness, dreams, obsessions, jokes, slips of the tongue – have a kind of deep logic of their own, rooted in the fears and longings of childhood and, even before that, in our biological origins. It has also given us a way of understanding how family relationships in childhood lay down a template for our later functioning as adults.

Many people approach Freud's ideas with some fairly strong preconceptions. Even if you don't think you know much about his ideas, you will probably react to his name and the term 'Freudian' with some thoughts, feelings and associations and you may find it useful to be aware of these as your own starting point.

Sex is often the first thing that comes to mind when Freud's name is mentioned; people will say that 'he was obsessed with sex', 'he thinks everything is to do with sex'. You could argue that one of the legacies of Freud was to make sex something of an obsession in modern society. Whether that is really a legacy of Freud, or whether it owes more to broader social and economic forces, is of course another question – and a big one. What we will see, though, is that Freud's use of the term 'sexual' was fairly broad.

You may also be aware of the therapeutic technique known as psychoanalysis which Freud developed, which has spawned a thousand cartoons featuring couches and Freud lookalikes with pencils and pads. Certainly, a lot has been written about the efficacy or otherwise of psychoanalysis and its potential for abuse. We will not be covering this in any detail here, because this is a book about psychosocial development and not about therapeutic techniques. But it does rightly form a large part of most people's image of what Freud was 'all about'.

You have probably also come across the idea of 'the unconscious' as a driving force within us but outside our control which underlies the aspects of our behaviour that seem to defy rational explanation. The aim of psychoanalysis is often described as to make the unconscious conscious. Freud's theories about how the unconscious worked were developed through his experience of the practice of psychoanalysis, and the case histories he recorded.

And you may be aware of doubts about Freud's claim to be offering a genuinely scientific or objective theory, or concerns about Freud's attitudes and assumptions (particularly towards women) or about whether his ideas can be generalised in the way that he did generalise them. These are important questions which will be discussed later in this chapter.

Many people also find some of the language in which Freud's ideas are expressed rather off-putting, or even at times a bit absurd, though many of them have passed into everyday speech ('penis envy', 'phallic symbol', 'anal personality'). It is important to try to look behind the language and the sometimes startling imagery and try to get some sense of the underlying ideas.

We will now attempt to sketch out some of the main themes in Freudian thinking, with the warning that this is necessarily a very partial account of a rich and complicated set of ideas which Freud himself changed and developed repeatedly during his lifetime, and which has been developed further in many different ways since his death.

THE UNCONSCIOUS

Freud didn't begin his professional career in psychiatry but in the field of pathological medicine and neurology. At the age of 29, while working in Paris with a French physician called Charcot, he encountered the treatment of 'hysteria' using hypnosis. At that time 'hysteria' was a term used to refer to physical symptoms which had no apparent physical cause. Freud was impressed by the fact that observable physical symptoms could be caused not only by infection or by injury, but simply by distressing *ideas* in a patient's mind. And he was impressed by the fact that unconscious thoughts could be accessed and patients apparently treated by talking to them under hypnosis to neutralise these powerful ideas.

When being treated by hypnosis, the patient listens while the doctor talks. Freud turned this on its head by developing a form of therapy in which the patient talks while the therapist listens. In other words he moved on to what a patient of his early collaborator, Josef Breuer, described as 'the talking cure' (Freud and Breuer, 1955 [1895]: 30). This is now the basis of the practice of many helping professionals who would not regard themselves in any way as Freudians. He then developed this further into a technique which encouraged the patient to 'free associate'. This allows exploration not only of the patient's conscious thoughts, but of connections of which the patient herself may not be consciously aware, and proved to be a more effective way of getting in touch with the unconscious mind than hypnosis.

▬▬▬▬▬▬ Free association ▬▬▬▬▬▬

In free association, the patient is asked to respond to a word or an idea with the first thing that comes into her head, without thinking about it and without holding anything back. It's a bit like the parlour game 'elbow tennis', in which players have to say as quickly as possible the first word that comes into their head in connection with a word chosen by the previous player. However, in free association the patient is not required to demonstrate a connection between one word and the next. On the contrary, the technique is based on the assumption that there will always *be* some link, though the patient may not be aware of it.

When one of the authors was giving a lecture on this subject one Christmas, he tried hard to think of two completely unrelated words and came up with 'tangerine' and 'anger'. Later he realised that there *was* a Christmas-linked connection for him between these words. He does not like tangerines but his parents always put one in the very toe of his Christmas stocking. After the unwanted and unexciting tangerine, there were no more presents.

Another more obvious connection has since been pointed out to us: that the word 'anger' is actually embedded in the word 'tangerine'. And this is a good example of the kind of punning word play that Freud saw, along with 'slips' and jokes, as a clue to unconscious meaning. He believed that, by exploring the links that our minds make without us being consciously aware of it, we obtain glimpses of the contents of the unconscious.

As a result of his explorations, Freud became convinced that his patients' neurotic problems were rooted in traumatic events in infancy, and that these events were basically sexual. Again and again they seemed to be telling him that their fathers had sexually assaulted them. He came to the conclusion that most psychological problems in adulthood were caused by what we would now call sexual abuse in childhood. This theory is known – rather inappropriately – as the *seduction theory*.

When Freud presented this theory to a distinguished scientific audience in 1896, it met with a chilly reception, and he found himself ostracised and professionally isolated. His views later changed, as they did about many aspects of his theory, in the light of further work with patients and of the analysis of himself which he carried out. He recognised his own sexual fantasies about family members, but knew that these were not related to actual abuse (Gay, 1988: 93–4). This led him to reject the view that all 'hysteria' was caused by sexual abuse, and to explain it more in terms of the fantasies arising from unconscious wishes and desires, and the view that sexual feelings are present and active from the earliest infancy. From the last part of the twentieth century, as the prevalence of sexual abuse has become more widely recognised, Freud has been criticised (most notably by Masson (2003), as will be discussed later) for changing his mind over the reality of the events described by his patients.

Suppressed desires

As a result of changing his mind over the seduction theory, Freud moved on from his original perspective that 'hysterics' suffered mainly from reminiscences, to the idea that the primary problem was not so much memories – or suppressed memories – as suppressed *desires*. His view was that we have all kinds of desires, not all of which can actually be met, and some of which we cannot even safely admit even to ourselves. Desires which we are aware of but which we don't allow ourselves to act upon we *suppress*. Other desires we *repress*, which means that we push them right out of our conscious mind altogether.

But Freud believed that unconscious desires could not be completely contained. It is as if we were to put the lid on a pan of boiling water, so that we can no longer see its contents. We may have put the lid on the pan but we are nevertheless made aware, in various ways, of the heat and pressure inside. The contents of the unconscious, Freud thought, emerged in disguise in various ways: in jokes, in slips of the tongue (the famous 'Freudian slip'), in dreams and in physical and psychological symptoms of distress. The technique of 'free association' is supposed to provide a means of tapping into them.

It was certainly not a new idea of Freud's that we are not always aware of all the contents of our mind. If you reflect on this for a moment you will see that this is actually self-evident. We are not always thinking about everything that is in our memory. If someone mentions your last summer holiday, it is probable that, until they mentioned it, it was not in your thoughts at all. At times we may even be unable to retrieve something from our memory and into consciousness, even though we know quite well that it is there. 'It's on the tip of my tongue', as we say.

But such memories are like library books which are not currently being read, and which may occasionally be hard to find if we can't remember what subject they were filed under. In the terminology of Freud's earlier model of the mind these things are *preconscious*, rather than unconscious. Freud's conception of the *unconscious* was much more dynamic than this. He saw the unconscious not as a kind of static library or storehouse but as a powerful, active player in the dynamic system that was the human mind. It was a source of energy, and it contained things which were in some sense dangerous. Desires, unlike memories, have urgency about them. And the unconscious is timeless – it does not distinguish between past and present.

THE STRUCTURE OF PERSONALITY

Freud moved on again from being primarily interested in the distinction between conscious and unconscious, to making a new distinction between parts of the mind known in English as the *ego* and the *id*. (Freud's translators used these rather technical-sounding Latin terms for the everyday German words 'ich' (I) and 'es' (it) which Freud himself used.) In this new model, the *id* – or 'it' – contains the instincts: the inherited part of ourselves, our basic biological drives, and it operates on the *pleasure principle*. It is:

> a cauldron full of seething excitations ... It is filled with energy ... but ... has no organisation ... only a striving to bring about the satisfaction of instinctual needs subject to the observance of the pleasure principle ... (Freud, 1964 [1933]: 73)

The *ego*, or 'I', is a part of ourselves that develops from the id as a result of experience, and is the part of ourselves where conscious thought takes place.

> The ego is that part of the id which has been modified by the direct influence of the external world... The ego represents what may be called reason and common sense, in contrast to the id, which contains the passions ... in its relation to the id it is like a man on horseback, who has to hold in check the superior strength of the horse ... (Freud (1961 [1923]: 25)

According to Freud, the ego operates on the *reality principle.* It deals not only with the powerful instinctual demands arising from the id, but also with the demands of the external world, and with what it has learnt through experience. One of the jobs that the ego does is the job of repressing desires which cannot safely be allowed into consciousness. The part of the ego that does this job is necessarily itself unconscious. This meant that Freud's previous model of the mind as being made up of separate layers, of conscious, preconscious and unconscious, could no longer convey the complexity of the relationship he now saw between the conscious and unconscious parts of the mind.

In order to explain how the unconscious part of the ego decided what must be repressed, Freud introduced the idea of the *superego* ('uber-ich' – over-I – in German). The *superego* is a kind of 'deposit' left behind in our minds from our childhood relationship with our parents and others who were in charge of us. It contains rules and restrictions which a child would originally have received from adults ('That's naughty', 'You mustn't do that', etc.), but which in due course become internalised. The superego is therefore the seat of conscience and self-criticism. To give a simple example of how this process of internalisation operates: a small child does not think to wash her hands after using the toilet. She has to be told to do so, and starts to do so in order to conform to adult wishes. By the time we are adults, however, we wash our hands not to please others, but because it feels uncomfortable not to do so.

To understand more clearly how these different parts of the mind work together, try this activity:

▬▬▬▬▬ Activity 2.1 ▬▬▬▬▬

Imagine you see something in a shop that attracts your attention; perhaps an expensive piece of clothing that you think would really suit you, or the latest electronic gadget. You really want to possess it; in that moment it has become the object of your desire. Think about how you might respond to this, and the part the id, ego and superego might play in your response. What might you do if the id dominates? The superego? The ego? What kind of response is most likely for you? If you do this activity with others, you will probably notice a different range of responses.

Comments on Activity 2.1

The id will draw you towards instant gratification of your desire without thinking about the consequences. At worst, this could lead you to shoplifting! More likely you will reach for your credit card without thinking about how much you already owe on it, or whether you can afford to spend the money. You will make an 'impulse buy'.

The superego will speak to you in the voices of your parents, and frame your internal debate in moral terms. Perhaps, 'That's far too extravagant. How could you think of spending all that money on yourself?' Or 'That's too showy. You can't go out dressed like that.' Or conversely, 'You deserve it', or 'That's the kind of thing that will convey the right image, the sort of thing that people like us wear/own.'

The ego will be aware of the voices of the id and the superego, and will try to balance them out, and look at the reality of your situation. Do you need it? Would you wear/use it? Can you afford it? Do you have to buy it today or would it be better to go home and think about it, and perhaps do some more research? And so it will help you to make a considered decision.

Returning to the language of nature–nurture: the superego in Freud's model is clearly the product of 'nurture', while the id is the product of 'nature'. The ego has the job of balancing the competing demands of id and superego, and the demands of external reality. So in Freudian terms the ego is the mature, reality-based part of ourselves; very different, and confusingly so, from the way we tend to use the word in everyday language when we describe someone as 'having a big ego', meaning that they have a high opinion of themselves and like to have everything their own way. Freud wrote 'Where id was, there ego shall be' (1964 [1933]: 80). He was talking about the aims of psychoanalysis, but it also describes his view of human development, as the ego emerges over the course of childhood as a force that can control the impulses of the id and temper the demands of the superego.

THE SHAPING OF PERSONALITY: UNCONSCIOUS PROCESSES

We've seen that in Freud's model, the individual starts with certain basic instinctual needs. The id constantly demands the satisfaction that comes from meeting those needs. The ego has the job of mediating between the demands of the id, the demands of the external world and the demands of powerful others (the parents), who end up being internalised (or *introjected*) as the superego.

A person grows as a distinct and separate personality as the result of her ego performing its own unique balancing act. Each individual ego develops strategies for negotiating the competing pressures upon it and finds ways of resolving dilemmas, which in some cases will mean suppressing inconvenient things from consciousness.

If all goes well, the individual will progress to a stage where she can cope with adult life. But things can go wrong along the line, which may hamper growth. For example, traumatic events may be experienced which are beyond the capacity of the individual to properly cope with, or needs may go unmet. Difficulties can occur in any number of ways which, if not successfully resolved, will result in the individual being stuck to some degree.

Psychological defences

Freud saw the ego as employing a whole range of *defences* as a protection against anxiety. His daughter Anna later developed the concept of defences further in her book *The Ego and the Mechanisms of Defence* (Freud, 1968 [1937]), drawing on material from her pioneering work in child analysis. Another child analyst, Melanie Klein, who we will discuss later, also made an important contribution to the understanding of defence mechanisms with her concepts of splitting, projection and projective identification.

Defences are *unconscious* processes. They prevent the conscious part of the ego from having to face the disturbing or uncomfortable feelings which may come from:

- increases in instinctual tension - tensions coming from the id: needs and desires demanding to be met
- a bad conscience - i.e. pressures from the superego
- reality - a threat to the individual's safety and well-being in the real world.

These defences are necessary at the time – the best that can be done in the circumstances – but they can sometimes subsequently become obstacles to development.

To consider this more closely, have a look at the following activity:

━━━━━━ Activity 2.2 ━━━━━━

Jenny

This small child aged four lives alone with her mother (Mandy) who is highly volatile and unpredictable. Occasionally Mandy treats her kindly, but at other times Mandy erupts into frightening rage and violence, hitting her, depriving her of food, and threatening to abandon or kill her. Mandy also isolates her. Jenny doesn't know anyone else other than Mandy's friends. She does not know other children of her own age.

How would Jenny deal with this situation psychologically? How would she explain to herself what was going on? How would she comfort herself?

Please note: we are not asking you to guess what Freud might say about this. We are asking you to consider what you yourself think, based on your own experience and your own imagination.

Comments on Activity 2.2

The first thing that strikes us about this scenario is that a child cannot deal with it like an adult. An adult is aware of other possibilities, the possibility of escape, of sources of help (though, having said this, we need to acknowledge that choices and sources of help are limited for some adults too, for example vulnerable older people or people in abusive relationships). Her mother may abuse her, but to Jenny, Mandy is also the world, the source of her nourishment, the provider of her home.

A child also does not think like an adult in terms of logic, cause and effect and so on. (See Chapter 4 for a discussion of cognitive differences – differences in the structure of thought – between children and adults.)

The second thing that strikes us is just how intolerable it would be for a little child of this age to admit to herself that she was in real danger from the adult who cares for her, or that her mother was a bad person, or that her mother did not have her best interests at heart. The anxiety of this would be too much to bear and she needs to protect herself from it.

But Jenny is very little compared to Mandy. There is no way in reality that she can defend herself from what is going on. All she can resort to are psychological defences. She might tell herself, for example: 'This isn't really happening to me' or 'This isn't real', just as we do as adults, at least at first, when brought some terrible news such as news of a bereavement. This defence is known as 'denial' (another Freudian term that has entered everyday language).

Or she could tell herself that the Mandy who mistreats her is a different person from the Mandy who is kind to her. The kind Mandy is her real mum. This defence is known as splitting.

Or perhaps she could tell herself that she is bad, and that she deserves the treatment that Mandy gives her. This does not sound a very comfortable position to take, but it may well be less frightening to think of herself as bad, than to think of the large person who controls her life as being bad. This defence is known as turning against the self, or identification with the aggressor (she is adopting Mandy's view of her). In our experience, it is extremely common among children who have been seriously abused (as are denial and splitting). Even very little children – who from an outsider's perspective are quite obviously powerless – often blame themselves for abuse perpetrated against them.

The point about these defences is that they are necessary, the best that Jenny can do in the circumstances to protect her sanity. They are less damaging in the short run than facing the full reality of the situation. But in the long run, they may leave her with a seriously defective way of dealing with the world.

Jenny may grow up routinely blocking out painful feelings, or feeling of any kind. She may grow up with the habit of 'splitting' – holding in her mind contradictory stories at the same time. She may grow up with a view of herself as worthless and bad.

Most children do not have challenges as great as Jenny's in our example to contend with, but all children have to deal with an imperfect world, using whatever psychological resources are available to them. The use of unconscious defences is a part of the normal process of development, and the kinds of defences used can be related to an individual's developmental stage; they develop through life. Various attempts have been made, from Freud onwards, to label and classify the different mechanisms of defence, and to evidence them in action. In reviewing the research in this area, Cramer (2006: 18) contends that grouping defences into broad categories makes research more reliable.

A distinction can be drawn between mature and immature defences, but of course this depends on the actual life stage of the individual concerned. What is a mature defence for a 4-year-old like Jenny will be an immature defence if it persists into adult life, which unfortunately it is likely to do if the anxieties it was mobilised to cope with are extreme and potentially overwhelming.

Cramer sees a developmental progression in the emergence of different defences, and looks at the defences of denial, projection and identification. We will follow this, and also look here at the related Kleinian concept of projective identification.

- *Denial.* Probably most of us have observed, at first or second hand, the way that people go initially into denial to protect themselves against the impact of some catastrophic event – a sudden bereavement for example – and will only gradually allow themselves to face the fact that this event has actually taken place. Denial can take different forms. There is 'looking and not seeing' (Cramer, 2000: 50), the non-perception, or misperception of something unpleasant or threatening. This primitive form of denial is available to even the youngest babies, and Cramer cites evidence for this from research with children subjected to extreme stress and deprivation. Then, as the child's cognitive abilities develop, it becomes possible to reframe uncomfortable realities through strategies such as maximising, minimising, reversal and 'undoing'. Anna Freud gives an example of a child taking nasty medicine while constantly repeating, 'like it, like it' (Freud, 1968[1937]: 84). Fantasy comes to play an important part in this process. For example, children's play is often concerned with pretending that they are grown up, therefore avoiding the recognition of their powerlessness in relation to the adult world. It is also an acting out of identification, discussed below.
- *Projection* is a process whereby unacceptable feelings or unacknowledged aspects of the self are split off from conscious awareness and experienced as belonging to another person (or it could be a group of people, an animal or some inanimate object). For example, people in the helping professions may deny their own vulnerability and project these feelings onto those whom they help. Someone in a dispute with their neighbours or work colleagues may attribute all the aggression and unreasonableness to the others, see themselves simply as a victim and be unable to acknowledge their own anger and part in the dispute. A mild-mannered, conforming individual may own, and be very attached to, a fierce or unruly cat or dog which allows them unconsciously to express another side of themselves. You will see from these examples that the objects of projection will themselves often have some of the characteristics that are being projected; service users actually are vulnerable, the neighbours may be unreasonable and the cat or dog out of control. What is characteristic of projection, though, is the black and white split; it is all the other person and nothing to do with the self. Projective processes are particularly common in intimate relationships, as we discuss in Chapter 7, and an understanding of projection is also an aspect of a systemic approach, which recognises that the problem in a family or a group is not always located where it appears to be at first sight (Chapter 9).
- *Identification* can be both a defensive and a developmental process (Cramer, 2006: 95). As we grow up, we model ourselves both consciously and unconsciously on parental figures, and experiment with adult roles through play and fantasy to arrive at our own identity. We will discuss this further in relation to learning theory and gender roles (Chapter 5) and the movement towards an adult identity in adolescence (Chapter 7). When identification is used as a defence, it seeks to side-step the anxieties and uncertainties of one's own developmental journey by becoming like a significant other. In Chapter 7 we will see how this can happen in adolescent identity foreclosure. We also saw in Activity 2:2 above how Jenny identified with Mandy's negative view of herself. Identification with the aggressor can also lead to the victim of abuse or bullying becoming an

abuser or a bully themselves. Identification can also be a defence against loss. Becoming more like the person who has been lost, perhaps through bereavement, can be a way of trying to hold on to something of them.

- *Projective identification* is what happens when the recipient of projected feelings takes them on and identifies them as their own. Thus we can speak of feelings being projected *into* rather than *onto* someone. As with projection, the originator of the feelings will have split them off from conscious awareness, but it may sometimes be possible for a feeling that has been projected into someone else to be made available through them, and re-experienced and taken back on board by the projector. This is like mirroring, which we will discuss later, in that it reflects back an image of the self that can be recognised and used developmentally. The mechanism through which this happens is called *countertransference*.

Transference and countertransference

The way in which feelings from past relationships affect present ones is known in Freudian terms as *transference*, which is a specific kind of projection Freud noticed that his patients often reacted to him as if he were someone from their past, often a father. Initially he saw this as an obstacle to the work of psychoanalysis, but transference eventually became recognised as a key concept through which psychoanalysis could bring alive the past rather than merely talking about it. And transference is not limited to the consulting room; it affects many different kinds of relationships. We saw an instance of this in the example of Matthew in Chapter 1 (Activity 1.3) where his mother described Matthew's behaviour to the visiting teacher as being 'just like his father', and saw herself as powerless to influence him in any way. We considered how she might now be transferring onto Matthew the feelings of angry and intimidated helplessness that she experienced in her earlier relationship with his violently abusive father. The transference effect will be even more powerful if her own father also behaved in this way, and this is quite likely. People do often seem to choose a partner who has something in common with a parent, and this can be understood in terms of the Oedipus complex, discussed below, or within the framework of attachment theory, which we will discuss in Chapter 3. There is also likely to be transference onto the teacher as an authority figure, and this will compound Matthew's mother's angry and powerless feelings in this situation. One of the clues that transference is at work is the strength of the feelings that are aroused; this is because they usually relate to early childhood.

The term *countertransference* is used to describe the feelings experienced by the analyst in response to their patient, and it is a useful concept not just for psychoanalysts and therapists but for anyone in a professional helping relationship with another. These feelings can come both from the worker's own experience and from what is projected into them by the person they are working with. For example, Matthew's teacher in Activity 1.3 might find himself feeling very angry at Matthew's mother's response to his concerns about her child. He may also feel helpless. This could be to do with Matthew's mother's unexpressed feelings being experienced by the teacher through projective identification (see above), or to do with something in his own experience (perhaps his parents behaved in a similar way to Matthew's, or perhaps there are other things going on in his working life that make him feel helpless). Or it could be a combination of both of these.

PSYCHOSEXUAL STAGES

If Jenny – in Activity 2.2 – had been 13 when the mistreatment started, the emotional and intellectual resources available to her would be different. They are different again for a baby subjected to abuse. Freud saw emotional development going through several stages (see Table 2.1), with each stage having its characteristic goals and its characteristic defensive strategies.

Table 2.1 Psychosexual stages

Stage	Age
Oral	First Year
Anal	Roughly ages 2-3
Phallic (Onset of Oedipus complex)	Roughly ages 4-6
Latency period	Age 7 to adolescence
Genital	Adolescence onwards

More controversially perhaps, Freud called these stages 'psychosexual' stages. And this is because he saw them as being based on the child's changing focus of *sexual gratification*. (Many people find this a somewhat shocking concept, even nowadays, because we are accustomed to thinking of childhood as a time that is free, or relatively free, of preoccupation with sex.)

During the *oral* stage the principle source of gratification is food and the comfort obtained from sucking, the latter being as important as the nourishment itself.

> The baby's obstinate persistence in sucking gives evidence at an early stage of a need for satisfaction which, though it originates from and is instigated by the taking of nourishment, nevertheless strives to obtain pleasure independently of nourishment and for that reason may be termed sexual. (Freud, 2003 [1949]: 24)

Freud's definition of 'sexual' in the above quote is worth noting. Many people might agree with most of this sentence but might use the word 'sensual'. Alternatively, they might say that the gratification obtained from suckling was 'like sex' or 'analogous to sex', if they think that sex is primarily about reproduction, but acknowledge that it carries a whole range of other functions to do with pleasure, intimacy and so on. But a woman who enjoyed breastfeeding her baby might have no difficulty in recognising it as a sexual experience. Freud's reputation is that he says everything is to do with sex. He certainly *does* give sex a very central role but, as this quote shows, his definition of 'sex' is quite broad.

In Freud's model, people can get *fixated* at different stages for various reasons, which is to say they hang on to some aspects of behaviour characteristic of that stage – or *regress* (i.e. go backwards) to such behaviour at a time of stress. The orally fixated person has the mouth as their primary 'erotogenic zone', and tends 'to *identify* with others rather than to relate to them as others' (Rycroft, 1995: 122). This is because the oral stage is the most primitive stage, a time when a baby has not yet learnt that self and others are really separate things. (See Chapter 4 for further discussion on the growth of a child's sense of objects as separate to self.) Food and comfort come through sucking and taking in milk, and the mother who nurses him at the breast, or the carer who holds the bottle, are taken for granted as being there to serve his need. We often regress to an oral stage when we are ill and we find childhood foods comforting. And adolescence – a time of rapid advance towards independence – is also characterised by periodic regressions to dependence, as any parent will know. The teenager helplessly searching for a vital item in the chaotic bedroom from which parents have been banned for months while shouting, 'But you *must* know where it is!!' has regressed in that moment to the childhood stage when he was secure in the knowledge that if he signalled his distress loudly enough his parent would be able to make it better, whatever its cause.

During the *anal* stage, according to Freud, the anus and defecation are the major source of sensual pleasure. And at this stage of ego development, control of the body and socialisation of impulses are the child's major preoccupations. A basic but very important example of body control usually acquired during this stage is that of toilet training, when a child learns to resist the impulse to defecate whenever the urge takes her and to control and defer it.

So compulsive orderliness and excessive pleasure taken in power and control are, in the Freudian scheme of things, examples of anal fixation. The pleasure we take in orderliness and control was seen by Freud as akin to the pleasure taken by a child proudly looking into the potty after defecating and then presenting some particularly fine stools to his parent for admiration. Like other ideas of Freud's, this idea has entered everyday speech: the word 'anal' is sometimes used of someone who is very controlling and orderly ('I'm very anal about my CD collection'). Interestingly the phrase 'tight-arsed' is used of someone who is mean, though we do not know whether the latter term followed or preceded Freud. Taking pleasure in cruelty (sadism) – again to do with power and control – is also supposed to be characteristic of the anal stage (though sadism can also be oral – hurting through biting and devouring).

During the *phallic* stage the focus – for both boys *and* girls in conventional Freudian thinking – is the penis. (This is of course very controversial – and raises questions about how Freud viewed the sexes.) Fixation in the phallic phase might result in an adult who sees sexual activity as a test of potency, as opposed to an adult who has progressed to the *genital* stage, who would see it as the expression of a relationship.

It is during the phallic stage that the famous *Oedipus complex* is supposed to come into play. The name comes from the Greek myth of Oedipus as told in Sophocles' tragedy *Oedipus Rex*. As an infant Oedipus was left to die on a mountainside because it was prophesied that he would kill his father, the king, and marry his mother. But he was saved by a kindly shepherd, and went on unknowingly to fulfil the prophecy. He inherited his father's kingdom, brought down a curse upon his people and gouged out his own eyes in remorse when he discovered what he had done. The idea of the Oedipus complex is that, at the phallic stage, both boys and girls desire to have an exclusive sexual relationship with their opposite-sex parent, and become murderously jealous of their same-sex parent. This is countered however by, firstly, fear of the same-sex parent (in boys this is supposed to be a fear of actual castration by their father) and, secondly, contradictory feelings of love for the same-sex parent. At this stage girls are supposed to become aware of their own lack of a penis ('penis envy').

Freud saw the Oedipus complex as being resolved by identification with the same-sex parent, and suppression of desire for the opposite-sex parent. So, for example, by identifying with his father a boy can, as it were, vicariously have a sexual relationship with his mother – and no longer feel the need to kill his father. This then paves the way for a mature adult relationship which is not based on dependency or the need to control.

Control

Control is most obviously associated with the anal stage of development, but issues of control feature throughout the developmental process. Eating disorders are self-evidently oral in that they are concerned with food, and what is taken in (or not) by way of the mouth. However, they are usually understood as being concerned with control. The anorexic, very often an adolescent, seeks to control her own appetite and body, and also ends up controlling those close to her; unable to make her eat, they can only watch helplessly as she starves herself. This can be seen as a denial of oral dependency, and very often features a conflicted relationship with her mother, and a battle for control which is played out over food. Anorexia can also be seen as an attempt to turn back the developmental clock and deny progression to adult sexuality – Freud's genital stage.

Phallic sexual behaviour, which places potency above relationship (seen in its most extreme form in rape and other manifestations of sexual violence) is also associated with control and power over others. Sexual desire and aggression are strongly linked, as they are in the myth of Oedipus.

The goal of a healthy developmental process is to establish a sense of autonomy and control over oneself which is secure enough not to need to resort to a defensive exercising of control over others.

Having accomplished the resolution of the Oedipus complex, the child then enters the *latency* phase until adolescence. This is viewed as a relatively quiet period, in psychosexual terms, between the struggles of the Oedipal phase and the struggles of adolescence.

The final phase of development (for Freud, that is: Erik Erikson, discussed below, suggested three further stages) and therefore not one which a person can be fixated in, is the *genital* phase, when the individual seeks a sexual partner as a substitute for the opposite sex parent, and as another and more permanent way of resolving the Oedipal conflict. (Sometimes, of course, the partner chosen is of the same sex.)

We are about to move on to discuss some developments of Freud's ideas. The following activity is to give you an opportunity to 'take stock' of what we have covered so far:

━━━━━ Activity 2.3 ━━━━━

Can you think of examples – among people you know – of people who might be described as having oral fixations, anal fixations or fixations from the phallic stage, in Freud's sense?

Do you find that these concepts shed any light on behaviour (whether other people's or indeed your own)?

Thinking of the genital stage, can you think of examples of people who have chosen partners who remind you of one of their parents?

Can you think of instances from your own experience of unconscious processes and defences?

At the beginning of this discussion, we asked you to consider your own preconceptions about what Freud was 'about'. Having considered this again, what do you think about Freud's ideas about sex – and its importance in human development?

What would you consider to be the major problems with Freud's theory, and what would you see as its strengths?

Comments on Activity 2.3

We can't comment on the people you know, of course, but it seems in our experience that certain characteristic patterns of behaviour are observable which could be described in Freudian terms as anal, oral and so on. It seems useful – and makes some sense to us – to think of these as patterns which come from different stages of childhood.

It seems quite common for people to choose as a partner someone who has something in common with a parent - e.g. appearance, character, role. For example, one of the authors had an aunt, oldest and favourite daughter of her bank manager father, who married a man who worked in a neighbouring bank and went on to become a bank manager himself.

Instances of unconscious processes seem quite common in everyday life. An example which one of us has encountered is projected anger as in:

'Of course I personally don't mind, but everyone else in the team is very angry with you.' In that instance the speaker may quite genuinely not be aware of being angry herself, having split off her angry feelings and projected them onto, or into, the other members of the team. If the other members of the team don't actually feel angry, this is projection. If they do, then it may be projective identification (or it may be their own anger for their own reasons).

Although we've argued that Freud's definition of 'sexual' is broader than most people's, and in many instances the word 'sensual' could perhaps be substituted, Freud's preoccupation with the sexual drive is an issue for many people. It was one of the reasons that Carl Jung split with Freud.

Some other criticisms of Freud are discussed at the end of this chapter.

DEVELOPMENTS OF FREUD'S IDEAS

Freud's ideas have proved to be very fertile ground for other thinkers and theorists, both in his own time and in the years since. It would be impossible here to give an account of all the different strands that have emerged, split off from, or been influenced by Freudian thought – they are so numerous and diverse. Alfred Adler, for example, split off from Freud in 1911. Carl Jung did likewise soon afterwards, falling out with Freud on a number of points after being a close colleague and disciple. This pattern of close personal and intellectual relationships followed by acrimonious splits was followed throughout Freud's life. It resembles the rivalry between father and son which he saw as part of the Oedipus complex, and perhaps helps to explain why he thought this idea so important.

The Freudian tradition threads its way through many aspects of intellectual life. It has influenced not only psychology but philosophy, literature, literary criticism and the creative arts. For example, surrealist artists such as Dali were much influenced by Freud, and the ideas of the French psychoanalyst Jacques Lacan about language have contributed to the development of postmodernist critical theory. Some of those who developed Freud's ideas would see themselves as remaining within his framework, others as moving on from it, branching off from it or making connections with other schools of thought. There have been feminist reworkings of Freud's and Lacan's ideas, for example in the work of Dorothy Dinnerstein, Nancy Chodorow, Julia Kristeva and Juliet Mitchell.

The development of psychoanalytic theory was deeply affected by historical events. Freud and many of his followers were Jewish and in the 1930s and 1940s, along with other intellectuals, found themselves forced to flee from Nazi persecution. Freud and his daughter Anna and Melanie Klein settled in England while other major figures, such as Erich Fromm, Karen Horney, Herbert Marcuse and Erik Erikson, emigrated to the United States. This geographical dispersal led to theoretical development taking rather different courses. In Britain, what is known as 'object relations theory' became the most important idea, while in the United States, 'ego psychology' became influential. Both developed thinking about the processes by which, as infants, we learn to relate to the outside world and develop a sense of who we are – the balancing act.

For the remainder of this chapter we will briefly look at the ideas of two members of the British object relations school, Donald Winnicott and Melanie Klein, and at the related ideas of Erik Erikson about ego development, to which we will be referring again later on in this book. Another member of the British object relations school, John Bowlby, and the Attachment Theory which he developed, will be discussed in more detail in the next chapter.

OBJECT RELATIONS AND EGO DEVELOPMENT

In early Freudian theory, people are seen as seeking to gratify primitive instinctual needs. An individual's relationship to others is seen in terms of 'drive reduction', the extent to which that relationship can be used to meet basic instinctual needs (e.g. for food and – of course – for sexual/sensual gratification). Later, Freud began to focus more on relationship in his work on the Oedipus complex, and in his conception of the superego as an internalisation of a parental figure.

However, in the various developments of Freud's ideas described as object relations theories, the development of the *relationship* between an individual (the 'subject') and others (the 'object') takes centre stage. The word 'object' is used here not in the sense of a 'thing' but in the sense in which we refer to the object of a sentence. (In the sentence, 'I love my mother', 'I' is the subject and 'mother' is the object in grammatical terms.) In object relations theory, too, the focus shifts away from the Oedipal drama and the role of the father to the earliest stages of infancy and the child's relationship with its mother or primary carer.

The mirror

In object relations theory, human relationships are a prerequisite to a sense of selfhood. It is only through an intimate relationship with her primary carers that an individual can arrive at a sense of difference between self and others. Erikson wrote that our ability as adults to trust others stems in the first instance from learning as a child to trust that when our mother goes away, she will come back:

> The infant's first social achievement ... is his willingness to let the mother out of his sight without undue anxiety or rage, because she has become an inner certainty as well as an outer predictability. (Erikson, 1995 [1951]: 222)

This process of building up a sense of trust which will survive the process of separation is at the heart of attachment theory, which we will examine in the next chapter. Not all children ever do have this experience, of course. If you know anyone who experienced neglectful or very inconsistent parenting early in life (or if this applies to you yourself) you will probably agree that people with these experiences do indeed often find it very hard to trust others in adult relationships. So this basic sense of trust in infancy seems to be a precursor to satisfactory relationships later in life. Donald Winnicott (1896–1971) used the analogy of a mirror to describe how this works (Winnicott, 2005 [1971]: 111–18). All small children must rely on others to meet their basic physical and emotional needs. And Winnicott suggested that, if these needs are reliably met when they are expressed, then it is as if the carer is *mirroring* the child. A need seems to the child to bring a corresponding response, just as when we look into a mirror, our mirror-image produces actions that correspond to our own, and we see reflected back an image that we recognise as ourselves.

So, as a result of having her needs consistently met, the child would conclude (if not actually in words) that 'If I express my needs, they are met. If I express my feelings, they are recognised and acknowledged as valid. My carer knows who I am.' This, Winnicott suggested, gives her a sense of possessing power, an *illusion of omnipotence* (Winnicott, 2005 [1971]: 11). As a result of this experience, the child is freed up to be creative, to make demands of life and to spontaneously express needs and feelings. Through having her self mirrored and her needs recognised the child develops what Winnicott called a *true self*. People learn who they are by having their needs and feelings reflected back, just as we can only come to know what our own face looks like by seeing it reflected in a mirror.

But children are not necessarily mirrored. Needs can be ignored, feelings can be dismissed, demands can be rejected or responded to negatively, for instance with anger, punishment or ridicule. And a child who does not have the experience of her needs being reliably met at this crucial early stage, or of her feelings being accepted as valid, will fail to develop a sense of trust and fail to properly develop a sense of herself as an autonomous being. In fact, Winnicott thought, for a child who has not been 'mirrored', human interaction in general becomes terrifying, and the child attempts to defend herself by developing a *false self* in which she denies her own feelings and needs and instead tries to anticipate the reactions of others. An extreme form of this would be the 'frozen watchfulness' of badly abused children, who do not play or explore but simply watch the adults around them, trying to guess what they are going to do next. But of course many of us have at least some difficulty in asserting our needs, and many of us feel more comfortable giving way to other people and meeting their needs. (This seems to us to be particularly common among those, like many readers of this book, who are drawn to work in the caring professions.) Even in a very happy home environment, after all, a child's needs cannot always be mirrored. Winnicott was clear about this when he talked about the 'good enough' mother (Winnicott, 2005 [1971]: 10 and elsewhere). As Erikson said about early childhood:

> Even under the most favourable circumstances, this stage seems to introduce into psychic life … a sense of inner division and universal nostalgia for a paradise forfeited. It is against this powerful combination of a sense of having been deprived … and of having been abandoned that basic trust must maintain itself throughout life. (Erikson, 1995 [1951]: 224)

Winnicott described the process of weaning as one of disillusionment (Winnicott, 2005 [1971]: 13). He was talking about the difficult process of giving up the exclusivity of a physically and emotionally nourishing relationship with a mother figure and allowing in the wider world: other foods, other relationships, other experiences. He thought that one of the things that can help children across this bridge from mother to the outside world is the use of a *transitional object*: the favourite teddy or piece of grubby old blanket which is invested with huge emotional significance and which must never be lost until it is outgrown.

So it is an important part of a child's development that his needs should not always be met immediately and absolutely. Gradually the parent enables the child to accept that, though the world can provide something like what is needed and desired, it will not do so automatically nor at the very moment the need arises or the desire is felt. The gap between wish and fulfilment stimulates the child to develop his own resources of creativity and resilience.

Good breast and bad breast

Melanie Klein (1882–1960) put less emphasis than the other object relations theorists on the external world and more on the child's internal fantasies. And she presented what many find a rather bleak and disturbing picture of what is going on in the mind of a small human being. Klein suggested that babies from an early stage simultaneously feel intense love and murderous, sadistic hatred towards the same object: the mother, and in particular the mother's breast. (If you don't believe that babies can have such violent feelings, look closely the next time you see a baby in a rage.)

The love felt by the baby for his mother relates to the comfort offered by the mother, while the hatred relates to the absolute power that the mother has to give and withhold this comfort. (Because, as we've just noted, no mother can hope to respond to *every* need.) To begin with, Klein thought, babies deal with these contradictory feelings by the classically Freudian mechanisms of *splitting* and *projection*. Instead of seeing the mother as one person, the baby splits her in his mind into two different people, or two different things – the 'good breast' and the 'bad breast' in Kleinian terminology. The rage which the hungry baby feels when food is not forthcoming is projected outwards onto the 'bad breast' which the baby then experiences as attacking and frightening. However, it is necessary for the child to move on from this position (the *paranoid-schizoid* position) because failure to do so could in her view lead to schizoid/paranoid disorders in later life, including (so Klein thought) schizophrenia.

The move from the paranoid-schizoid position takes the child to the depressive position, which starts to appear at about three months. At this stage she comes to see the mother as a whole person, so that:

> disappointment with the mother no longer turns her into something wholly bad and dangerous: damage is no longer feared as total destruction. A good experience does not mean heaven forever; its loss is no longer the end of the world but is … mitigated by the hope of good experiences in the future. (Segal, 2004: 38)

In the depressive position the child is able to experience and tolerate *ambivalence*; that is, to have contradictory feelings of love and hate towards his mother at the same time. But guilt also appears at this stage when the child realises that his own feelings are ambivalent, and feels badly about the violent and negative feelings he has towards his mother. This guilt can be assuaged by finding a way of making *reparation*, that is, by expressing the love that he feels alongside the hate. Contrary to what its name might suggest, this position is essentially a healthy one, based on reality rather than fantasy:

> The loved and hated aspects of the mother are no longer felt to be so widely separated, and the result is an increased fear of loss, states akin to mourning, and a strong feeling of guilt, because the aggressive impulses are felt to be directed against the loved object … The very experience of depressive feelings in turn has the effect of further integrating the ego, because it makes for an increased understanding of psychic reality and better perception of the external world, as well as for a greater synthesis between inner and external situations. (Klein, 1986 [1946]: 189)

Klein talks about positions rather than stages, conveying the idea of an oscillation between positions rather than an orderly progression from one stage to the next: 'Some fluctuations between the paranoid-schizoid and the depressive positions always occur and are part of normal development' (Klein, 1986 [1946]: 191). We repeatedly revert to a schizoid position at times of difficulty and stress. For example, in a quarrel with a loved partner we may temporarily see them as wholly bad and malicious, and ourselves as wholly blameless and good. But Klein thought that real caring relationships require us to negotiate the difficulties of the depressive position, in which ambivalence has to be faced.

Klein described the integration of the ego as beginning with the depressive position, when the world begins to be experienced as a coherent whole, and the self which experiences it begins to feel coherent too. Erikson, whose work we will now discuss, saw the development of the ego as a lifelong process which begins in a similar way, with the baby learning to trust the world in which he finds himself.

Erikson's stages

Erik Erikson (1902–1994) saw the ego developing through a series of stages at each of which it faces a 'crisis', which must be resolved for the individual to move on to the next stage (see Erikson, 1995 [1951]: 222 ff). This is a classically Freudian model, both in its conception of stages, and in its suggestion that there are characteristic issues that have to be resolved at each stage before a person is fully capable of moving on. Indeed, the first five stages in Erikson's model do correspond to Freud's oral, anal, phallic, latency and genital stages. But a major difference is that Erikson's model spans the whole life cycle and not just childhood.

Also, while Freud referred to stages of *psychosexual* development, Erikson paid more attention to the social context of development and referred to *psychosocial* stages. Although there are many criticisms that can be levelled at his framework, it does provide a useful starting point for discussion of change across the human lifespan – and we will be returning to it in later chapters. His stages are summarised in Table 2.2.

As you can see each stage has a favourable outcome and an unfavourable outcome. The actual outcome for any individual would depend on how well the particular 'crisis', or challenge, of that stage had been successfully met. You'll also notice that an unfavourable outcome in one stage makes it more difficult to fully meet the challenge of the next stage. Thus, as we've already discussed, Erikson saw the task of the first stage (equivalent to Freud's oral stage) as being the establishment of a sense of trust. Clearly if it is not possible for an infant to establish a sense of trust in the environment because it is not a secure one, it would be more difficult to achieve the sense of autonomy which is the next stage (the anal stage, in Freudian terms). In turn it would be harder to develop the capacity for initiative which is the optimum outcome of the next (phallic) stage. This will then put the child at a disadvantage when she reaches the next stage and starts school, because it will make it more difficult for her to apply herself to learning, so that she risks ending up with a sense of inferiority which she will carry into adolescence and adulthood, and which will affect her capacity to achieve the subsequent developmental tasks. Social factors will play their part too; in a context where it is hard to find secure and meaningful employment it will also be hard for her to develop a vocational identity and feel she is making a contribution to society.

Having said this, Erikson's model does not say that you have to have completed one stage before you go on to the next. In fact everyone is likely to have some unresolved issues from earlier stages (exactly as in the original Freudian model). But too much baggage from earlier stages will impede progress.

A new stage of life, according to Erikson, does however offer opportunities not only to tackle the new challenges that it presents, but to go back and deal with unresolved issues from earlier stages.

Table 2.2   Stages of psychosocial development

Life Crisis	Favourable Outcome	Unfavourable Outcome
First Year *Trust v. Mistrust* The child needs consistent and stable care in order to develop feelings of security	Trust in the environment and hope for the future	Suspicion, insecurity, fear of the future
Second and Third Years *Autonomy v. Shame and Doubt* The child seeks a sense of independence from parents	A sense of autonomy and self-esteem	Feelings of shame and doubt about one's own capacity for self-control
Fourth and Fifth Years *Initiative v. Guilt* The child explores her environment and plans new activities	The ability to initiate activities and enjoy following them through	Fear of punishment and guilt about one's own personal feelings
Age Six to Eleven *Industry v. Inferiority* The child acquires important knowledge and skills relating to her culture	A sense of competence and achievement. Confidence in one's own ability to make and do things	Unfavourable reactions from others may cause feelings of inadequacy and inferiority
Adolescence *Identity v. Role Confusion* The young person searches for a coherent personal and vocational identity	Ability to see oneself as a consistent and integrated person	Confusion over who and what one is
Young Adulthood *Intimacy v. Isolation* The adult seeks deep and lasting relationships	The ability to experience love and commitment to others	Isolation; superficial relationships with others
Middle Adulthood *Generativity v. Stagnation* The individual seeks to be productive and creative and to make a contribution to society	The ability to be concerned and caring about others in the wider sense	Lack of growth; boredom and over-concern with oneself
Late Adulthood *Integrity v. Despair* The individual reviews and evaluates what has been accomplished in life	A sense of satisfaction with one's life and its accomplishments; acceptance of death	Regret over omissions and missed opportunities; fear of death

Sometimes, for example, a person entering a 'midlife crisis', at the beginning of Erikson's sixth stage, may revisit unresolved issues from early adulthood and adolescence. (We'll discuss this further in Chapter 7.) And how the transition to adulthood is negotiated will in turn relate to earlier childhood experiences when the first steps were taken towards independence from parents. It is also common for new parents to find that the experience of parenthood reawakens their own unresolved early childhood feelings. This is often a contributory factor in postnatal depression.

And in a family, of course, different members will be going through different stages at any given time. This creates a complex web of interactions which we will discuss further in Chapter 9, when we look at family systems.

As good a way as any of looking at Erikson's model is to test it against your own life:

Activity 2.4

What stage are you at in your life? Look through the stages you have already been through and see whether you agree with Erikson about the issues that were important at each stage.

Which stages do you think you negotiated most successfully? Which ones do you think you negotiated less successfully? (Everyone carries some 'baggage' from unresolved issues in earlier life – 'unfavourable outcomes' in Erikson's terminology.)

What do you see as the main drawbacks of Erikson's model?

Comments on Activity 2.4

One criticism of Erikson's model is that it is too linear and prescriptive. It may sketch out the issues we deal with, or try to deal with as we grow older, but it does not allow sufficiently for the many different routes that we may take.

You may also have felt that this model fits better with middle-class life in North America and Europe than it would in other cultures where decisions are made much more collectively and individuals have less choice (or no choice at all) about issues like marriage and career.

CRITICISMS OF FREUD AND HIS SUCCESSORS

We asked you earlier (in Activity 2.3) to consider what you saw as the main problems with Freud's model. We will conclude this chapter by discussing some of the criticisms that are commonly levelled at Freud and psychodynamic theory. Some of these apply primarily to Freud and some are more general criticisms of a wider range of psychodynamic approaches.

Originality

We have seen how later theorists built on the work of Freud, who is often seen as the founding father of psychoanalytic theory. But the claims that are made for Freud's ideas as original have also been challenged. Perhaps, for practical purposes, it makes little difference precisely who contributed to the development of these ideas, for they certainly do have their precedents. For example, if you look at the writings of the Greek philosopher Plato (who lived nearly two and a half millennia before Freud), you find a dynamic model of the human mind in which it is likened to a chariot in which the rider is the soul while the two horses pulling it are reason and desire (1973: 51).

Likewise in Sophocles' play *Oedipus Rex* (written nearly two and a half millennia ago), Jocasta, the wife and mother of Oedipus, says:

> Many a man before you
>
> In his dreams, has shared his mother's bed (Sophocles, translated by Fagles, 1984: 215)

Webster (2005) in particular argues that Freud's ideas are actually much less original than is usually thought.

Scientific method

Freud presented his theory of personality and human development as scientific, and sought acceptance from the scientific community of his day. However, it is questionable whether his methods were scientific in the way in which that term is usually understood. His methods, which relied on his clinical observations, could not eliminate his own subjective feelings and prejudices. That said, modern perspectives on scientific method accept that objectivity is never possible, and that the observer will always affect the outcome. In social research it is accepted that qualitative research, which looks in depth at the experience of a few people, has a different kind of validity from quantitative research, which may be more rigorous in terms of samples and control groups. In this respect Freud could be seen as a participant observer, and a qualitative researcher *par excellence*.

Personal bias

Freud's use of self-analysis as part of the foundation for his theories is open to some criticism. As well as using material from the analysis of his patients, he subjected himself to the same process of analysis and used the results as the basis for his developmental theories. As his biographer Peter Gay observes, 'Many of Freud's most unsettling ideas drew on acknowledged, or covert, autobiographical sources' (Gay, 1988: 90). The primacy which he gave to the Oedipus complex reflected the powerful relationship he had with his father; the theory was developed in the period immediately after his father's death. This bias made it difficult for him to look beyond the confines of his own cultural, social and gender position.

Patriarchy and feminism

Freud didn't understand women – he famously referred to female sexuality as a 'dark continent' (Freud, 1959 [1926]: 212). His concept of penis envy has attracted anger and scorn from feminists at the idea that women should be defined by their absence of a penis. But his case histories do show an understanding of how women were made ill by their social situation. Dorothy Dinnerstein has reframed penis envy in a way which is more consistent with feminism by talking about the little girl's envy of 'the social prerogatives which it (the penis) confers' (Dinnerstein, 1987: 52n). And there were plenty of women among Freud's intellectual and professional colleagues who played an important role in the development of psychoanalytic theory and practice. His daughter Anna was one of the most significant of these. He encouraged and supported her development as an analyst and was happy at the end of his life to see her as his intellectual heir who would carry on his work.

Seduction theory

Freud has been much criticised for changing his mind about believing what his patients told him about their experience of sexual abuse. As we have seen, Freud's theories were constantly evolving and changing throughout his life, and his position on seduction theory was part of this process. It is not the case, as his most vehement critics (e.g. Masson, 2003) maintain, that he abandoned a belief in the reality of sexual abuse altogether. For example, he wrote in one of his public lectures in 1916:

> You must not suppose, however, that the sexual abuse of a child by its nearest male relatives belongs entirely to the realm of fantasy. Most analysts will have treated cases in which such events were real and could be unimpeachably established. (Freud, 1963 [1916–17]: 370)

Much has been written on this issue, and you will have to read more in order to make up your own mind about it. Some suggestions for further reading are given at the end of this chapter.

Cultural specificity

It can be argued that the theories presented here were developed in relation to Western two-parent nuclear families in the first half of the twentieth century, and there is no reason to assume that they can be applied equally in different cultural contexts. And Western family life has itself changed: higher divorce rates have led to more complex family structures, and a child's parents may not remain a couple for very long. With the exception of Alfred Adler, most psychoanalytic theorists, from Freud onwards, have paid little attention to sibling relationships (though see Mitchell, 2003). However, these can be of immense importance. Sibling relationships, unlike those with parents and children, will often span all of life's stages, from childhood to old age. And when parents are unavailable, they can go some way to compensating for that lack. For example, in many families in southern Africa, where parents have died of AIDS, the bond between brothers and sisters is all that holds the family together.

Clearly you must make up your own mind about the strengths and weaknesses of Freud's ideas, and those of his successors. However, we would suggest that for all their shortcomings these ideas remain of value. Freud and other psychodynamic theorists have shed light on dimensions of human development which are not illuminated in the same way by any other body of theory. They give us a way of thinking about how we find our place in the world and of understanding the forces which drive us to seek relationships, and they explain why the quality of our earliest relationships is so fundamental to our well-being for the rest of our lives. In the next chapter we will look at attachment theory, which is concerned with how these relationships are established, and what happens when they go wrong.

CHAPTER SUMMARY

- In this chapter, we looked at the development of Freud's ideas about the unconscious.
- We looked at Freud's conception of the structure of the personality (ego, id, superego).
- We saw how personality is shaped through unconscious processes, and looked at the psychological defences of denial, projection and splitting, identification and projective identification, and at transference and countertransference.
- We then looked at his theory of psychosexual development (from oral, through anal and phallic stages, into the struggles of the Oedipus complex and the latency period and finally into the genital stage).
- We discussed developments of Freud's ideas, including those which (loosely) can be categorised as object relations theories; some of the ideas of Winnicott (the mirror, the true and false selves, the transitional object), Klein (good breast and bad breast, the paranoid/schizoid and depressive positions). We also looked at Erikson's concept of psychosocial development.
- We concluded by looking at criticisms of Freud and psychodynamic theory.

In the next chapter we will look at *attachment theory*, a body of theory that developed out of object relations theory.

Tangled Webs

You will probably be able to find examples of the unconscious at work in all of our case studies, but we have suggested the following two cases to consider in relation to the themes in this chapter. Both deal with people who are struggling to resolve one of the life crises that Erikson describes.

Zak Renton (Case K). Zak is having difficulty with the adolescent task of establishing his identity. He has a very close relationship with his mother – Deanna describes them as being 'like a little married couple'. You could see him as stuck at the Oedipal stage of development, and he is now having difficulty expanding the horizon of his relationships to allow anyone else in. He is closely identified with his mother, and he is using this as a defence against the anxiety of beginning to find his own place in the world. He is also using the defence of projection to deal with feelings which neither he nor his mother, both described as 'gentle', are able to experience or express directly. He is projecting his anger into Derek by 'winding him up' in a way that might be seen as manipulative if its unconscious nature is not recognised. He is also projecting his feelings of uselessness and frustration into Jade and Rob. Their countertransference is strengthened by factors in their own experience; Jade is new and quite inexperienced, and Rob has become over-identified with Derek. Both are frustrated by the lack of support from other agencies for their work with Zak. If they are able to recognise the feelings that Zak stirs up in them as projective identification, it may be possible for them to use their countertransference to help him to own and integrate these feelings.

Deanna Whitworth and Zoe Scott (Case L) are finding it hard to adapt to their new roles as parents. Deanna is using the defence of denial both in relation to Zoe's drinking and to her own

(Continued)

(Continued)

difficulty in coping with this in addition to the demands of parenthood and work. As she talks to Brendan she uses minimisation and humour to play down the problem. We can also see projection at work here as Deanna, who has needed to see herself as a strong, coping person since childhood, projects her denied vulnerability onto Zoe, and therefore may unconsciously need Zoe's drinking problem to continue. We only see the situation and this couple's relationship through Deanna's eyes, and denial makes her an unreliable narrator. It is likely that there are also projections on Zoe's side, and that she too is denying the extent of her drinking. Deanna is increasingly absenting herself from the family, perhaps identifying with her absent father. It is probable that their baby Sophia is not receiving the mirroring that she needs from either parent at the moment, and that her apparent compliance may be a false self.

 You can access Tangled Webs by visiting **https://study.sagepub.com/tangledwebs**

━━━━ Further reading ━━━━

On Freud and his ideas

Freud, S. (2003 [1949]) *An Outline of Psychoanalysis*. London: Penguin.

This is a short and perfectly readable summary of his ideas by Freud himself, not quite completed due to his death. Unlike some of his successors, Freud writes in a clear and lucid style.

Jacobs, M. (2003) *Sigmund Freud*. London: Sage.
Rycroft, C. (1995) *A Critical Dictionary of Psychoanalysis*, 2nd edn. London: Penguin. Contains explanations of all the many terms and concepts.

On developments of Freudian theory

Elliot, A. (2002) *Psychoanalytic Theory: An Introduction*. Oxford: Oxford University Press. An overview including Klein, Winnicott, Erikson, Lacan and others.
Erikson, E. (1995 [1951]) *Childhood and Society*. London: Vintage.
Segal, J. (2004) *Melanie Klein*, 2nd edn. London: Sage.
Winnicott, D.W. (2005 [1971]) *Playing and Reality*, 2nd edn. London: Tavistock/Routledge.

Criticism of Freud

Frosh, S. (1997) *For and Against Psychoanalysis*. London: Routledge.
Masson, J. (2003) *The Assault on Truth: Freud's Suppression of the Seduction Theory*. New York: Ballantine Books.
Webster, R. (2005) *Why Freud Was Wrong: Sin, Science and Psychoanalysis*, 3rd edn. Oxford: Orwell Press.

A SECURE BASE

THE IMPORTANCE OF ATTACHMENT

TANGLED WEBS

Any of the cases in Tangled Webs would be relevant reading for this chapter. The relevant questions to ask are (in the case of children): What kind of messages are these children being given about their worth? What are they learning about the availability of others to help them when they are distressed? What are they learning about the reliability of others? What message are they getting about how best to get the most they can out of others? Cases you might like to look at are **Caitlin Smart (Dudley)** and **the Dudley/Harris family (Cases A and G)**, and **Tracey Green (Case J)**. Tracey is a social worker dealing with the Dudley/Harris family, so you could ask yourself how her experience might affect the way she sees them.

 You can access Tangled Webs by visiting **https://study.sagepub.com/tangledwebs**

At the end of the previous chapter we looked at the development of Freud's ideas by object rela-tions theorists. Attachment theory, the subject of this chapter, is an object relations theory *par excellence*. It is based on the proposition that the way we relate to others throughout our lives (subject–object relations, in other words) is shaped by our first relationship with our primary carer, who traditionally and still usually is the mother.

John Bowlby, who one might describe as the 'father' of attachment theory, was a psychoanalyst and a member of the British group of object relations theorists which also included Winnicott and Klein. His emphasis was very different from Klein's, however, and he was less interested in speculating about fantasies that go on in children's minds and more interested in developing a scientific approach that drew on verifiable, objective research on human and animal behaviour. Nevertheless, in modern attachment theory, which has developed from Bowlby's original ideas, you can still find ideas that owe a debt to Freud.

Attachment theory has been and continues to be very influential in the development of policy and professional practice. It has had its critics, but research in the rapidly developing field of neu-roscience is now emphasising the crucial role that our early attachments play in the development of our brains and our cognitive and emotional functioning. It has been particularly important in fields where assessing parenting is a central issue. In Britain, for example, health visitors, social workers, teachers and others working with children and families are often involved in addressing questions such as the following. All of them are related to attachment:

- Are a child's needs being adequately met within this relationship?
- Can the relationship change?
- Would the damage done by disrupting this relationship be outweighed or not by the benefits of providing other more consistent carers?
- Could the child settle with new carers?
- If so, what therapeutic work would be needed to make that possible?
- Is the respite and support offered to a family by a shared care arrangement likely to be beneficial to relationships in that family?
- Does a child's rejection of their foster carers reflect a real problem with those particular carers, or is it the result of the child's difficulties with attachment that would be a problem in any relationship?

Writers such as Howe (1995, 2005), Berlin et al. (2005) and Juffer and Bakermans-Kranenberg (2008) use attachment theory as a reference point for developing and evaluating strategies for assessment and intervention in child care practice. And of course it is also vitally important in the field of fostering and adoption practice (Schofield and Beek, 2006; Golding, 2008).

In any of the caring professions – or indeed in life generally – you are certain to encounter many people who have problems with attachment. Attachment theorists argue that many other psy-chological problems actually have their roots in difficulties in early attachment relationships and that early attachment has strong links with mental health in adult life, the ability to form relationships, the ability to parent and the ability to deal with loss (see Chapter 7). And devel-opments in neuroscience are shedding new light on the relationship between attachment and cognitive development (which we will discuss in Chapter 4).

The following activity may help you to gather your own thoughts on the subject:

====== **Activity 3.1** ======

a   Think of a child you know who seems to have some problems in relating with his/her parent(s) or carer(s). What is it that makes you think there is a problem? How does it affect the child?
b   Now think of an adult you know who seems to have difficulty with intimate relationships. What makes you think that there is a difficulty? What are your theories about what may have caused the difficulty in the first place?

Comments on Activity 3.1

a   You may have mentioned that this child is reluctant to go to his/her carers, or seems anxious in their presence. Alternatively, you may have said that the child seems excessively clingy to his/her carers, and seems very anxious if separated from them at all. Or you may have said that the child appears to cling indiscriminately to any adult. Among the effects on the child, you may have noticed: poor concentration, difficulty in making friends, difficulty in judging social situations.
b   You may have mentioned an adult who seems to have difficulty in committing themselves, and is always ending relationships because they feel trapped.

Or an adult who is unable to talk about their feelings with their partner – or seems to talk about them compulsively. Or perhaps someone who always seems to let themselves be abused and dominated in relationships, and can't seem to end them, no matter how unhappy they feel ... If you know anything about this adult's childhood, you will probably notice that their relationship with parents/carers was problematic in some way. There may have been neglect or abuse, or abandonment of some sort. Or the parents may have been excessively controlling or excessively protective.

We'll now have a look at Bowlby's contribution to thinking about these matters.

JOHN BOWLBY AND 'MATERNAL DEPRIVATION'

Although a trained psychoanalyst, and a member of the British psychoanalytic community, John Bowlby (1907–1990) was critical of those psychoanalysts who focused (in his view) too much on fantasies and imaginary fears, such as a small boy's supposed fear of castration by his father, as if there were not enough real dangers in the world. He thought Klein and the Kleinians in particular were excessively interested in children's fantasies about their parents, and suggested (in the paper which he presented to qualify as a full member of the Institute of Psychoanalysis) that it would be much more fruitful to look at their parents' real characters (Bowlby, 1940). Bowlby was interested in the *external* factors that influence a child's development.

Bowlby was also interested in reconciling the insights of psychoanalytic theory with ethology (the study of animal behaviour) and with verifiable, empirical research in general. However, he was part of the psychoanalytic community, and though his ideas are expressed in much more down-to-earth 'common-sense' terms than those of some other writers in the psychoanalytic tradition, they recognisably follow the same pattern. As in classical Freudian theory, Bowlby's ideas included the concept of various unconscious strategies that come into play when needs can't be met at different stages, including strategies such as splitting or excluding things from consciousness (Bowlby, 1997 [1969]: 32). Like Freud, he saw these strategies being carried into later life.

Bowlby's particular interest was in the effects of separation of children from their parents. *Attachment, Separation* and *Loss* were the titles of the three volumes of his most famous work (Bowlby, 1997 [1969], 1998a [1973], 1998b [1980]). In 1950 he was asked by the World Health Organisation to carry out a study of children separated from their parents. (This was in the post-war context, when bereavement, evacuation, deportation and displacement had disrupted millions of families in Europe.) He looked at children separated from parents in various ways and interviewed disturbed adolescents and adults. He found a strong link between what he called 'maternal deprivation' and problems in adult life such as delinquency, mental illness and difficulties in parenting.

Bowlby's definition of 'maternal deprivation', in his original thinking, included loss of the mother or separation from the mother, as well as things like neglectful or abusive mothering. Both the word 'maternal' and the word 'deprivation' are targets of criticism, the former because of its exclusive emphasis on the mother, as opposed to the father and other carers, the latter because it conflates several very different things. As attachment theory has developed, it has taken on board some of the criticisms in both these areas.

In addition to these studies on the long-term effects of maternal deprivation, Bowlby and his colleague James Robertson also looked at the short-term effects on children of separation from their mothers (see Robertson and Bowlby, 1952). They made a series of films which graphically and painfully capture the process, and which have helped to educate generations of childcare professionals and to change childcare practices (*A Two Year Old Goes to Hospital* 1952; *Young Children in Brief Separation* 1967–71). What they observed was that children went through several stages:

1   A stage of *protest*, including crying, screaming, trying to find the mother and so on.
2   A stage of *despair,* when the child becomes listless and apathetic.
3   A stage of *detachment*, when the child seems to lose interest in the missing parent and starts to become involved again in other activities, though this involvement may be quite superficial and unengaged.

This last stage seemed to Bowlby to be the result of defensive mechanisms coming into play which meant that the child *repressed* (to use the Freudian term: Bowlby also used the phrase *defensively excluded*) feelings of grief and anger. If they were never resolved in any way, could these painful, angry, distressing feelings lead to the long-term problems which his other research seemed to indicate were associated with so-called maternal deprivation?

As you will see, attachment theory tries to bring these different observations together into a coherent whole.

Bowlby and social reform

Bowlby's interest in this topic was not, however, primarily academic. He was passionate about the need of children for love and security and he was influential in bringing about many changes that we now take for granted. For example, parents in the 1950s and 1960s were routinely told not to visit their children in hospital, because 'it only upsets them'. Bowlby decided that this was nonsense. Children did not get more upset when their parents visited, they just felt safe enough to *show* how upset they already were. Bowlby was a key figure in bringing about a change towards the modern approach of encouraging parental contact. Likewise, he challenged what he called 'the astonishing practice' of separating mothers and babies immediately after birth which was common in the 1950s. He described this practice as a 'madness of Western society' which he hoped would never be copied by 'the so-called less developed countries' (Bowlby, 1990 [1953]: 180). It is, of course, no longer normal in the West.

THE BIOLOGICAL ORIGINS OF ATTACHMENT

A much-quoted comment of Bowlby's, made in 1951, was that 'mother love in infancy and childhood is as important for mental health as are vitamins and proteins for physical health' (Bowlby, 1951, cited by Rutter, 1981: 15). He saw the need for a close relationship – an attachment – between child and carer (and particularly *mother*) as being a basic biological need. And, like the rest of the object relations school, he didn't see this relationship as being important only insofar as it met basic primary needs: sexual needs and the need for food. He saw it as a need in its own right. We can easily observe, not only in humans, but also in other mammals, how strong the bond is between a mother and a child. Both mother and baby animals of many species become distressed and agitated if they are separated, and mother animals will often fight ferociously to prevent a baby being taken from them. Bowlby quoted, for example, the following vivid description from a piece of research in which baby monkeys were separated from their mothers for five-minute periods:

> Separation of mother and infant monkeys is an extremely stressful experience for both mother and infant as well as for the attendants and for all other monkeys within sight or earshot of the experience. The mother becomes ferocious ... the infant's screams can be heard over almost the entire building. The mother struggles and attacks the separators. The baby clings tightly to the mother and to any object which it can grasp to avoid being held or removed by the attendant. With the baby gone the mother paces the cage continually ... bites at it and makes continual attempts to escape. The infant emits high-pitched screams intermittently and almost continuously for the whole period of the separation. (Jensen and Tolman, 1962, cited by Bowlby, 1998a [1973]: 85)

So both mother and baby monkey called to each other and signalled their distress, and the mother made frantic efforts to get back to the baby. These are examples of what Bowlby termed *attachment behaviour*, but attachment behaviour also includes behaviour by the child that has the effect of attracting the mother's interest in a positive way, such as smiling, and indeed *any* behaviour that has the function of bringing mother and child together. And it is by observing the amount of attachment behaviour that we gain some sense of how strong an attachment exists. For instance, from the account just quoted of a baby monkey being separated from the mother, we conclude from the behaviour of both mother and baby that a strong attachment exists between the two. But it is important to note that a *strong* attachment is not necessarily the same thing as a *secure* attachment.

Attachment and animal experiments

Bowlby was interested in learning from animal experiments. But such experiments are controversial for two reasons: firstly, there is a question about *ethics*. Secondly, there is the question as to whether they are valid. Can information from animals tell us anything about human beings? The sociologist, Erica Burman, for example, emphatically rejects this (Burman, 1994: 87-9).

The most well-known animal experiments in the field of attachment were carried out by Harlow and his collaborators (Harlow, 1963). In one experiment, baby rhesus monkeys were separated from their mothers within 12 hours of birth and placed in cages with two types of surrogate mothers: one made of soft cloth and one made of wire. They found that the babies preferred the cloth mother, spending their time cuddled up to it, even if the experimenters arranged things so that it was the wire mother that actually provided milk. Babies raised with these surrogate mothers, or with no mothers at all, grew up incapable of normal sexual or social behaviour, and were neglectful and abusive mothers to their own babies.

There must be serious ethical questions about such experiments, but there *do* seem to be striking parallels here with human experience. (Indeed the striking parallels with humans could be argued to be one compelling reason why these experiments should be regarded as unethical.)

Bowlby believed that attachment behaviour is innate, part of our 'nature', and he theorised that this behaviour had evolved for a specific reason. A baby (human or animal) needs to explore to learn about the world. It cannot permanently be physically in contact with its mother. But it also needs to retain some proximity to the mother, on whom it depends for food and protection. The effect of attachment behaviour is to act as a kind of invisible elastic, maintaining a link between mother and child. Too much separation, whether in terms of distance (too far away), or in terms of time (too long), increases the anxiety levels of mother and child and increases the amount of attachment behaviour. When closeness is restored, attachment behaviour can go into abeyance and other behaviours can be resumed. Attachment behaviour is about *homeostasis* (a term we will come back to in Chapter 8), which means maintaining a steady state.

The effects of this can be observed quite readily. If you are a parent, for example, you will probably be familiar with the scenario in which you are sitting in a room with your children playing round you and you then decide to move to another room. After a period of time you find that your children have followed you. They may not necessarily want anything in particular from you, and they may well quietly resume their games when homeostasis has been re-established. For a more extreme example of attachment in action, you only need to consider the reactions of both parent and child when they accidentally lose one another in a busy street.

Parents, mothers, carers

You may have noticed that we sometimes use the word 'mother' to describe a child's primary attachment figure, which was also Bowlby's practice. In the case of some animals, there can be little doubt that the mother *is* the primary attachment figure (and indeed in some species, the males take no part in childrearing, and may not even have any way of knowing which are their own children). But, of course, children can and do have attachment figures other than the mother. And, even if the main attachment figure *is* the mother, they may well have other figures who are also important sources of protection and comfort. A criticism of attachment theory, as originally expounded by Bowlby, is that it makes the assumption that there has to be one single primary focus of attachment behaviour. In all cultures to some extent, and in some cultures to a great extent, childcare is of course a task that is *shared*, not only by mothers and fathers but also by grandparents, sisters, brothers, uncles, aunts and friends.

THE SECURE BASE AND ATTACHMENT BEHAVIOURAL SYSTEMS

One way of looking at attachment is that the attachment figure is a kind of emotional anchor, a source of security, or, in the expressive phrase coined by Bowlby's collaborator Mary Ainsworth, a *secure base*. In the absence of the attachment figure, there is insecurity. Attachment behaviour is designed to restore the sense of security that comes from knowing that the secure base is there in case it is needed.

But on occasion the secure base will not be there. There will be unavoidable separations of one kind or another and there will also be occasions, more frequent and long-lasting for some children than others, when the mother or primary carer is physically there, but is not really available as a source of comfort, perhaps because she is preoccupied, or because she is angry with the child, or for some other reason, such as ill health, either physical or mental. Post-natal depression, for example, is estimated to affect 10–15 per cent of new mothers in the UK (Mind, 2013).

Children will adopt different behavioural strategies, depending on their circumstances, to obtain as much support as they can. Attachment behaviour is modified in the light of experience and each individual adopts a different repertoire of characteristic attachment behaviours. This repertoire, together with the response of the caregiver, Bowlby called an attachment *behavioural system* (Bowlby, 1997 [1969]: 304).

There are some children who grow up with no real sense of a secure base at all. Such children can be described as being in a state of *dissuagement*, a state of permanently having an unmet need (Heard and Lake, 1986: 434). This is an extremely difficult situation to be in, and the child will resort to various defensive manoeuvres in order to minimise separation anxiety and/ or to try to obtain support. The idea of defences is of course a concept derived directly from the Freudian model and, like Freud, Bowlby did not see these defensive patterns as merely temporary behaviours. He saw them being internalised by degrees into what he called an internal *working model* of the world, which an individual carries with him into later life (Bowlby, 1997 [1969]: 110–13).

We hope you can see how these ideas lead outwards from what begins as a relatively straightforward idea about the biological origins of attachment, into a theory about how human personality develops, and how relationships in early childhood shape and influence behaviour and relationships throughout life.

The following three propositions, extracted from Bowlby's book *Separation* (1998a [1973]: 235), may help to clarify what we have just been discussing:

1 '... when an individual is confident that an attachment figure will be available to him whenever he desires, that person will be much less prone to either intense or chronic fear than will an individual who has no such confidence.'
2 '... confidence in the availability of an attachment figure, or lack of it, is built up slowly during the years of immaturity - infancy, childhood and adolescence - and ... whatever expectations are developed during those years tend to persist relatively unchanged throughout the rest of life.'
3 '... the varied expectations of the accessibility and responsiveness of attachment figures that different individuals develop during the years of immaturity are tolerably accurate reflections of the experiences those individuals have actually had.' [This last proposition, as Bowlby went on to say, was controversial in analytical circles because many psychoanalysts, such as Klein, put so much more stock on fantasy than on actual objective experience.]

We will return to these ideas later, in the discussion about *internal working models* and about *secure* and *insecure* attachment. The following activity is to give you an opportunity to think about how different patterns of relating to others can become established in childhood:

Activity 3.2

Think of three or four children, preferably of similar ages, from different families, and think about how they relate - or related - to their parents (or to their primary carers if these are not their parents).

Assuming that all children are seeking the reassurance that their carers are available to them for support, but that this is not equally available to all children all the time, what do you notice about the different ways in which these children gain their parents' attention? Can you see ways in which these children have adapted their attachment behaviour to meet the particular circumstances in which they find themselves?

Comments on Activity 3.2

The possibilities here are, of course, endless. The following are a few patterns which we have noticed:

- Some children learn that presenting symptoms of illness is a good way of attracting parental interest and attention. This is particularly so, of course, when parents are anxious about health. We have encountered children who have developed what seem like quite intractable health problems, which have consumed a good deal of their parents' time, yet which seem to disappear when the children are with other carers.
- Sometimes children of parents who are emotionally fragile can seem unusually 'grown-up', 'independent' and 'well-behaved'. Perhaps these are children who have learnt from experience not to make excessive demands on their parents, and they need to become like parents themselves in order to look after them?
- Some children, on the other hand, seem to subject their carers to an incessant barrage of demands as a way of reassuring themselves that their carers are available to them.
- Youngest children often continue to use 'cuteness' to attract positive attention at a much later stage than their older siblings did. ('Acting cute' is a form of attachment behaviour.) The older children in the family, faced with younger and 'cuter' rivals, have needed to develop other ways of getting parental attention.

We will return later to look in more detail at patterns established in childhood.

THE GROWTH OF ATTACHMENT

Unlike many animal species, human infants do not show obvious attachment behaviour from birth. But this does not mean that attachment is not developing from the very beginning of life. Attachment is a two-way process between baby and mother, and develops out of the interaction between them. Earlier, when we referred to Bowlby's description of research on monkey mothers and babies you will remember that the mothers' distress on separation was as great as that of the babies, and you may be able to draw on your own experience for examples of the close bond between parent and newborn baby.

We will now look at the stages in the development of attachment in childhood. If you look at the attachment literature, you will find some variation in the terms used and in the indicative ages given for each stage. One would expect, in any case, that there would be some differences between individuals in respect of the speed at which they develop. But, taking the ages as rough guidelines only, the following are the stages through which attachment is thought to develop. (The indicative ages which we have used here are from Howe et al., 1999: 19–21.)

1. Pre-attachment (0–2 months)

This stage is characterised by *undiscriminating social responsiveness*. At this stage babies enjoy social interaction. They are interested in human voices and human faces. But they can be left with different caregivers without seeming to be distressed. Experiments on monkeys carried out by Harlow (1963) and others in the 1960s and 1970s showed that very small baby monkeys could be separated from their mothers without causing any long-term difficulty, but that older babies separated from their mothers for the same period, showed long-term behavioural problems: this suggests that for monkeys too there is a pre-attachment stage. Also of relevance here are the findings of cognitive psychology, which we'll discuss in the next chapter. Piaget's model would suggest that at this very early age the baby would have no concept of the mother or carer as a separate individual with her own existence. At this stage the baby does not even know that objects exist when she is not looking at them. (According to Piaget the concept of 'object permanence' does not develop until about six months.) However, the newborn baby is most easily able to focus visually on objects which are at the same distance from him as the face of the person who is holding him and feeding him (Bowlby, 1997 [1969]: 327), so it is not surprising that this should quickly develop into a preference for this carer – usually the mother. If all goes well, her responses will be attuned to his cues – smiles, cries, babbling, arm and leg movements – and will set up the kind of mirroring process described in Chapter 2, which is the groundwork of a secure attachment.

2. Attachment-in-the-making (3–6 months)

We now see *discriminating* social responsiveness developing. Babies start to show different responses to different people. They respond more to familiar people than to strangers and they become increasingly focused on their main carer, smiling and babbling more when they are relating to her and being more easily comforted by her when distressed. The baby and his carer give each other feedback and become more attuned to each other, and the baby's mood, whether of pleasure or distress, is 'held' or regulated by the carer's response in the same way as she holds him physically in her arms.

3. Clear-cut attachment (7 months to 3 years)

During this stage a child will *actively seek proximity and contact* with his main carer whenever the distance between them becomes too great. And the child will display full-blown separation anxiety when the carer leaves the room. By this stage, of course, the child is learning to move independently, so he can take more control over the distance between himself and his carer. As well as becoming more active in seeking out the carer, the child will also become more active in maintaining contact. For example, the child will read the situation and alter his behaviour accordingly in order to optimise the response from the carer. (So we see *different* attachment behavioural systems developing, depending on circumstances, as discussed above in Activity 3.2.)

4. Reciprocal relationship (from 3 years)

As the child becomes more mobile and spends more time away from the carer, the pair enter a reciprocal state in which they share responsibility for maintaining equilibrium. Increasingly, a feeling of security can be maintained even during temporary separations – linked to cognitive developments which allow the child to think in more sophisticated terms about things like time and space, the reasons for a carer's absence and so on. (The child can feel that the carer is 'there for him', and hold her in mind even when she is not physically present.) Cognitive developments also allow the child to begin to be able to see things from the carer's point of view and to adjust behaviour accordingly, understanding that their carer also has goals and plans. The relationship becomes more of a partnership.

The description of the reciprocal relationship stage which we have just given does suppose that, by and large, the relationship between carer and child has gone well. Rather different patterns would otherwise emerge. Whatever pattern is established by this stage, though, will become the *internal working model* that the child will use as a standard to guide interactions with other people – and will carry on into the rest of his life. In adulthood, these attachment patterns have a profound effect on the way in which we choose and relate to our partners, and the attachments we make with our own children, and they with us.

INTERNAL WORKING MODELS

What differences in behaviour are noticeable between children who have a secure relationship with their carers and those who don't? Have a look at the following activity:

━━━━━━━━━━ **Activity 3.3** ━━━━━━━━━━

What characteristic behaviours might lead you to think that there was a secure relationship between a child and her carer? What behaviours would lead you to feel that the relationship was problematic?

The fact that children behave differently suggests that they have different ideas in their minds. What ideas might those be?

Comments on Activity 3.3

You may have described a secure relationship as being one in which a child goes easily to her carer, but seems confident enough of her carer's support to leave the carer's side and explore. A securely attached child has learnt the basic lesson of trust which you may remember Erikson saw as the first developmental task (see Chapter 2). The child has the belief that the carer can be depended upon. You may also have mentioned eye contact, mutually rewarding physical contact and mutually rewarding verbal communication.

In the case of an insecure attachment, you may have thought either of clinginess or

(Continued)

(Continued)

the opposite: the child avoiding or ignoring the carer (or perhaps you may have thought of children who exhibit a strange combination of both of these). Some children seem to have the idea in their minds that there is no point in going to their carers for support – or that to do so might actually do more harm than good. Other children seem to see it as their job to look after their carers rather than the other way round, or to feel guilty about the burden they are to their carers. Such children may seem over-preoccupied with the carer, constantly watching the carer for approval, or constantly checking that the carer is okay.

You may have mentioned a lack of specificity about the relationship: the child treats other adults just the same way as she treats the carer. You may have mentioned a lack of mutuality: eye contact, touch or verbal communication do not seem to be pleasurable or rewarding to either party.

Insecure children exhibit a number of different characteristic ways of behaving (different attachment behavioural systems). We will discuss different patterns of insecure attachment later on. For the purpose of the present discussion though, what we would like you to note is that children in different kinds of relationships (secure and insecure) appear to have different ideas in their minds about what they can expect from their carer, what is expected of them, and what is an appropriate way to behave.

We are thinking beings and our actions are based on ideas about the world that we carry in our minds, based on previous experience. We avoid fire and hot things, for example, because we have in our minds the idea that they can cause injury and pain. The same, Bowlby suggested, applied to attachment behaviour:

> … each individual builds working models of the world, and of himself in it, with the aid of which he perceives events, forecasts the future, and constructs his plans. In the working model of the world that anyone builds, a key feature is his notion of who his attachment figures are, where they may be found, and how they may be expected to respond. Similarly, in the working model of the self that anyone builds, a key feature is his notion of how acceptable or unacceptable he himself is in the eyes of his attachment figures. (Bowlby, 1998a [1973]: 236)

As David Howe puts it, internal working models, contain 'expectations and beliefs about (1) one's own and other people's behaviour; (2) the lovability, worthiness and acceptability of the self; and (3) the emotional availability and interest of others, and their ability to provide protection' (2011: 35. Original emphasis). A securely attached child will have a working model of the world in which she herself is worthy of love and attention, others are expected to be responsive and reliable (at least in the absence of evidence to the contrary) and relationships with others are seen as rewarding and fun. (This corresponds roughly with the idea of a child who has been 'mirrored' to in Winnicott's terminology, as discussed in the previous chapter.) But what about a child whose caregiver is unpredictable, unavailable or rejecting? In such circumstances, according to attachment theory, children develop a working model to help them cope, as best they can, with a difficult situation. So the child will adjust her behaviour to get as many of her needs met as possible by making allowance for the parents' needs, behaviour and limitations. For instance, a child who gets more attention when poorly may begin to adopt a sick role, or a child whose parents fly into a rage when too many demands are made, may learn to pay close attention to her parents state of mind before asking for anything at all, and a child whose parents are simply too busy or preoccupied to notice the child's needs may learn to cope for herself as much as possible. Children will also use *defensive exclusion* (or 'denial' as Freud would have called it) to shut away from consciousness feelings or aspects of reality in order to help them manage their anxiety, and when this happens the resulting model is sometimes described as 'faulty' in the sense that it sacrifices the child's need for an accurate representation of reality in order to help the child cope in the present moment. For instance, children with grossly neglectful parents (like Jenny in Activity 2.2 in the last chapter) will think of all kinds of excuses for the neglect in order to protect themselves from concluding that their parents do not care about them. They may tell themselves that they deserve the neglect, or that they prefer things the way they are. Such models are sometimes described as 'faulty' but, while it is true that they may involve accepting what looks to an outsider like a very distorted reality, the word 'faulty' can be misleading. The important point to get hold of is that these models are functional. They are developed to make the best of a less than satisfactory situation, and in that sense are not faulty at all. Looking at this in evolutionary terms, James Chisholm notes that:

> A mother who is stressed (often because she is struggling to secure resources or because she has little social support) is less attentive to her infant than a mother who is not stressed. As a result of her lack of attentiveness, her infant's HPA system [the hypothalamic-pituitary-adrenal system, which controls reactions to stress] will be repeatedly activated. Repeated activation of an infant's HPA system then 'in-forms' the infant that the environment is dangerous, and sets the infant on the developmental pathway that results in a fear system that is calibrated for a dangerous environment. As a result the individual will have a heightened awareness of danger, as well as a quicker reaction when danger is present. (Chisholm and Sieff, 2015: 167)

Winnicott's concept of a 'false self' (see previous chapter) is a similar idea to this notion of a working model developed to cope with adversity, and indeed this sort of idea is very much in the psychodynamic tradition. As we've seen, Freud saw defences coming into play to protect an individual against the anxiety that comes with needs not being met, and suggested that defensive mechanisms, once established, become part of our makeup, so that as we move into adult life, they continue to affect our behaviour, even though the original situation in which they developed may no longer apply. In the same way, as we form new attachments as we move through life, these will be affected by the working models we established in early childhood. In other words, adults who have internalised 'faulty' working models as children may continue to try to form relationships on the basis of a model which is not necessarily applicable to the new situation.

Of course working models can change over time, but this does not necessarily happen in a straightforward way. Foster-carers of children from neglectful and abusive environments, for instance, soon find that offering a child the loving and safe environment that they have lacked, does not simply undo the behaviours and feelings that the child has brought with them from the past, which may persist for years, and even, to some extent, for a lifetime. There are a number of reasons for this, including neurological ones, but also reasons to do with the nature of working models themselves. For one thing, as Howe notes, 'there is a tendency for internal working models to become self-fulfilling and self-confirming as others react to our expectations of how we think they will behave' (2011: 36). We have probably all encountered shy people, for instance, whose fear that no one is interested in them results in behaviour that comes over as stand-offishness. As a result, people will tend to avoid them, thereby confirming the part of their working model that says 'I am not of interest to other people.' What is more, defensive exclusion may mean that models can't be updated in the light of new experience. For instance, if part of your working model is that you have told yourself that you don't need anything from other people, and have repressed your own needs from consciousness, then you may continue to act as if your needs did not exist. Working models may well also include *splitting* (see p. 29) to allow the co-existence of incompatible ideas. For example, 'My mum loves and cares for me very, very much' co-exists in the same mind as 'Unless I am very, very careful, my mother punishes me and tells me she never wanted me.' This prevents the development of a coherent sense of self. (People prone to splitting never know what they *really* think or who they *really* are.) Defensive exclusion may also remove the opportunity to process painful feelings, such as grief or anger, resulting in repressed feelings from the past which get in the way of present relationships.

MARY AINSWORTH'S ATTACHMENT CLASSIFICATION SYSTEM

Everyone's working model is unique, but attachments do fall into certain patterns. Mary Ainsworth, a collaborator of Bowlby, developed the Strange Situation Test and proposed a classification, based on these studies of mother and baby interactions, which included three categories of attachment: *secure, anxious-avoidant* and *anxious-ambivalent* (Ainsworth et al., 1978). A fourth category, *disorganised* attachment, has since been recognised and there are also some individuals who have not experienced any type of attachment at all who can be termed *non-attached*. So we now have five categories, as follows. We will now discuss these in turn, but the reader should note that we are simplifying here, and that other classifications of attachment, with additional categories, can be found in the literature.

Secure

The child shows a clear preference for the mother (or other primary carer) over others. The carer is sensitive to, and responds to, the child's attempts to communicate. The child is confident that the carer is available to give support and takes pleasure in the presence of the carer. The child shows distress on separation from the carer. On reunion they seek some reassurance, but then settle again. In adulthood, they are '*autonomous* in that they can reflect without too much distortion, on their own thoughts, feelings and behaviour … [and] behave non-defensively' (Howe, 2011: 81. Original emphasis).

Anxious-avoidant

This is also known as 'insecure-avoidant' (the word 'anxious' and the word 'insecure' are used interchangeably in this context) and one might describe it as the 'aloof' strategy. The child doesn't show much distress on separation from the carer and when she returns, the child ignores or avoids her. The child does not seek out physical contact and is watchful and wary around the carer. Her play is inhibited and she shows little discrimination between her carer and others, including strangers. This pattern emerges when the parent is insensitive to, or rejecting of, the child's needs. The child has therefore learnt to minimise needs for attachment (through defensive exclusion) in order to avoid rebuff. It is as if the child is saying: 'Who cares? I didn't want it anyway.'

David Howe writes that, 'for adults classified as avoidant, the tendency to downplay the importance of attachments and the anxiety felt in the context of close relationships remains characteristic', while 'vulnerability, emotional need, and feelings of anxiety are downplayed for fear that thinking about such matters might activate the attachment system, triggering reminders of past rejection' (2011: 107).

Anxious-ambivalent

Also called 'insecure-ambivalent' or 'resistant', this might be described as the 'clingy' strategy. The attachment is very visible but not secure. (This distinction sometimes confuses professionals assessing parent–child relationships, who may see the attachment as being 'strong' because it is so very visible). Here, the child is distressed on separation but does not settle down on reunion. The return of the carer is longed for, but when it comes it is not reassuring: the separation anxiety continues. The anxious-ambivalent child is frightened to go off and explore the world, because she is uncertain about whether the carer will be there when needed. This pattern is the result of a parenting style that is not consistently hostile or rejecting, but is inconsistent, and where parents are lacking in empathy for the child's needs. Not surprisingly a history of separations from parents, and threats of abandonment, are also associated with this strategy. The child may adopt all kinds of strategies to keep the attention of the carer. Role reversal may take place, for example, where the child cares for the caregiver, paying more attention to the caregiver's needs than her own. But at the same time the child is angry about the unreliability of the carer, though this anger may be defensively excluded, so that the child is not consciously aware of it.

As Howe notes, the adult version of ambivalence tends to be referred to as the *'anxious, preoccupied or entangled'* pattern (2011: 136. Original emphasis). For such adults 'persistent feelings of anxiety and doubt mean that distress and attachment behaviours tend to be displayed at maximum strength [which] results in behaviour that can be interpreted as immature, silly and over-the-top', and they have a 'great need for repeated reassurance… There is a pervasive fear that other people are not sufficiently interested in the self, that their love, availability and attention cannot be taken for granted' (2011: 136).

Disorganised

This occurs when the carer is viewed by the child as frightening (as in abusive situations) or as frightened (as for example when the carer is unable to protect the children, or is herself or himself an ongoing victim of abuse). Either way, the carer is not available as a source of comfort or reassurance, though the child has nowhere else to go. Indeed, in the case of abusive situations, the carer may simultaneously be the main *source* of danger or fear, *and* the only place to go for comfort. The relationship between Jenny and her mother Mandy described in Chapter 2 (Activity 2.2) is an example of this kind of situation, in which there is no 'right' response. Children exhibiting disorganised attachment may show a confused mixture of both ambivalent and avoidant responses (for example, seeking to be held, but then looking away and avoiding eye contact). Or they may simply 'freeze', showing neither positive nor negative reactions to separation and reunion. As Howe puts it:

> Fear pervades the internal working models of disorganized children. It dysregulates their emotions, overwhelms their cognitive capacities, and damages their ability to develop an integrated state of mind with respect to all attachment matters… Frightening attachment-related information is kept out of mind. It cannot be integrated into the individual's mental representation of experience. Therefore it is defensively excluded in so complete a way that traumatic memories and painful feelings are segregated and put out of conscious awareness… [so they] cannot be processed, analysed or reflected upon. (2011: 155)

Children with disorganised attachment tend to be heavily overrepresented in the workloads of childcare professionals, and it is disorganised attachment that is most likely to produce long-term behavioural and mental health problems in adulthood, so exploring this further has become the priority of research. Indeed Green and Goldwyn (2002: 840) conclude that, 'there has been … a shift of emphasis in attachment literature away from the importance of the distinction between attachment security/insecurity to that between attachment organisation/ disorganisation.'

Children whose attachment is disorganised will develop what Howe (2005) describes as 'brittle behavioural strategies' which seek to impose some control on their frighteningly out-of-control world, which means that (at least in situations of relatively low stress) their attachment behaviour is no longer completely disorganised. As these children grow up, these strategies may take many different forms. Behaviours such as compulsive self-reliance, compulsive compliance or compulsive caregiving seek to impose control on the self, and minimise dependence on caregivers, while controlling strategies such as aggression seek to coerce caregivers into meeting their needs. Addictive behaviours can also be seen as a way of meeting attachment needs; when a person has developed an internal working model in which other people cannot be relied on as a source of support or comfort, drugs or alcohol may become a substitute for human relationships (Flores, 2004). Or indeed another compulsive behaviour may take this role, such as comfort eating, gambling, or the use of pornography.

Children who show disorganised attachment are likely to have carers who have themselves been unable to resolve childhood experiences of loss and trauma (Main and Hesse, 1990). Intolerable feelings arising from these experiences are then triggered by the stresses that arise when they become parents themselves, and they dissociate, going 'mentally offline' (Howe, 2011: 154) and no longer being able to respond appropriately to their children's needs.

Incidentally, the use of the term 'disorganised' to describe this kind of attachment had been questioned by Crittenden (2008) and other recent researchers, on the basis that (a little like the concept of 'faulty' models), it is misleading. These authors see it as a highly functional and complex strategy for staying safe in circumstances where parenting is frequently chaotic and dangerous by adapting the attachment style to the demands and threats of the moment, alternating as necessary between compulsive anxious-avoidant and controlling anxious-ambivalent modes. For a summary of Crittenden's Dynamic Maturational Model of attachment, including her attachment 'wheel', see her website (Family Relations Institute, 2011–2018).

Non-attached

This applies to children who have had no opportunity to form attachments of any kind. For example, it applies to children raised from an early age in some kind of institution, where, even if they are adequately fed and clothed and so on, they may have no opportunities to form personal relationships with carers. It may also apply in some cases to families where the carer is totally unavailable emotionally, as the result perhaps of mental illness. Non-attached children show serious problems in social relationships. They may show little preference for, or interest in, one person rather than another. They have difficulty in controlling their impulses. Their cognitive development may be impaired (Rutter, 1981).

═══════ Activity 3.4 ═══════

a   Thinking about adults that you know (perhaps the ones you thought of in Activity 3.1), can you think of some whose way of relating to others could be described as anxious-avoidant and of some whose way of relating to others could be described as anxious-ambivalent?

b   If you would like to consider how your own childhood relationships affect your relationships now, one way to look at it would be to write down a list of messages that you characteristically received from your parents – positive ('You are special'), negative ('I'm too busy to attend to you') or neutral. You can then consider how these messages have affected your characteristic stance in relation to other people. *Please note though that this can be surprisingly distressing. It may be best done as a structured and facilitated small group discussion with people you trust, when you can compare and contrast your responses with those of others.*

Comments on Activity 3.4

a   Most of us probably know people who are avoidant or ambivalent in relationships, sometimes to surprising extremes. If you are familiar with the childhood history of these people, you may well see, we suspect, that the parents were either rejecting or unresponsive (in the avoidant case) or inconsistent (in the ambivalent case).

(Continued)

(Continued)

b If you decided to do the second part of the exercise, you will probably have noticed how powerful some of those parental messages are in terms of the emotional response they produce – and it may have struck you that these messages from your childhood do indeed affect the way you deal with the world now. One could argue that this is a demonstration of internal working models in action. (Parent message cards, incidentally, on which a large number of such messages are written out, one per card, can be used as a therapeutic tool: the idea being to sort them into two piles, those that apply and those that don't – or those that you would wish to pass on to your children – and those you would not.)

DEVELOPMENTS OF ATTACHMENT THEORY

Privation and deprivation

Research by Michael Rutter and others confirms Bowlby's original insistence on the importance of early life experiences on children's long-term psychological development. In a study published in 1998, Rutter and his collaborators in the English and Romanian Adoptees Study Team, found that gross early privation was a major cause of cognitive deficits among Romanian orphans adopted in the UK and concluded that 'psychological privation was probably a more important factor in this than nutritional deprivation' (Rutter et al., 1998: 465). But Rutter has pointed out that Bowlby's concept of 'maternal deprivation', as originally formulated, was a confusing one because it lumps together many different factors, and because the words 'maternal' and 'deprivation' are both somewhat misleading.

He argues that things such as cognitive delay and language delay in children from deprived backgrounds may be due to lack of *stimulation* in those environments. This is a different thing from the lack of emotional warmth, which research by Rutter and others confirms is linked to deviant and anti-social behaviour in later life. Emotional warmth and cognitive stimulation are different factors, and the lack of each of them has different effects, though in certain environments, both may be lacking.

Importantly, Rutter also argues that *privation* (that is to say, a chronic *lack*) rather than deprivation (that is, a specific *loss*) is what causes long-term psychological problems.

> Loss of an attachment figure, although a major factor in the causation of short-term effects, seems of only minor importance with respect to long-term consequences …
> Indeed the evidence strongly suggests that most of the long-term consequences are due to privation or lack of some kind, rather than to any kind of loss. (Rutter, 1981: 121)

The 'maternal' part of 'maternal deprivation' is also questioned because it implies a unique importance to the mother. Modern attachment theory recognises that the primary attachment figure does not have to be the mother, and indeed that children can and do have a number of different attachment figures: 'The chief bond need not be with a biological parent, it need not be the chief caretaker and it need not be with a female' (Rutter, 1981: 127).

Recent developments in neuroscience

Rutter's work linked emotional and cognitive development, and the fast-developing area of neuroscience research is shedding more light on how the two areas are linked. Neuroscience is the study of the development of the brain, and how it operates with the rest of the nervous system to shape emotion, cognition and human behaviour. Technical developments such as brain scans have made new areas of information available, and work in this field of research is still progressing rapidly.

Findings from neuroscience research give strong support to the principles of attachment theory developed by Bowlby and his successors. A picture emerges of the critical importance of the first three years of life, when the right hemisphere of the brain is undergoing an explosion of development. The right brain operates in an intuitive, holistic fashion and is associated with unconscious processes, as opposed to the left brain, which develops later and is involved in the logical and linear functions that are necessary for the acquisition of language and the development of reasoning powers (Gerhardt, 2004: 36, 51). So it is the right brain that is involved in the processes of attachment, and dominates the first years of life, while the left brain becomes more important later.

The biology of the brain is too complicated to describe in detail here, but, briefly, what happens in the early period of rapid growth is that new pathways and connections (known as 'synapses') are made between different cells in the brain (neurons) and the nervous system. The speed at which the brain develops at the beginning of life is phenomenal – 'equivalent to a rate of 1.8 million new synapses *per second* between two months' gestation and two years after birth' (Eliot, 2001: 27, quoted by Balbernie, 2001: 240). However, only those connections which are reinforced by regular use will survive and develop, producing a system of established or 'hard-wired' neural pathways. And it would seem that attachment patterns are among the pathways that are established and reinforced in this way. Ainsworth argued that attachment is 'built into the nervous system in the course and as a result of the infant's experience with the mother' (Ainsworth, 1967: 429, quoted by Schore, 2000). The work of Schore and other neuroscientists has confirmed Ainsworth's view, and begun to explain, and continues to explore, the processes through which this takes place.

One area where neuroscience has given support to previous thinking about human development is the importance of eye contact and visual perception. Both attachment theory and Winnicott's concept of mirroring in object relations theory (see Chapter 2) recognise the importance of this in early infancy, and research evidence shows rapid change and development at about eight weeks in the part of the brain that processes visual information (Schore, 2001: 17). This sets the stage for a period of development characterised by rich visual communication and exchange, when an unconscious synchronisation takes place between carer and infant, and the infant learns to feel connected, held and secure. Genetics research is shedding more light on 'critical periods' like this in brain development. More is being discovered about the way in which certain genes throw switches in the brain to enable it to respond to environmental stimuli, which then makes possible the rapid neurological development which must take place in a very specific window of opportunity, as is the case with visual perception, which may not develop at all if this window is missed (Ridley, 2004: 163–7).

Schore (2000; Schore and Schore, 2008) describes attachment theory as a *regulatory* theory: the unconscious exchanges between the infant and his carers give him the means to begin to regulate the power of his feelings. If his carer is attuned to him, she will reflect back and amplify his pleasurable feelings (for instance by responding to his babbling with her own affectionate baby-talk) and soothe his unpleasurable feelings (for instance by cuddling and rocking him and making reassuring noises to him when he is crying and distressed). This is the very first step towards having another view of himself and his experience of the world, which will eventually enable him to 'mentalise' – a term coined by Peter Fonagy et al. (2002) and associated with the acquisition of a theory of mind (something we will discuss more fully in our next chapter).

Neuroscience points to a close connection between emotional and cognitive development: 'Research suggests that emotion operates as a central organising process within the brain' (Seigal, 1999: 4, quoted by Balbernie, 2001: 237). It also demonstrates just how complex the relationship between nature and nurture is, as a consensus emerges that the physical development of the human brain is designed to be moulded by the environment it encounters, particularly in the early years of life (Schore, 2001: 14).

Bowlby broke new ground by bringing together two previously separate disciplines: psychoanalysis and the study of animal behaviour. Present-day neuroscience continues in this multidisciplinary tradition as it develops its psychoneurobiological model of human development.

Attachment in later life

Bowlby's work focused on babies and young children, but present-day attachment theory takes a much longer view, and presents a case for the importance of an understanding of attachment across the whole lifecourse (Howe, 2011). We will find ourselves revisiting attachment theory in the later chapters of this book which deal with adolescence, adulthood, old age, bereavement and disability.

Increasingly, links are being made between disorganised attachment in children and the kinds of mental health problems which can occur in adulthood when these attachment issues are unresolved. These include personality disorders (Crittenden and Newman, 2010), eating disorders (Barone and Guiducci, 2009), drug and alcohol abuse (Schindler et al., 2005) and also post-traumatic stress disorder (Kobak et al., 2004). And the effect of these problems extends way beyond the individuals concerned, and poses questions of social and economic policy for the whole of society:

> The behavioural and mental problems shown by the majority of those who have suffered early trauma and maltreatment point to the heavy cost, both social and material, that societies pay when children are raised in environments where stress, disadvantage, poverty, violence and neglect are endemic. (Howe, 2011: 196)

CRITICISMS OF ATTACHMENT THEORY

As we have noted, Rutter took issue with some of the earlier formulations of attachment theory. Both their emphasis on mothers and their claim that children were essentially 'monotropic' (forming a primary attachment to just one person) can be criticised from both a feminist and from a multicultural point of view.

We would suggest that not only mothers but also many fathers would object to the restricted roles to which Bowlby sometimes seems to consign them. However, those roles were seen as the norm in the immediate post-war period in which Bowlby was writing.

A number of feminist writers (for example, Burman, 1994) have criticised Bowlby for 'tying women to the home', by implying that if the mother leaves her child at all, this will result in long-term harm. In fact, it has been argued that one reason that Bowlby's ideas became popular when they did is that they provided a rationale for taking women out of paid work following the war years when so many women had joined the industrial workforce, and expecting them to stay at home rather than compete for jobs with men returning from the war. Attachment theory could be used as a pretext for not providing good day-care facilities, for example, or for denying women an equal role with men in the workplace. From a multicultural point of view, one could also argue that the insistence on the monotropic mother–child bond has the effect of setting up the European/North American 'nuclear family' as the model for childrearing, ignoring the more communal approaches that are the norm in other parts of the world. In other words: attachment theory, in its original formulation, is distinctly 'Eurocentric'. Even within the terms of Western culture, overemphasis on the monotropic mother–child bond seems to undervalue other relationships, such as those with the father, grandparents and siblings.

It can even be argued that if a child relies too exclusively on care from one person, her mother, this may in the long run itself be damaging, placing undue pressure on the mother which will itself harm the relationship if she is worn out, or bored, or becomes resentful of the child. And these days, unlike in the 1950s, it is very common, and frequently an economic necessity, for a mother to return to work in the first year after her baby's birth.

However, although these criticisms can be made about attachment theory as originally formulated by Bowlby, it would be a mistake to discard Bowlby's ideas about the importance of attachment, merely because his conception of what attachment might consist of was limited by the particular perspective of his own times.

Bowlby's ideas were related to the ideas of other object relations theorists such as Winnicott, and also to the ideas of Freud himself. One lasting legacy of Freud seems to be an increased recognition of the deep emotional needs of young children and of the profound damage that can be done if these needs are ignored. Bowlby translated this insight into a theory which has proved to be something that can grow and develop in the light of new evidence, and into a practical concern which has been a major influence on public policy, and on the way we think about children and their needs.

CHAPTER SUMMARY

- In this chapter, we looked at John Bowlby's ideas about the importance of early attachment for long-term psychological health.
- We considered his ideas about the biological origins of attachment and attachment behaviour.
- We looked at the stages in the development of attachment.
- We considered the idea of 'internal working models' – of self and others – learnt in early relationships and carried into later life.

- We looked at Mary Ainsworth's classification system for secure and insecure attachment (the latter being divided into anxious-avoidant and anxious-ambivalent – disorganised attachment and non-attachment are two additional categories).
- We considered developments of Bowlby's theory in work by Rutter and recent research in neuroscience.
- We looked at criticisms of attachment theory from feminist and multicultural points of view.

In this and the previous chapter we have been looking primarily at emotional development. In the next chapter we will move on to look at cognitive development: the development of thinking.

Tangled Webs

Since attachment theory is equally relevant to thinking about children's relationships and adult's relationships it should be applicable to every single case study in Tangled Webs. However, in some cases you have more information than in others about the individual's early history. At the beginning of this chapter we suggested the cases below to consider through the lens of attachment theory. Our more general advice would be that, rather than use attachment theory to try and 'diagnose' an attachment problem in terms of the five categories given above (which are very 'blunt instruments' given that each one applies to a large slice of the entire population), you should concentrate more on thinking (in the case of children) about what kind of internal working model they are likely to develop in their present circumstances. In other words: what expectations and beliefs are they likely to be building up about their own lovability and worth, and about the emotional availability and interest of others. In the case of adults, you might consider what kind of working model they seem to have internalised in their childhood.

Caitlin Smart (Dudley) and the Dudley/Harris family (Cases A and G). Caitlin, according to her teacher, is very quiet and withdrawn. She is also behind with schoolwork. Her mother is chronically depressed, with low self-esteem, and, when her partner Lee is away, will retire to bed pretty much all day, leaving the children to look after themselves. Caitlin's father, who she no longer lives with, was violent towards her mother. Lee, her current step-father figure puts her mother down and warns Caitlin and her sisters not to end up like her. He favours his son, and tells Caitlin he doesn't want her in the room when he's watching TV because she 'stinks of piss'. There are more details in the case studies, but it is clear that Caitlin has been given some pretty negative messages both about her own lovability and about the availability of others.

Tracey Green (Case J). Tracey is a social worker, and she appears in several case studies in her professional role, but if you look at her own history, she too has received many negative messages about her own worth and the availability of others. However, these have been offset by some more positive experiences. Her father abandoned her at a young age. She had a positive experience of being cared for by her grandmother, but this didn't last and she was removed from her grandmother in a rather traumatic way. Then (like Caitlin) she lived with a mother who was being violently abused by her partner, and for a time became a kind of protector of her younger sister. She returned to her grandmother, but then had to come into care at the age of 8. However, the couple who fostered her proved to be stable and dependable carers, and in her teens she had some therapy to help her work through some of the more painful experiences in her life. Again, there is more material in the case study, but you will see that, over the years, she has been given very different messages about her own worth, the availability of others and their ability to protect herself and her siblings. To complicate things further, you will see she has also suffered many losses, both as a result of bereavement and of separation.

 You can access Tangled Webs by visiting **https://study.sagepub.com/tangledwebs**

══════ Further reading ══════

Foundations of attachment theory

Ainsworth, M., Blehar, M., Aters, E. and Wall, S. (1978) *Patterns of Attachment: A Psychological Study of the Strange Situation.* Hillside, NJ: Lawrence Erlbaum.
Bowlby, J. (1990 [1953]) *Childcare and the Growth of Love.* Harmondsworth: Penguin.
Bowlby, J. (1997 [1969]) *Attachment.* London: Pimlico.
Bowlby, J. (1998 [1973]) *Separation.* London: Pimlico.
Bowlby, J. (1998 [1980]) *Loss.* London: Pimlico.
Holmes, J. (2014) *John Bowlby and Attachment Theory*, 2nd edn. London: Routledge.

General introductions to attachment theory and its application

Howe, D. (1995) *Attachment Theory for Social Work Practice.* Basingstoke: Macmillan.
Howe, D. (2005) *Child Abuse and Neglect: Attachment, Development and Intervention.* Basingstoke: Palgrave.
Howe, D. (2011) *Attachment across the Lifecourse.* Basingstoke: Palgrave Macmillan.

(The present authors have leaned particularly heavily on this last book, which is very useful for understanding how childhood attachment problems may play out in later life.)

Neuroscience and attachment

Gerhardt, S. (2004) *Why Love Matters: How Affection Shapes a Baby's Brain.* Hove: Routledge.

4

THE EMERGENCE OF REASON

THE DEVELOPING ABILITY TO UNDERSTAND

TANGLED WEBS

This chapter is about how children understand and think about the world in a different way to adults. If you want to think about some cases before you read the chapter, you might like to look at **Xenia Veloso (the Veloso family, Case I)** or at **Caitlin Smart (Dudley)** and **The Dudley/Harris family (Cases A and G)**. Notice the ages of the children and, drawing on your own experience of children (or even your own childhood memories) ask yourself what would be different about the children's understanding of what is going on, as compared to the adults.

 You can access Tangled Webs by visiting **https://study.sagepub.com/tangledwebs**

Suppose you are a teacher in a nursery school. In your class is a 4-year-old boy whose mother has to go to hospital for an operation. She is a lone parent with no relatives in the area, and it is going to be necessary for the little boy to go to a foster home for seven nights. How do you help a 4-year-old make sense of the fact that he must go and live with strangers for a week? It's not just a matter of making him feel cared for, or of helping him cope emotionally, and giving him an opportunity to express his feelings (as Bowlby advocated), vitally important though that is. It is also a matter of making the facts intelligible to him. What is a hospital? What is an operation? What is a foster home? What, for that matter, is a *week*? All these concepts need explaining.

This chapter represents something of a change of gear from the two previous chapters. We have been considering how childhood experience influences emotional development. We are now going to look at how a child learns to make sense of the world. We are moving into what is known as cognitive psychology – or, more specifically, into developmental cognitive psychology.

In particular, we are going to focus on the work of Jean Piaget. If Bowlby is the father of attachment theory, Piaget could perhaps be described as the father of developmental cognitive psychology. Just as with Bowlby, many of Piaget's ideas have been challenged by subsequent research, and we are not offering them here as the 'last word'. Nevertheless, because of Piaget's importance in the development of thinking in this field, the easiest way to introduce this topic is to begin with Piaget and then discuss some of the problems with his ideas that subsequent research has identified and look at some of the other theories and theorists who can contribute to our understanding of cognitive development.

We began this discussion by making a distinction between cognitive development and emotional development. But in reality the two are closely interlinked. If you look back after reading this chapter at the developmental ideas of Freud or Bowlby, or those of Klein or Erikson, you will see that each stage presupposes a level of cognitive development also. Children cannot reach an understanding about their relationship with others, for example, until they are able to grasp that others do actually have a separate existence.

As discussed in the previous chapter, a secure emotional base allows exploration and learning to take place. We mentioned how an insecure baby monkey that puts all its energies into attempting to find comfort does not explore as much as does a monkey that is confident that its mother is available when needed – and any teacher will confirm how difficult it is to get troubled children to settle and concentrate in class. So a solid emotional base gives the security that supports learning. But the reverse is also true. Learning about how the world works helps us to make sense of troubling events. Moves and losses, for example, are particularly difficult for children at an age when they are old enough to know what is happening but not old enough to make sense of it. It is easier for a child to spend a week away from home when that child is capable of grasping the concept of 'a week'.

For those who work with children, it is important to have some understanding of cognitive development as well as emotional development because the two go hand in hand.

COGNITIVE PSYCHOLOGY AND COGNITIVE DEVELOPMENT

To us as adults, most of the time, it seems as if the outside world – the world of people, objects and events – is just self-evidently *there*. But in fact all that we can ever know about that outside world comes to us in the form of millions of electrical impulses that reach our brains from our various sense organs: light-sensitive cells in our eyes, cells in our ears that are sensitive to vibrations in the air, pressure sensors in our skin. The 'world' that we feel ourselves to inhabit is not 'just there' at all, but is something which we have somehow reconstructed from these countless signals. Once in a while we may get a sense of this. You have probably had the experience of seeing someone out of the corner of your eye and noticing all kinds of details: a beard, glasses, a slight stoop. But then you look round and see it was only a coat hanging on the back of a door. All those details were just intelligent guesses made by your brain on the basis of the limited information available.

Cognitive psychology is the branch of psychology that deals with the interpretation of sensory events: how they *register* (perception), how we store them in memory and retrieve them, how we learn from experience and make use of images, symbols, concepts and rules in thinking, reasoning and problem solving. In short it is about how we process and interpret *information* (in contrast to psychodynamic theory which is more about how we process *feelings*).

And this business of processing and interpreting information is a skill. Some skills are innate and present at birth (horses are born with the ability to walk) but some skills have to be learnt. The study of human development suggests that most of these cognitive skills are not present at birth, not even very basic ones such as the ability to understand that the patterns of colours in front of our eyes represent objects out there in the world. Although the skills have to be learnt, the process of learning follows pathways that may in themselves be innate (as with the growth of the body), influenced by a complex interaction of genes and environmental triggers, as we saw in Chapter 1.

The following activity may help you to start to think about the different ways in which children function cognitively at different ages.

═══════════ **Activity 4.1** ═══════════

Think of a child of 4 or 5 years old that you know or have worked with. What is different about the way this child thinks and understands the world, from the way adults think about the world? What kinds of ideas does this child - and others of this child's age - characteristically find difficult to grasp?

Comments on Activity 4.1

Some things you may have thought of:

1   Geography - small children have little grasp of geography, not only in the sense of factual information about the world, but in the more fundamental sense of being unable to grasp ideas such as distance (if you go on a journey with a small child,

(Continued)

(Continued)

she may repeatedly ask, 'Are we nearly there?'), or the idea that, say, a different town may still be in the same country.

2   Time - you may have thought of examples where small children have similar difficulties with adult ideas of time as they do with space. 'Next month' does not mean much to a 5-year-old.

3   Money - small children have difficulty with the concept of money. When you go to a shop and receive change, they have difficulty understanding what change is, however carefully it is explained to them. Small children may think that change is simply a gift.

LEARNING TO MAKE SENSE OF THE WORLD

When dealing with children, adults (including many adults whose job involves working with children) are prone to make one of two incorrect assumptions:

- *That children think and understand just like we do.* For example, if you are a parent, you might possibly have had an experience like the following, which once happened to one of the authors. A family is setting off in the car on the annual holiday which has been discussed for months. Twenty miles down the road, the youngest child suddenly asks: 'By the way, where are we going?' The holiday *may* have been discussed for months, but unfortunately the adults had never done so in terms which were comprehensible to this child.
- *That children don't think at all about the world about them.* Some parents discuss all kinds of adult matters in front of their small children, and, if the wisdom of this is queried, simply say: 'Oh, don't worry about him, he's not listening to us and anyway he doesn't understand ...'.

The big insight of the Swiss psychologist Jean Piaget was that both those assumptions about children are untrue: children do think, as adults do, but they don't think in the same way as adults. This insight came to him early in his career when he was working on intelligence tests and realised that children regularly made the *same kinds of mistakes*. There was a pattern to their mistakes, in other words, which suggested that they were thinking in a consistent way that had a logic of its own, even though this was not consistent with adult logic.

Jean Piaget, who died in 1980, was born in 1896 in Switzerland. Although one of the most famous names in developmental psychology, he in fact did not see himself as primarily a psychologist at all, but as a biologist and a philosopher. He described himself as a 'genetic epistemologist'. Epistemology is the philosophy of knowledge, so what he meant by this was that he was interested in the origins of knowledge.

Piaget believed that a child is actively involved in the development of her own thinking and he saw the active search for knowledge as being something that children do, and want to do, for its own sake, and not just as a means to other ends. In Piaget's view a child finds her way through successive stages of cognitive development rather like a scientist, experimenting and developing ever more sophisticated models to explain the world, until eventually a level is reached where she is able to reason abstractly, think about hypothetical situations and organise rules about the world in her mind. Piaget saw cognitive development moving – in all children – through several stages, each one of which is characterised by a different way of thinking about and understanding the world. And he identified four factors that might be involved in this developmental process:

- physical maturation (that is, actual physical changes in the brain during childhood, resulting in the emergence of new abilities)
- experience
- social transmission (what we learn from other people)
- equilibration (a concept which we will explain and discuss a little later on).

Given that Piaget saw all children, regardless of culture, as going through the same basic stages, one might think that he would see physical maturation as being a major factor. But Piaget did not think that physical maturation could explain much of the change. His reasoning was that although children in different cultures go through the same stages of cognitive development, they reach different stages at different speeds, whereas if it was purely a matter of brain growth, one would expect the speed to be constant across cultures.

Experience and social transmission are (of course) factors in a child's learning, but Piaget did not take the view that our knowledge and understanding are simply the sum of what we have experienced or been taught. His view was more that children would use the information presented to them by experience as experimental data with which to develop their thinking about the basic rules that operate in the world. So children with very diverse experiences would nevertheless come to the same basic conclusions and develop their thinking along essentially the same paths because basic properties of the universe, like time and space and number, work in the same way everywhere. You could learn the concept of number, for example, in any environment, though some children may begin by counting marbles, others by counting stones.

As far as social transmission is concerned, teaching could be used to speed up a child's progress, provided that it was pitched at an appropriate level. There are some things that a child simply cannot be taught below a certain age. Certain ideas cannot be grasped until other more basic ideas are in place, just as one cannot place a building block one metre above the floor until there is a pile of other building blocks beneath it to hold it in place. Outside factors make a difference, but the essential driving force of cognitive development is something from *within* the child.

ASSIMILATION, ACCOMMODATION AND EQUILIBRATION

The basic building block of learning, according to Piaget, is what he called a schema. 'Schemas' are basic patterns of coordination between perceptions and actions. Grasping at a colourful object, for instance, could be described as a 'schema'. When a child encounters a new object or situation, she will try to deal with it in the first place by applying ideas and habits learnt from dealing with other objects and other situations. For example, if she is familiar with eating Smarties, she may try to eat other round, brightly coloured objects like beads or small parts of toys like Lego. This process Piaget called *assimilation*.

However, when a new object turns out not to fit into an old schema, schemas then have to be changed to fit the new object. In the example above, when the child finds that the object doesn't taste like a Smartie she will probably stop trying to eat it and explore other ways of playing with it. She will also revise her ideas about small round coloured objects, recognising that they don't always have the same properties. This process Piaget called *accommodation*.

Mental growth involves both assimilation and accommodation. The only way we can deal initially with a new situation is to try to apply ideas learnt from other situations (assimilation), but no one would progress with learning about the world if they did not modify their ideas in the light of experience (accommodation). This process of combining assimilation and accommodation he called *equilibration*.

So more complex ideas develop from simpler ones through an alternating process of assimilation and accommodation. And Piaget argued that this process could only take place in a certain sequence. More complex blocks could only be put in place when simpler ones have already been laid. This is why Piaget (unlike Vygotsky, whom we will discuss later) saw experience and social transmission as being of secondary importance in learning. No amount of information or stimulation could impart a new idea to a child unless she was at a stage where she was able to grasp it.

We have now used the analogy of building blocks twice, because this seems to sum up the assumption behind Piaget's theory, which is known as *constructivism*. Before going on to look at Piaget's stages of development, the following activity is an opportunity to consider this analogy:

Activity 4.2

Piling up building blocks is one metaphor for human development. Another might, for example, be going on a journey. Are there any other metaphors that could be used for human development? Do different metaphors make us look at the process in a different way?

Comments on Activity 4.2

The metaphor of building blocks may seem to be a reasonable way of describing human learning – and it may be – but one should always be careful about the power of metaphors. For example, you might have described learning as being like colouring in a picture, or of accumulating useful objects in a sack. If so, you may have noticed that the implications of these analogies are different. With building blocks, you have to start at the floor and work upwards. But with colouring books and filling sacks, you don't have to start in any particular place, or perform tasks in any particular order.

In thinking critically about Piaget's ideas, one question you could ask is whether building blocks are the best metaphor. Does colouring fit better? Or are some aspects of learning like building and others like colouring?

Critics of Piaget often point out that development doesn't follow quite such a neatly ordered sequence as the model suggests. The same criticism could be made of other kinds of 'stage' models of human life (for example, Erikson's model discussed in Chapter 2): often we don't move neatly through different stages so much as go back and forth between different states or levels.

Table 4.1   Piaget's stages of cognitive development

Stage	Approximate Age
Sensori-motor	0-18 months
Pre-operational	18 months to 7 years
Concrete operations	7-12 years
Formal operations	12 + years

STAGES OF COGNITIVE DEVELOPMENT

Piaget identified four basic stages in the development of a child's thinking, illustrated in Table 4.1. It should be emphasised that the approximate ages are a rough guide only: the stages are defined by the level of abstraction that the individual is capable of.

We'll now look at the stages one by one:

The sensori-motor stage (0-18 months)

Piaget proposed that babies start with basic physical reflexes, learn to modify these and then extend them by a process of assimilation and accommodation until – at the end of this stage – they are able to hold representations of things in their minds and plan out what they do. He thought that development in different areas – the understanding of space, say, or of number, or of cause and effect – proceeds in parallel. They all require the same basic underlying structures of reasoning. For example, sensori-motor development occurred alongside development of the idea of *object permanence*: the idea that objects still exist, even when you can't see them. Thus, a child starts out with little or no idea that objects really exist at all. (Why, after all, should a baby be able to know that the colours and shapes that she sees are anything more than just colours and shapes?) The child then progresses to a point where she doesn't just see objects but actively looks for them. Alongside this development, the child is similarly progressing in terms of sensori-motor control from movements which exist for their own sake and have no other purpose, to movements which are not only purposeful but planned in advance.

The pre-operational stage (18 months to 7 years)

At the conclusion of the previous stage, the child was beginning to hold representations of things in her mind. This ability develops in the pre-operational stage when representations of many kinds are used with increasing sophistication. The child acquires language, learns to make and interpret pictures and uses one object to represent another in imaginative play (a box is a car, a doll is a baby). So the *meanings* of objects and events are now being manipulated as well as the actual objects which the child learnt to manipulate in the previous stage. This is a major advance in the ability to think. But, as you probably concluded in Activity 4.1, a child during this stage still thinks in a very different way from an adult.

The following are some of the ways in which, Piaget suggested, the thinking of a child is different during this stage:

- The child tends to be *egocentric*. This is not necessarily to say that the child is *selfish* but that the child finds it difficult to see things from a point of view other than her own. For example, a child talking on the telephone may point to something in the room and refer to 'that thing over there', seemingly unaware that the person on the other end of the phone cannot possibly know what she means. Or a child playing hide-and-seek may hide her face, without realising that the rest of her body is just as visible to others as it was before, even though invisible to her.
- The child is prone to *centration*. She tends to fix her attention on one aspect of a situation and ignore other aspects. She has difficulty in recognising that a situation may have a number of dimensions. To give an instance encountered by one of the authors: a child of 4 is talking with his mother about how everyone he knows goes to the same school. This is an interesting idea which hasn't struck him before. 'But how come I know granny then?' he asks. 'She doesn't even *go* to my school!' Struck with the idea of school as the place where you get to know people, he has failed to hang on to the idea that there might be other contexts too in which you can meet people.
- There is a *lack of reversibility* in the child's thinking. This means that the child is unable to mentally reverse a series of events or steps of reasoning. To us as adults it follows that if we take three Smarties away from a pile of twenty, there will be twenty Smarties there again if we add another three. Or, if some water half fills a glass and we pour it into a mug, it will still half fill the glass when we pour it back again. There is a whole range of actions which we understand to be reversible. But these things are not self-evident to a pre-operational child. The word *operation* in Piaget's terminology refers to these reversible logical processes. The term *pre-operational* thus refers to the stage when the child has not learnt to use 'operations'. We mentioned earlier the inability of small children to grasp the concept of giving change in shops. Buying something, paying for it and receiving change is a good example of an operation in Piaget's sense. The price of the item bought and the change, we as adults understand, add up to the amount handed over to the shopkeeper. If we change our minds about the purchase and return the item, we will get back the price of the item which, with the change, adds up to precisely the same as the money we first handed over. But this is very difficult to explain to a 5-year-old.

So a child at this stage has a 'pre-logical' understanding of the world, based on subjective impressions and hunches, rather than on logical thinking, and based on a view of the world that has themselves at its centre. That is, after all, how it subjectively *appears* to all of us, but as we grow older we learn that this is not really the case. One aspect of this is that children at this age in particular are prone to 'magical thinking'. The following conversation is reported by Piaget with an 8-year-old child (child's words in italics).

You have already seen the clouds moving along? What makes them move? – *When we move along, they move along too.* – Can you make them move? – *Everybody can, when they walk.* – When I walk and you are still, do they move? – *Yes.* – And at night, when everyone is asleep do they move? – *Yes.* – But you tell me that they only move when somebody walks. – *They always move. The cats, when they walk, and then the dogs, they make the clouds move.* (Piaget, 1930: 62)

Those who work with children have to watch out for the combination of magical thinking and egocentrism which can make pre-operational children in particular feel that they are responsible for events which in reality have nothing to do with them: a traffic accident in which a relative was injured, perhaps, or their parents' divorce.

The following activity is a further look at the practical implication of pre-operational thinking.

Activity 4.3

Suppose you are a doctor or nurse, explaining to a child of 6 why he needs to have an operation – and what will be entailed.

Bearing in mind that a child of 6 thinks in a different way from adults, how should you go about this?

Comments on Activity 4.3

- Many people, when talking to children, are careful to adopt a kind and reassuring tone of voice, to talk about things familiar to the child and to use words which the child is likely to know – and all these things are of course important. But it is also important to ensure that the ideas presented to the child are comprehensible at his age.

- Because children at this age tend to centration, a complex discussion of the kind 'on the one hand, on the other hand' is likely to mean nothing to the child.

- The child's concerns may be focused on particular aspects of the situation which can be quite different from an adult's. To give an example: it may be that the thing that most worries the child is not the operation at all but having the bandages removed later, because he is terrified of pulling off sticky plasters.

- The child may come with powerful preconceptions which are quite irrational ('People who have surgery always have their legs removed', 'My illness is a punishment because I hit my little brother'). It might be a good idea to ask the child to describe his understanding of the situation – though of course the child may not want or feel able to tell you all his thoughts.

Being aware of children's very different ways of thinking is of course only part of successful communication with children. There are a lot of other issues too: awareness of a child's emotional needs and of his relationships, for example. And any adult trying to communicate with a child, such as a doctor or nurse in the above example, needs to be aware of the huge power difference between an adult and a child. But being aware of children's levels of cognitive understanding remains very important.

▬▬▬▬▬ Theory of mind ▬▬▬▬▬

Closely related to 'egocentrism' in Piaget's sense is the concept in cognitive psychology that is known as a 'theory of mind'. What is meant by this is an 'ability to explain and predict the behaviour of others by attributing to them mental states, such as beliefs, desires, emotions or intentions' (Gallagher and Frith, 2003: 77). In other words, having a 'theory of mind' means that we try to understand other people's actions by forming theories about what is going on in their heads.

Having a 'theory of mind' is necessary in order not to be egocentric, because it is about recognising that 'other people have a different perspective from ours' and that 'to understand their behaviour we have to take account of their perspective as well as the state of the world from our own perspective' (Gallagher and Frith, 2003: 77). Research into brain development is increasingly recognising the link between attachment (which we discussed in Chapter 3) and the development of a theory of mind, or mentalisation; 'understanding of minds is hard without the experience of having been understood as a person with a mind' (Fonagy and Target, 2005: 334).

The development of a 'theory of mind' in children can be tested in experiments such as a 'change of location' task in which children 'witness a character placing an object in one location and then leaving the room. In the character's absence, children witness the object being moved to a new location. Children are then asked where the character will look for his object upon his return' (Bernstein et al., 2007: 1375). If children understand that the character has a different perspective from their own, then they will suggest that the character will look in the place where he left it. If they have difficulty with understanding that the character has a different perspective, then they suggest that he will look in the place where *they* know it to be. Bernstein et al. note that 'children younger than about 4 years of age typically state the latter option' (2007: 1375).

Simon Baron-Cohen (1989, 1997) proposes that difficulty in developing a theory of mind is a specific developmental problem characteristic of autistic children, and uses the term 'mindblindness' to describe this.

The concrete operations stage (7–12 years)

In this stage the child is now able to grasp what Piaget called 'operations'. A child at this stage will have no difficulty grasping that when water is poured from a tall container to a broad one, it is the same amount of water and will come back to the original level when poured back into the first container. But, although the child becomes at home with external, *concrete* operations of this kind, she is still less at home with more abstract kinds of operations.

During the concrete operations stage, Piaget thought, there is a gradual waning of egocentric thinking (to repeat: this word is meant here in a cognitive sense and not a moral one). There is an increasing ability to *decentre*: to recognise and take into account the fact that many phenomena have several dimensions to them.

The child now grasps the idea of *reversibility* and growing logical insights lead to the development of concrete operational structures such as *classification* (sorting things out into categories), *seriation* (placing things in a logical order: of size, for example) and *conservation* of size and number (for example, water poured into a different shaped container is still the same amount of water).

The reason that a pre-operational child has difficulty with conservation of size and number is that she understands them in a *perceptual* way, as a description of the way things look, whereas the concrete operations child has got hold of the idea that number is not just about appearances. Likewise, a child at the pre-operational stage can find the way from A to B if it is a familiar route but she does so on the basis of remembering things on the way, and could not make a map of the route, while a child at the concrete operations stage could do so.

Another example of this shift is in the understanding of what are called *relational* terms (for example: 'This colour is *darker* than that one'). It can be shown that a concrete operations child understands that such terms describe a *relationship* between two things (between two colours in our example). But a pre-operational child sees words such as darker, bigger and so on, more as synonyms for 'very dark' or 'very big'. Once again, the concrete operations child is using logical concepts to organise experience, while the pre-operational child is relying on perception.

The contrast is apparent again in *classification*. Small children have difficulty with the idea of categories within other categories. We mentioned, for example, when discussing Activity 4.1 that small children have difficulty with the idea that a different town may still be in the same country. A statement such as 'We're driving from London to Bristol, but we'll still be in England', may be baffling to a pre-operational child. The concrete operations child is at home with such concepts.

But while able to use these sorts of rules and structures, a child at the concrete operations stage still finds it difficult to think in a self-conscious way about the rules she is using.

Comparisons with psychodynamic stages

If you compare Piaget's concrete operations stage with Freud's psychosexual stages, or Erikson's psychosocial ones, you'll find that it corresponds roughly to what Freud called the latency period (a period when the turmoils of the Oedipus complex were set aside while the child pursued more outward and practical concerns). Erikson saw this as a stage whose successful outcome was a sense of competence and achievement, and confidence in one's own ability to make and do things. These seem broadly consistent with Piaget's view of this stage as one in which concrete operations are mastered. While Piaget's model is not a psychodynamic theory, and does not even purport to address the same kinds of questions, Piaget did have a psychoanalytic training.

The formal operations stage (12+ years)

According to Piaget the stage of formal operations is normally reached at the beginning of adolescence and it is the final stage. This does not mean, of course, that Piaget was suggesting that a 12- or 13-year-old functions in exactly the same way as an adult in every respect (the ways in which this stage is different will be the subject of Chapter 6). But he thought that, when it comes to using rules and solving problems, a young person at this stage does indeed operate in much the same way as an adult. Piaget's theory would suggest that 11-year-olds, though very proficient in all kinds of ways, are less flexible in the way they think about problems and new situations than 14-year-olds – who, on the other hand, operate with much the same degree of flexibility as adults.

At the formal operations stage we are able not only to master basic, concrete operations, but also to perform operations *with* operations. Faced with a problem, we are able to:

- be self-consciously deductive (consciously going into problem-solving mode, so to speak) and consider all the possible ways a problem might be solved
- use abstract rules to solve a class of problems
- reflect on the rules we are using and be aware of our thought process
- use 'higher order' or analogical reasoning, for example making connections between problems that at a surface level seem quite different, but which have some likeness in terms of their logical structure.

The following experiment (Piaget et al., 1977, described in Goswami, 2011a: 405) may make this slightly clearer. Piaget and his colleagues gave children a set of jumbled pictures and asked them to sort them into pairs. So, for example, given pictures including: *dog, feather, vacuum cleaner, car, dog hair, ship, bird* … etc., they might pair *bird* and *feather*, and *dog* and *dog hair*. Children at the concrete operations and formal operations stage do not find this difficult. Children at the pre-operational stage will tend to pair pictures in idiosyncratic ways of their own.

Children were then asked to *pair up the pairs*. Thus, for example, the pairs *dog* and *dog hair*, and *bird* and *feather* might go together as they both describe a similar relationship (as might the pairs *pilot* and *aeroplane*, and *driver* and *car*, for instance). This is an example of 'higher order' analogical thinking, because the participants were being asked to make connections not on the basis of anything visible on the cards, but on the basis of types of relationships. They were being asked to consider the rules that they used to form the pairs in the first part of the experiment, and then to find a second level of rules which could be used to pair up the rules themselves. In other words, they were being asked to make rules about rules, or to categorise categories. This was possible for young people in the formal operations stage, but it was too abstract for concrete operations stage children.

PIAGET'S MODEL: CHALLENGES AND DEVELOPMENTS

As we said at the beginning of this chapter, Piaget's model cannot be taken as a definitive account of cognitive development. Criticisms of Piaget's theory come from many different quarters, and other theorists have made important contributions to the field.

Vygotsky and the role of language and culture

One notable aspect of Piaget's thinking is the surprisingly secondary importance he assigns to language and social interaction. The Russian psychologist Lev Vygotsky (1896–1934) put much more emphasis on language and saw the capacity to learn through instruction as a basic feature of human intelligence.

Vygotsky was born in the same year as Piaget, but the context of his work and the history of its influence on Western psychology were very different. He died while still in his thirties, having produced a considerable body of work, but this did not become widely known in the West until much later, until the 1960s and 1970s when the cultural divide between East and West was beginning to break down. Vygotsky was active in the early, idealistic days of the Russian communist revolution, and his thinking is strongly influenced by the Marxist view of social, cultural and historical processes as driving the development of individual and collective consciousness.

One of Vygotsky's most influential concepts is that of the *zone of proximal development*. This describes the gap between what a child can accomplish unaided and what she can do with help from adults or more capable peers (Vygotsky, 1978: 86). His view that 'the only good learning is that which is in advance of development' (1978: 89) differs from Piaget's view that a developmental stage must be reached internally before advances in learning can take place, and it shows how Vygotsky conceptualises development as an interactive process between the individual and society.

Language is one of the most important mediums through which this interaction takes place, and consequently Vygotsky attached much more importance to the role of language than Piaget did. He suggested that the role of language and instruction is so crucial in guiding action that, when it is not provided externally, we learn to provide it for ourselves. Piaget saw the fact that small children chatter to themselves as an example of egocentrism, because the child chatters away and it doesn't occur to her that what she is saying means nothing to anyone else, and because private speech disappears as the child grows older. But Vygotsky saw language as basic to thought and suggested that a child using private speech was giving instructions to herself as a strategy to keep her focused on a task. Private speech, in Vygotsky's view, did not disappear, but simply became internalised as the interior monologue which goes on in our heads even as adults (Vygotsky, 1962).

In fact Piaget's exploration of the underlying conceptual structures which children use when solving problems could have been flawed by the fact that he did not address issues to do with language. It is possible, for instance, that children may actually possess concepts such as object permanence but may not demonstrate this if adults put questions to them in a way that they cannot grasp. To complicate this, the opposite can also be true. Children may be taught to repeat a rule, but without understanding the underlying concept. One of the authors once poured water from a tall glass into a wide one and asked a 7-year-old whether the amount was the same or not. 'The same', she said, but then added: 'I know because my teacher told me.'

The contradictions in these examples make more sense if we understand them as examples of learning in the zone of proximal development, where the interactions with adults are a part of the learning process. Followers of Vygotsky use the term 'scaffolding' to describe the educational methods that adults can use to help children move from one stage of understanding to the next (Wood et al., 1976: 90). Vygotsky's model of development is rather different from the 'building block' model of Piaget and others. It is a relational one, which arises out of the Marxist concept of a dialectical process, a back and forth interaction between two different perspectives which leads to the emergence of a new understanding.

Building blocks and stages

Some research seems to confirm Piaget's ideas about different kinds of thinking at different stages. But a lot of experimental evidence now suggests the various cognitive milestones are reached much earlier than Piaget envisaged. There is experimental evidence, for example, that the concept of object permanence is present at least as early as three months. Renée Baillargeon (1987) devised an elaborate apparatus whereby a toy car rolled down a track. A screen could be placed in front of part of the track and a box could be placed behind that screen either *next* to the track or *on* it, so that it looked as if the car could not get past it. In both cases the car could in fact pass the box. She compared babies' responses to the apparently 'possible' event of the car reappearing from behind the screen when the box had been seen to not be in its way and the apparently 'impossible' event of the car seeming to have passed through the box. She found that babies stared for much longer at the apparatus in the 'impossible' case. If they had no concept of object permanence, Baillargeon argued, why would the 'impossible case' be any more interesting than the other case? Later work by Baillargeon and colleagues, using similar experiments, has continued to explore the way in which infants perceive and interpret objects, and is showing that there are several different cognitive systems involved in interaction with each other (Baillargeon et al., 2011: 41). They have also carried out experiments which show that these very young children can be 'taught' to perceive confusing objects and events correctly even though this would normally be beyond what would be expected at their developmental stage (2011: 30). In Vygotsky's terms this could be seen as an example of learning in the zone of proximal development, with the researchers providing 'scaffolding'.

Other researchers have challenged what Piaget said about 'egocentricity' and demonstrated that small children *are* able to view many types of problem from points of view other than their own (for example, Cox, 1991). It can also be demonstrated that children as young as 2 can make deductions by analogy. This is done by showing children how to do one task with one set of materials, and then giving them another analogous but different task with a different set of materials. They do better at the new task than children not previously shown the analogy. Chen et al. (1997) even claim to have demonstrated analogical reasoning in children less than a year old.

One challenge to Piaget's theory comes from the simple observation that babies at only three days old will imitate an adult sticking out her tongue. How can a baby know that the tongue of another person is in some way equivalent to her own, if she has not yet learnt to interpret the signals in her optic nerves as objects at all? It seems that Piaget's 'building block' model, in which each block can only be put in place when the previous block is already there, may be too rigid. Or, at least, it does not apply to every aspect of cognitive development. Perhaps a more complicated analogy needs to be found which allows for the fact that some aspects of the structure are already in place at the outset, and that others can emerge at different speeds?

It is also the case that forms of thinking characteristic of children do not simply disappear in adulthood. Adults can be prone to magical thinking of various kinds. In particular, when facing trauma or bereavement or acute stress, adults can regress to childlike ways of thinking, demonstrating how cognitive and emotional functioning can often be interlinked and interdependent.

Modularity

There are also challenges to Piaget's idea that cognitive development necessarily unfolds 'across the board' as newer and more powerful thinking skills are acquired and applied to different areas. Jerry Fodor (1983) is associated with the idea that the mind consists of a number of separate systems ('modules') which have evolved to deal with particular functions. A number of different modules have been suggested including language acquisition, 'visual analysis of objects and space', 'theory of mind' and face perception (Kail, 2004: 446). One would predict from a modular model that development could occur unevenly rather than 'across the board', and certainly it is not hard to find evidence that this can be the case. For example, there are high-functioning autistic children who have remarkable mathematical abilities but who have difficulty with 'theory of mind', and dyslexic people who are very intelligent in other respects but who have difficulty in writing. (For those interested in these debates, Annette Karmiloff-Smith (1995) proposes a model somewhere between that of Fodor and that of Piaget.)

Brain development

Finally, although Piaget did not emphasise physical maturation as a major factor in the development of our thinking, it is known that the brain continues to grow and develop throughout childhood and adolescence and into adulthood. It is almost certainly the case that some of the cognitive changes that occur in the course of childhood can be explained, not in terms of 'equilibration' producing a gradually more sophisticated model of the world, but in terms of the changing capacities of the brain itself (that is, to use computer terminology, in terms of 'hardware', rather than simply 'software'). As we have already seen in previous chapters, neuroscience is currently an area of intense research activity which continues to produce new knowledge about cognition and how it relates to the development and functioning of different areas of the brain. So, for instance, Casey et al., describing the structure of the brain at different ages, conclude that 'brain regions subserving primary functions such as motor and sensory systems mature before higher-order association areas that integrate these primary functions (e.g. prefrontal cortex)' (2005: 242), which would suggest a physical basis for some of the increasing mental sophistication which Piaget described. So would the evidence (discussed by Spear, 2000: 422, in a review of literature on the effects of brain development in adolescence) that adolescents who physically mature early do slightly better in IQ tests than adolescents who are late to mature.

Increased understanding of brain function is producing new developmental models. Information processing models, which have their origins in Piaget's work, show in detail how the brain's neural network develops, and how and where in the brain different kinds of information are processed, and therefore which processes will occur later rather than earlier. These later developing areas are those that enable the processing of complex information through logic and reasoning (Halford and Andrews, 2011: 715). Neuroconstructivism (Mareschal et al., 2007) is another recent model which takes account of the emerging understanding of how biological and environmental factors interact in the development of the brain (we described this briefly in Chapter 1). Indeed, it challenges the computer analogy of the brain that we used above, which separates experience-dependent 'software' from biological 'hardware', proposing that they cannot be studied and understood independently of each other, and that the 'software' of experience changes the underlying 'hardware' (Westermann et al., 2011: 725).

Concluding comments

Although we have concentrated on Piaget's model of cognitive development in this chapter, we hope we have made it clear that there are alternative models, and also many things that are still not fully understood about cognitive development. It is important to recognise that cognitive development does not simply take place in the individual brain, but in relationships and interaction with others in a social and cultural context. It cannot be rigidly separated from emotional and moral development, and the processes by which we learn to take our place in society, which we will consider further in later chapters. Nevertheless, Piaget's insight that children do think in *systematically* different ways from adults does, we suggest, remain valuable, and his account of the *qualitative* differences in the ways in which people think at different stages seems to us to remain valid and relevant (even if reality is rather more complex than the model allows). As we said earlier, many people make the mistake of assuming, on the one hand, that children don't think at all or, on the other, that they think in exactly the same way as adults. Piaget helped us to recognise that children's minds are just as full of thoughts as the minds of adults, but that those thoughts may work in very different ways at different ages.

CHAPTER SUMMARY

- In this chapter we looked at the concept of cognitive psychology and at cognitive development, including its relationship to emotional development as discussed in the previous chapters.
- We then looked at the work of Jean Piaget and his ideas about the nature of human cognitive development. His key insight was that children's thinking differs from adult thinking in consistent, systematic ways.
- We introduced some of Piaget's basic concepts including *assimilation, accommodation* and *equilibration*, as well as specific uses of the terms *schema* and *operation*.
- We then described Piaget's stages of cognitive development: the *sensori-motor* stage, the *pre-operational* stage, the *concrete operations* stage and the *formal operations* stage, looking at the characteristic thinking that Piaget suggested occurred at each stage.
- We looked at challenges to Piaget's model and Vygotsky's emphasis on the importance of language and learning through instruction, and at more recent developments in cognitive theory.
- We concluded that while Piaget's original insights remained useful, they should not be seen as the 'last word' on cognitive development, a subject which is still being explored, debated and argued about in the scientific community.

We have now looked at Piaget's theory of cognitive development and at psychodynamic theories. Though they may seem worlds apart, they do have in common that they are attempts to map out what goes on in people's heads. This is in stark contrast to the behaviourists, whom we will consider in the next chapter.

Tangled Webs

In any of the cases where children are involved, it is worth asking the question: how would this situation look from the perspective of a child of this age, who does not have an adult's understanding of the world?

The cases we suggested at the beginning of the chapter were:

Xenia Veloso (Case I: the Veloso family). At the age of 6, Xenia (according to Piaget's framework at least), is still at the pre-operational stage of cognitive development, which is to say that she may find it hard seeing things from other perspectives than her own, and she will tend to think in a 'pre-logical' way based on feelings and appearances, rather than on reasoning things out. She will also be prone to 'magical thinking'. One can only speculate about how this may shape her understanding of the situation. It's possible, for instance, that she will hold herself responsible for things that she really isn't responsible for at all. She may find it difficult to understand the role of Tracey or Deanna in the way an adult might do (that is: simply as human beings doing their job), and may imagine them to have powers or agendas which they in fact don't have. (Chris Beckett recalls as a small child being given a parking ticket when he was waiting in the car while his mother popped into the shop. He imagined his mother might be sent to prison and, very frightened, tore the ticket to pieces.)

Caitlin Smart (Dudley) and **the Dudley/Harris family (Cases A and G).** Caitlin is 8, and so two years older than Xenia, and perhaps less prone to magical thinking, but we should bear in mind that her cognitive development may be somewhat behind for her chronological age, and also that 8-year-olds (seen as being at the stage of concrete operations in Piaget's model) still have difficulty with abstract ideas as compared to adults and think in more concrete and literal ways. And the circumstances which may be leading her to the mistaken impression that she is to blame for the unhappiness of other family members (her critical stepfather and depressed, withdrawn mother) have been part of her life for some years. At 6, her brother Josh is the same age as Xenia.

 You can access Tangled Webs by visiting **https://study.sagepub.com/tangledwebs**

Further reading

On Piaget

Boden, M. (1994) *Piaget*. London: Fontana.

On Vygotsky

Daniels, H. (ed.) (2017) *An Introduction to Vygotsky*, 3rd edn. Hove: Routledge.

(Continued)

(Continued)

On cognitive development

Goswami, U. (ed.) (2011) *The Wiley-Blackwell Handbook of Childhood Cognitive Development*, 2nd edn. Oxford: Blackwell.

Taylor, L. (2005) *Introducing Cognitive Development*. Hove: Psychology Press.

MAKING CONNECTIONS

IDEAS FROM BEHAVIOURISM

TANGLED WEBS

This chapter is about the ways in which certain behaviours become habitual when they are associated with some sort of pay-off (or 'reinforcement'). Towards the end of the chapter, we discuss the application of this idea to the acquisition of stereotypical gender roles: the way that boys learn to behave 'boyishly' and girls learn to behave 'girlishly'. You could look at any of the cases and ask yourself, 'What is this person's characteristic way of behaving, and what is the pay-off for that person that encourages this behaviour?' A couple of cases you might like to look at are: **The Dudley/Harris family (Case G)** and **Derek Harrow (Case B: Rob Thomas and Derek Harrow)**.

 You can access Tangled Webs by visiting **https://study.sagepub.com/tangledwebs**

Every day, when John comes home from work, he opens the fridge and eats some cheese. If he stopped to think about it, he'd say this wasn't a good idea because he has a bit of a weight problem, but, for some reason, he just keeps doing it. Jacky invariably lights up a cigarette after a meal, and, when she's very anxious, she will often smoke one cigarette after another. Malik is ten years old and, if he finds something difficult in his class at school, he will begin to act up, interrupting the teaching and picking fights with other children.

These are habits, characteristic patterns of behaviour. We all have them. Often they are harmless, or even beneficial, but sometimes they can be destructive either to ourselves or to others. In Malik's case, for instance, his behaviour gets in the way both of his own learning and that of the other children in his class. People in the helping professions, whether social workers or nurses, teachers or doctors, often have to try to think of ways of managing destructive patterns of behaviour that adults or children have somehow got into. But where do these habits come from? Since we are not born opening fridges, or smoking cigarettes, or messing about in classrooms, we must have learned these behaviours somehow, but it's a very different kind of learning than the one we talked about in the last chapter. Jacky doesn't smoke as a result of some logical process of reasoning. John would probably be hard pressed to explain why and when he got into his comfort eating habit. Malik almost certainly doesn't know why he feels the need to disrupt his class on such a regular basis.

So what is the reason for Malik's behaviour? If you think about it for a moment, you may well conclude that it happens because it has some sort of consequence which feels good. Perhaps he likes the fact that it gets him a lot of attention? Or perhaps it provides a welcome distraction from the uncomfortable feelings he gets when something seems difficult to understand? What we are talking about now is a kind of learning that's simply about making connections: connections between a situation, a behaviour and a consequence. And this kind of learning can take place without any kind of reasoning process, or even without conscious thought. Animals learn in this way, and animal trainers typically operate by rewarding behaviours they want to encourage, building connections between a command, a particular behaviour and a pleasurable reward.

A whole branch of experimental psychology is based on this idea of learning by association. Once called *connectionism*, then *behaviourism*, this body of ideas is also referred to as *learning theory*, with the methodology associated with it often being called *behaviour analysis*. The characteristic style of this school of psychology is an experimental method, based on the physical sciences, in which connections are only asserted to exist when this can be proved statistically in a controlled experiment. The original behaviourists typically tried to avoid speculating about what is going on inside the heads of their subjects, and even to avoid words like 'feelings' and 'thoughts'. In the heyday of behaviourism, in the mid-twentieth century, some of its practitioners argued that all learning and all behaviour could be explained in terms of these kinds of connections between situations, actions and consequences. Unlike the other ideas we have discussed in the last three chapters, learning theory does not offer a model of development and is certainly not a stage theory, in any shape or form. It is simply a series of generalisations about how new behaviour is learnt. What is more, much of the material we will now discuss comes from animal experiments and not from the study of human beings at all. And, that being so, the reader might well ask why have we included it at all in a book on human development?

There are a number of reasons. Firstly, this way of looking at things provides an important contrast to the theories discussed so far, a reminder that development doesn't have to be looked at as a stage process, or as an 'innate phenomenon which leads to an inevitable sequence of behaviours' (Dillenburger and Keenan, 1997: 14). Secondly, it describes a mechanism of learning which can be very helpful for thinking about many aspects of social development, including the learning of gender roles, which we'll discuss at the end of this chapter. (How do boys learn to behave in stereotypically 'boyish' ways? There's a good case for thinking that, in large part, it's because they're rewarded for doing so, and rewarded for avoiding behaviour that is stereotypically 'girlish'.)

Thirdly and finally, learning theory looks at patterns of behaviour and asks a very simple question, not 'what is the origin of this behaviour?' but 'what is it that keeps that behaviour going?' This has been a fruitful source of ideas for schools of therapy that avoid the psychoanalytic emphasis on delving into the past, and look instead at the here and now. So learning theory has had important practical applications, and has been an important influence in the caring professions. Many parenting programmes, for instance, teach parents to look at the way they inadvertently reward their children's problem behaviour. Cognitive behaviour therapy (which we'll also come back to) works by getting people to look at their own behaviour in the same kind of way.

This way of looking at behaviour cannot be used to answer all the questions we might want to ask about human development but, in conjunction with other ideas, it makes an important contribution to our understanding of how we are shaped by circumstances into the people we become. One might argue that the learned connections described in this chapter are the nuts and bolts (or building blocks, or atoms) of which other phenomena, described elsewhere in this book, are constructed. For instance, attachment behavioural systems (discussed in Chapter 3) could be seen as made up of many learned connections of this kind.

Before going any further, though, you might like to use the following activity to review your own experiences of learning by association:

Activity 5.1

Can you think of examples in your own experience where a particular sensation (sight, sound, taste, smell) regularly evokes a particular response? Can you think of an instance where a particular set of circumstances seems to bring about an automatic response in you?

Comments on Activity 5.1

Most people can probably think of particular smells, or pieces of music that set off associations. Certain pop songs, for example, are often evocative, calling to mind a whole string of memories of the time when that particular song was commonly being played, and of feelings associated with that time. The smells of certain kinds of disinfectant immediately call to mind for some people childhood fears about hospitals and operations. These are instances of connections which are learnt when things come together at the same time.

(Continued)

(Continued)

An example of a certain situation seeming to bring about an automatic response is this: if you are a driver, you will probably have had the experience of getting in your car and being on the way to work before you realise that in fact it is the weekend, and you were not intending to go to work but to drive in the opposite direction. Being in the car set you off on a chain of actions so familiar that you didn't even think about it. Smokers trying to give up often report that certain situations - the end of a meal, for example - trigger an intensely strong desire to light a cigarette.

CLASSICAL CONDITIONING

Ivan Pavlov (1849–1936) was a physiologist, not a psychologist, and his primary interest was in the digestive system: he received a Nobel Prize for his work in this area. As part of this work, however, he became interested in finding out what stimuli set the digestive juices flowing. He demonstrated that dogs start to salivate at the sight or smell of food and that this appeared to be an innate, involuntary *reflex*, like the automatic knee-jerk reaction when one is struck above the knee. Pavlov then tried sounding a buzzer every time food was given to the dogs. He found that after a while the dogs started to salivate as soon as they heard the buzzer. An innate reflex had been 'conditioned' so that it occurred in response to a new stimulus. This is what he termed a 'conditioned reflex' and this particular type of conditioning is known as 'classical conditioning'.

Pavlov then went on to explore exactly how this kind of connection worked, by experimenting with different possibilities. Some of his key concepts can be summarised as follows:

- **Extinction** - Pavlov found that if a dog had been conditioned to salivate in response to a buzzer that preceded food, it would then continue to salivate in response to the buzzer alone. However, this effect did not last forever. If the buzzer ceased to be followed by food, then after a while the conditioned reflex would wear off and the sound of the buzzer would no longer result in salivation. In Pavlovian terms, the conditioned reflex had become 'extinct'. To give a human example: a quitting smoker may for a long time feel a strong craving for a cigarette after a meal. But after some time that craving fades, until a point is reached where the end of a meal does not trigger a desire to smoke.
- **Spontaneous recovery** - but Pavlov also found that, if a conditioned reflex has been allowed to become extinct, it can very quickly be re-established. So a dog may have been conditioned to salivate at the sound of a buzzer, and this conditioned reflex may then have been allowed to become completely extinct, so that the dog does not salivate at all in response to food. But if the buzzer now starts to be sounded at feeding time again, the original conditioned link will reappear rapidly at full strength, much more quickly than it would appear in a dog which had never previously been conditioned. In other words, even though the link has been extinguished in terms of behaviour, some record of it clearly remains in the dog's brain. Again, we can use the comparison of a quitting smoker. After a sufficient time has elapsed, this person may no longer feel a craving for a cigarette at the end of a meal. But if that person takes up smoking again, all those conditioned connections seem to reappear very rapidly at full strength.

- **Generalisation** - if a dog has learnt to salivate to a buzzer, this response will tend to generalise to other sounds also. For example, the dog will salivate not only if it hears a buzzer but also if it hears an electric bell. (This concept has some similarities with Piaget's assimilation, discussed in the previous chapter.)
- **Discrimination** - however, while generalisation occurs by default, dogs can be trained to finely discriminate between different stimuli. If you are the owner of a cat or dog you may have observed how animals can learn to distinguish the particular engine sound of the family car, and respond to this one sound, while ignoring all others.

These basic concepts are central to learning theory. What you may notice about them is that, unlike either psychodynamic theories or Piaget's theory of cognitive development, these concepts of conditioning, extinction, spontaneous recovery, generalisation and discrimination do not purport to describe anything that might be going on in the dogs' minds. They are purely and simply descriptions of relationships between different types of stimulus and observed and measurable responses.

The insistence of behaviourists that only observable behaviour should be studied can seem perverse. But of course we cannot know directly what goes on in the mind of another person, let alone an animal. It is possible to train a pigeon to discriminate, say, between red and other colours but it is impossible to know what red actually looks like to a pigeon. Indeed, two *people* cannot know whether the colour red looks the same to each of them.

Therapeutic approaches derived from behaviourism do not try to get inside the patient's mind to the extent that psychoanalysis does. Instead, they are aimed at finding practical ways of unlearning behaviour that is causing problems, or learning new behaviour.

BEHAVIOURISM

A very influential figure in psychology in the middle of the twentieth century, J.B. Watson (1878–1958) was the one who actually coined the term 'behaviourism'. He was an enthusiastic advocate of the use of conditioning techniques to make people conform to the needs of society, and was extremely confident in their ability to actually do so, as the following quote illustrates:

> Give me a dozen healthy infants ... and my own specified world to bring them up in and I'll guarantee to take any one at random and train him to become any kind of specialist I might select. ... (Watson, 1931: 104)

He was also a pioneer of the use of sexual imagery as an advertising tool, believing that if people could be taught to make a connection (even if an unconscious one) between a brand of cigarettes, for example, and sex, it would make them buy more. His views were parodied in Aldous Huxley's famous futuristic novel *Brave New World*:

> Patiently the D.H.C. [Director of Hatcheries and Conditioning] explained. If the children were made to scream at the sight of a rose, that was on grounds of high economic policy. ...

'A love of nature keeps no factories busy. It was decided to abolish the love of nature, at any rate among the lower classes. ... Hence those electric shocks.' (2014 [1932]: 18)

In Huxley's novel children were shown flowers and given an electric shock. An electric shock causes an involuntary response of pulling back. A flower does not normally provoke this response, but could be made to do so by associating flowers with shocks. This is an example of classical conditioning, which, as we've seen, is about connecting a new stimulus to an existing basic reflex. The new stimulus is connected to something that provokes an automatic response – and, incidentally, also gives pleasure or pain, though Pavlov did not concern himself with these subjective experiences.

But Watson argued that rewards or punishments were not necessary to make a connection between two things. Simply the fact that two things occurred together was enough. The connection would be stronger if the two things occurred together *frequently* or if they had occurred together *recently*. Thus an animal placed in a maze might wander around until it found its way out. If placed back into the maze it would find its way out more quickly, not necessarily because it had been rewarded for finding its way out, but simply because finding its way out was the last thing it did in the maze. A human parallel here might be our example of getting in a car and driving without thinking along a familiar route. It is not as if this is particularly rewarding: it is just that this is what you did last time you got into the car. You might also notice that if you use a certain word in conversation that you don't often use, you will often find yourself repeating the same word in later conversations the same day.

OPERANT CONDITIONING

Animal trainers have known for centuries that animals can be taught to behave in certain ways when this behaviour is followed by a reward, and discouraged from behaving in other ways with punishments. Parents, of course, have also applied this principle to children. This kind of learning is different from that studied by Pavlov because it is not just about conditioning innate reflexes (such as salivation or a fear response) to new stimuli but about connecting voluntary behaviours to stimuli. It has become known as *operant* conditioning, for reasons which we will explain, as opposed to Pavlov's *classical conditioning* (also known as *respondent conditioning*).

Concepts such as extinction, generalisation and spontaneous recovery apply to operant conditioning also. And the original researchers into operant learning, no less than Pavlov, avoided speculating about insight or thought on the part of animals. Animals are simply seen as trying various behaviours more or less randomly at first. Those that are followed by a positive outcome become part of the animal's repertoire, while those that are followed by a negative or neutral outcome do not. It is a process analogous to Darwin's theory of natural selection – those that prove successful survive, while those that don't, die out – except that it applies to behaviours rather than to genetic variations:

> In both operant conditioning and the evolutionary selection of behavioural characteristics, consequences alter future probability. Reflexes and other innate patterns of behaviour evolve because they increase the chances of survival of the species. Operants grow strong because they are followed by important consequences in the life of the individual. (Skinner, 1953: 90)

B.F. Skinner (1903–90) was the inventor of the term 'operant conditioning' (although he was not the first to explore this kind of learning) and he was a dominant figure in post-war behaviourist research. His classic experimental tool was the so-called Skinner Box, consisting of a cage in which there was a food dispenser with a lever above it. In the most basic version of this experiment, a rat presses the lever and the food dispenser drops a pellet of food into the tray beneath it. Not surprisingly, when this happens on a regular basis, the rat goes on pressing the lever in order to get the food.

In Skinner's terminology, the rat's original pressing of the lever is termed an *operant behaviour*, meaning a behaviour that occurs with no obvious stimulus, as opposed to a *respondent behaviour*, an example of which would be pulling your hand away from a hot stove, or Pavlov's dogs involuntarily salivating at the smell of food (hence 'operant conditioning', as opposed to 'respondent conditioning').

Reinforcement

In Skinner's experiment above, the rat was rewarded with a pellet of food when it pressed the lever, and this increased the frequency of the lever-pushing behaviour. This is known as *positive reinforcement*. *Negative reinforcement* of a behaviour means that something unpleasant is *removed* as a consequence of it. In the context of Skinner's experiment, negative reinforcement would be something like an electric shock which the rat can only stop by pressing a lever. Think back to the example of Malik which we gave at the beginning of the chapter. If the reason he disrupts the class is that he likes the attention it brings him, that would be an example of *positive reinforcement*. If he does it because it stops him having to concentrate on work that makes him anxious because it seems too difficult, then that would be an example of *negative reinforcement*.

Punishment, which reduces a behaviour rather than increasing it, can also be positive or negative. A 'positive' punishment would have been giving the rat an electric shock as opposed to the positive reward of a pellet of food when it pushed the lever; clearly this would not have reinforced the rat's behaviour but would have had the opposite effect of deterring it. And a 'negative' punishment would be something that took the food away when a lever was pressed (see Figure 5.1).

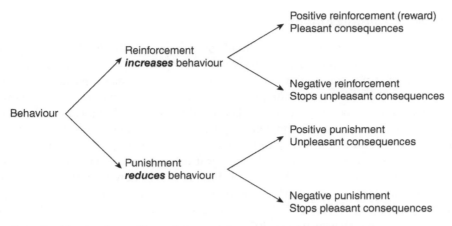

Figure 5.1   Positive and negative reinforcement and punishment

If a particular stimulus occurs regularly with a reinforcer, that stimulus itself can become a positive reinforcer. This is the principle behind 'click training' which is used by many dog-owners and trainers. The dog is taught to make an association between the clicking sound and the reward of food. The click can then be used on its own as a reinforcer, with the advantage that it can be easily given *at the exact moment* that the behaviour you want to reinforce is happening. Of course, if you don't ever follow a click with food, the connection between click and food will in due course become extinct, and the click will no longer be effective as a reinforcer.

Skinner and the mind

As we've noted, behaviourists study observable behaviour rather than processes within the mind. But Skinner was at pains to say that he was not denying that there were such things as thoughts and feelings, or that these were important. What he did argue was that we are accustomed to think of such things in the wrong way.

He wrote, for example, that 'what is felt or introspectively observed is not some non-physical world of consciousness, mind or mental life, but the observer's own body'. What went on in that 'world within the skin' was, he argued, the product of the external environment which 'made its first great

contribution during the evolution of the species, but [which] exerts a different kind of effect during the lifetime of the individual, and the combination of the two effects is the behaviour we observe at any given time'.

His point is that, when we explain things in terms of what is going on inside our minds, we are not really explaining anything. For example: if you say 'I did X because I was angry', this begs the question as to what 'anger' really is and what causes it.

'When what a person does is attributed to what is going on inside him', Skinner wrote, 'investigation is at an end' (1974: 17, 18).

Schedules of reinforcement

Skinner's experimental work consisted essentially of altering the patterns of reinforcement and seeing the effect this had on behaviour. To give one example, Rat 'A' is rewarded with a pellet every time it pushes the lever. Rat 'B' only gets a pellet every 20 times it pushes the lever. Not surprisingly, rat 'A' learns lever-pushing behaviour more quickly than rat 'B'. But now suppose that both rats stop being given food pellets at all for lever-pushing. For which rat would lever-pressing behaviour become extinct more quickly? People tend to guess that rat 'A', which had always been rewarded for lever-pushing, would be slower to give up pushing the lever. In fact, though, experimental evidence shows that it is the opposite that is the case. The rats that are only rewarded occasionally for lever pushing go on trying to push the lever for longer. They learn the behaviour more slowly – and they also unlearn it more slowly. This helps to explain the persistence of some addictive behaviours; gambling, for instance, where rewards are extremely unpredictable (Svanberg, 2018: 64).

Shaping

As we've said, Skinner's techniques resemble those of animal trainers – and some of his students did in fact go on to become animal trainers. He and his co-workers set themselves tasks like training pigeons to play skittles in a miniature bowling alley or to knock a ping-pong ball to and fro (Skinner, 1960). You clearly can't get an animal to learn a behaviour as complex as this in the same way as you get it to learn something simple like lever-pushing. If you adopted the method of just waiting for the bird to start playing skittles by chance, and then reinforcing this behaviour, you would wait forever. What Skinner did was this:

- ensured the pigeon was hungry
- established a strong conditioned connection between food and a certain sound (for instance a clicking sound, as described above)
- every time the pigeon did anything even vaguely approximating to the required task, he made the clicking sound and then gave it the food. (This was important because a click can be done at precisely the moment that the behaviour he wanted to reinforce occurred.) For example, he might start by making the clicking sound every time the pigeon pecked at the ball
- once ball-pecking had become established, he would then move on to another stage and, let's say, only click when the ball was pushed in the general direction of the skittles
- once that was established, he would then take it a stage further and, say, only click when the ball was knocked more than a certain distance in that direction
- and so on ...

This process is called *shaping* and is a powerful training technique with many applications. Its particular strength is that it avoids setting the person or animal being trained up to fail. At every stage, the trainee is encouraged to continue to produce operant behaviour: in other words, to keep trying. By contrast, if the pigeon was only to be rewarded for completing the full task, *none* of its intermediate behaviour would be reinforced, and so it would have no reason to even begin to change its behaviour in the right direction. And if the pigeon were trained by punishing it for doing the wrong thing, then this would have the effect – as a result of generalisation – of reducing active behaviour of any kind.

Discrimination

Using techniques like this, it has been possible not only to teach animals to do complicated tricks, but also to teach them extraordinary feats of discrimination. For example, pigeons (not known for their large brains) can be taught to distinguish a photograph of one person from 100 other people, even if they were all taken against the same range of backgrounds and even if that one person was shown in 100 different poses (Herrnstein et al., 1976).

The strength of different reinforcers

Learned behaviours normally extinguish over time if they are not reinforced – positively or negatively – any longer. As we've seen, the rates of learning and 'unlearning' a given behaviour depend in part on the schedules of reinforcement used. But the kind of reinforcer used also makes a difference. Interestingly, an exceptionally powerful *positive* reinforcer has been found to be the drug morphine. When rats received an injection of morphine for pushing a lever, lever-pushing never completely became extinguished, even if morphine stopped being given and even if the experiment was carried on past the time when there could possibly still be an actual physical dependency on morphine (Walker, 1984: 63).

The only other means of shaping behaviour comparable in power to this were strong positive punishments such as a powerful electric shock. (We believe that there are strong ethical arguments against giving animals powerful electric shocks, even though we are reporting the findings of experiments where such things have been used.) Given such a shock for pushing a lever, an animal might never push that lever again, regardless of the length of time that had passed (Azrin, 1959, cited in Pierce and Cheney, 2004: 156). Given the tendency of responses to generalise, this means that positive punishment like this can have a generally inhibiting effect on learning.

Indeed, in some adverse circumstances, the behaviour that animals learn is to *do nothing at all*. This phenomenon is called 'learned helplessness'. In yet another cruel experiment, Martin Seligman (1975) subjected one group of animals (call them group X) to electric shocks in an environment where they were strapped in and could not do anything to get away. A second group, Y, was not subjected to this experience. Both group X and group Y are then given a shock-avoidance task (that is, a task where they are given shocks which can be stopped by, for example, pressing a lever). What was found was that the group X animals performed less well on the shock-avoidance task than the group Y animals. A simple behaviourist explanation would be that the group X animals had (of necessity) been doing nothing when the shocks stopped in the first part of the experiment. The behaviour of 'doing nothing' had therefore been negatively reinforced, so that this was the behaviour that they adopted when placed in the second situation. Perhaps this helps to explain how some people become very passive and unable to help themselves.

Before moving on, you may like to pause to look at the relevance (or otherwise) of what we have been discussing to human development, bearing in mind that all the findings discussed so far are based on experiments with dogs, rats and pigeons.

━━━━━━━━━━ **Activity 5.2** ━━━━━━━━━━

1 Skinner found that the rats unlearned behaviour more slowly when that behaviour had only intermittently been reinforced. Can you think of any parallels here with attachment theory?

2 How might learning theory help us to understand the development of addictive behaviour?

3 Can you think of situations where human beings are placed in a similar situation to the helpless rats in Seligman's experiments? Can you think of instances of 'learned helplessness' in human life?

Comments on Activity 5.2

1 One parallel that may have struck you is that children who have been anxiously attached – whose attachment behaviour has only intermittently been reinforced – find it harder to cope with moves, let go of old attachments and make new attachments, than children who have been securely attached.

2 John's comfort eating and Jacky's smoking, with which we started this chapter, are examples of habits which could become addictions. 'Addiction is a process rather than an end point, and can be understood as a habit that has become dysfunctional, and is hard to break' (Svanberg, 2018: 11). Learning theory gives us insight into the mechanics of this process, though it is also important to understand it as a way of trying to deal with adverse life experiences such as abuse and trauma. Svanberg quotes a study that found that 100 per cent of people attending substance misuse services had been exposed to traumatic situations (Gielen et al., 2012, cited in Svanberg, 2018: 59). The two explanations do not contradict one another, though. If a person can distract themselves from painful feelings arising from trauma by, for instance, comfort eating, then what we are saying is that comfort eating is negatively reinforced by the relief it offers from the painful feelings.

3 Many children in abusive situations are in much the same position as Seligman's rats, since the abuse is something outside of their control. Certainly, depression in adult life is a common result of childhood abuse, as is a feeling of not being in control. People in institutional care – old people, for example, or people with mental illness – often experience a huge reduction in their control over their own lives, and often exhibit a kind of learnt passivity (there will be more on this in Chapter 11). You may also have been struck by the fact that these animals were in a no-win situation. Children in seriously abusive situations can be in the same position: the most dangerous thing in their lives is also their only source of physical care. You'll remember that attachment theorists suggest that the most dysfunctional form of anxious attachment – disorganised attachment – arises in these kinds of circumstances.

COGNITION AND BEHAVIOUR

Although Skinner, Watson and others tried to avoid any sort of speculation about what was going on in the minds of humans and animals, and to focus purely on the observable and measurable phenomena of behaviour and stimuli, the experimental evidence does make such an approach hard to sustain. There are phenomena which cannot easily be explained without postulating internal maps or models that animals and humans carry in their minds, and thanks to advances in neuroscience we now have much more knowledge about how the brain works than we did in Skinner's and Watson's day. It is no longer a widely held view that it might be possible to explain human behaviour without looking at the workings of the mind.

One result of the breaking down of barriers between cognitive and behavioural approaches has been the development of *cognitive behaviour therapy* (usually known as CBT). This brief, focused therapy is based on the work of Aaron Beck (1963, 1964, cited by Westbrook et al., 2011: 2–3). It is widely used in the NHS in the UK to help people to change thought patterns and behaviours that are causing them problems. It uses the ideas of learned behaviour, conditioning and reinforcement which we have already described, but, unlike earlier behaviourism, it also takes account of what is going on in people's minds, and a CBT therapist will help clients to recognise their negative thought patterns as part of the process of learning to change their behaviour. These negative thoughts are understood as being based on a system of core beliefs and 'schemata', which are information-processing structures built up from early childhood (Westbrook et al., 2011: 355). We have already met the term 'schema' in our discussion of Piaget in Chapter 4, but it is used more widely in CBT to include emotional as well as cognitive, physical and behavioural dimensions.

To bring about changes in behaviour, CBT uses reinforcement by setting clear, achievable goals agreed between therapist and client, maybe starting with very small steps (see the discussion of shaping above). For example, somebody with agoraphobia might start by aiming to be able to stand on their front doorstep, or they might not aim to do anything at all, but to keep a record of the pattern of their negative thoughts about venturing outside. The important thing is the reinforcement they gain from completing the task successfully.

Activity 5.3

Think again about Malik, described at the beginning of this chapter, whose behaviour disrupts his class and prevents him from learning. If you were his teacher, how might you go about understanding and dealing with this behaviour using some of the ideas we've outlined above?

Comments on Activity 5.3

You may have thought about the two types of conditioning, classical and operant.

Malik's interrupting and picking fights is not a self-evidently involuntary behaviour, like the salivating of Pavlov's dogs. One could see that a teacher could **shape** it through operant conditioning, using reinforcement to discourage the disruptive behaviour and encourage the desired behaviour of focusing on learning. We talked earlier about the kinds of reinforcement Malik may be obtaining from his behaviour; the positive reinforcement of the attention he gets, and the negative reinforcement of the distraction from a task he finds difficult and stressful.

However, operant conditioning gives us quite a limited and mechanistic view of a teacher's role, which does not take account of the different personalities, backgrounds and experiences of children (as opposed to rats and pigeons). You may have gone on to think about using insights from cognitive behaviour therapy by engaging Malik himself in the process of changing his behaviour, exploring negative thought patterns and ensuring that any goals you set for him are achievable. Finding out from him what he is thinking and feeling will help you as his teacher to decide what kinds of reinforcement will be most effective. If he is primarily seeking attention, you could ensure that he gets this for good behaviour just as much as for bad behaviour, and you might also be looking out for any reason why he might be looking for attention at the moment (perhaps a new baby in the family, or a parental separation) and exploring his feelings about this, so that they get the attention they need. If the main problem is that he finds the work too hard, you could explore his negative thoughts about this ('I'm stupid'; 'It's no good trying; I'll never be able to do it') and ensure that the tasks he is set are achievable, if necessary with extra learning support, so that his learning behaviour is reinforced by the reward of success and he no longer needs to distract himself and others from learning.

OBSERVATION AND SOCIAL LEARNING THEORY

One cognitive factor that can be demonstrated to be a part of learning in animals – and which we all know to be a part of learning in human beings – is *observation*. Animals consistently learn tasks more quickly if they have previously observed other animals completing them, than if they are only taught by the traditional operant conditioning procedures. In fact, learning from observation seems to be very deep-rooted. (In the previous chapter we mentioned that one-day-old babies can copy simple movements such as sticking out the tongue.) Albert Bandura (1977) explored observational learning in human children. In his basic experiment, a child is shown a live or filmed model doing something, and is later observed to see how much of the model's behaviour she copies. Bandura identified several variables that influenced the amount of copying that occurred:

- Children were more likely to copy models identified as high prestige in some way. (Advertising agencies have presumably discovered the same thing, since they routinely use celebrities to endorse products.)
- They were more likely to copy models similar to themselves in some way.
- They were also more likely (not surprisingly) to copy models that they had seen rewarded for their actions.
- He also found that there was a distinction between acquiring the capability of performing a task and actually copying it. So, for example, children who didn't mimic a certain action after seeing it, could do so if asked (again, perhaps, not a very surprising finding).

Bandura's work formed part of the basis for an area of psychology known as social learning theory, which uses ideas from learning theory to look at how we acquire complex social behaviour. This can be applied to any aspect of social behaviour, for example, how do we learn the behaviour that is characteristic of our culture or our social class? However, we want for the rest of this chapter to concentrate on just one area, which is obviously a crucial one in the study of human development: the acquisition of gender roles. At the beginning of the chapter we suggested that simple learned connections could perhaps be seen as the building blocks or atoms from which more complex learning is constructed. Gender development provides an illustration of this.

But before going any further, you may find it useful to look at the following activity. This will give you an opportunity to consider what you have read so far about learning theory by trying to apply it to the question of gender roles.

━━━━ Activity 5.4 ━━━━

Looking back at the ideas from learning theory which we've discussed (operant conditioning, classical conditioning, observational learning, generalisation, discrimination, etc.), consider how these might apply to the way that children learn different 'masculine' or 'feminine' gender roles.

Comments on Activity 5.4

Ideas you may have mentioned are:

- Different behaviours are positively or negatively reinforced, by parents or other adults (that is, aggression is encouraged more in boys, playing with dolls is discouraged, etc.).
- Observational learning means that boys will tend to copy male role models (at home, on TV and elsewhere), and girls female role models. Boys will also tend to copy males who are seen as successful and having high status, while girls will tend to copy famous, high-profile girls or women.

- From an early age different stimuli are offered, even in connection with meeting basic needs for food and warmth (girls are given pink cups, boys blue, for example).
- You may also have considered ways in which connections learnt in one context tend to generalise to others – or children may learn to discriminate very subtly different clues as to what is appropriate for boys and what for girls.

LEARNING AND THE ACQUISITION OF GENDER ROLES

Men and women – and boys and girls – behave in different ways in all kinds of respects. Until recent times, most people would have assumed that this was mainly the result of 'nature' – boys and girls are simply born different – but there has been a growing awareness that many, and some would argue most, or even *all*, of these 'masculine', and 'feminine' characteristics are the result not of nature but of nurture. From a sociological point of view, one would say that gender roles are 'socially constructed': that is, created by the particular circumstances and dynamics of a particular society. From a psychological perspective (the main perspective of this book), one would say that they are *learnt* – and learning theory provides some ideas about the mechanisms through which this might come about.

For the remainder of this chapter we will give a brief tour of some of the research in this area.

Differences in attitudes to masculinity and femininity

Gender stereotypes can be very different in different societies. In ancient Greece, for example, there was once a crack army regiment consisting entirely of gay men. The Sacred Band of Thebes, as it was known, apparently played a crucial part in many battles. In our own time, gay men still tend to be stereotyped as 'unmanly', and homosexuality has only recently been permitted in the British and American armed forces, but in the ancient world, men whose sexual preference was for other men were sometimes seen as being *more* manly than men whose preference was for women (see Boswell, 1996: 62–4). And in Iranian culture, some of the familiar stereotypes of most Western cultures are reversed, with men being seen as more emotionally expressive than women (Epstein, 1997, cited in Bussey, 2011: 613).

Operant and classical conditioning and gender roles

Many researchers have suggested that behaviours such as aggression or dependency are differentially rewarded depending on whether they are produced by boys or girls. Baby boys have been found to be given more physical stimulation than girls, whereas girls are touched and talked to more (see Golombok and Fivush, 1994: 77–88).

Boy and girl children are also exposed to different learning environments. Different toys are given to them, and different things are drawn to their attention ('Look at that fire engine, John!' 'Look at that pretty dress, Jane!'). Also 'some behaviors are reinforced, punished or extinguished more often in one sex than the other' (Blakemore et al., 2009: 180), with children being rewarded for taking part in 'gender-appropriate' and discouraged from taking part in 'gender-inappropriate' ones. So, even if it were not the case that things like aggression and dependency per se are reinforced differentially, play *is* selectively reinforced that will develop different patterns of behaviour – a form of 'shaping'.

As we noted above, appropriate activities are even colour-coded in our culture to assist children to choose the 'right' activities, and to allow them to generalise their social learning about gender. To give an example from the personal experience of one of the authors: a 9-year-old boy is going through a Lego catalogue, pointing out the space models, cowboy models, aircraft models and so on. Coming to a page depicting models made with pink bricks, he instantly dismisses it as 'girlie stuff', turning to the next page without a second glance. (The 'pinkstinks' campaign recognises and challenges the power of this kind of colour-coding: (Pinkstinks, online)).

Interestingly, researchers have found that boys are more likely to be discouraged from 'girl-appropriate' activities than vice versa, and that fathers more than mothers do the job of discouraging them (Leaper and Friedman, 2007). Girls are not discouraged from 'boy' activities to the same extent, but are equally discouraged by both parents (Langlois and Downs, 1980). Other children also exert pressure to conform to accepted gender-roles, and again, boys are more likely than girls to be discouraged by their peers from activities which are seen as gender-inappropriate (Blakemore, 2003).

There are also more subtle messages which children receive from parents and teachers which help to build up their core beliefs about what they can and can't do, which are less obviously based on gender. Research shows that parents tend to underestimate their daughters' competence in sport and maths, while overestimating it for their sons (Bussey, 2011: 619).

Observational learning and gender roles

Bandura showed that children are sensitive to the characteristics of the model they use, and are more likely to copy those that seem 'like them'. It therefore seems likely that children will tend to model themselves on the same-sex parent. (The picture is complicated by the fact that, in a traditional family or in a single-mother family, or indeed a modern primary school, where women teachers heavily outnumber men, role models are of course much more to hand for girls than for boys.)

Children will notice the behaviour of a large number of models of both genders and work out which behaviour is more *typical* of their own sex. Perry and Bussey (1979) showed 8- and 9-year-old children a series of videos in which a number of men and women were shown choosing between pairs of gender-neutral items (for example: banana or apple). If all the members of one gender were seen to have made the same choice, then, if the children were presented with the same options, they would tend to make the same choice as the models of their own gender. In a different stage of the experiment, one of the adults consistently made a different choice to the rest of his or her gender, and in this case, the children would tend to discount this person as a role model. The implication of this seems to be that, even if a boy sees his father changing the baby's nappy, for example, or a girl sees her mother mending the car, they are much less likely to copy this behaviour if their wider experience suggests to them that this is not typical behaviour for the respective genders.

A number of experiments have also found that girls will imitate male role models more readily than boys will imitate female role models, so boys seem to be particularly resistant to imitating gender-atypical behaviour (Blakemore et al., 2009: 183). You will remember that Bandura (1977) found that children would be more likely to copy models they saw as prestigious or powerful. In a society where more power is still held by men, this preference for powerful role models would be consistent with the finding that boys are more reluctant to imitate women, than girls are to imitate men.

Other factors in gender differentiation

Learning theory, and particularly social learning theory suggests a number of *mechanisms* whereby children learn gender roles, but it does not have anything to say about how those different roles came to be considered the norm in the first place. This is a sociological and political question of the kind that we will come back to in Chapter 10, but which the reader is encouraged to explore more widely in the literature on feminism, patriarchy and gender politics.

We should also note that the fact that, while children's adoption of gender-specific behaviour can be very clearly shown to be shaped by training and reinforcement, as discussed above, this does not necessarily mean that biological factors do not also play some role. (To put this another way, the fact that 'nurture' clearly plays a major role, does not mean that 'nature' does not also have some part to play.) As Blakemore et al. (2009: 16) note, 'during prenatal development male and female children are exposed to a different hormonal environment over several months of their development.' Some children are exposed to 'atypical levels of prenatal hormones for their sex' such as girls with congenital adrenal hyperplasia (CHA), who are exposed to high levels of androgens, and there is some evidence that these girls have more of a preference for stereotypically 'boyish' toys than other girls (see Blakemore et al., 2009: 152–7: see also Berenbaum and Hines, 1992), and are more aggressive on average than other girls (Blakemore et al., 2009: 158). There are complicating factors that make the findings of these CHA studies difficult to interpret – for instance, hormone levels are not the only things which distinguish these girls from other girls: they are also born with abnormal genitalia, which are usually then surgically modified – however, Blakemore et al. (2009: 156) suggest that there is compelling evidence for innate differences. Among the evidence they cite is that, even among rhesus monkeys there appears to be a gender difference, with males preferring to play with stereotypically boyish toys, and females preferring stereotypically girlish toys: Janice Hassett and her colleagues looked at whether rhesus monkeys preferred to play with wheeled toys or plush toys and concluded that:

> As is the case with sex differences in children's toy preferences, only male monkeys
> showed a significant preference for one toy type over the other, preferring wheeled
> over plush toys. Unlike male monkeys and like girls, female monkeys did not show any
> reliable preference for either toy type. (2008: 362)

Given that rhesus monkeys are unlikely to be influenced by role models on television and so forth, the fact that their preferences reflect those of human children does suggest a 'nature' element in gender preferences, but of course none of these imply in any way that either boys or girls *should* have certain preferences, or that there is something wrong with them if they do not. They only suggest that, even without social pressures, some preferences might still be more common for one gender than for the other.

Another indication of just how complex this whole question is comes from the experience of transgender and non-binary people who are born to a certain biological sex, are socialised within the same society as others, and yet still feel themselves to belong to a different gender to the one that would normally be assigned to them on the basis of their body type, or, in the case of non-binary people, reject exclusive identification with either gender. There will be more on the transgender experience in the next chapter.

LEARNING THEORY AND HUMAN DEVELOPMENT

As already noted, gender roles are only one of many areas to which learning theory and social learning theory can be applied. Social learning theory could also be used, for example, to look at the ways in which different patterns of behaviour are learnt by people from different social classes or ethnic backgrounds, differences which, again, in the past have often been seen as innate rather than learnt.

Learning theory has its limitations: there are biological factors and cognitive factors in development which cannot usefully be explained merely in terms of learnt connections. It can also be misused (as Aldous Huxley's satire colourfully illustrates). But it can be useful as a way of understanding the influence of the external environment in shaping our behaviour. This kind of learning could be seen as one of the basic building blocks upon which the construction of social roles is based.

The following activity is an opportunity to consider the value of this point of view in a practical context.

Activity 5.5

Suppose you are a member of staff on a team that provides support to adults with learning disabilities living in supported group homes in the community, the aim of the team being to promote independence. One of the group home residents, Angie, arrives in your office having got in a muddle with her benefits, with the result that she currently has no money and is in a very distressed state.

You give her some sympathy, calm her down, make her a cup of tea and then go off and sort the whole thing out on the phone with the benefits office.

Angie is very grateful.

But what could be the drawbacks of this response from a behavioural point of view – and what might have been a better response?

Comments on Activity 5.5

While Angie saw your response as helpful and has no complaints whatsoever, you may not have really done her a good turn if your aim is to promote independence. What you have done is to reinforce the behaviour of bringing her problems to you to sort out (positive reinforcement being provided by the tea and sympathy, and negative reinforcement being provided by the anxiety of having no money, which has now been taken away). You might have done better, for example, to have talked Angie through what she needed to do, given her a phone and then given her the tea and the encouragement after she had sorted it out for herself. That way you would have been reinforcing her own problem-solving behaviour.

Incidentally, the learning is not all one-way in such situations. Just as you were reinforcing Angie's

'helpless' behaviour, she was no doubt reinforcing your helpful behaviour by being happy and grateful when you had sorted it out for her. This seems to us to be a common pattern in the work of the helping professions: dependency can be rewarding for both the professional and her client, so it keeps getting reinforced.

You might also have considered how both your behaviour and Angie's might be unconsciously influenced by the socially constructed stereotypes that you have each learned and internalised about disability and gender. You may both find it difficult to overcome the assumption that because Angie has a learning disability she won't be able to manage a difficult situation like this. And might you both also have some gender-related assumptions about confidence, independence and problem-solving?

CHAPTER SUMMARY

- In this chapter we considered the tradition in psychology known as connectionism, behaviourism or learning theory, which explores the ways in which we connect events and actions. We began by looking at the work of Pavlov and the basic concepts of 'classical conditioning'.
- We looked briefly at J.B. Watson (who coined the word 'behaviourism') and considered the idea of learnt connections based purely and simply on proximity.
- We looked at operant conditioning (conditioning that links behaviour with particular stimuli) and the work of B.F. Skinner in this area.
- We described the concept of 'learned helplessness' and looked at stress.
- We then looked at cognitive aspects of learning which cannot easily be explained in purely behavioural terms, and then at observational learning and at social learning theory.
- We discussed the application of learning theory to the question of how children acquire gender roles.

Up to now we have looked at general theories of human growth and development, most of which have focused mainly on childhood. In the next section, however, we will look not at a particular theory, but at a particularly crucial stage of life: adolescence, the time of transition from childhood to adulthood.

Tangled Webs

We have suggested in this chapter that learned connections between stimulus, response and reinforcement could be seen as the building blocks of many different kinds of patterns of behaviour that we develop over our lives. (We have suggested that they can be used to explain how children learn to behave in ways that adults deem gender appropriate as an example of that.) We have also just suggested (in Activity 5.5) that professionals and their clients influence each other's behaviour, often unintentionally, by reinforcing certain responses. You are likely, therefore, to be able to find examples in most or all of the Tangled Webs cases of behaviour that may have been learnt in these kinds of ways. The following were the two cases we suggested you might like to look at:

The Dudley/Harris family (Case G). In this family you can see how certain patterns of male and female behaviour may be learnt both through observational learning (by observing the parents and how they behave) and through direct reinforcement. In the case of Chloe, Hannah and Caitlin, their stepfather Lee's behaviour towards them makes it easier for them to retire to the kitchen with their mother to watch TV, as Lee wants them to do, than to stay in the family living room with him and Josh, who, like his father, is waited on by his mother and sisters and is learning that bullying behaviour is acceptable. Although the case study says nothing about how Lee would react if any of the three sisters tried to behave in a stereotypically boyish way, it's not difficult to imagine how such behaviour might be punished by scorn and ridicule.

The girls' disengagement at school could also be seen as a kind of learned helplessness. Given their history and family circumstances, they probably have not been rewarded very much in their lives

(Continued)

(Continued)

for thinking for themselves or taking the initiative, and the behaviour of keeping quiet and out of the way may well have been negatively reinforced, in that it had resulted in a reduced likelihood of unpleasant consequences occurring.

Derek Harrow (Case B: Rob Thomas and Derek Harrow). By contrast, Derek's background has taught him to behave in a way that's consistent with a particularly tough and aggressive version of masculinity. Again the case study doesn't say very much about the details of his upbringing, but it is not difficult to imagine the kinds of reinforcement and punishment that might have shaped him in this way, including scorn and disapproval if his behaviour was ever in any way girlish, and paternal attention and approval for behaviour that conformed to his father's idea of masculinity.

Derek has a habit of throwing his weight around. There may be many different reasons for this, but given the fact that he is larger and stronger than most of his peers, you can see how this behaviour might have resulted over the years in desired outcomes which have served to keep it going. These might include practical outcomes such as other boys backing down, deferring to him and letting him have his way, but also the powerful release that comes from the opportunity to act out a pent-up emotion.

 You can access Tangled Webs by visiting **https://study.sagepub.com/tangledwebs**

Further reading

On learning theory/behaviourism/behaviour analysis

Baum, W. (2005) *Understanding Behaviorism: Behavior, Culture and Evolution*. Oxford: Blackwell.
Pierce, W.D. and Cheney, C.D. (2004) *Behavior Analysis and Learning*. Mahwah, NJ: Lawrence Erlbaum Associates.
Powell, R., Symbaluk, D. and Macdonald, S. (2002) *Introduction to Learning and Behaviour*. Belmont, CA: Wadsworth.

On cognitive-behavioural therapy

Westbrook, D., Kennerley, H. and Kirk, J. (2011) *An Introduction to Cognitive Behaviour Therapy*, 2nd edn. London: Sage.

On gender role development

Blakemore, J., Berenbaum, S. and Liben, L. (2009) *Gender Development*. Hove: Psychology Press.
Bussey, K. (2011) 'Gender Identity Development', in S.J. Schwartz, K. Luyckx and V.L. Vignoles (eds), *Handbook of Identity Theory and Research*. London: Springer, pp. 603–28.

6

WHO AM I GOING TO BE?

ADOLESCENCE, IDENTITY AND CHANGE

TANGLED WEBS

This chapter deals with adolescence and with identity, something which comes to the fore as an issue in adolescence, though it is important throughout life. If you would like to look at some cases before reading further, we suggest you might choose **Deanna Whitworth (Case L: Deanna Whitworth and Zoe Scott)**. Deanna is an adult, but ask yourself what kind of adolescent experience she has had. Two adolescents you could look at are **Derek Harrow (Case B: Rob Thomas and Derek Harrow)** and **Zak Renton (Case K)**. Ask yourself what kind of adolescence they are having, and what challenges face them as they move towards adulthood.

 You can access Tangled Webs by visiting **https://study.sagepub.com/tangledwebs**

The previous two chapters have looked at acquiring an understanding of the world and learning behaviour. This chapter looks at how each individual builds up a sense of her own identity. This is something we have to do throughout our lives. To a greater or lesser extent we have to revise and rebuild our identity every time our circumstances change. Whether the change in question is becoming a parent, getting divorced, or winning a million pounds on the national lottery, you can no longer just go on being the same old you afterwards, no matter how much you might want to. But the question of identity is *particularly* central to adolescence, when we make what is arguably the biggest transition of all: the shift from being a child to being an adult. For this reason it seems appropriate to locate our discussion of identity in a chapter which also focuses particularly on the adolescent transition.

CULTURE AND BIOLOGY

The transition from childhood to adulthood is of course in part a biological process: a time of physical growth and change, a time when secondary sexual characteristics appear, the stage at which for the first time we become capable of having children of our own, and this biological change is key to the new identity we need to build. But the stage of life between childhood and adulthood which we call 'adolescence' is only partly defined by biology. It is also a psychological transition and it takes place, and is shaped by, its social context, meaning that it is seen differently in different societies, just as childhood and adulthood themselves are seen differently. And since society itself is constantly changing, the social context is different in each generation, and the experience of adolescence itself is different as a result.

Adolescence, as we now understand it, is the result of social changes that took place over the last two centuries. Segregation between adults and children became much more marked in societies after the so-called industrial revolution, when most of the population moved from the countryside to cities, universal schooling began and most parents either went out to work in a factory or office, or worked at home. In pre-industrial societies (that is to say, in Western Europe and America in the past, and the many countries around the world today where most people still work on the land), these conditions do not necessarily apply. Children do not necessarily go to school at all, or for very long, and both adults and children are involved in similar daily activities and routines, such as caring for domestic animals or harvesting crops. There is, of course, still a *biological* transition between childhood and adulthood, but the change in *role* (see Chapter 10) may be in many ways very much less pronounced. For children in such societies, 'What are you going to do when you grow up?' might seem an odd question, for you are going to carry on doing what you already do.

The significance of adolescence is therefore different in non-industrial cultures, and the period of transition may be briefer. Marriages will tend to take place much earlier, for instance, particularly for girls, and may be arranged by parents, rather than negotiated by young people themselves, and adolescence, in the sense of a lengthy transitional stage distinct both from childhood and adulthood, may not really exist. Thus, a teenager from the small Pacific nation of Samoa commented that she had never heard of adolescence until she left her own country and came to New Zealand:

Sometimes I think that we [in Samoa] are children for most of our lives. ... It does not matter how old you are, [for] if you are not considered worthy or responsible enough by your elders then you will not be treated as an adult. You really have to earn your place in the Samoan culture. So adolescence as a developmental stage is foreign to our culture. (Subject #3, Tupuola, 1993, cited by Kroger, 2004: 5–6)

Of course the major biological changes we associate with adolescence *are* common to all cultures – the onset of fertility, rapid growth and physical and biochemical change. But, not only between different societies, but even within a single society, each individual will experience these changes in a different way. The changes do not take place at the same time, or in the same order, for boys as for girls (the growth spurt usually starts earlier in girls). There are also substantial differences in the timing of these changes from one individual to another.

Early maturing boys feel more positive about themselves and about their bodies ... are likely to be more popular, and to do well in their schoolwork ...

[But] a number of writers have shown that girls who mature significantly earlier than their peers are less popular (among other girls), more likely to show signs of inner turbulence ... and to be less satisfied with their bodies. (Coleman, 2011: 34)

Here, we see the timing of biological changes interacting with an individual's social environment (an early maturing girl may be less popular with her peers), just as in the earlier quotation from a young Samoan we saw the interaction of biological changes and cultural context (growing up in Samoa is completely different to growing up in New Zealand). As in so many areas of human development, the experience of adolescence, for any given individual, is not simply biological, not simply a matter of individual psychology, and not simply a socially constructed phenomenon either, but a complex interaction between all of these elements.

In this chapter we will be looking primarily at adolescence as it occurs in societies which have industrialised (many of them now moving towards a post-industrial era, as industrial production moves to countries like China). But it is important to remember that, even in this context, young people go through this transition with many different cultural expectations, which themselves change over time. This key question of social context is something that is relevant to *all* the transitions we discuss in this book, including even birth and death. We focus on it in particular in Chapter 10.

TRANSITIONS

Later in this book we will look at many different life changes including the mid-life transition, becoming a parent, bereavement and growing old, but the transition from childhood to adulthood is certainly one of the biggest transitions we have to make.

Transition is defined by the *Concise Oxford Dictionary* as 'passage or change from one place or state or act or set of circumstances to another'. Any such change in human life involves a psychological readjustment, a coming to terms with an ending and a coming to terms with things being different. Even an event as trivial as a cancelled evening out involves an adjustment of this kind. We may be annoyed, disappointed, temporarily at a loss as to what to do with ourselves until we have accepted that the evening we had in mind is not going to happen and we begin to plan a new one. Major events, though, require substantial psychological work which may take months or years and may never be fully completed.

Various models have been proposed to describe this process of adjustment, often originating in the study of bereavement (see Chapter 12), since bereavement is one of the most difficult transitions that most people have to go through. The following summary of the stages involved in dealing with transitions is paraphrased from Sugarman (2001: 144–9), who herself draws on Hopson (1981). As with other stage models discussed in this book, the reader should not be deceived into thinking that people necessarily progress through stages in an orderly, linear fashion. As we discuss further in Chapter 12, in reality we move back and forth many times before reaching the end of the process, assuming that we ever quite reach the end at all.

1 **Immobilisation:** this is the initial response of being stunned, frozen, dazed. (Typical comments which we make in the aftermath of both positive and negative events are: 'I can't believe this is happening', 'It feels like a dream', 'It hasn't sunk in'.)
2 **Reaction:** (a) elation or despair: after a period of time, our initial stunned response gives way to a sharp mood swing (either up or down depending on the nature of the event). (b) minimisation: this initial post-shock reaction is typically followed by some kind of minimisation. 'For a positive transition', as Sugarman writes, 'the feelings of elation become dampened as more ambiguous or less desirable concomitants of the transition become apparent or are confronted ... Similarly, the importance or likely impact of a negative event may be played down' (2001: 146).
3 **Self-doubt – (and sometimes depression):** this phase is characterised by fluctuations in energy level, doubt as to our own ability to manage ('I was really pleased to get this new job', we might say, 'but now I'm wondering whether I'm really up to it') or perhaps self-blame ('If only I'd not let her go out that night, she'd still be here today'). It may involve considerable anger and depression.
4 **Accepting reality and letting go:** until now we have been hanging on to the old order of things as they existed prior to the new event. There has been an element of denial and we have been clinging on in defiance of the new circumstances. At some point, these old attachments have to be broken in order to allow us to move on. These may include ties of affection to other people, or to old habits, or old beliefs. We may feel grief and anger at this, but if we are not completely stuck, there will be a gradual recognition of the need to put the past behind us.
5 **Testing:** as we let go of the past, we become free to explore the new circumstances in which we find ourselves. We can try out new identities and start to form new attachments.
6 **Search for meaning:** 'putting the past behind us' does not mean denying that it ever happened. During this phase, we look back at the past from our new viewpoint, reappraise it and try to make sense of it.
7 **Integration:** the transition process is complete. 'We feel "at home" in the new, post-transition reality' (Sugarman, 2001: 148). New behaviours and new ideas about ourselves have become part of our sense of our own identity.

Successful negotiation of a transition puts a person in good shape to deal with other transitions in the future. But a transition which has not been successfully negotiated may make it difficult for people to cope successfully with adapting to new life changes. To give a well-known example, it is difficult to make a commitment to a new partner if one is still attached to and grieving for a previous partner: hence we speak about the need to 'get over' a previous relationship before embarking on a new one.

The following exercise invites you to consider and compare the way we adjust to different kinds of event:

━━━━━━━━ **Activity 6.1** ━━━━━━━━

1   You have been planning an exciting holiday with a partner or friend for some time and are much looking forward to it. Not long before the day of your departure, your friend applies for a new job which will mean that he/she can't come on the holiday and it will have to be cancelled. Suppose you have just received the phone call. What would your initial reaction be – and what stages would you then go through?
2   Out of the blue, your partner announces that she/he has found someone else and wishes to end your relationship. What would your initial reaction be and what stages would you then go through?
3   Looking back at your own teenage years and early adulthood, can you chart the stages you went through between the time you thought of yourself as a child and the time you thought of yourself as an adult?

Comments on Activity 6.1

1   We suspect that you will have found yourself going through stages of disappointment, anger at your friend, guilt for feeling angry and so on, but eventually reaching a point where you were able to give up on the old plan and either make some new plan, or rearrange the plan for a later date, so that instead of grieving over what did not happen you are once again looking forward to something that will happen in due course. You might even have found some advantages in having postponed your original plan.

2   Obviously, this would be different in every individual situation. We would guess, though, that there would typically be an initial reaction of disbelief, followed by distress and attempts to change the partner's mind, or to cling onto some elements of the old relationship, for example, by saying you wished to remain friends. This could be seen as an attempt on your part to minimise and normalise the situation. Self-doubt and anger with your partner would likely follow for a long period before you reach a stage of being able to let go of the attachment and perhaps begin to think about new ones.

3   People take many different paths through adolescence, but you will probably have noticed yourself experiencing grief at the loss of childhood (when Christmas presents stop being exciting, for example) and ambivalence and fear about becoming an adult, but then gradually coming to terms with the change.

Although two of these questions relate to major life changes and one relates to a comparatively temporary problem, we are suggesting that there will have been a somewhat similar pattern of response in each case.

Transitions and adolescence

The transition from childhood to adulthood is not a sudden event like, say, a bereavement or a lottery win, but it is nevertheless an event to which we have to adjust. We have to adjust to becoming a sexual being and forming new kinds of relationships, we take on new responsibilities and new freedoms, and we have to begin thinking about having to earn a living and choosing an occupation that will, to some extent, define us. As with other transitions, adolescence involves a letting go (of childhood and everything that goes with it); it involves forming new attachments (with an increasing emphasis on relationships with friends and sexual partners); and above all (as we will discuss shortly) it involves trying out new identities and building a new adult identity with which to embark on adult life.

But is adolescence really a single transition, a single event, or is it really a number of different ones? Graber and Brooks-Gunn (1996) suggest that we should look at adolescence as a transition containing a number of distinct 'turning points' and they suggest that dealing with these turning points is more difficult when, for instance:

- *Atypical timing* of turning points creates additional stress. For example, as discussed earlier, an unusually early or late onset of puberty, which puts a young person out of step with his or her peers, may be difficult and stressful.
- *Too many* turning points come together, so that there are too many things to deal with at once.
- *Context* is not supportive of change. As we'll discuss shortly, some family environments are not supportive. Nor are some school environments. To varying degrees, society in general may not be supportive. A young person who finds he is gay may find he has less support, for example. A disabled young person may find that society is resistant to allowing her an adult status (something we discuss in Chapter 8).

IDENTITY VERSUS ROLE CONFUSION

As we have already noted, all transitions involve renegotiating your identity, and none more than the adolescent transition, which you begin as a child and end as an adult. In Chapter 2, we discussed Erik Erikson's stage model (see p. 40ff) which divides the whole lifespan into eight 'psychosocial' stages, each of which is marked by a distinctive life 'crisis' or task, a reasonably successful resolution of which would provide the individual with qualities which would assist with other tasks ahead. And in this model he described the characteristic crisis of adolescence, the fifth stage, as *identity versus role confusion*. Erikson was writing in very different times. His book *Identity, Youth and Crisis* (Erikson, 1994) was first published in 1968 (during the adolescence of the authors of this book!). Nevertheless, his ideas about identity development in adolescence remain influential and have been the basis of much research in more recent times.

Erikson thought that during the adolescent stage, a combination of rapid growth, sexual maturity and a growing awareness of adult tasks ahead, leads (as all transitions must do) to a questioning of the 'sameness and continuities relied on earlier' (Erikson, 1980 [1959]: 94). Of course, children do have a sense of identity before adolescence but, as we move towards adulthood, we need a sense of ourself that will be able to deal with new demands and expectations that come with being an adult. Successful resolution of this stage will lead to a secure sense of 'ego identity', meaning that the individual has developed a defined personality within a social reality which she understands, and has a secure sense of herself as a consistent person. Of course, as is the case with all the crises that we face at various stages, there is no guarantee that we will successfully resolve this stage during adolescence itself. This depends in part on the 'inner capital' (Erikson, 1980 [1959]: 94) we have been able to accumulate as we negotiated previous crises, just as in future crises in adult life, we will draw on the inner capital we manage to accumulate as we negotiate the adolescent transition. 'The danger of this stage is *identity diffusion*' writes Erikson (1980 [1959]: 97, original emphasis). Losing the security of old continuities and samenesses when new ones are still not in place can be very frightening. We may adopt a whole range of different strategies to avoid facing the situation we find ourselves in, or to manage the anxieties which it provokes. 'To keep themselves together', for instance, adolescents often 'temporarily overidentify, to the point of apparent complete loss of identity, with the heroes of cliques and crowds' (Erikson, 1980 [1959]: 97).

Identity status

Looking further into the way that adolescents negotiate this difficult business of finding a new identity, James Marcia (1966), and Kroger and Marcia (2011) defined four different kinds of 'identity status' found among adolescents. These are:

1 **Identity diffusion** (see Erikson's use of this phrase above): an identity status characterised by the avoidance of commitment, indecision about major life issues, and escape into diversionary activities intended to avoid anxiety. The stereotypically 'difficult' teenager who lies in bed, watches TV and refuses to think about or discuss the future might be said to be in a state of identity diffusion. Gullotta et al. comment that in their dealings with others, identity-diffused young people tend to be tense and insecure. As they note, 'how hard would it be to present yourself to others if you have no idea who you are?' (2000: 83).

2 **Identity foreclosure**: a status characterised by the acceptance of others' values (those of parents, for example, or teachers), rather than self-determined goals. The teenager who does not seem to question or rebel against adult expectations at all might be said to be in a state of identity foreclosure. Such a young person might seem to adults to be less of a 'problem' than the identity-diffused teenager, but in fact is likewise failing to tackle the challenges of adolescence because she is relying on identification with others, and introjection of their values and priorities, rather than seeking her own identity. Gullotta et al. comment that 'foreclosed late adolescents have relatively constricted personalities' and are 'immature in their social behavior styles... frozen in their developmental progression, rigid in their overcompliance, and generally unadaptive' (2000: 84).

3 **Moratorium**: a status of intense identity crisis characterised by active attention to major decisions and exploration of possibilities for the future, but not yet resolved in firm commitments. So, like the identity-diffused young person, a young person at the moratorium stage is avoiding making a commitment, but is doing so constructively, because it is constructive to consider actively

all the options before making a serious decision. Moratorium is an *uncomfortable* position, which individuals may be tempted to avoid by opting for foreclosure.

4 **Identity achievement**: individuals with this status have resolved their crises and made firm commitments to ideals and plans, based on their own thinking and not simply on ideas imposed by or uncritically accepted from others. In Erikson's terms, they have successfully negotiated the challenge of this stage of life.

Two of these statuses – moratorium and diffusion – are characterised by lack of commitment to particular goals or values while two – foreclosure and achievement – are characterised by *commitment* to a particular set of goals and values. But, looking at it in another way, moratorium and identity achievement are both about active *exploration* of new adult identities, while diffusion and foreclosure are both about avoiding the anxiety involved in such exploration. So these four identities statuses can be seen as the four parts of a quadrant with two dimensions: the presence or absence of commitment, and the presence or absence of exploration.

These kinds of identity status are not *stages* in identity formation, in that young people do not necessarily move through them in linear order. In fact, as discussed above in relation to transitions (and elsewhere in the book in relation to stage models of various other kinds), stage models in general are usually a considerable simplification of the uneven and back-and-forth process which, in reality, characterises most major psychological transitions. But if you refer back to the 'transitions' stages discussed earlier in this chapter (p. 112), one could say that foreclosure and identity diffusion both relate to the early three stages. Moratorium might be said to correspond to what were referred to there as 'letting go', 'testing' and 'search for meaning', and identity achievement to 'integration'.

One of the features of Erikson's model is that at later times of transition, we may revisit unresolved issues from earlier stages. As we'll discuss in the next chapter, the mid-life transition is sometimes marked by revisiting issues that were prematurely foreclosed in adolescence or at the beginning of adult life. For example, permanent relationships or careers or parenthood entered into too early may, when revisited later, be seen as examples of foreclosure: commitments made, not for positive reasons, but in order to avoid the anxiety of leaving matters unresolved. And in the same way, adolescents will often revisit issues left unresolved from childhood.

Gullotta et al. (2000: 92–3) suggest that patterns of identity diffusion would tend to be characteristic of young people from rejecting, detached families. Identity foreclosure would tend to be a pattern with child-centred families in which there is strong pressure to conform to the values and beliefs of the parents. Moratorium is, they suggest, characteristic of active families which encourage autonomy, self-expression and individual differences. They associate identity achievement in adolescence with homes with 'high praise, minimal parental control and secure attachments'.

━━━━━━━━━━ **Activity 6.2** ━━━━━━━━━━

Drawing on your own adolescent experience (or that of other people you know), think about how the process of identity achievement unfolded. Can you identify examples of foreclosure, moratorium and diffusion?

Comments on Activity 6.2

Looking back, did you have some regrets about risks not taken? These might be areas of foreclosure, such as taking advice that led you to go straight from school to take the qualification route to a safe career, ignoring the voice in your head that urged you to travel the world or pursue your passion for making music. Or maybe you settled down with your first boy- or girlfriend, and the relationship didn't turn out well as you both matured and grew apart? On the other hand, you may be appalled by some of the risks you took in the course of finding your way in life. Perhaps too, you remember the discomfort of the moratorium stage, when you felt confused and uncertain of what you wanted or were capable of, and wanted independence one minute and security the next. Often it will only be with hindsight that the process of identity achievement can be seen at all clearly; the difference between identity diffusion and moratorium is largely whether one emerges from it or not; at the time they may feel very much the same.

Neurological development in adolescence

The rapid psychological changes that occur in adolescence have a neurological underpinning, as well as environmental, cultural and biochemical ones. Much has been discovered in recent years about the structure and functioning of the adolescent brain, and this area of research continues to develop rapidly.

It used to be thought that brain development was complete by the end of childhood, but it is now known that during adolescence the brain develops almost as rapidly as it does during the period of infancy which we discussed in Chapter 3. And along with this development, as in the early years of life, goes a process of synaptic pruning, as those neural pathways which are not reinforced by use disappear, while those which are regularly used become more efficient. Another process occurring in the brain during this period is an increase in myelination. Myelin is a substance which sheaths and protects the brain cells and neural pathways, making the brain function more efficiently but at the same time restricting its capacity for change (Music, 2011: 188).

The limbic system, the area of the brain that drives both emotion and the exploration of new behaviour, and therefore risk-taking, is also developing rapidly during adolescence, while the frontal lobes, which are associated with self-regulation and what is called 'executive function', do not catch up developmentally until early adulthood (Hare et al., 2008, cited in Music, 2011: 188). Understanding this helps to make sense of the impulsive and sometimes extreme behaviour which is typical of adolescence, and is part of the experimentation involved in the process of identity formation.

Hormonal changes also contribute to these behaviour patterns. Hormones are of course involved in the process of puberty, but are also part of the process of brain development. For example, dopamine, the feel-good hormone, is a powerful neurotransmitter, facilitating connections between neurons in the brain, and its production increases markedly during adolescence (Ernst and Spear, 2009, cited in Santrock, 2012: 88). Another hormone which becomes more active in adolescence is melatonin, which regulates sleep patterns, and research has now shown that there is a biochemical basis for the adolescent's difficulty in getting out of bed in the morning, while wanting to stay active late into the night (Carskadon and Acebo, 2002, cited in Coleman, 2011: 36).

All this rapid development makes the teenage brain particularly vulnerable, while also making risk-taking behaviour more likely. It has been shown that drugs and alcohol are more likely to do lasting damage to the brain in adolescence than in later life (Crews et al., 2007, cited in Music, 2011: 189).

Another part of the brain that develops rapidly in adolescence is the system which connects the left and right hemispheres of the brain. This means that complex information can be processed more readily and in a more sophisticated manner (Giedd, 2008, cited in Santrock, 2012: 88). This makes possible the higher level of cognitive functioning that characterises Piaget's formal operations stage, which we described in Chapter 4.

Moral development

One aspect of this capacity for more sophisticated cognitive functioning relates to moral judgements. Lawrence Kohlberg (1927–87) spent his academic career developing a theory of moral development which has been influential in the fields of philosophy, psychology and education. Piaget had already done some work in this area; Kohlberg built on this to identify three levels of moral development, each broken down into two stages, making six stages in all, which can be summarised as follows in Table 6.1:

Table 6.1　Kohlberg's moral stages (summarised from Kroger, 2004)

Pre-conventional morality (childhood)	1. Avoiding punishment
	2. Instrumental - self-interest within relationships
Conventional morality (early adolescence)	3. Mutual expectations within relationships
	4. Upholding society's rules
Post-conventional morality (late adolescence/adulthood)	5. Social contract - rules not absolute
	6. Personal system of moral principles

The progression is from a simply behaviouristic avoidance of unpleasant consequences like punishment and disapproval through a deepening understanding of the nature and obligations of one's relationships to others, both in the closer bonds of family and friendship and in the wider networks of society, ultimately moving beyond adherence to rules, laws and social conventions to develop a personal sense of morality, or conscience. Adolescence is a key period for the development of moral judgement, which requires the ability to move beyond black and white thinking and consider complex factors in relation to each other. As Kroger points out, Kohlberg saw this development of moral reasoning as an important part of identity formation (Kroger, 2004: 91). He also believed that education could play an important role in moving children and young people from a lower stage to a higher one (Kohlberg, 1980).

Kohlberg's research method involved posing hypothetical dilemmas such as the 'Heinz dilemma', in which Heinz is unable to afford an expensive drug for his sick wife. He is unable to persuade the manufacturer of the drug to sell it to him at a lower price, and so he steals it. The research subjects are invited to consider and evaluate the morality of Heinz's actions. His work following the same individuals over a period of time supported his hypothesis of a stage theory – people did not return to a lower level once they had reached a higher one, and further research has confirmed this (Kroger, 2004: 113). However, he also found that many people never reached the highest level, even in adulthood (Colby et al., 1983).

Research also confirms a link between Piaget's stage of formal operations and the more advanced stages of moral reasoning. But as Kroger points out, the 'cognitive level appears as a necessary but not sufficient condition for one's mode of moral reasoning' (Kroger, 2004: 113).

It is important to note that Kohlberg's research looked at judgement and reasoning rather than action, which is a very different thing, and that it is based on hypothetical rather than real-life situations. There is evidence that people react to real-life dilemmas with a lower level of moral reasoning than they use in considering hypothetical questions (Kroger, 2004: 109). Kohlberg's theory has been questioned in other ways too, for example in relation to gender and cultural specificity (see Kroger, 2004, Chapter 4 for a full discussion of this). However, his work remains important in highlighting the moral dimension of development and the role of education in supporting this.

Identity, ethnicity and culture

Establishing an identity in adolescence can present particular challenges for young people who are members of ethnic minorities. One reason for this is that they may be faced with competing – and very different – models of adult identity. A British Muslim teenager of Pakistani descent, for instance, has to define her own identity not only in relation to the norms of the majority (white, Western, secular) culture, but also to those of her family's culture, which may subscribe to radically different values in relation to religion, sex, the role of women, marriage, family, authority, and so on. For ethnic minority teenagers, trying to establish a separate identity from their own parents, while at the same time taking pride in their identity as a member of the tradition which their parents represent, requires the 'capacity to surf between two cultures and negotiate their identity in such a way that they maintain their links with their family and achieve full citizenship' (Sabatier, 2008: 186).

Not surprisingly, therefore, ethnicity has been found to be a more important identity issue for those from minority cultures than it is for those from the majority culture (Phinney and Alipuria, 1990). And the same study found self-esteem among young people from ethnic minorities in particular to be correlated with their interest in and commitment to their own ethnic identity. Phinney (1989, 1993) has also proposed a model of ethnic identity development, based on Marcia's categories discussed earlier, in which there is a move from 'unexamined ethnic identity' to 'ethnic identity search' to 'achieved ethnic identity' through the processes of exploration, resolution and affirmation.

We need to be aware that recent scholarship in this area is increasingly recognising the complexity of ethnic identity. Different social identities, such as gender and sexual identity, intersect and interact with ethnic identity, and 'it is important not to assume homogeneity in ethnic identity experiences within or among ethnic minority groups' (Umaña-Taylor, 2011: 803, 805).

RELATING TO OTHERS

Having talked about what is going on 'inside' young people during adolescence, we'll now consider what adolescence means in terms of relationships with other people. This is of course a two-way question. How do adolescents relate to others – and how does the behaviour of others affect adolescents?

Autonomy and the peer group

There are considerable cultural variations in the amount of autonomy that smaller children are given. There are also large cultural variations in the amount of autonomy that even an adult can expect. However, it must fairly generally be the case that one of the changes that normally occurs in adolescence is that young people are given, and expect, more autonomy. There are several kinds of autonomy though, which don't necessarily all go together. Steinberg and Silverberg (1986), looking at levels of autonomy among 12- to 16-year-olds, thought it would be more useful to break the idea of autonomy into several categories. These were:

- *emotional autonomy*, in which the individual relinquishes childhood dependence on her parents
- *resistance to peer pressure*, in which the individual becomes able to act upon her own ideas, rather than conform to those of peers
- *a subjective sense of self-reliance*, in which the individual feels free of excessive dependency on others, takes initiatives, and has a feeling of control over her life.

What these researchers found in their survey of young people was that as 'emotional autonomy' increases, 'resistance to peer group pressure' decreases. There seemed to be a kind of trade-off. Young people become more reliant on their peer group as they become less reliant on their family of origin.

Ryan and Lynch (1989), however, argue that what Steinberg and Silverberg's first category really measured was not emotional *autonomy*, but emotional *detachment*. Their view was that children who scored high on this measure are actually lacking in emotional support at home and so tend to compensate by relying heavily on their peer group. In their view, securely attached adolescents were actually better placed to achieve genuine autonomy than emotionally detached ones, who would tend to be easily led by their peers rather than genuinely determining their own course in life.

Gender differences

Stage models of development (at adolescence and other stages) have often been guilty of offering male development as the 'norm', and either ignoring female development or tagging it on as an afterthought. Freud's Oedipus complex is a case in point. And, as Carol Gilligan has pointed out, Erikson's well-known developmental chart ('Stages of a Man's Life', rather than 'Stages of a Person's Life') also seems to assume that the 'male' developmental route is the primary one.

In her influential book *In a Different Voice*, Gilligan (1982) suggested that girls construct identity in a different way to boys, characteristically linking identity to *intimacy* while boys are more prone to link identity to *role* and to ideas of *autonomy*. She contrasts 'a self defined through separation', which she suggests is characteristically male, with 'a self delineated through connection', which she sees as characteristically female (Gilligan, 1982: 35). She notes that, while Erikson does himself suggest that 'for women, identity has as much to do with intimacy as separation, this observation is not integrated into his developmental chart' (Gilligan, 1982: 98).

Drawing on the work of Nancy Chodorow (1978), Gilligan argues that 'given that the primary caretaker in the first three years of life is typically female, the interpersonal dynamics of gender identity formation are different for boys and girls' (1982: 7), because girls experience themselves as being alike to their main carers while boys experience themselves as being distinct.

> Since masculinity is defined through separation and femininity is defined through attachment, male gender identity is threatened by intimacy while female gender identity is threatened by individuation. Thus males tend to have difficulty with relationships, while females tend to have problems with individuation. (Gilligan, 1982: 8)

Gilligan was concerned with moral development (she was originally a colleague of Kohlberg's) and here she found significant gender differences, with women tending to give more weight to relationships and the responsibility of caring for others, while men gave more weight to abstract principles of justice and law.

We don't want to make sweeping generalisations about differences between male and female behaviour, but it is definitely worth thinking about Gilligan's suggestion that the characteristic female route to establishing an adult identity is different from the characteristic male one, built on very different foundations.

SEXUALITY AND GENDER

The biological foundation on which the social and psychological phenomenon of adolescence is built is the onset of sexual maturity. For both boys and girls, coming to terms with new sexual feelings and new social pressures about sex is, of course, integral to adolescence and a major driving force behind the changes that occur during this stage. 'Adolescents ... cannot simply add new sexual feeling to an old self' (Cobb, 1995: 129). These new feelings (and the new social expectations that go with them) are one of the main reasons that an adolescent needs to build a new self.

How this happens varies enormously between individuals, cultures and points in time. As Jeanne Brooks-Gunn and Roberta Paikoff observe, 'the study of sexuality is a perfect example of why person, time, context and period must be considered simultaneously' (1997: 190). Among other things, this means that the experience of one generation is only partly relevant to the experience of the next. The authors of the present book, for instance, both grew up in the 1960s and 1970s, a period when sexual norms were very different to those that apply today. Contrary to stereotypes about the permissive '60s, sexually explicit material is much more widely available in 'Western' countries in the twenty-first century than it was then (with graphic depictions of sexual acts now readily available on the internet) and there is generally (though not universally) more acceptance among the parental generation of sexual activity by teenagers. It is not surprising that findings by researchers suggest that young people are becoming sexually active at a younger age than they were in the 1960s or 1970s (Coleman, 2011: 134–6).

But in spite of what appears to be a much higher degree of frankness about sex and sexuality than existed in previous generations, or exists now in more traditional cultures, sexuality remains a difficult area. Young people receive mixed messages from the world around them – on the one hand, there are injunctions to abstain from sexual activity outside of committed relationships, while on the other hand, there is the pressure to prove themselves and acquire status through sexual experience – with boys continuing to receive different messages to girls. And perhaps it is not just a question of mixed messages but of a certain ambivalence about intimacy which is part of the condition of being human. 'The struggle between intimacy and autonomy', observe Brooks-Gunn and Paikoff, 'is played out on the sexual stage as well as in relationships with parents, ... peers, and siblings' (1997: 209).

Societies differ but in any society adolescents have to come to terms with physical changes, respond to new desires and manage new expectations, in a wider context that also includes managing sexual risks, negotiating intimacy and autonomy, maintaining the esteem of their peer group and taking account of the expectations and sanctions of the adult world. How they meet these challenges is in turn influenced by a range of factors. A number of studies look, for instance, at the factors linked to the age at which young people become sexually active. Laflin et al. (2008) found that higher academic achievement and (perhaps not surprisingly) importance attached to religious belief were both factors associated with sexual abstinence in boys and girls in a US sample. L'Engle et al. (2006) found that adolescents exposed to more sexual content in the media are more likely to be sexually active. Crockett et al. (1996) found that the most significant factor influencing the timing of the start of sexual activity was parental circumstances. Being the children of separated parents and having a mother who was a teenage parent were also factors which, for both boys and girls, were associated with becoming sexually active earlier. Whitaker and Miller (2000) found that teenagers who talked to their parents about sex were likely to initiate sexual activity later than teenagers who did not, with peer influence being stronger on the latter group, as would be predicted from the finding of Ryan and Lynch discussed earlier that lack of parental support resulted in increased reliance on the peer group (1989).

But, while a lot of research studies look at questions like the timing of first sexual intercourse, the experience for young people is of course a good deal more complicated than can be captured simply by statistics relating to specific events.

Sexual identity

Becoming a sexual being is part of the whole process of identity formation. Like other aspects of identity formation, it depends not just on an individual developmental process but on the family, social and cultural context in which this takes place, as we have described above. Attitudes to sexual activity depend on the meaning that young people attach to sex, and how sex fits in with their wider picture of themselves and the world.

Young people do not simply begin to engage in sex as a result of being 'slaves to their hormones' though of course biology is part of it. (Hormones are important but their effects are mediated by social context: see Moore and Rosenthal, 2006: 74 ff). There are a whole range of reasons why young people choose to engage in sex, or abstain from it. Brooks-Gunn and Paikoff (1997: 200), for instance, cite African-American sources suggesting that some girls consent to sex as a price to pay for the protection conferred by boys against other boys. And sexual activity may be important too as a marker of growing up or for the status it confers within a young person's peer group. Janet Sayers cites the recollections of a woman in her forties recalling her experience of her first kiss:

> All we talked about [when we were 13] was had you been kissed, and had you had
> your periods. All the girls were desperate to be kissed. I don't think it mattered if it was a
> gorilla that kissed them. It was more a thing to tell my friends – that I'd had my first kiss –
> rather than the kiss itself. (Sayers, 1998: 88)

It will not come as a surprise to many readers that researchers find differences in the attitudes of boys and girls, with boys tending to see sex as a means of demonstrating their status and maturity, while girls tend to see it more as an expression of love and intimacy (Moore and Rosenthal, 2006: 133–6), though these differences can be overstated, and are probably not as marked as they were in the past.

Other factors apart from gender play a part here. The same authors also report less marked differences between boys and girls among 'a middle-class Anglo-Australian sample' as compared to the differences between boys and girls among homeless teenagers (Moore and Rosenthal, 2006: 135). Most (though not all) boys and girls in the middle-class group identified 'love, caring and affection' as the primary motivation. Among the homeless group, though, while girls also identified 'love, caring and affection' as their primary reason for engaging in sex, 'many of the homeless boys responded to the harshness of their lives with an unequivocal rejection of romantic values' (2006: 135).

To what extent gender differences are due to biological difference, and to what extent they are due to different 'sexual scripts' inculcated by social conditioning, is difficult to unravel (see the discussion on gender differences in Chapter 5), but research does confirm that the 'double standard' does still exist in terms of messages given to boys and girls about the acceptability of sexual behaviour. Discussing a review of 30 different American studies on this topic carried out since 1980, Mary Crawford and Danielle Popp conclude that, while some groups 'still endorse the absolute double standard that prohibits sexual intercourse outside marriage for women, more generally the orthodox double standard has made way for new kinds of double standards that are subtler but perhaps equally effective as a means of social control' (2003: 22–3). For example, girls continue to be labelled as 'sluts' by their peers if considered to be too sexually active, but there is no equivalent word for promiscuous boys.

Different 'sexual scripts' may even alter something as basic as what people mean by 'having sex'. Diamond and Savin-Williams (2009) discuss the differing definitions revealed in a number of in-depth studies of adolescent sexual behaviour. Girls tended to take a narrower view than boys, and were less likely to count anything other than full intercourse as 'having sex', which is consistent with the kind of double standards already discussed (2009: 482). Young people in the US who had pledged not to have sex outside marriage for religious reasons also took this narrow view, in some cases retracting the disclosures of sexual activity which they had made a year earlier (Rosenbaum, 2006, cited in Diamond and Savin-Williams, 2009: 483).

The extent to which people define their desires in relation to their social learning and their expectations of themselves also becomes apparent when we unpack the concept of sexual identity. *Sexual identity, sexual orientation* and *sexual practices* are different things, which may or may not be congruent with each other. Our *sexual identity* is how we define ourselves (for example homosexual, bisexual, heterosexual), *sexual orientation* describes our sexual preferences and desires, and *sexual practices* describe our actual behaviour. (Coleman, 2011: 147). Figures from a longitudinal study of US youth show that significantly more young people admitted to having experienced same-sex attraction than would define themselves as gay or lesbian (Savin-Williams and Ream, 2007, cited in Savin-Williams, 2011: 681–2). This anomaly can be explained by the fact that although Western societies have moved a long way in the last half-century towards a greater acceptance of different sexualities, assumptions about sexuality are still overwhelmingly *heteronormative.*

Even now gay and lesbian young people will pick up the message from many different sources that being gay is not an acceptable identity, that it is not compatible with being a 'real' man or a 'real' woman – and so on. In the UK, for example, young people would have to cope with the widespread use of the word 'gay' as a term of abuse among their peers. And this is even more the case with acceptance of transgender identity.

Recent research and writing about adolescent sexuality has moved towards a more inclusive view, in which sexual diversity is normalised rather than defined as a problem. An example of this is Dillon's model of sexual identity formation, which can be applied equally to people of all sexualities (Dillon et al., 2011: 658). His model moves from what he terms compulsory heterosexuality (the heteronormative assumption) through exploration and experimentation to commitment. He links it with Marcia's model of identity formation, where the developmental task is to steer between the extremes of diffusion and foreclosure to reach a personally congruent identity which can be owned and lived. It is also important to note, as Savin-Williams does, that sexual identity is not just an issue for adolescence which is then settled for life (Savin-Williams, 2011: 681). It can, and often does, change in the course of adulthood.

Gender identity

Even more fundamental than which gender you are sexually attracted to, perhaps, is the question of which gender, if either, you feel you belong to. Children may from an early age feel that they do not belong to the gender that their parents and the world have assigned them to, but this is a question which will often come to a head with the increased autonomy of adolescence and the physical changes of puberty. Increasing numbers of young people are identifying as transgender; an indication of this is the almost trebling of referrals to the NHS Gender Identity Disorder Service in the UK between 2015 and 2017 (Gender Identity Development Service, online). These difficulties with gender identity, however, do not inevitably lead to individuals becoming transsexual, that is, embarking on medical treatment leading to gender reassignment. Carmichael and Davidson (2009: 916) found that 80 per cent of children presenting with atypical gender identity find a solution other than gender transition (cited in Wiseman and Davidson, 2012: 534). Many are able to find their own unique position as transgender or 'trans' individuals. For instance, 'Alex, now 17, increasingly refuses to be defined as male or female, but prefers more simply to be referred to as Alex' (Wiseman and Davidson, 2012: 535).

Bernadette Wren, describing working with transgender adolescents in the context of 'queer theory' based on the work of Judith Butler (1990), writes that 'The postmodern way is to see gender not as monolithic and linear, but as a creative compromise in endless negotiation with the self, other and culture (2014: 275). This creativity is captured by Jack Halberstam in the use of the term 'Trans*' as the title of their book about the history and cultural and political context of gender variability. The asterisk is used as in the wildcard of internet searches, indicating endless possibilities. However, there is a tension between this notion of gender fluidity and the need of adolescents for some fixed points in their sense of identity when so much in their bodies and lives is changing. The challenge for parents, families and professionals involved with transgender adolescents is to support them in managing and finding their way through this uncertainty towards an adult gender identity without premature foreclosure.

PROBLEMS IN ADOLESCENCE

In the UK media and public debate, adolescents, teenagers or youths are frequently depicted as *problems*. There is – and has been for many years – a great deal of adult concern about youth crime, anti-social behaviour, teenage pregnancy, drug and alcohol use and so on. But the stormy and rebellious stereotype of adolescence can be overstated. For many people adolescence is not an exceptionally stormy period. In some cases, in fact, it could be argued that adolescence is *not stormy enough*, since a lack of any challenging behaviour during adolescence might sometimes indicate that a young person had opted for 'foreclosure', rather than risking the state of 'moratorium' required to build a genuine adult identity.

Not everything the adult world sees as problematic is a problem for the young person concerned. Adolescent psychologists today tend to approach the problems of adolescence by looking at the factors that contribute to risk and resilience and take a view that focuses on strengths rather than problems. This positive youth development model has become particularly influential in the USA (Lerner et al., 2009). However, it is true that a number of problems come to the fore in adolescence, or peak at that time, and we will consider some of these.

The incidence of depression, for instance, is relatively high during adolescence (Seroczynski et al., 2003). This may in part be linked to hormonal changes, but it is also a product of the multiple challenges involved in this period of life: as we noted earlier, depression is a common feature of transitions of all kinds. Drug and alcohol use also become widespread, although patterns vary considerably from country to country, and also over time. A longitudinal study of American high school pupils shows a peak of substance use from the mid-1970s to the early 1980s, then a decline, followed by another rise in the early 1990s, since when it has levelled off. Patterns also varied considerably for different drugs (Chassin et al., 2009: 725). A survey of the health behaviour of adolescents across Europe and the US carried out for the World Health Organisation in 2009–10 (Currie et al., 2012) found that in England 22 per cent of girls and 31 per cent or boys drink at least once a week at the age of 15, and 43 per cent of girls and 38 per cent of boys of this age report having been drunk on at least two occasions (155–7). Twenty-four per cent of 15-year-old girls and 22 per cent of boys had used cannabis, and 9 per cent of both boys and girls had done so in the last 30 days (166–7). Some countries in Europe had higher rates than this, and others lower. Boys mostly reported higher rates of drinking and drunkenness, but the gender gap narrowed between 1998 and 2006 (161).

Eating disorders usually appear in adolescence or soon afterwards. 'Anorexia nervosa ... occurs primarily in pubertal girls, and bulimia nervosa generally appears in slightly older teenage girls or women in their early twenties' (Polivy et al., 2003: 523). Suicidal behaviour – very rare in childhood – also sees an abrupt rise in adolescence (Windle et al., 2000: 261), though the incidence of such behaviours varies considerably according to the particular social context. (In the USA, for example, suicide rates are more than twice as high for Native Americans aged 15–24 as for the rest of the population [Seroczynski et al., 2003: 558].) At present, in both the USA and the UK, attempted suicide and deliberate self-harm are much more common in girls than boys, but completed suicide is more common in boys (Coleman, 2011: 122; Seroczynski et al., 2003: 557). Adolescence is also a peak time for criminal behaviour, with the peak age for offending in England and Wales being 18 for boys and 15 for girls (Coleman, 2011: 116), with the majority of those who become offenders in adolescence being 'adolescent-limited offenders' whose offending is largely confined to their adolescent years (Agnew, 2009: 75). There are different ways of looking at the emergence of deviant behaviour in adolescence and researchers have identified and explored both socio-economic factors and familial ones. Barber (1992) suggests that a developing individual needs both psychological autonomy and behavioural boundaries. Young people whose parents have difficulties with allowing them psychological autonomy will tend to be more likely to withdraw and have internalised problems. Young people whose parents have difficulties with setting behavioural boundaries will tend to have external problems, which would include delinquency.

Deviance and identity

But it is possible to argue also that deviant behaviour, particularly when it occurs in economically deprived areas, may be driven by quite similar needs to socially acceptable behaviour such as choosing a profession and acquiring the necessary qualifications. As Coleman observes 'being without a job makes it more difficult for young men to find appropriate adult roles, as well as encouraging aggressive behaviour as a mark of status and power in the community' (2011: 202).

So, in a way, offending behaviour by adolescent boys in such a context could be seen as an attempt to acquire the status of a man. (And indeed many of the adolescent behaviours which worry adults – smoking, drinking, having sex – are activities that are considered perfectly acceptable for adults but not for children.)

In the same way, some adolescent girls perhaps choose to become pregnant at a very early stage for similar reasons. Being a parent is, after all, a recognised adult role, an adult *identity*, and for some it must seem like the only adult identity that is attainable. Coleman (2011: 151–2) notes that teenage pregnancy is highest in urban areas, and among the most socio-economically disadvantaged groups. There is a higher incidence among girls brought up in care than in the general population. The following is the explanation given by a 16-year-old for her decision to become a parent:

> … when I got to around 14, I was in a children's home and all I felt was that no one
> loved me, no one ever loved me, no one ever would love me, and that's when I decided I
> wanted me own family, and so that's what I done. (A 16-year-old participant in a study by
> Dennison and Coleman, 1998, cited in Coleman, 2011: 151)

ADOLESCENCE AND ATTACHMENT

Adolescence is not something that occurs to individuals in a vacuum, and we have already discussed the wider social context within which it occurs (and without which we would have no distinct concept of adolescence at all). It is also important to consider the much more immediate context, the context of family and relationships with adults.

Factors that make for a successful adolescent transition to a confident adult identity seem to include:

- Parental involvement and connectedness with young people. 'Diffused' young people have been found to score lower on the scale for emotional attachment to parents than other young people and lower on independence (Perosa et al., 1996; Willemsen and Waterman, 1991). Seeking autonomy is not about ending close relationships with parents and family, but actually takes place most effectively within the context of close relationships with both parents.
- Parental acceptance of conflict and of their children's own emotions. 'Absence of conflict has characterised the family environment of foreclosed family relationships' writes Kroger (2000: 108, citing Perosa et al., 1996; Willemsen and Waterman, 1991) while Bronstein et al. (1993) conclude that where parents accept and support non-hostile expression of emotions by their children, this is linked with their greater ability to cope with the transition from childhood into adolescence.
- Parents' ability to set firm boundaries, without being controlling or unresponsive. As Kroger (2000: 52) puts it, referring to work by Baumrind (1991): 'An authoritative (in which warmth and nurturance are coupled with firm control) rather than an authoritarian or permissive parental style of child rearing has been associated with greater self-reliance, social responsibility and achievement motivation in later childhood and adolescence.'

Maccoby and Martin (1983) classified parenting types on two dimensions ('demandingness' and 'responsiveness') resulting in the four categories shown in Table 6.2.

Research seems to show (Coleman, 2011: 90–91) that on measures such as self-esteem and avoiding risk behaviour such as drug use, adolescents brought up in 'authoritative' families score the highest. Adolescents brought up in 'indulgent' households are on average less mature, more irresponsible and more conforming to their peers. Adolescents brought up in 'indifferent' households are more impulsive and more likely to get involved in high-risk behaviour.

Table 6.2   Parenting types (after Maccoby and Martin, 1983)

		Demandingness	
		High	Low
Responsiveness	High	Authoritative	Indulgent
	Low	Authoritarian	Indifferent

Another way of putting all this would seem to be that the adolescent transition takes place best within the context of a *secure attachment* and that young people with an insecure attachment to their parents or carers will find it harder to establish a secure adult identity. Bowlby's *secure base*, you may remember, was something that the securely attached child was supposed to be able to internalise and carry forward as a source of confidence and security in adult life.

What we would also predict from attachment theory is that those adults who themselves experienced insecure, and particularly disorganised, attachments to *their* carers as children, will find it harder to provide this kind of security to others, perhaps particularly during the challenging and testing time of the adolescent transition. Parents who were themselves insecurely attached, for example, may find it difficult to reconcile being firm with being caring and supportive, and may attempt one at the expense of the other, or lurch unpredictably between the two. They may need help with striking this balance.

COPING SKILLS AND RESILIENCE

In recent years, there has been an increased interest in the nature of the resilience that enables some individuals to cope more successfully than others with difficult life events. Resilience is not simply a character trait that some people have and others do not, and it is important to look at resilience as it interacts with the stress factors that are present to a greater or lesser extent in all young people's lives: a young person who seems superficially not to be very resilient, may in fact just be dealing with more serious or more numerous stress factors than another young person who appears to be coping better. Stress factors can be at an individual, family or community level, and they often occur together; for example, poverty is likely to be accompanied by poor physical and mental health for the individual and/or other family members, insecure housing, poor nutrition, limited educational opportunities and so on. The more stress factors a young person is exposed to, the greater the likelihood of a poor outcome (Appleyard et al., 2005, cited by Coleman, 2011: 212). Some stress factors are to do with the normal transitions and changes of adolescence, while others may come from specific events, such as illness, bereavement or moving to another school, town or country. And some, like poverty, are chronic, while others, like a serious accident, are acute. All in all, risk and the way it interacts with resilience in adolescence presents a complex picture which requires a 'multilevel approach' (Compas and Reeslund, 2009: 562).

Since working to promote resilience seems an interesting alternative to responding to problems after the event, a number of researchers have explored the question of what qualities and/or coping strategies enable some adolescents to deal more successfully with stresses than others. Two broad groups of ways have been identified, in which people respond to stressful events:

- emotion-focused - aimed at managing the uncomfortable feelings that the stressor evokes (there are several possible sub-categories of this: for example, approaches based on rumination as against approaches based on distraction)
- problem-focused - aimed at tackling the stressor itself (Lazarus and Folkman, 1984, Lazarus, 1993, cited in Frydenberg, 2008: 39).

It would seem that emotion-focused coping strategies become more common with age, while problem-focused strategies are not closely related to age (see Compas, 1995). In fact, which is the best approach to take will depend in part on the situation. In situations which it is possible to control, a problem-focused strategy is appropriate, but in situations which it is not possible to control, an emotion-focused strategy is more appropriate and in fact a problem-focused approach is likely to be counter-productive, since it will not work and will therefore add to feelings of failure and inadequacy. Beardslee and Podorefsky (1988), for example, in a study of teenagers with depressed parents, found that those teenagers who recognised that they could not cure the depression itself coped better.

Successful coping in this and other studies seemed to be linked therefore not only to emotional factors, but also to cognitive factors (the ability to think through a situation, see it from different points of view, and arrive at a realistic appraisal of the extent to which it can be controlled). Coping skills can also be taught and Compas (1995) reports several pieces of research evidence which show, for example, that the teaching of basic coping skills in school does have positive outcomes.

Erica Frydenberg (2008: 23–4) suggests that there is an additional third group of coping strategies which could be described as 'dysfunctional coping'. This would include things like turning to drugs and alcohol. In Frydenberg's (Australian) study, these seem to become more prevalent at the age of about 15. Frydenberg also notes an increased tendency towards self-blame in the older adolescent group, and the importance of friendship networks in enabling young people to cope effectively with stress, suggesting that young people with specific social skills deficits will generally be more vulnerable to stressful events. Teaching social skills then becomes another strategy for promoting resilience.

The coping strategies used by boys and girls tend to be different, in line with the gender differences we have already noted in relation to intimacy and autonomy. Girls are more likely to turn to family and friends for support and assistance, while boys are more likely to adopt a problem-focused approach rather than talking to others about how they feel (Coleman, 2011: 219).

Like risk factors, factors contributing to resilience can be considered at individual, family and community levels (Garmezy and Rutter, 1983, cited in Coleman, 2011: 215). Evidence from a number of longitudinal studies highlights the importance of the presence of a consistent and reliable adult (not necessarily the parent); 'the role played by one adult who cared about the individual, and who was available at significant turning points, appears to be absolutely central to the development of resilience in the face of adversity' (Coleman, 2011: 216).

Of course resilience is necessary to cope with challenges all through life, right up to the end, and all life transitions are challenging. But, as we have already argued, adolescence is an especially challenging transition in a society where becoming an adult involves making choices between many different possible futures. It is perhaps even more challenging, at a time of rapid social change, when all choices carry risks and uncertainties and where options that were available in previous generations (home ownership, a job for life) are either no longer available, or much harder to attain. We suggest, therefore, that it is important to recognise that some of the problems associated with adolescence are a reflection of the magnitude of the challenge.

The following activity invites you to apply some of the ideas we have been discussing to one of the kinds of situation where adults and adolescents often find it difficult to understand each other.

Activity 6.3

Ben is an able boy. Up to the age of 15 he performed well at school, particularly in maths and science, and expressed a keen interest in a career in medicine, which was a source of considerable pride to his parents. They themselves both left school at 16 and now run a small convenience store, and they have cherished the hope that their son, who is their only child, would become a doctor ever since his talent for science became evident in primary school.

But from the age of 15, Ben's motivation began to slip. He turned in poor homework, or, increasingly, simply failed to complete homework at all. He began to miss classes, and sometimes whole days of school, and, when in school, he was often disruptive, talking and joking in class and distracting other pupils.

When teachers attempt to challenge him about this change in his level of motivation, he shrugs, and is monosyllabic, reluctant to engage in any kind of dialogue. He is just the same at home, refusing to discuss the situation with his parents. When pressed he simply walks out, staying out very late with friends with whom he smokes cannabis, drinks, plays video games and watches TV. His performance in exams has plummeted. Medical school, and indeed university at all, will cease to be an option unless he does something about this. But when this is pointed out to him, and he's asked what his plans are, he refuses to answer.

'It's as if,' his mother says, 'he thinks he can just spend the rest of his life smoking weed and watching TV with his mates.' His father, with some bitterness, adds, 'I notice he doesn't mind helping himself to food out of the fridge whenever he wants it, though. I wonder how he thinks it gets there?' Both parents work long hours, opening the shop at 6 a.m. and closing at 10 p.m., and they feel that Ben is throwing away opportunities that they would dearly love to have had.

What can be said about Ben's current identity status? How might his parents and other adults be most helpful to him?

Comments on Activity 6.3

Ben would seem to be exhibiting the obvious signs of identity diffusion, in that he is simply showing no willingness to work on or think about the problem of what he is going to do in the future. Since of course he will at some time have to earn his own living, one could argue that he is simply in denial, 'hiding his head in the sand'. And of course this is not uncommon among teenagers, enjoying the autonomy that comes with the approach of adulthood, but dreading the responsibilities that adulthood also brings.

However, things may be a little more complicated than that. It would appear that the expectation that he become a doctor has been placed upon Ben from an early age by his parents. It may be that medicine doesn't appeal to him. Or perhaps, whether it appeals to him or not, the fact remains that if he simply pursued that career, he would always feel as though it was something that he'd accepted, rather than something he had chosen. In other words, what

seems to his parents and teachers like Ben recklessly abandoning a clear and promising career path may in fact for Ben be the only way he knows of avoiding identity foreclosure.

This is not to say that his diffused state is a viable long-term option, but it may be a way of putting on the brakes, until such time as he is ready to move into a state of moratorium and start exploring options for himself. He might feel more supported if he could be reassured by his parents that more than one option would be fine with them. It will also be helpful for him if his parents, while expressing their concern and providing clear boundaries, can find ways to convey to him that he is loved and valued for who he is now and not just for what he might become. If there are other significant adults in his life besides his parents and teachers, maybe people who can be role models for a variety of different paths into adulthood, this will be helpful too.

CHAPTER SUMMARY

- In this chapter we began by looking at the relationship between biology and culture (a version of the nature–nurture question) with particular reference to puberty, which is both a biological change and a culturally determined one.
- We then looked at another topic with particular relevance to adolescence – the psychology of the characteristic stages which human beings go through when responding to new circumstances of whatever kind.
- There is a general consensus that achieving an adult *identity* is the major challenge for young people going through adolescence and we looked at the various stages and factors in the development of a sense of identity. We considered the question of ethnic and cultural identity.
- We looked at recent research findings about the development of the adolescent brain, and at cognitive and moral development in adolescence.
- We looked at the changing nature of adolescents' relationships with others, including their parents and with their peer group. We looked at the concept of autonomy and how it relates to identity.

- We looked at gender differences in relation to identity and at suggestions that the relationship between autonomy, identity and intimacy is different for girls and boys.
- We considered how boys and girls adjust to themselves as sexual beings and, in some cases, confront the fact that they do not identify with the gender to which they have hitherto been assigned.
- We considered the increase in crime and self-destructive behaviour that occurs in adolescence and how this relates to the discussion about identity.
- We looked at different parenting styles and how the behaviour of adults and the quality of adult attachments impact on the adolescent transition.
- We looked at another topic which is highly relevant to adolescents but is important at every stage of life: the quality of *resilience*.

Many of these themes will be carried on into the next chapter where we look at early and middle adulthood and the changes and transitions that occur within the long period from the end of adolescence to the beginning of old age.

─ Tangled Webs ─

There are several adolescents among the Tangled Webs case studies. You can also consider the adults and ask yourself what kind of adolescence they had or might have had, or look at the younger children and consider what kind of adolescence may be in store for them. The three examples we gave at the beginning of this chapter include two adolescents and one adult.

Deanna Whitworth (Case L: Deanna Whitworth and Zoe Scott). Deanna is an adult but she describes an adolescence in which her father left the family home when she was eleven, and her mother had serious health problems and was a heavy drinker. As she describes it, she had to take on responsibility herself for running the family home and being a carer for her mother. This is a kind of foreclosure, in that Deanna in many ways would have had to set aside the experimentation and exploration that is normal in adolescence in order to take on an adult role which she hadn't chosen for herself. It's worth considering what impact this experience is likely to have had on her attitudes and choices in adult life.

Derek Harrow (Case B: Rob Thomas and Derek Harrow). Derek is big and throws his weight around, he is involved in serious crime, and he uses drugs: he is the kind of adolescent that people think about when people talk about out-of-control youth and anti-social behaviour. In fact, though, he has an unusually difficult adolescent transition to negotiate. Many young people get involved in crime or deviant behaviour of one sort or another during their teenage years, causing worry to their parents, and then grow out of it, but in Derek's case, the family pressure is to be involved in crime, and he shows (at least according to Rob) some signs of regretting this and wanting to do something different. So unusually, foreclosure for him might mean simply joining the family business (which is a mixture of criminal and legitimate activities) under his father's leadership, while (and again, this is according to Rob, who of course has his own agenda), identity achievement might involve breaking away from that, and working with animals, possibly at a high price in terms of family acceptance. Added to this are the challenges that face young people from ethnic minorities (in his case Romany), as they try and negotiate their own identity while retaining what they value about their own ethnic community. While he might appear to be a typically identity diffused young person, there appear to be elements of moratorium in his position too, and it is this, perhaps, that makes Rob feel that the system should be there to help him.

Zak Renton (Case K). Zak would appear to be a classic example of an identity diffused young man in that his life is focused on getting through the day with as little anxiety as possible (the kind of behaviour that Erica Frydenberg described as 'dysfunctional coping' [p. 129]), and there is almost no sign at all of him committing himself in any way to the task of building some sort of adult future for himself. There are many reasons why he might find this difficult, one of which is surely that his mother Lily herself finds the adult world very difficult. She has a serious mental health problem and perhaps she herself has only partially negotiated the transition into adult life, even though she is now in her thirties?

  You can access Tangled Webs by visiting **https://study.sagepub.com/tangledwebs**

━━━━━━━━━━ **Further reading** ━━━━━━━━━━

Coleman, J. (2011) *The Nature of Adolescence*, 4th edn. Hove: Routledge.

An account of the whole range of issues relating to adolescence, put in a social context.

Frydenberg, E. (2008) *Adolescent Coping: Advances in Theory, Research and Practice*. Hove: Routledge.

Kroger, J. (2004) *Identity in Adolescence: The Balance between Self and Other*, 3rd edn. London: Routledge.

Moore, S. and Rosenthal, D. (2006) *Sexuality in Adolescence: Current Trends*, 2nd edn. Hove: Routledge.

ACTING LIKE A GROWN-UP

CHALLENGES OF ADULTHOOD

TANGLED WEBS

The very broad subject of this chapter is adulthood up to the onset of old age. Any of the case studies would be relevant reading here. In each case, the sorts of question you might ask yourself are 'What does adulthood mean to this person?' 'How is this person coping with challenges of adulthood, such as parenting, work, and maintaining adult relationships?' Some adults you could look at are: **Rob Thomas** and **Tracey Green (See Case B: Rob Thomas and Derek Harrow; Case J: Tracey Green), Lee Harris** and **Lisa Dudley (see Case G: The Dudley/Harris family)** and **Maryam Begum's family (Case E)**.

 You can access Tangled Webs by visiting **https://study.sagepub.com/tangledwebs**

What do we mean by 'adult' and what is different about being an adult from being a child? The most basic aspect of adulthood is that you have finished growing, you won't get any taller, your body has completed its development, you are, in fact, 'grown-up'. But the idea of being adult or grown-up also carries a sense that you have completed another kind of growth, meaning that, unlike a child, you should be allowed and/or expected to make choices which previously would either have been closed to you completely, or made for you by others. Thus, for instance, in Britain, a person under the age of 16 cannot give legal consent to sex and is required to attend school, but after that point, you can consent to sex, and you can choose whether or not to attend school, while at 18 you are allowed to buy alcohol and vote. The exact ages at which the law allows people to make various decisions varies from one jurisdiction to another – in many American states it is illegal to buy alcohol until the age of 21, for instance, and in Scotland 16-year-olds were allowed to vote in the 2014 independence referendum – but the general principle holds that, as you become a grown-up, you are both permitted and expected to make more choices by yourself. You have, in short, become responsible for yourself. But of course, once you become an adult, you remain so for the rest of your life, a much longer period than the whole of childhood, and one might question whether it makes sense in psychosocial terms to see adults at very different ages as necessarily having a great deal in common with one another. Does a young woman of 20, for instance, have more in common with an 80-year-old than she does with a girl of 15?

One way round this is to divide adulthood up into several distinct developmental stages, as we've done in previous chapters with childhood (for instance: Piaget's stages discussed in Chapter 4 and Freud's in Chapter 2). But this too presents problems because there are so many different routes through adult life. Some people become parents in their teens, for instance, others don't become parents until their forties or don't become parents at all, meaning that, while parenthood is one of the most important and transformative events in adult life, it can't be neatly assigned to a particular stage or age. In this chapter we will look at early and middle adulthood as distinct stages – the periods, roughly speaking, from 20 to 40, and from 40 to the onset of 'old age'– but we should make clear that this is a very rough and ready distinction: these two stages cannot be clearly separated in a straight-forward way.

A third stage of adult life – old age – will be given a separate chapter of its own (Chapter 11). This is because it has a number of characteristics that make it rather distinct. We should emphasise though (not least because the authors are approaching old age themselves!) that old people are also adults.

BEING GROWN-UP

When we say 'let's sort this out like adults' or tell someone to 'grow up and stop acting like a child', what do we actually mean? What is the essential quality that marks out adulthood and prompts us to label some adults as childish, or adolescent, when they fail to conform to it? Before going any further, you may like to consider your own views on these questions.

━━━━━━━ Activity 7.1 ━━━━━━━

With apologies to any younger readers, we are assuming that you are at some stage in your adult life. Looking back on your own experience, or at the experience of others:

At what point in your life did you start to think of yourself as an adult? Why? What had changed from how you were before?

If we divide adult life up into young adulthood, middle adulthood (middle-age) and late adulthood (old age), which group do you belong to? Is it easy to decide? How do you view adults in the other two groups? What is different about them and what do you have in common with them that you do not have in common with adolescents or children?

Comments on Activity 7.1

Many adults would say that they don't actually feel like an adult to themselves. (We probably all have times when we wish the real grown-ups would come along and solve our problems for us.)

Nevertheless, there is a time in life when we stop thinking of ourselves as a boy or a girl and start thinking of ourselves as a man or a woman. This may or may not coincide with the time that the rest of the world starts to see us in that way. As to the quality that distinguishes adult life from childhood or adolescence, we can't guess what you decided about this, but in discussions with groups of adult students, the word that tends to come up is 'responsibility'.

Having reached adulthood, a person must take responsibility for themselves and for others around them. As we pointed out earlier, this is reflected in laws which allow adults to make choices and take on responsibilities which are restricted or forbidden for younger people. It is also reflected in the disapproving use of the words 'childish', 'immature' or 'adolescent' to refer to adults seen as acting irresponsibly. This is not to say that children and young people cannot themselves act very responsibly: in Britain alone, the 2011 census showed that almost 178,000 under-18s were acting as carers for family members with disabilities or health problems (Carers UK, 2014). It is also the case that, for some people, even when they are adults in the legal sense, it may be a struggle to get society to let them take responsibility for their own lives (for adults with disabilities, and sometimes for older people, as we'll discuss further in Chapters 8 and 11). There is also a growing trend for young people to remain economically dependent on their parents for some years after they have become adult, in part because, in most circumstances, the benefits and student finance systems in the UK regard young people under the age of 25 as at least to some extent the financial responsibility of their parents.

But we can probably agree that young carers are in danger of 'losing out on childhood' if they are expected to take on too much responsibility, and we can probably also agree that in most circumstances it is inappropriate to treat older people or disabled adults like children who cannot make choices for themselves.

DEVELOPMENT, CONTINUITY AND CHANGE

As we have noted, the period of 'adulthood' covers by far the largest part of our lives, but these years have historically attracted much less attention from those who study and theorise about human development than have the years of childhood. Kevin Durkin explained this apparent lack of interest in adulthood by observing that many developmental psychologists have taken the view that the process of development is completed with the achievement of adulthood (Durkin, 1995: 597). We are already grown up, in other words, so there is nothing more to say about our psychological development. However, readers of this book, who are most likely to be young or middle adults, will probably agree that reality is rather more complex than this.

Some perspectives on adult life do emphasise the stability and continuity of the personality as developed through childhood and adolescence, but there are also stage models that focus on continuing change and development. The course of adult life is a complex interplay between the biological, the psychological and the social, between who we are, the kind of world we find ourselves living in, the choices we make, and what happens to us. We need to be able to look at adulthood in a number of dimensions at the same time – and we need to take into account that, as adults ourselves, we are participant observers and our point of view will alter according to where we stand. (Each time the authors revise this chapter for a new edition, we notice that our own perspective has changed. For instance there was a lot of emphasis on the mid-life crisis in the first edition – Chris was in his early forties at the time – but this seems rather less central now that both authors are in their sixties and we are thinking rather more about the concept of 'old age'.)

The branch of psychology that looks at development across the whole of life, and not just childhood, is known as 'lifespan psychology'. This is not a unified theory, but a broad perspective encompassing a number of academic disciplines, including sociology, history, anthropology and biology. Baltes (1987) identified the seven main principles of the lifespan perspective:

- development is a lifelong process
- development is multidimensional and multidirectional
- the process shows plasticity - that is, it can be affected and changed by life experience and circumstances
- it involves both gains and losses
- it is an interactive process between the individual and their environment
- it is culturally and historically embedded
- it is a multidisciplinary field of study.

It is interesting that Baltes developed his thinking about lifespan psychology from a starting point of studying the problems of ageing – as Kierkegaard observed, life can only be understood backwards, but it must be lived forwards (Kierkegaard, 2001 [1843]: 18).

(There are some links between this perspective and the more sociological *life course* approach, which we will also consider in Chapter 10. This has developed in recent years in response to a world where social structures and cultural norms are constantly changing, as a way of understanding how this shifting landscape affects human development at an individual level throughout the life course.)

Continuity

Though important processes of change and development can be traced in adult life, it is also possible to see aspects of continuity across the lifespan. McCrae and Costa's work on personality in adulthood is based on a number of American longitudinal studies, where the same group of people are studied over a long period of time (like Baltes, their starting point is gerontology: the study of old age). They used a five-factor theory of personality based on basic traits – neuroticism, extraversion, openness, agreeableness and conscientiousness – and found that, after the age of 30 people's personalities remained relatively unchanged (McCrae and Costa, 2003: vii).

The different attachment styles which we discussed in Chapter 3 are an aspect of our personalities which seem to be carried over into adult life, and have a profound influence on our choice of partner, our intimate relationships, and also on other important areas of life such as our interactions with our workplace and our community. The work of Mary Main and others has demonstrated the persistence of these patterns of attachment, and she has developed the Adult Attachment Interview, which is used as a diagnostic tool in psychological work with adults, including couple therapy (Main and Goldwyn, 1994). In the interview, adults are asked to describe their childhood experiences and relationships, and the manner in which they do this is used to assess their attachment style. Main's four categories of adult attachment – secure, dismissing, preoccupied and unresolved – correspond to the secure, avoidant, ambivalent and disorganised attachment behaviours which can be observed in babies and young children. Security is measured by the degree to which the adult interviewed is able to engage with the interviewer to tell a coherent story about their childhood, with an integrated balance of positive and negative feeling. *Dismissing* adults will have difficulty in recollecting childhood experiences and feelings, while *preoccupied* adults' narratives will be full of unprocessed negative emotion. *Unresolved* states of mind in adulthood are the legacy of the dysfunctional parenting that leads to disorganised attachment in childhood, and for unresolved adults feelings and fears from the past are constantly intruding into the present, making it difficult for them to manage relationships, particularly with partners and children; 'early loss, abuse, neglect and trauma, if unresolved, retain the power to seriously disturb thought and feeling across the lifecourse' (Howe, 2011: 183).

Attachment behaviour in adults is seen, of course, in their choice of partner; the couple relationship is the natural successor to the attachment to caregivers in infancy and childhood and the hope is that it will become a secure base for adult life. But it is different from early attachment relationships because it is interdependent, with each partner both providing and seeking a secure base. When things go well, partners will move flexibly between the dependent and depended-on positions. Securely attached adults, who are comfortable looking back at their childhood selves from an adult perspective as described above, are more likely to be able to do this.

The process of choosing a partner – the chemistry of 'falling in love' – ultimately defies analysis, whatever theories are advanced. However, it is clear that early attachments are influential – as we noted in Chapter 2, we will often choose a partner who has something in common with one of our parents. Other unconscious processes at work involve mirroring, splitting, projection and identification, which we discussed in Chapter 2. Clulow and Mattinson suggest that in forming relationships we are working to a script which goes:

> I love someone who reflects part of myself, sometimes a hidden or unacknowledged part of myself; I feel good with a you who either shares my feelings, expresses them for me or helps me defend myself against them. (Clulow and Mattinson, 1989: 52)

While attachment styles may tend to be lifelong, adults can continue to change and develop through their closest relationships, those with partners and with children. We have already seen how crucial the parent–child relationship is to the child's development, but the extent to which adults are changed by the experience of parenthood is often overlooked.

Narrative

One perspective on the life course is to see it as a narrative, a story with a beginning, a middle and an end. We have been influenced by that approach in this book in deciding to begin it with the story of the birth of a baby. The viewpoint here is that of the individual whose life is under discussion – what sense do they make of their story? Is it a comedy, a tragedy or a romance? Among others, Dan McAdams has developed a narrative theory which sees a person's life story as 'a personal myth that an individual begins working on in late adolescence and young adulthood in order to provide his or her life with unity or purpose and in order to articulate a meaningful niche in the psychosocial world' (McAdams, 1997: 5). According to McAdams, different elements of the narrative emerge at different developmental stages, with the narrative tone, images and themes being laid down in childhood, the belief systems and characters developed in adolescence and young adulthood, and the narrative denouement in middle adulthood, with later adulthood given over to review and evaluation.

As we have seen in the discussion of adult attachment above, the ability to construct and communicate a narrative of one's early life is an indication of secure attachment, which in turn leads to a greater resilience in coping with life's difficulties. In a more recent book Dan McAdams argues that those individuals who are most productive and dynamic (he uses Erikson's term 'generativity', which we will discuss later) are those who can tell a positive story of their lives:

> Narrative research shows that especially productive and caring American adults often identify an early advantage in their lives that (they believe) established for them a secure and coherent inner self. (McAdams, 2005: 139)

In a review of developments in personality psychology, McAdams (2010: 536) concludes that 'personality develops as a dynamic constellation of dispositional traits (the person as actor), characteristic goals and motives (the person as agent) and integrative life stories (the person as author)'.

Many of the ideas we discuss in this chapter and in the rest of this book are based on specific research studies, of a particular group of people in a particular geographical and cultural location at a particular point in history, and it is important to bear that in mind when deciding how useful these theories are in shedding light on our experience here and now. We will be looking in more detail at the importance of the wider social context to an understanding of human growth and development in Chapter 10. In the rest of the present chapter we will take a broadly chrono-logical approach, because this is the most accessible way of thinking about it – but it is not the whole story.

STAGES AND TRANSITIONS

The best known stage theory of adulthood is Erik Erikson's. We have already discussed his stages of childhood and adolescent development in Chapters 2 and 6, and we gave an overview of his model of development through the human lifespan in Chapter 2 (pp. 40–42). Many other stage theories have been advanced, and Leonie Sugarman's book on lifespan development gives a com-prehensive overview of these (2001: 68). Some models describe a process of growth and devel-opment followed by a process of decline in later life for, as Peter Coleman and Ann O'Hanlon observe, 'a simplistic perspective of the lifespan as "rise and fall" is deeply embedded within Western Culture' (Coleman and O'Hanlon, 2017: 9). However, not everyone who writes about adult development takes this view. Coleman and O'Hanlon note, for instance, that, for Carl Jung, 'midlife was a crucial turning point when the individual was provided with new opportunities for development' and for what he called 'individuation' (2017: 12). Erik Erikson also takes a more positive view of adult development, and proposes that continuous growth is possible across the lifespan, concluding, if all goes well, with wisdom and integration in old age. (These contrasting narratives of pessimism and optimism will be of particular importance when we come to look at old age in Chapter 11).

Daniel Levinson (1978), in a book which popularised the concept of the 'mid-life crisis', offered a model of a man's life which typically unfolded through a series of stable (structure-building) stages and transitional (structure-changing) phases. (See also Levinson and Levinson, 1996, which looked at women's lives in a similar way.) Others have also focused on transitions, for instance Lowenthal et al. (1975) whose work was based on interviews with men and women at the point of leaving school, marriage, children leaving home and retirement. We have already looked at the transition cycle proposed by Hopson (1981) in Chapter 6 (p. 112) and we will return to the subject of transitions when we discuss family systems in Chapter 9.

Transition is concerned with change, which always involves loss. This is most obvious in sad life events such as bereavement or divorce, but elements of loss are also present in happy events such as marriage (or forming a live-in relationship) and graduation, as familiar roles and contexts give place to new ones. Events, predictable and unexpected, positive and negative, play a significant role in determining the course of adult life and can also have an impact on stress levels and affect physical and mental health, particularly when several significant life events occur within a short space of time. Holmes and Rahe (1967) compiled a ranking of the life events most likely to cause stress. The top ten most stressful events include, as you might expect, close family bereavement, divorce or separation, imprisonment, personal injury or illness, redundancy and retirement, but also include the positive changes of marriage and marital reconciliation. Other positive events such as pregnancy and the birth of a child also rank highly, as does change in financial status or employment, irrespective of whether it is for the better or for the worse. When this ranking was re-examined in 1995 it had not changed significantly, except that the overall levels of stress experienced had risen, and marriage had moved down the list, presumably because it does not now usually involve the same degree of lifestyle change as in the past (Sugarman, 2001: 143), since marriage tends nowadays to be a choice made by couples who are already living together, rather than, as would often be the case in the 1960s, by couples who would be moving in together for the first time.

Although transitions are important, and it is helpful to pay attention to them as we consider development in adult life, we must be wary of seeing stage theories as a neat progression from one stage to the next. Erikson himself made no such claims for his model and objected to writers who tried to make an *achievement scale* out of his stages, or made the assumption that at each stage 'a goodness is achieved which is impervious to new inner conflicts or to changing conditions' (Erikson, 1995 [1951]: 247 [footnote]). We would suggest that what is most useful about stage theories is the insight that new developmental tasks become progressively more difficult if other developmental tasks have not yet been completed. This basic idea is common to all theoretical models in the psychodynamic tradition. In attachment theory, for example, establishing a secure base is seen as the necessary precursor to confident exploration of the world.

It is also helpful to think of change as proceeding according to a 'social clock' as well as a biological clock, as suggested by Neugarten et al. (1965). This describes the effect of social and cultural norms and expectations about the 'right' time to make life decisions and transitions such as getting a job, settling with a partner or having children. And of course these expectations will differ across different cultures and social groups and in different historical periods. An example of this is the increase in recent years in the average age at which women have children. In 2016, the average age for first-time mothers in England and Wales was 30.4, having been increasing steadily since 1975 (ONS, 2017a). This trend is mirrored in most Western countries. Reflecting on the factors which might be influencing this change will suggest that changes in employment patterns, gender roles and economic pressures are all playing a part.

YOUNG ADULTHOOD

There are a number of features of early adulthood which, if not universal, apply fairly widely to this age-range in modern industrialised societies:

- It is the peak time for human physical performance in most areas. Muscle tone and physical strength, for example, peak at around the ages of 25-30.
- Most people leave their parental home during this period and set up home separately.
- Most people marry or set up a couple relationship during this period.
- Careers tend to be established in this period.
- Many people have children during this period.
- Daniel Levinson (1978) also proposed (writing specifically about young men) that at this time of life, we characteristically form and live out a 'Dream', or vision of what our life is going to be about.

Most of these things are of course culture-specific, as we'll discuss further in Chapter 10. In traditional, pre-industrial cultures, the idea of a career may be unknown in the Western sense and marriage and leaving the parental home may take place in a very different way. There have also been changes in Western culture in recent years, with a trend towards a longer period of education and dependence on parents, and more fluidity of relationships and later childbearing. This pattern led Jeffrey Arnett (2004) to suggest that the years between adolescence and the end of the twenties should be seen as a separate developmental stage, characterised by freedom, exploration and instability, which he terms *emerging adulthood*.

You will remember from Chapter 4 that Piaget's four stages of cognitive development concluded with the 'formal operations' stage, which he described as being attained in adolescence. In adulthood, there is no qualitative change in thinking comparable to the changes which occur in childhood, but there will be further cognitive changes through learning from experience as adulthood progresses, and there are often specific tasks to perform, at work or at home, so that cognitive development may become more specialised and focused on particular areas. More recently discoveries about the brain's capacity to change and develop throughout life in response to experience (as described, for example, by Norman Doidge, 2007), have given neuroscientific confirmation to the understanding of cognitive development as extending beyond childhood and adolescence. We also saw in the last chapter that Kohlberg saw moral development as extending into adulthood.

Intimacy and identity

Erik Erikson saw the challenge of early adulthood as being the establishment of intimate relationships with other adults, following on from (and building on) the earlier adolescent struggle to establish one's own identity:

> The strength acquired at any stage is tested by the necessity to transcend it in such a way that the individual can take chances in the next stage with what was most vulnerably precious in the previous one. Thus the young adult, emerging from the search for and the insistence on identity, is eager and willing to fuse his identity with that of others ... even though [this] may call for significant sacrifices and compromises. (Erikson, 1995 [1951]: 237)

His suggestion was that only when we are secure and confident in our own identity can we take the risks involved in genuine social and sexual intimacy of a lasting kind. He went on to say that 'the avoidance of such experiences because of a fear of ego loss may lead to a deep sense of isolation and consequent self-absorption'. Some empirical support for his view that identity achievement is an important prerequisite for successful adult relationships is provided by an extremely long-term study by Kahn et al. (1985), who looked at the progress of a group of male and female college students over an 18-year period from late adolescence to their late thirties. The researchers found that those who seemed to have established a strong sense of their own identity during college also had the more enduring marital relationships 18 years on. Men who seemed to lack a well-developed sense of identity in late adolescence were more likely to remain single into mid-life. But women who had likewise had difficulty in establishing a secure identity in late adolescence had usually gone on to marry, but then typically had had problems in maintaining stable marital relationships.

As this study illustrates, it clearly is not the case that everyone enters adulthood having successfully resolved the issues of adolescence and, as Kroger (2000: 151) comments, 'a number of existing longitudinal studies of adolescent identity development have produced samples with fewer than half of subjects attaining the status of identity achievement by young adulthood'. So the task of identity formation may well continue into adult life, like other tasks associated with earlier stages of development.

Most people would probably agree with Erikson that establishing intimate adult relationships is an important theme in early adulthood. Erikson added that some partnerships amounted to 'an isolation à deux, protecting both parties from the necessity to face the next critical development – that of generativity' (1995 [1951]: 239). This is one way in which identity development can be foreclosed, as we discussed in relation to adolescence in Chapter 6. And couple relationships often run into difficulties when one partner wants to continue with the development of their identity and the other does not. This may lead to conflict over whether and when to start a family, but it can also lead to problems when one partner develops a different and broader outlook on the world, perhaps through travel, a new job or a university course.

Difficulties in young adulthood

A limitation of models such as the ones we have been discussing is that they are essentially descriptive. For those who are working with young adults and who are looking for practical tools to help them in their thinking, this may be frustrating. In rather the same way, a car mechanic seeking guidance on how a particular type of engine works and what is likely to go wrong with it, might not find it very helpful to be given purely descriptive information about how a sample of cars behaved over their working life. Of course there is not and never will be a human equivalent of a car service manual, and this book is not in any case about intervention, but there are many people who are having difficulties with the demands made upon them as young adults, and who are struggling with intimacy along with unresolved challenges from previous stages. Their difficulties may become apparent through, for instance, offending behaviour, drug or alcohol misuse, relationship and parenting problems or mental health problems. These issues may bring them into contact with professional services of one kind or another. So it may be helpful to consider the following scenario and see whether any of the ideas we have discussed so far are of any assistance.

═══════════ **Activity 7.2** ═══════════

Karl

Suppose you are a community psychiatric nurse working in a drug and alcohol service, and that one of your patients is a man named Karl, aged 24. Karl left school at 16. He has never had a job that lasted longer than a few weeks. He has a long string of criminal offences (burglary, shoplifting).

He is a heroin addict and is believed to have been a heroin user since the age of 17. He has two children by two different partners. Both partners have said that he has been violent towards them. A child protection agency has established that Karl recently left his youngest child (Sarah – aged 6 months) on her own when he went out to obtain drugs. He is attending youth services at the insistence of the child protection agency, who have made it clear that they will take steps to prevent Sarah remaining in Karl's care if he does not address his drug habit. Sarah's mother, Leanne, who is 17, is also a drug user. She is often depressed, and has little self-esteem. In spite of Karl's violence towards her, she cannot imagine leaving him as she looks to him for security.

If you look at Karl specifically as a young adult, within the cultural expectations of young adulthood that now exist, does this illuminate his problem in any way? (In other words, what is there about being a young adult in particular that may contribute to his problem?)

And what about Leanne? In what ways are her problems similar to Karl's and in what ways are they different? Supposing you yourself were 24 years old, what difference might this make to how you work with Karl? And how about if you were 54?

Comments on Activity 7.2

Clearly drug use, criminal activity and so on are not unique to early adulthood. But it may have struck you that the expectations which are placed on young adults may be a pressure for some which could lead to drug use, offending and so on. Whatever the limitations of models such as that of Levinson, most people would agree that tasks like establishing a 'Dream', forming love relationships and taking up an occupation are indeed typically associated with early adulthood – and that not being able to manage them would be seen by many as a kind of failure.

Karl will be aware of these expectations, but in attempting to meet them (to establish intimate relationships, to become a parent, to enter the world of work) he may in effect be trying to run before he can walk. The sense of failure that results may well be a contributory factor in his drug use and violence, even though the end result of such behaviour is to set him back even further. And his partner Leanne is suffering from a similar sense of failure, but we can see how the gender difference leads them to adopt different coping strategies which bring them into conflict with each other. Leanne is trying to deal with it by clinging to intimacy at all costs rather than

struggling for the kind of autonomy that Karl is trying to achieve through his violent and criminal activities.

The reason why these adult demands are so hard for him to meet may well be that he has entered adult life without the necessary resources that would come from the successful resolution of challenges earlier in life. He almost certainly did not achieve a secure identity in his adolescent years. He may very well never have acquired the capacity to trust that comes from having one's needs mirrored in infancy. Perhaps any work with him will need to start by helping him to feel less ashamed of having to learn to walk before he can run.

Additionally, we need to be aware of the social dimension which is sometimes missing from purely psychological models. Karl's problems may well be rooted in his personal history, but they may also be exacerbated by his social environment. For example, he may come from a community where there are few educational or employment opportunities. If Karl was black, racism could have put additional obstacles in the way of his entering the world of employment.

(Continued)

(Continued)

Finally, on the question of your own age and how this might affect your work with Karl, it may have struck you that if you were the same age as Karl, he might find this very threatening, since you have managed to achieve a position of responsibility and authority which has eluded him. This is something you might need to bear in mind. He might well find it less threatening if you were 54 (old enough to be his parent), though other difficulties might arise if he has difficulty relating to his own parents, or if part of his problem is that his own parents have not let him grow up (see Chapter 9 for further discussion of this).

MIDDLE ADULTHOOD

The age of 40 is often seen as a marker of mid-life, a pivotal point. Levinson (1978) found in his sample of men that 80 per cent had been through a period of some personal turbulence about the 40 mark, and this popularised the notion of the mid-life crisis (though other researchers, e.g. Farrell and Rosenberg (1981) have found less extreme patterns of conflict). However, the idea had been around for a lot longer. Carl Jung had a serious mid-life crisis which led to a mental breakdown. This personal experience led him to develop the concept of individuation, which he saw as the developmental task of the second half of life, opening up the possibility of a new kind of creativity after the focus on relationship and reproduction in the earlier years of adulthood. Individuation can be described as 'a kind of Pilgrim's Progress without a creed, aiming not at heaven, but at integration and wholeness' (Storr, 1973: 89). In 1965, Elliott Jaques wrote a paper entitled 'Death and the mid-life crisis', which explored the effect of reaching mid-life on creativity by examining the careers of artists and writers, as well as drawing on material from his psychoanalytic experience (Jaques, 1965). He concluded that the challenge of this particular transition is to be able to accept the knowledge of one's own death, and to find a creative way of living with this knowledge.

This puts the mid-life transition in stark terms. So when we say jocularly that 'life begins at 40', we may either be denying the reality that we are already half way through life, or else recognising the possibility of a different kind of new beginning – or quite possibly a bit of both! It seems a natural point at which to review commitments made in earlier life and consequently also a time when men and women sometimes decide to end some old commitments, and strike out in new directions. (Levinson found, for example, that this was a common time for divorces and house moves.)

This is a phase of life which necessitates – as do the changes in adolescence – a reappraisal of one's identity. And the mid-life crisis may not only parallel adolescence in some ways, but may also include elements of adolescent behaviour. (If you have seen the film *American Beauty* you will remember, for example, how the hero got himself sacked by insulting his boss, bought himself a showy and expensive car, and developed a crush on one of his teenage daughter's school friends, while his wife threw herself into a torrid affair with a work colleague.)

Among the issues commonly encountered at this stage of life are the following:

- *Some physical decline* – this is not sudden, of course, but from this time onwards we are likely to become more aware of things such as greying hair, skin wrinkles and so on, as well as a gradual reduction in physical performance. Athletes, for example, will be past their physical peak. Clearly, exercise and a good diet can slow this down, but the very need to be aware of such things may for many people be a change. We are also likely to become more aware of peers who have suffered serious health problems.
- *A decline in fertility for women* – during their forties, women's fertility reduces. What happens at a biological level is that the ovaries start to miss out on hormonal signals from the pituitary gland to release eggs. The pituitary then produces more hormones to compensate. (This is an example, incidentally, of a biological 'feedback loop' – a concept we will return to in Chapter 9.) So hormonal balances change until, at around 50 or 55, the ovaries stop functioning and a woman reaches the menopause: the end of the reproductive phase of her life. Research tends to show (see for example Whitbourne, 1996) that the menopause is a transition whose impact has been somewhat exaggerated in popular mythology, but nevertheless it is an important and fundamental change to be adjusted to.
- *Adolescent children and the 'empty nest'* – parents in middle adulthood and onwards will have the experience of their children growing up and leaving home, though this can fall at very different times for different people. Parenting an adolescent provides many new challenges and may bring up unresolved issues from the past. The impact of children actually leaving home is also likely to be an event which has very different meanings for different people. The impact of the 'empty nest' on parents who have devoted themselves principally to childcare and homemaking may be greater, for example, than the impact on parents whose energies have gone into their career.
- *Fewer career options* – career changes become more difficult, because, qualifications being equal, employers tend to favour suitably qualified younger men or women to older ones. (One example of this attitude is provided by the information given on its website by the Australian High Commission in London to prospective skilled migrants: 'You must be under 50 when you apply.')
- *Own parents entering old age* – the older generation getting old and dying becomes a fact of life from this point onwards. It may become necessary to provide care for parents or other elderly relatives. Or the death of parents may result in major reappraisals of one's own position in the world.
- *Letting go of dreams* – a man of 40 once remarked to one of us that from now on he was going to have to accept that he was just an ordinary person. Certain hopes and dreams that might have provided direction in earlier life may now have to be relinquished. If you haven't become a rock star yet, it is unlikely to happen now. In some cases, the dream to be relinquished may be the dream of becoming a parent.

One could perhaps summarise the mid-life transition as a time of life when it becomes necessary to relinquish an identity as 'young'. Clearly, as with all such transitions, there is likely to be an element of grieving and denial involved in this. However, if one can let go of young adulthood, new possibilities open up. Many of the challenges associated with middle adulthood which we listed above have positive as well as negative sides. Children leaving home can free up time and energy for other projects. Letting go of old dreams too can be a release from a pressure, as well as a source of sadness. In some cultures menopause itself is apparently positively welcomed

(Neugarten et al., 1963). Even the death of parents, however sad in itself, is quite often experienced as a freeing from old ties, and some people report, following the death of a parent, that they feel like an adult for the first time.

For many in middle adulthood, accumulated experience is a valuable resource. When recognised by others, this is a source of authority. (Most people in senior positions in politics, business and elsewhere, for example, are in middle adulthood.) Mallory (1984) found that 'identity achievement' increased with age (using Marcia's terminology which we discussed in the last chapter), while 'identity diffusion' decreased. Mallory found that identity achievement was higher for men and women aged 40–47 than for men and women aged 30–37 (for whom 'foreclosure' ratings were higher). This would suggest that, on average, the over-40s were more secure in their own identity than young adults.

Generativity

Generativity versus stagnation, in Erikson's model, is associated most strongly with parenthood and reproduction, arising naturally from the previous stage of intimacy:

> Generativity, then, is primarily the concern in establishing and guiding the next generation, although there are individuals who, through misfortune or through special and genuine gifts in other directions, do not apply this drive to their own offspring. (Erikson, 1995 [1951]: 240)

The focus on the production of the next generation associates this stage most strongly with middle adulthood, but of course many people are still in early adulthood when they become parents for the first time. It makes sense that intimacy precedes generativity in psychological development (just as sex precedes childbearing in a purely biological sense), but clearly they are not two distinct stages.

However, Erikson viewed generativity as something associated with participating in society and working towards goals beyond one's own immediate needs, as well as just with the bringing up of children. He made the connection, for example, between generativity and work. (This link is paralleled, as he noted, in Marxist thinking where both 'production' and 'reproduction' are seen as the means by which a particular social system perpetuates itself.) But again, occupational role is as important to many in early adulthood as it is in middle adulthood.

With the move into middle adulthood, there is a change of focus. Summing up the concerns raised by adults aged 40–65 whom she interviewed, Jane Kroger writes:

> Although issues directly related to biological changes were not frequently mentioned, changes in procreational and sexual capacities were clearly on the minds of some participants. However, of greater interest for most seemed to be a new psychological awareness of their own mortality and how meaningfully to fill whatever time there was that remained for them. In addition, the wish to contribute to the welfare of the general community surfaced in ways not described by previous age groups. ... And ... community recognition of individual contributions was highly valued by many in the process of midlife self-definition. (Kroger, 2000: 168)

Erikson's concept of generativity is quite difficult to pin down, and his proposal to link it to middle adulthood seems inappropriate when he also links the idea to parenthood. Nevertheless, Kroger's comments perhaps illustrate a certain quality that is typical of middle adulthood (though not unique to it), in which there is a concern to contribute to – and be recognised by – the wider community.

Difficulties in middle adulthood

As we said earlier in relation to young adulthood, the ideas we have been discussing are quite descriptive and may seem to be of limited use when it comes to practical questions. Again, the best way of testing them may perhaps be to look at some examples of difficulties that might be faced in middle adulthood and consider how to approach them.

Of course the difficulties faced by adults in their middle years can come into all the same categories as the younger adults we discussed earlier, but the most common problems will change: specifically, adults in this age range are more likely to be having difficulties with adolescent children, and far more likely to be caring for elderly relatives. Loss of career through redundancy, ill health or early retirement is also more likely in middle adulthood.

The following activity looks at two case examples of adults in their middle years.

Activity 7.3

What themes do you notice in the following two cases? If you were a mental health worker, what approaches might you take in trying to help?

- Jill (50) – coming from a large African-Caribbean family, Jill incurred the anger of both her parents as a young woman when she chose not to start a family, in order to pursue a career in the Civil Service, her ambition being to become the first black woman to head a government department. She works extremely hard, and very long hours, and has always had a fairly limited personal life. As a result of her ability and efforts, she has risen to a senior post in the Department of Health, overcoming both sexist and racist obstacles. However, a few months ago she had a heart attack and had to take extended sick leave, with the possibility that she would not be able to return to her old job and would have to consider early retirement. She became very depressed during her enforced idleness and made an attempt on her own life. She is now in hospital being treated for depression.
- Sue (45) – the youngest of four, and the only girl, in a suburban white British family, Sue grew up with parents who pushed their sons to achieve, and seemed to value their daughter's achievements very little. Sue didn't leave home until the age of 24 when she married an older man and became a housewife and mother. She is proud of her two confident, well-adjusted children, both of whom have now left home. She has recently started a job as a learning support assistant in a local school, which she very much enjoys. But her mother has now died and her three brothers now expect Sue to give up her part-time job to care for her father,

(Continued)

(Continued)

pointing out that all three of them are the main breadwinners for their families, while Sue's income is small and she is supported financially by her husband. She agrees with them about her duty, but the prospect fills her with such dread that she has become ill.

Comments on Activity 7.3

Loss of a career and caring for older parents are both themes which become more common in middle adulthood. For both women, work was important to their identity and the loss of work – or the threat of it – was a blow. For both these women, these typically middle-adulthood challenges may also interact with painful issues from earlier stages of life, as well as with gender and cultural issues. Caring responsibilities are more likely to be carried by women than men throughout their adult lives, and as a result they are more likely to face difficult choices between career and family.

In Jill's case, it would appear that she had to cut herself off from her family of origin to some extent in order to pursue her career. It is also possible that she may have had some regrets about not having children, but felt she had to make a choice between career and children (it would be more unusual for a man to feel that he had to make such a choice). Having made significant sacrifices in order to invest in her career, the possible loss of it must be a major blow. She has built an identity for herself around her career, rather than around personal relationships. On what is she now going to build a sense of meaning and purpose in her life?

Sue's family background seems to have resulted in her settling for 'identity foreclosure'. She never established herself as an independent adult as a young woman and perhaps only managed to escape the parental home by accepting a new parental figure in her older husband. However, she has gained some confidence from doing a good job as a parent and the 'empty nest' has for her been an opportunity to spread her wings and to begin to seek an identity of her own. This is now being placed under threat by the pressure from her brothers to once again subordinate her own needs to those of other people. This has brought up old struggles, never fully resolved, from her earlier years.

As a mental health professional (social worker, psychiatric nurse, occupational therapist, psychologist or support worker) you might use a counselling or cognitive behavioural approach to help these women to express their feelings about the difficulties they are facing and to understand them in terms of the ideas we have outlined above, and to try to find a more positive way of responding to their situations. In Jill's case this might involve exploring the possibility of reconnecting with her family and cultural roots, from which she seems to have become alienated. In Sue's case, she may need support to question the family assumptions she has grown up with about gender roles and become more assertive about her own needs. For both of these women the loss, or threatened loss, of occupational role is significant, and insights from the Model of Human Occupation (Kielhofner, 2008) used by occupational therapists may be very relevant. This focuses on the three aspects of human occupation, productivity, play and activities of daily living, as they are carried out over time and in a social and cultural context.

Many adults in middle years, as well as younger adults, will have had difficulties in dealing with the challenges of earlier stages, and this may make it more difficult to deal with the new challenges that they now face. And many, however well they faced previous challenges in their lives, will have extra challenges piled on them which they had not expected and which will force them to radically revise their expectations. In addition, the two things may come together: new challenges and old issues. Old unresolved issues ('baggage', 'unfinished business') may be brought to a head in middle adulthood by a new crisis that was unexpected but is nevertheless typical of middle adulthood: difficulties with adolescent children, the break-up of a marriage or long-term relationship, loss of a valued career, the needs of ageing parents. This kind of interaction between old issues and new events will be explored further in Chapter 9, when we look at family life cycles.

So in understanding the challenges of adult life we need to be aware of past issues as well as present ones. There is a third factor, too, which we need to consider, which is the opportunities and options available for meeting these challenges. These will vary hugely for different people in different social circumstances, and we will explore this in Chapter 10.

CHAPTER SUMMARY

- In this chapter, we looked at what is meant by 'adult'. While there is a huge difference in the issues faced by adults at different ages and in different circumstances, a common theme is that adults are expected to take responsibility.
- We then looked at different ways of thinking about the course of adult life. We discussed lifespan development and themes of continuity and change and the narrative approach.
- We considered stage theories and the importance of transitions, and the effect of life events on development in adulthood.
- We then looked at themes of identity, intimacy and generativity across the course of adult life, using Erikson's theory as a basis for our discussion, but also considering others' work on these themes.
- We then looked at specific features of young adulthood, and discussed the kinds of problems that may be characteristic of this life stage.
- In the next section we looked at the mid-life transition and middle adulthood. We looked at the themes that are common to this period, and some of the typical problems that can occur.
- We concluded this section with a more general discussion about the interaction between challenges in life, unfinished business from the past, and the different opportunities that are available to different individuals in different circumstances.

In the next chapter we will look at the particular challenges faced by people with disabilities as they embark on and progress through adulthood, and in the chapter after that we will shift our focus from the individual to the family. For families collectively, as well as individuals, face challenges, carry legacies from the past, and adapt to many different circumstances.

━ Tangled Webs ━

There are many adults included among the Tangled Webs cases. These are the ones we suggested at the beginning of the chapter:

Rob Thomas and **Tracey Green (see Case B: Rob Thomas and Derek Harrow; Case J: Tracey Green).** Rob is in middle adulthood. He is 41, divorced, and living with Tracey who is ten years younger. Rob has two sons from his marriage, and feels badly about having let them down by leaving their mother. It is a source of friction between himself and Tracey that she wants to have children and he doesn't want to start another family, feeling that he should give his time to the children he already has. One thing we can see in action here is the idea of 'social clocks' discussed in this chapter: Tracey's clock is, in effect, telling a different time to Rob's and one might argue that part of the difficulty between them is simply the fact that they are at different stages of adult life, and have different priorities as a result, however well matched they may or may not be in other respects.

Lee Harris and **Lisa Dudley (see Case G: Dudley/Harris family).** These two have a similar age gap to Rob and Tracey. Lee is 47 and so, like Rob, in middle adulthood, but he approaches this stage of life in a very different way, making himself the dominant figure in the family by controlling his partner Lisa and her three daughters in various ways which possibly include some that have not as yet come to light, but certainly include the use of constant put-downs to sap their confidence and to elevate the status of himself and his son as the men of the family. It is hard to fit this behaviour into the schema in which middle adulthood is a time of generativity, but part of generativity is about establishing one's standing in the community and perhaps Lee *is* seeking to achieve something a bit like this, albeit in a negative and abusive way, by making himself the indisputable head of his family. Lisa, who is 34, appears to be struggling with two of the most characteristic challenges of adult life. In place of intimate relationships which might be a source of support and encouragement she has had relationships with a series of violent and/or controlling men, and she is frequently unable to cope with her children when she is on her own.

Maryam Begum's family (Case E). All eight named members of this family are adults, and so all of them could potentially be looked at through the lens of the ideas in this chapter. We can see Kabir, at 24 a young adult, struggling to establish an adult relationship with Gary, and a gay identity, while still attempting to be what his family of origin wants him to be, and we can see, in his older brother and his younger brother (Monty and Sajid), two other young adults, one of whom feels he has to make a brutal break with his origins to establish himself as an adult in his own right, while the other is perhaps putting adult life on hold as he tries to meet his family responsibilities. Their mother Amina meanwhile, aged 52, and with her three sons grown up, is struggling with one of the challenges that are typical of middle adulthood, and particularly of *women* in middle adulthood **(see Sue in Activity 7.3 above, for instance)**, and is having to put her own needs on hold in order to cope with the demands of her demented and sometimes violent mother-in-law.

 You can access Tangled Webs by visiting **https://study.sagepub.com/tangledwebs**

Further reading

Howe, D. (2011) *Attachment across the Lifecourse*. Basingstoke: Palgrave Macmillan.

Kroger, J. (2000) *Identity Development: Adolescence through Adulthood*. London: Sage.

Sugarman, L. (2001) *Life-Span Development, Frameworks, Accounts and Strategies*, 2nd edn. Hove: Psychology Press.

ACCESS TO ADULTHOOD

GROWING UP WITH A DISABILITY

— TANGLED WEBS —

This chapter considers the particular challenges facing people with disabilities as they grow up and move through life. There are two cases in Tangled Webs involving disabled people. They are: **Jenny Quinton and Gloria Johnson (Case C)** and **The Sullivan family (Case H,** but see also **Case F: Max Sullivan and Gloria Johnson)**. The questions to ask yourself are: 'How different is the experience of this disabled individual from that of another individual of the same age and background without a disability?' 'How different is the experience of this person's family?' and 'What makes their experience so different?'

 You can access Tangled Webs by visiting **https://study.sagepub.com/tangledwebs**

In a delivery room in a maternity hospital, a mother is about to give birth after an eight-hour labour. There are four people present: the mother herself, the baby's father, a midwife and a doctor. Everyone is trying to encourage the exhausted mother ('Keep pushing!', 'You're almost there!', 'Don't forget your breathing!').

Then the father shouts out excitedly, 'I can see its head!'

Suddenly, a fifth human being is in the room ...

This account of a birth is identical to that at the beginning of Chapter 1. But let us suppose now that, as the baby emerges into the world for the first time, the four adults present become aware of a birth defect not previously picked up by antenatal tests: the baby's fingers are missing perhaps, or she has no eyes. Imagine how different the reaction will be in these circumstances to what it would otherwise have been.

Many impairments are picked up antenatally nowadays, others do not become apparent until some time after birth, and some happen later on as a result of illness or accident, so this scenario is only one of a number of possible ways in which parents find out that their child has an impairment of some kind. But if you imagine the response of the people present at this particular child's birth, it may help to illustrate a point that we will keep coming back to in this chapter: disability is not just about impairments, but also about the reactions of others.

Since this is a book about human growth and development, a key point here is that one of the things that other people often do to disabled people is to infantilise them, which is to say that disabled people are treated as if they were children, and can in all kinds of ways find themselves prevented or impeded – by society at large, by those around them, and even by anxious and overprotective loved ones – from moving, as other people do, through the stages of development which we have been discussing so far in this book.

People with disabilities can face formidable obstacles to having a satisfying work career, or of making a contribution to the community. They may be discouraged from having sexual relationships, or from having children. So, just as people with disabilities often have difficulty gaining access to many facilities that other people use, such as buses, toilets and public buildings, they may even have to struggle to gain access to the rewards and responsibilities of adulthood itself. For this reason, it seemed important to devote some space to looking in particular at the developmental issues faced by people with disabilities, although we can only give a very general overview here.

DEFINING DISABILITY

As we have outlined above, disability can take many different forms and can affect people at different stages of their lives. It is a complex concept, both because it covers such a wide range of conditions and because it involves an interaction between the individual and society. The terminology used in this area can be confusing too. You will find that some writers use the word *disability* to refer to the specific difficulties encountered by the person with an impairment (the inability to walk, for example, in the case of a person whose impairment is having no legs) and *handicap* to describe the social restrictions resulting from that. In common parlance, on the other hand, 'disability' or 'handicap' are often used interchangeably to cover all these different meanings, though handicap is now thought by many to have negative connotations. Many terms that have been used in the past to describe different impairments have acquired – or have always had – deeply negative connotations: 'spastic', 'idiot', 'moron', 'imbecile', 'cripple', 'retarded'. We will discuss the power of language to stereotype and exclude in Chapter 10 (p. 193ff), but for the moment we will simply note that terminology inevitably shifts over time as thinking and understanding change, and that it is important to listen to the preferences of people with disabilities themselves when we choose our words.

Social and medical models

In this chapter, we will use the word 'impairment' to describe the physical or cognitive difficulty (inability to walk, for instance, or a sensory deficit, or difficulties with some aspect of cognition), but we will use the word 'disability' to describe the extent to which the person concerned is disadvantaged. The important point here is that the extent to which a person is disadvantaged by an impairment depends on the social context. For instance, if John had polio as a child and is not able to walk very far unaided, that is an *impairment*. But, if John finds it hard to get around that is a *disability*, and just how *much* of a disability it is will depend, not simply on the severity of his impairment, but on factors such as the layout of streets, the accessibility of buildings, trains and buses, and the availability of mobility aids.

This distinction between impairment and disability originated with the Union of the Physically Impaired Against Segregation (UPIAS, 1976), an organisation of disabled activists described by Colin Barnes (2012: 13) as 'undoubtedly the most influential organisation in the history of social model thinking'. The social model of disability to which he refers is based on the idea that it is normal for a society to contain individuals with mental and physical impairments, and that disability is largely a consequence of *society's* failure to recognise this and to make provision which would allow such individuals to be included in mainstream activities. In contrast to this idea of disability as something created by society, the older *medical* model viewed the disability as being purely to do with the individual concerned.

As Tom Shakespeare points out, not *all* of the problems faced by people with impairments are within the power of society to abolish, and 'there is a danger of ignoring the problematic reality of biological limitation' (2014: 28), but the fact remains that the degree to which an impairment causes disability depends a great deal on the social context. Short-sightedness or long-sightedness, for example, are undoubtedly impairments, but they are not serious disabilities in a society where spectacles are readily available. Dyslexia is an impairment too, but the extent to which it is a disability depends on a range of factors including the importance of writing in a given society (dyslexia is presumably not a serious problem in a preliterate community), the availability of help with writing, and the level of public recognition that the writing or reading problems caused by dyslexia are nothing to do with general intelligence.

Peggy Quinn (1998) offers an historical example. On the American island of Martha's Vineyard there was for a period such a high incidence of congenital deafness among the population that it ceased to be regarded as abnormal and even most hearing people learned to use sign language. In such a context – and similar communities still exist in various parts of the world (Kuster, 2010) – deaf and hearing people share a common means of communication, and deafness, while still an impairment, is nothing like as serious a disability as it is in a largely hearing society where signing is understood only by a few.

Towards a more integrated model

The last five decades have been a period in which disability studies have developed as an academic discipline, alongside an increasingly influential user movement, and 'the combination of political activism and scholarship has helped generate a shift in perceptions of disability both nationally and internationally' (Barnes, 2012: 23). The United Nations Convention on the Rights of Persons with Disabilities, adopted in 2006, recognises in its preamble that:

> disability is an evolving concept and ... results from the interaction between persons with impairments and attitudinal and environmental barriers that hinder their full and effective participation in society on an equal basis with others. (UN, 2006:1)

The WHO *World Report on Disability* (2011: 3–4) begins its answer to the question, 'what is disability?' by stating that it is 'complex, dynamic, multi-dimensional and contested', and goes on to say that it 'should be viewed neither as purely medical nor as purely social ... A balanced approach is needed, giving appropriate weight to the different aspects of disability.'

Although service users' voices have been influential in developing the social model, language can be a barrier for people with learning difficulties who want to participate in research, just as steps and narrow doorways can be a barrier for wheelchair-users. A mixed group of learning-disabled and non-learning-disabled researchers collaborated to produce an article giving the learning-disabled researchers' views on what they needed and what should be done to make things better for learning-disabled people (Docherty et al., 2010). Writing about the social model of disability, they say that:

> Anne Louise Chappell (1998) says that learning disabled people are left out of the social model of disability. The social model of disability is in writing, so that professionals can look at it. It's not accessible to learning disabled people. We might want to study the social model ourselves, but we can't because it isn't accessible. It should be in pictures and large print. (2010: 434)

Once again, we find – as we have already found in relation to gender roles in Chapter 5 and adolescence in Chapter 6 – that when something appears at first sight to be an essentially physical or biological matter, this turns out to be only the starting point. The biological fact exists, but its impact on the individual depends on the social context and on the meanings that society assigns to the biological fact.

VARIETIES OF IMPAIRMENT

Impairments vary greatly both in kind and degree and one must be careful not to generalise about them as if they were all the same. Some of the principal kinds of impairment are as follows, though within these categories there are still large differences and many people have more than one type of impairment:

- *Motor impairments* affect mobility and/or other physical abilities involving muscle control such as speech or use of the hands.
- *Sensory impairments*, which in practical terms means visual and hearing impairments.
- *Learning impairments* are those which affect cognitive ability, the ability to think, reason or acquire knowledge.
- *Autistic spectrum disorders* include 'difficulties in social communication and social interaction across multiple contexts', and 'restricted, repetitive patterns of behaviour, interests or activities' (DSM-15 diagnostic criteria, as cited by Boucher, 2017: 16). However, it is important to note that many people on the autistic spectrum also have abilities of various kinds that are 'significantly *superior* to those found in the general population' (Boucher, 2017: 48, our emphasis), and some autistic people (sometimes referred to as *savants*) have truly exceptional abilities in areas such as mathematics or music. Uta Frith (2003) cites the example of Stephen Wiltshire, who was able to draw buildings with very great accuracy entirely from memory. Autism, in short, is not necessarily entirely an impairment.
- Though they are not normally categorised as impairments or disabilities and will not be explored further in this chapter, long-term mental health problems such as schizophrenia or bipolar disorder, can, in a society which stigmatises mental 'illness', undoubtedly also result in disability in the social model sense.

IMPAIRMENTS AND DEVELOPMENT

Although advocates of the social model draw our attention to the fact that disability is in large part a socially constructed phenomenon, an impairment in itself can constitute an obstacle to an individual developing along the same path as people who do not have impairments, even if the individual concerned is given all possible support. A person with severe learning difficulties, for instance, may not necessarily be able to move through all the stages of intellectual development envisaged by Piaget, even in optimum conditions.

Motor impairments

Studies of the development of children with motor impairments (such as Cione et al., 1993) have found that these children tend to be behind other children developmentally in a general sense, but fall behind especially in areas such as development of the concept of 'object permanence' (as discussed in Chapter 4). This is perhaps not surprising given that motor impairments will make it more difficult to explore and manipulate physical objects.

Motor impairments have a variety of causes. They can result from cerebral palsy, for example, which is caused by brain damage at an early stage of development and can result in learning difficulties too. Or they can result from hereditary conditions such as spina bifida, which is a spinal problem and can lead to muscle weakness in the lower half of the body, including sometimes problems with bowel control. Some other motor impairments are the result of physical injury.

The *structure* of development has been found to differ from one type of motor impairment to another. Children with spina bifida–hydrocephalus often have verbal abilities well in advance of their performance abilities, while children with cerebral palsy seem to develop their abilities more evenly, though on average they are behind children who do not have impairments (see Hodapp, 1998: 150–4).

Sensory impairments

Blind children tend to be slower at developing skills in the areas of object permanence than sighted children (Warren, 1994). Without sight, a blind baby has far fewer cues than a sighted baby to tell her that an object still exists when it is out of reach, and often no cues at all. So it is not surprising that blind children take longer to grasp this concept.

Lack of sight leads to delays in a number of other areas of development. Motor skills and spatial skills are slower to develop (see Brambring, 2007). 'Babies move for the purpose of reaching something or someone that interests them', as Dale and Salt observe. 'Without vision, babies may not know that there is something to reach' (2007: 685). Language skills also develop in slightly different ways. Blind children are apparently slower in grasping the difference between 'this' and 'that' (Anderson et al., 1993). They are also apparently less prone than other children to 'overgeneralise', for example by using the word 'dog' to refer to all animals, but *more* prone to 'undergeneralise', for example by using the word 'dog' as if it referred to one particular dog only (see Hodapp, 1998: 132). Without sight, a child is less well placed to notice similarities between objects in the world at large.

In the case of deaf children, as one might expect, it is language development that takes a different course from that of hearing children. But here there are some interesting complications which again serve to illustrate the pervasive role of context and culture. These arise because deaf people have their own distinct and separate languages, such as American Sign Language (ASL) and British Sign Language (BSL). Apart from being signed rather than spoken, these languages have their own quite distinct grammar and sentence structure. 'ASL does not resemble English or BSL,' writes Steven Pinker, 'but relies on agreement and gender systems in a way that is reminiscent of Navajo or Bantu' (2007: 24). But British deaf children, when they learn to read and write, learn English, and have to use English in some form in order to communicate with most hearing people. This means that when studying the language acquisition of deaf children, it is necessary to bear in mind that, like children in a bilingual family, they may be working simultaneously on acquiring two quite distinct language systems. Researchers have found that deaf children who are exposed to sign language from an early age acquire it in much the same way – and in the same time scale – as hearing children acquire speech. The deaf babies of deaf parents even apparently 'babble' in signs at the age of 10–14 months (Petitto and Marentette, 1991).

Deaf children who acquire sign language at an early age from deaf parents are at a developmental advantage as compared to deaf children who, having grown up with hearing parents, are taught sign language at a later stage. Meristo et al. (2007) found that the former group performed at a level similar to hearing children on tests of 'theory of mind' reasoning (see Chapter 4), while children in the latter group lagged behind on these tests. This reflects the findings of Greenberg and Kushe (1989) that children who are deaf and whose parents are deaf as well progressed educationally more rapidly than deaf children with hearing parents. This is likely to be due to a number of factors. For one thing, deaf children of deaf parents can acquire sign language in the same informal way that hearing children acquire spoken language, whereas deaf children of hearing parents tend to be behind in all aspects of language development. But more generally, deaf parents understand, without having to think about it, the particular needs of deaf children, such as the need to find visual or tactile ways of getting a deaf child's attention. Like the deaf inhabitants of Martha's Vineyard discussed above, deaf children of deaf parents grow up in a family environment where deafness is 'normal' and therefore less of a disability.

Learning impairments

Among children with learning impairments, there are differences in the structure of development depending on the nature of the impairment. Children with Down's syndrome, for example, are strong on social skills but slow on language and mathematical skills. Children with Williams syndrome (a much less common genetically determined condition which also affects physical development) are strong on language skills and social skills, but weaker on spatial skills (see Hodapp, 1998: 54). But while children will experience particular problems related to their specific impairments, the extent of developmental delay across all areas is also undoubtedly linked to the expectations of parents, teachers and carers, the type of encouragement or discouragement that is offered, and the extent to which compensatory input is offered in particular areas of difficulty. The reader may recall Vygotsky's insistence on the importance of language and interaction with others for a child's cognitive development, discussed in Chapter 4.

Autistic spectrum Disorders

Autistic spectrum disorders become apparent at different stages for different individuals. For some children, 'socio-emotional-communicative [SCE] behaviours are absent or odd within the first 18 months of life' (Boucher, 2017: 75), while others seem to follow a completely normal developmental pathway for the first 18 months of life, only for SCE behaviours and language to 'decline significantly, and sometimes rapidly' (ibid.: 75), or if not decline then simply to plateau. Jill Boucher observes that:

> Home videos of children subsequently diagnosed as autistic reveal that by the end of their first year, most (but not all) such children are less likely than typically developing 1-year-olds to respond to their own names, to look at other people's faces or to follow another person's direction of looking or pointing. They are also averse to social touch. (2017: 76)

Long-term changes will depend greatly on the individual and 'even people with very low-functioning autism have some "splinter skills", or islets of relatively good ability' (ibid.: 46–7).

Emotional development

This discussion has so far related to issues to do with the acquisition of skills, but if impairments may result in children taking different developmental routes in respect of cognitive development, is it possible that impairments can also result in different pathways in respect of emotional development or the development of personality characteristics? You may remember that we noted in Chapter 4 that there was necessarily a close relationship between cognitive development and emotional development.

The following activity is intended to help you think about the particular challenges faced by people with disabilities.

━━━━━━ Activity 8.1 ━━━━━━

Below are the favourable outcomes which Erikson proposed for each of his eight stages of development:

1   trust in the environment
2   a sense of autonomy and self-esteem
3   the ability to initiate activities
4   a sense of competence and achievement
5   the ability to see oneself as a consistent and integrated person
6   the ability to experience love and commitment to others
7   the ability to be concerned and caring about others in the wider sense
8   a sense of satisfaction with one's life and its accomplishments.

What obstacles might stand in the way of achieving these outcomes for:

• a person with a sensory impairment?
• a person with a learning impairment?
• a person with a motor impairment?
• a person with an autistic spectrum disorder?

Comments on Activity 8.1

The following are a few suggestions:

In the absence of appropriate help, a child with a sensory impairment such as blindness, attempting to find her way in a world designed for sighted people, might well have difficulty establishing a sense of trust in the environment.

Similarly, in the absence of appropriate support, a person with cerebral palsy, who was unable to do things such as walk, dress herself or use the toilet, might have difficulty with a sense of autonomy.

A child with learning difficulties, in the absence of appropriate help, might well have difficulty in developing a sense of competence, when comparing herself with other children.

A child on the autistic spectrum is likely to have difficulty with trust in a social environment when she finds it hard to make sense of the motives, behaviour and feelings of other people.

Appropriate help, in all these cases, would need to include both resources that provide practical assistance (for example a wheelchair, mobility training, Makaton sign language) and the attitudes of those who provide it. Helpers need to understand the importance of enabling the person they are helping to do as much as possible for themselves, rather than just focusing on getting a task done, if they are to support them to realise their full potential. There are obviously resource implications here too; equipment and adaptations can be costly, and providing sensitive and empowering help will often take longer.

All of us, whether or not we are disabled, carry 'unfinished business' from the earlier stages of our life, and all of us find it hard at times to meet the challenges made on us in the here and now. People who have disabilities may have to carry additional emotional baggage from the past as well as deal with unusually difficult challenges in the present. Commenting on the high incidence of mental illness among people with learning impairments, Howells (1997: 77) observes:

> They have few opportunities to exercise choice, their expectations are low and they suffer from overprotection. Little scope exists to develop social networks beyond the family and paid carers. The result is too great an emotional investment in too few people. This, in turn, increases the significance of loss through bereavement and changes in staff.

FAMILIES, CHILDREN AND DISABILITY

In February 1972, a yellow and red calico duck beanbag sat expectantly in the crib in our new house … At 6 a.m. the morning before Valentine's Day I delivered our long-hoped-for child, a baby girl. The physician placed her briefly on my stomach, moved her to an examining table, and said, 'In just a few minutes, I'll come to the recovery room to talk with you.' When he stepped in, we heard 'Your baby shows signs of Down's syndrome (DS). Do you know what that is?'

… As I drank refreshing orange juice in the recovery room, Peter sat with his head in his hands, contemplating the necessary calls that would stun our parents about their first grandchild. We plunged into an unfamiliar world of confusion, numbness, disbelief. 'What's the baby's name?' a nurse asked.' We haven't decided.' We knew this was not Rebecca, the name selected for our baby if it were a girl. Within a few hours we decided on a name farther down our list, 'Sarah,' and added Kathleen as the middle name. Unconsciously, the naming process signified our recognition of the loss of our expected child and represented our first step in acknowledging the child who had arrived instead.

Over the 32 years of Sarah's life, enormous changes have occurred in our society, which now offers children and adults with disabilities, and their families, support ... that did not exist in 1972. Yet, there remains, unchanged, parents' common experiences of loss, mourning, and chronic grief, which extend throughout the life span and are exacerbated at times of transition. ... (Riesz, 2004: 371–2)

What is it like to discover your child has a disability? One of the most influential models was offered by Solnit and Stark (1961), who proposed that the birth of a child with an impairment was in some senses a bereavement. Parents had to go through a period of mourning for their dreams of a 'perfect' child and this would involve going through the stages associated with grieving: shock, denial, sadness and anger, adaptation and reorganisation.

It is worth thinking for a moment about what it would mean, not for the parents or the wider family, but for the child herself. What kind of start in life is it, if, like Sarah described above, your birth is not a joyful event but is the occasion for mourning?

Some readers may not feel comfortable with the idea of describing the birth of any child as being like a bereavement, but no one can seriously dispute that such a birth involves a major adjustment. The arrival of a child is a stressor in most families and the arrival of a child with an impairment is undoubtedly more of a stressor on the family system than the arrival of a child without an impairment. As Galpin et al. observe, families 'vary considerably in their ability to manage the challenges they face' (2017: 579). How well the family copes will depend both on the wider social context, and upon the characteristics of that particular family. At the societal level, widely held cultural beliefs might be a factor (in some cultures, the birth of a child with a disability is viewed as a punishment from God), while at the family level each family will have its own unique priorities, beliefs and values, built up over several generations. Some families might set great store by sporting achievement, for instance, others by intellectual achievement, and these families might be particularly affected by the birth of a child with physical or intellectual impairments. These kinds of historic factors can be described as 'vertical stressors', as opposed to 'horizontal stressors', which are events that operate at a particular time, like the birth of a child with an impairment. And it is when vertical and horizontal stressors intersect that things become especially difficult for a family (McGoldrick et al., 2016a: 21). We will return to this idea in more detail in our next chapter, when we look at the idea of families as systems.

Minnes (1988), looking in particular at families with children who had learning impairments, categorised these factors under the following headings:

- The child's own characteristics. The nature of the disability and the characteristics of the individual child, not surprisingly, make a difference. Many children with Down's syndrome are very affectionate and sociable. Some children with autistic spectrum disorders have very challenging behaviours or cannot settle down to sleep at night. Some children with physical disabilities need help with feeding, bathing and using the toilet all their lives.
- The resources of the family. Minnes broke this down further into 'internal' and 'external' resources.

    o 'Internal' resources are the personal characteristics of the family members and of the family as a whole. In particular, coping strategies that are focused on solving practical problems seem to be more adaptive than 'emotion-focused' coping strategies. According to Hodapp (1998: 81), 'In virtually every study, mothers who were focused on actively solving problems seemed better off than those focused primarily on their own emotional reactions.' This distinction between 'problem-focused' and 'emotion-focused' coping strategies was discussed in the section on Coping Skills and Resilience in Chapter 6 (p. 128ff).

o 'External' resources include such things as the family's financial resources and/or the availability of financial help, and the services and support networks that are available. We have already discussed how the extent that an individual is disabled by an impairment is dependent on the support available, the attitudes of others, and the provision made by the wider community. The same applies to families too.

- The family's perception of the child. The family's beliefs are also important. As Hodapp observes (1998: 81), some families may view a child as a special burden or responsibility placed upon them by God. Others may view the additional demands of a child with learning impairments as being 'unfair', and a brake on achieving what they saw as their legitimate aspirations in life. Family perceptions of the impairment are also a factor. In a study of stress experienced by parents of children diagnosed with autistic spectrum disorder, Brei et al. (2015: 629) note that, while the level of severity of the symptoms as rated by clinicians did not correlate significantly with parents' levels of distress, the parents' own perceptions of the severity of autism-related symptoms did significantly predict parental stress.

All developmental challenges are challenges for the whole family, and clearly this is very much the case with disability. A family with a disabled child may in some cases have a radically different life cycle from other families. For example, in a family where a child has serious learning impairments, the whole family may need to adjust to the fact that one of its members will never reach a stage of independent adult life.

And this process places great stresses upon the family. Higgins et al. (2005) found that caregivers of children with autistic spectrum disorders reported lower overall marital happiness than other families, while their families demonstrated less warmth and connection, perhaps not surprisingly given that, as Peter Burke notes, 'the impact on siblings of having a brother or sister with disabilities will increase the sense of being "left out"' (2004: 45). In a much older study, Gath (1977) found a higher incidence of divorce or marital dissatisfaction among parents of children with Down's syndrome. And Hodapp and Krasner (1995) likewise found the incidence of divorce among parents of school-age children with *visual* impairments to be 25 per cent, as against 15.3 per cent among a sample with non-disabled children. Burke notes too, that having to care for a child with a disability changes the employment options for parents. Childcare costs may be several times higher than for non-disabled children but 'the fact that a high proportion of woman carers have reduced employment prospects further stresses the family income ... at a point where costs are comparatively higher than for other families' (2008: 51). Emerson and Hatton (2007) found that the income of families of children with disabilities was 17 per cent lower than other families and that they were 'more than three times more likely than other families to be behind with hire purchase and insurance payments', and 'more than twice as likely than other families to be in debt' (2007: 568).

But the presence of a child with a disability can also result in positive growth. Marriages can be strengthened by the arrival of children with a disability, as well as broken, and extended families can be drawn together into a strong, mutually supportive system. Grossman (1972, cited in Hodapp, 1998: 70) carried out a study of older siblings of children with disabilities and found an almost exactly even split between predominantly positive and predominantly negative feelings. Feelings of resentment and frustration were reported by 45 per cent, while another 45 per cent described the experience of having a sibling with disabilities as being on balance a rewarding and enriching one. From a family systems perspective (see next chapter), a family's ability to adapt successfully to new challenges depends on its members' capacity to renegotiate the family structure. Perhaps the second group in Grossman's study came from families which had been able to change in this way. Perhaps the families of the first group had become 'stuck', unable to resolve and move on from their initial negative reactions.

Before reading further, you may find it useful to go through the following activity to help you think about families of children with disabilities.

━━━━━ Activity 8.2 ━━━━━

You are a social worker in a children's disability team. You have received a referral from a family who have twins aged 18 months and two older children aged three and five. One of the twins suffered brain damage at birth and has some physical impairment as a result; she is not yet able to walk or grasp and manipulate objects, unlike her twin, and she also has difficulty feeding herself and is very unsettled in her behaviour. Her parents are struggling to cope, and their doctor has asked if they can have respite care for their daughter. What factors would you consider in deciding how to respond to this request?

Comments on Activity 8.2

This family has a lot to cope with; having four young children so close in age would be stressful in itself without the additional factor of disability. They certainly need support and respite of some kind, but you have probably thought of a lot of questions you would want to ask about their situation before a decision was made about how best to provide this. How much help have the parents had, if any, in coming to terms with their child's disability, and how much is known about its diagnosis and prognosis? What effect has it had on relationships within the family? What resources can the family draw on, both from within their own family culture and from wider family, friends and community? Are there any aspects of the family culture which are adding further to the practical and emotional difficulties of coping with their child's impairment?

Failing to resolve initial negative reactions is a danger for families of children with disabilities and therefore a danger to the child herself, because healthy emotional development is not assisted by negative or ambivalent feelings on the part of one's parents. The process of adjustment will be greatly helped by clear information about the cause of the disability, about what to expect in terms of development and what parents and others can do to help the child reach her full potential. In this situation you would want to check whether all these issues have been fully explored, although of course there are not always clear answers to these questions. Support groups, where parents can access information and share experiences and strategies, can be very helpful.

Another danger is that parents may become so preoccupied with managing the particular special needs of a child with a disability, perhaps out of a desire to make the child become as 'normal' as possible, that they lose sight of the fact that the child has the same universal emotional needs as any other child. Such needs might include needs for fun, cuddles, exploration and so on and also needs for consistent care. This may affect the attachment relationship between parent and child; studies of attachment patterns in children with disabilities show that they are slightly more likely to be insecurely attached than others (Howe, 2011: 207). With this in mind, you would want to think carefully about the effect on attachment of respite care which separated this young child from her main carer. There is a difficult balance to be struck here between the parents' needs, the needs of the child and the needs of her siblings, which should be sensitively explored with the family in order to come up with a creative and workable package of support.

ADOLESCENCE AND DISABILITY

The developmental task of adolescence is widely agreed to be the construction of an identity of one's own with which to enter the adult world (see Chapter 6). Components of this identity differ from one individual to another, but are likely to include elements of the following:

- Autonomy – increasing independence from one's family of origin, which may include physically leaving home, as well as making one's own decisions and taking responsibility for one's own needs. This is linked to the increasing importance of a peer group as a source of support.
- Sexual identity – a sense of oneself as a sexual being, which arises from learning to successfully negotiate sexual relationships.
- Occupational identity – a sense of oneself as competent and able to provide for oneself and others, which comes from acquiring skills and work habits.

It would be wrong to generalise about all young people with disabilities as if they were a single homogeneous group, for there are enormous differences between the challenges that will be faced by, say, a young person of above average intelligence who is deaf, a person with Down syndrome, or a person who is quadriplegic. Nevertheless, there are some themes which do seem to run through the experience of many adolescents with disabilities.

Autonomy

Young people with disabilities may have their peer-group involvement limited or curtailed in various ways. They may attend special schooling, separate from other young people. In some ways, this may promote peer-group involvement, by allowing young people to mix with others who share the same kinds of experience, but it does also have the effect of isolating young people with disabilities from young people generally. In cases where young people with disabilities attend residential schools, or are bussed to schools at some distance using special transport services, this problem may be particularly pronounced. They miss out on getting to know young people in their own neighbourhood.

Mobility problems may also make informal socialising more difficult or impossible, as can intellectual impairments (some may lack the necessary linguistic or cognitive abilities) and visual impairments. There may be problems with gaining acceptance from non-disabled peers – or even reluctance to admit that they are peers – and difficulties with access, for physical or other reasons, to social and leisure facilities used by non-disabled young people in the same age group.

Becoming independent from one's family of origin may also be complicated – or made impossible – if one is dependent on one's family for basic physical care, such as dressing, bathing or going to the toilet. Whether these needs can be met in other ways will depend on financial resources and/or the availability of publicly funded services. Parents may also be in a position to hold on to control which they simply would have had no choice but to relinquish with an able-bodied child. For non-disabled children, establishing autonomy typically involves an element of wresting power from adults, as well as being granted it. Young people with disabilities may find this more difficult to achieve.

Sexual identity

Exploration of sex and sexual relationships is complicated for young people with disabilities for all of the reasons given above. Even access to information about sex may be more restricted, because adolescents typically acquire sexual information from their peers as well as from adults and, as we've seen, some young people with disabilities have more restricted contact with their peers.

Lollar (1994) makes the point that young people with spina bifida (and this would also apply to some with other conditions) have been subjected throughout their life to highly intrusive examinations and interventions, so that they will not have developed the same boundaries about their bodies as other young people, and may need particular help with this. Some young people with spina bifida may also have limited sensation in the genital area or, in the case of boys, be unable to have an erection.

Protectiveness on the part of parents and other adult carers may also result in a lack of sexual opportunities, which is not to say that protectiveness is necessarily unjustified in the case of young people whose limited cognitive abilities may otherwise place them in situations which they are unable to control or understand. Young people with disabilities are often more vulnerable to abuse and exploitation than are their non-disabled peers (see, for instance, Sullivan and Knutson, 2000). The tendency to infantilise people with disabilities can get in the way of parents, carers and others recognising disabled adolescents as sexual beings in the same way as their non-disabled peers.

Occupational identity

Depending on the nature of the impairment, and on the social environment, a young person with a disability may also have much more difficulty than non-disabled young people in finding a job and acquiring skills that will allow her to earn her own living and participate fully in the work of society. Drawing on a UK survey of nearly 24,000 men and women aged 19–59, a government survey found that 71 per cent of disabled respondents had no paid employment, as against 24 per cent of non-disabled respondents (Berthoud, 2006: 32). Though paid work is often an important part of occupational identity, leisure and social activities and the routines of daily living are important too, and people with disabilities may face obstacles in these areas also.

Writing in the foreword to the *World Report on Disability*, the late Professor Stephen Hawking, who had motor neurone disease, contrasts his own experience with that of the majority of disabled people:

> I rely on a team of personal assistants who make it possible for me to live and work in comfort and dignity. My house and my workplace have been made accessible for me. Computer experts have supported me with an assisted communication system and a speech synthesiser which allow me to compose lectures and papers, and to communicate with different audiences.
>
> But I realise that I am very lucky, in many ways. My success in theoretical physics has ensured that I am supported to live a worthwhile life. It is very clear that the majority of people with disabilities in the world have an extremely difficult time with everyday survival, let alone productive employment and personal fulfilment. (WHO, 2011: ix)

The routes by which people typically establish a separate identity during adolescence may be more restricted, or even closed in some cases, to young people with disabilities. The challenge for these young people and their supporters seems to lie both in challenging unwarranted obstacles and in finding alternative pathways to establishing a secure adult identity.

DISABILITY AND ADULTHOOD

Historically, even when young adults with disabilities left their family home, it was to move into institutional environments where they continued to be treated like dependent children:

> When the national health service was set up in 1948, the colonies or institutions which were built originally in the nineteenth century to segregate people with learning difficulties from the rest of society became 'hospitals' in which people were 'nursed' (all of their lives) and their problems were defined in medical terms. People with learning difficulties were seen as sick and in need of treatment. (Sperlinger, 1997: 6–7)

In the 1970s, one of the authors worked in a men's ward in an institution of this kind in which adults learning difficulties, whether aged 20 or 60, were uniformly referred to by themselves and staff as 'boys'. They had no opportunities for sexual relationships, other than furtive ones. They slept in dormitories and had no safe place for personal possessions. They had to ask for toilet paper when they needed it, though some of these men were of high enough intellectual ability to be able to read and write fluently. There are no longer hospitals in Britain like this, but it is still difficult for many people with disabilities to enter fully into what other people would regard as adult life.

Adult life does not mean 'independence', for, as Peggy Quinn points out, everyone, disabled or otherwise, depends on others 'for food, electricity, transportation, postal services and many other components of daily life' (1998: 160). But adulthood for most of us is a state in which we move from dependence to 'responsible interdependence' in which 'each person does what she does best and negotiates with others for the goods and services she needs to fill the gaps' (ibid.: 160). And for most adults, this state of responsible interdependence allows us to do many, if not all, of the following:

- moving out of the parental home and becoming responsible for one's own care
- engaging in sexual relationships and establishing a long-term sexual partnership
- becoming financially independent
- raising children
- leaving school and full-time education and moving into a career or occupation
- contributing to the community.

Of course, many people with impairments do all these things, and do them very well. But for many others some or all of them are difficult or impossible, not just because of the challenges created by their impairments, but because of the attitudes of society. In some cases, the level of disability that results can amount to a denial of access to adulthood itself. The group of learning-disabled researchers quoted earlier had this to say about the negative attitudes they had encountered:

The professionals, care managers, day centre staff, and parents and Joe Public judge us – all of them judge us – and they're frightened of change. A lot of learning disabled adults are in a rubber band system. They say 'You can go as far as that.' But if they see us progressing too far forward they say, 'Oh come back!' and pull us back. ... People say, *'you can't!'* all the time.

You can't get a job.

You can't get married.

You can't have a baby.

You can't have your own house.

You can't go out unless you're with someone else.

You can't get on a university course.

You can't have a normal life.

But now we can, and people need to learn that we can ... It's like Wolfensberger (1998) said, people think we're 'forever children' because we don't have the intelligence of a 'normal' adult. (Docherty et al., 2010: 435)

CHAPTER SUMMARY

- In this chapter, we looked at the interaction of physical and environmental/social factors that together constitute 'disability' (we used 'impairment' to refer to the purely physical/biological aspect). The restrictions that result from disability can in some circumstances amount to a restriction in access to the status of adulthood itself.
- We then looked at different types of impairment - learning impairments, motor impairments and sensory impairments - and considered the particular developmental challenges that each poses. As discussed in previous chapters, there are dangers in imposing a certain developmental pathway as 'normal' and this is apparent in the case of people with disabilities.
- We looked at the family context of children with disabilities, discussing both the initial reaction of a family to the arrival of a child with disabilities and the impact of disability on a family system (which, it would appear, can be both disruptive and strengthening).
- We then moved on to look at the particular issues faced by adolescents with disabilities, bearing in mind that adolescence is normally viewed as a time of establishing a separate identity.
- We concluded by looking at issues for disabled adults.

This chapter has emphasised both the family and the wider social context of disability. The next chapter will focus on family systems theory and the one after that will look further at the wider social context in which not only disability but all aspects of human growth and development unfold.

Tangled Webs

There are two Tangled Webs cases involving a disabled person, in one case an adult and in another a child. In both cases we hear from family members but not from the disabled people themselves, who may not even know they are being discussed.

Jenny Quinton and Gloria Johnson (Case C). Jenny is getting on for thirty. As a result of cerebral palsy she has significant motor impairments which limit her mobility and her ability to do things for herself such as bathing and shopping. They also make it more difficult for her to communicate clearly. Some help is available. She has a mobility scooter, and she has a number of carers including Gloria. There's no suggestion that she has any kind of cognitive impairment, nevertheless those around her do seem to act as if she is not capable of thinking for herself: shopkeepers talk over her head, and her carer Gloria and her mother, albeit out of genuine concern for her, talk about her behind her back. The fact that she is having a sexual relationship with an older, married man, is a big worry for Gloria and for her mother. We would guess that the relationship would be a concern for Jenny's mother even if she wasn't disabled, but Jenny would have much more choice as to how much her mother knew about it, or became involved. And though the relationship seems far from ideal, the fact is that Jenny has the same need for sexual intimacy as other 28-year-olds. As a grown-up, is she not entitled to make her own decision about whether or not this relationship is worth her while?

(Continued)

(Continued)

The Sullivan family (Case H, but see also Case F: Max Sullivan and Gloria Johnson). Jack Sullivan has some form of autistic spectrum disorder. We don't hear much in the case study about how he sees things, but we do have some information about the impact he has had on his parents. His father, Max, appears never to have fully come to terms with his son's disability and currently seems to find it difficult being around for him at home. His mother Penny seems to have had to take much more responsibility for him, and to be more engaged in thinking about his needs. He clearly makes huge demands on her: even a small and temporary change in the toilet arrangements in his school has thrown him. Disability affects the whole family's development and not just the individual. But of course the individual in turn must be affected by what the family can and cannot offer.

  You can access Tangled Webs by visiting **https://study.sagepub.com/tangledwebs**

═══ Further reading ═══

Hodapp, R.M. (1998) *Development and Disabilities: Intellectual, Sensory and Motor Impairments.* Cambridge: Cambridge University Press.

Summarises a large number of research findings and covers the Solnit and Stark and subsequent models on the birth of a child with a disability.

Lewis, V. (2003) *Development and Disability*, 2nd edn. Oxford: Blackwell.

Provides separate chapters on the development of children who are blind, deaf, have motor disabilities, have Down syndrome and have autism.

Quinn, P. (1998) *Understanding Disability – a Lifespan Approach*. London: Sage.

Covers each stage of the lifespan in a separate chapter.

NO MAN IS AN ISLAND

FAMILY SYSTEMS AND THEIR LIFE CYCLE

TANGLED WEBS

This chapter invites you to think of human growth and change as something that happens, not just to individuals but to families. If you want to look at some cases first (and you could look at any of the Tangled Webs cases for this), the sort of questions to ask are: 'How is this individual's behaviour a reflection of the functioning of their family?' 'What role does this individual play in his or her family?' 'What does this family need from this individual?' Some good cases to look at would be: **Maryam Begum's family (Case E)**, and **The Dudley/ Harris family (Case G)**.

 You can access Tangled Webs by visiting **https://study.sagepub.com/tangledwebs**

In the previous chapter we showed that a disability is not simply a characteristic of an individual, but is the product of an interaction between an individual and the wider social context in which he or she lives. This is an example of the more general point that human beings do not grow and develop in isolation. As the seventeenth-century poet John Donne famously put it:

> No man is an *Island*, entire of it selfe; every man is a piece of the *Continent*, a part of the *maine* ... (Donne, 1962 [1624]: 369)

People form parts of larger systems, pieces of a continent. It is within that context that we become the individuals we are. But there is more to it than that, for these larger systems themselves are subject to growth and change: relationships change, families change, communities and societies change. So in this chapter we are going to look at the growth and development of systems – specifically at *family* systems – and at how one can view human growth and development in terms of whole families rather than just looking at the growth and development of the individuals within a family. The next chapter will look at the even wider context of society at large.

We have included this chapter because family systems theory seems to provide a useful, unique and important perspective on child and adult development. But in fact family systems theory often goes unmentioned in the developmental literature. Accounts of systems theory and its application to families are found mainly in the family therapy literature, which is naturally orientated more towards the practical task of working with troubled families than towards advancing academic knowledge of human development.

There are many different approaches within the family therapy literature and there is no single 'founding father' or 'founding mother', as with some of the other theoretical models we have discussed, though Gregory Bateson (see Bateson, 1973) is described by one author as 'arguably the most influential early theorist' (Barnes, 2004: 18).

SYSTEMS THEORY

Originating in the work of the biologist Ludwig von Bertalanffy (1971), systems theory has its roots in mathematics, biology and cybernetics and deals with the way that parts come together in larger wholes. A system is a complex of interacting elements. An example of a very simple system is a room with a heating system controlled by a thermostat. The elements within this system – the room, the heating system and the thermostat – are linked together in a circular relationship: the temperature of the room affects the thermostat, the thermostat switches the heating on or off, the heating affects the temperature in the room and so on, as is illustrated in Figure 9.1.

Our bodies are systems like this. They are vastly more complicated, of course, consisting not just of three elements but of a large number of organs and tissues but, as in the example of the room and the thermostatically controlled heating, the different elements interact together. Heart rate and rate of breathing, for example, are affected by the level of oxygen in the blood, and the level of oxygen in the blood is in turn affected by heart rate and rate of breathing.

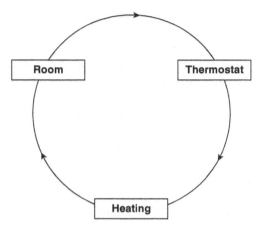

Figure 9.1   A simple system

If you look at it on a smaller scale, each organ is a system made up of a large number of cells. And if you look inside a cell, that itself is a system of interacting parts. Going to the other extreme, human beings are themselves a part of larger interlocking and overlapping systems: families, communities, organisations, countries, the biosphere. Each system is made up of 'subsystems' and is itself in turn a subsystem in even larger systems. There are many different 'system levels'.

Closed and open systems

Systems can be closed or open. A closed system is one which does not interact at all with the surrounding world. In open systems, there is an interaction with the world outside across the boundary of the system. A system has to have *some* sort of boundary to exist as something separate from its surroundings, but that boundary may be permeable.

Living systems characteristically are open systems. They have a semi-permeable boundary which does not cut them off completely from the outside world, but allows them to maintain some sort of equilibrium with it. The amoeba, for example, is a single-celled organism which has a semi-permeable membrane around it. Without the membrane, the contents of the amoeba would simply dissolve into the surrounding water, but if the membrane was completely impermeable, the amoeba would not be able to take in the water, nutrients and oxygen that it needs, or get rid of waste products.

Circularity and feedback loops

Circularity is a feature of systems in general. That is to say, the sequence of cause and effect in a system does not just go in one direction. In our thermostat example, one *could* say that the thermostat controls the temperature in the room (because it is the thermostat that turns the heating on and off), but it would be equally true to say that it is the temperature in the room that controls the thermostat (because the thermostat is a mechanism that responds to changes in temperature). The relationship between thermostat and room in this example is what is called a *negative feedback loop*. That is to say, an increase in temperature results in the heating being switched off, which then of course leads to the temperature dropping down again. A *positive feedback loop*, on the other hand, would exist if the thermostat was wrongly wired up so that an increase in temperature had the effect of turning the heating *up*. You can see that a positive loop would result in the room getting hotter and hotter indefinitely, while a negative feedback loop has the effect of maintaining temperature at a more or less constant level.

The term 'positive feedback loop' does not imply that this kind of feedback loop is necessarily beneficial. Positive feedback loops can be very dangerous. To give one example, part of the current concern about global warming is that rising temperatures may set in motion positive feedback loops which will cause even *faster* rises in temperature. (For instance, if higher temperatures result in the release of methane gas from frozen tundra, the methane will have a 'greenhouse' effect which will then result in further warming, more thawing of frozen land and the release of still more greenhouse gases to warm things up still more.) When positive feedback loops have harmful consequences of this kind, we tend to speak of 'vicious circles' or of things 'spiralling out of control'. But positive feedback loops can be beneficial if they result in a steadily improving situation, in which case they are referred to as 'virtuous circles'.

Just as positive feedback loops are not necessarily positive in their consequences, negative feedback loops are by no means necessarily negative in theirs. They are called negative because the feedback dampens down whatever stimulus set them off. In fact, far from being harmful, negative feedback loops are absolutely vital components of all living things, since life needs to maintain a state of equilibrium, or *homeostasis* (from the Greek words for 'same' and 'standing') in order to function. Maintaining equilibrium is of course precisely the purpose of a thermostat (the word comes from the Greek for 'heat' and 'standing'), which is a classic example of a negative feedback loop. Our bodies have their own remarkably efficient thermostatic mechanisms which, unless we are ill, keep our blood within half a degree or so of 37°C, the optimum temperature for our particular body chemistry, in summer or winter alike.

SYSTEMS AND FAMILIES

But what does all this have to do with families? Well, as we have said, every individual is not only a biological system, made up of numerous subsystems, but herself part of larger systems, including societies, communities, organisations, cultures ... and families. A group of people sharing the same environment interact and influence one another in many different ways. And, as Franklin and Warren write:

> if there is ... a sufficient level of contact between them, a global structure emerges that influences each of the actors in ways that cannot simply be explained by the impact of one individual on another; the whole is greater than the sum of the parts and cannot be explained completely by breaking it down into parts. ... Thus a system is born. (1999: 401)

This applies to all kinds of groups of people. Most of us are familiar with the way that a sporting team or a team at work gradually 'gels together' into some kind of an entity, but of course the members of families typically have a much higher level of contact over a much longer period of time. You may well have experienced the powerful and complex feelings, positive, negative, or both at once, that are set in train when the members of an extended family reunite at an occasion such as a wedding or a Christmas dinner, and the way that old patterns of behaviour, old rivalries and grudges and alliances, can very quickly reassert themselves, even after many years. In such situations, we observe the emergence of an entity that is greater than the sum of its parts.

To look at this entity which we call a family, and to consider it as a system, has the following implications, which have been found useful in practice in therapeutic work with families:

- If families are systems, they have properties which are more than the sum of their parts. So we cannot fully understand the behaviour of an individual in isolation, without looking at the system of which she is part.
- If they are similar to biological systems, families will operate to try to maintain a reasonably steady state. So, if a certain member of the family is habitually behaving in a certain way, this behaviour is likely to be serving the purpose of maintaining a steady state, even if the family members themselves do not recognise this.
- Communication and feedback between the parts of the system (that is, the members of the family) are an important part of the functioning of the system. So that, if we want to understand the family, we have to look at the way members communicate with one another, and not just at each individual in isolation.
- If you want to understand the behaviour of an individual in the family, you usually understand it better in terms of circular causality, rather than of linear causality. That is to say, the behaviour of an individual is not simply the cause of other events in the family, or simply the effect, but is linked to the rest of the family in a feedback loop. As with the thermostat and the temperature of a room, each one both controls and is controlled by the other.
- All systems are made up of smaller systems and are themselves part of larger systems.

Proponents of a systems perspective argue that when we think about human problems and try to solve them, we often fail to bring about change because we focus too much on individuals and not enough on the system of which they are part. A young offender, for instance, is working well with a probation officer and seems to be making excellent progress. But then, for no obvious reason, he seemingly throws it all away and goes out and offends again. There could be many reasons for this, of course, but one possibility is that the probation officer has neglected to look at the family context in which the offender is operating. Perhaps his offending serves some purpose for the family. It may provide a distraction, as we will discuss below, from other more alarming issues which might otherwise threaten the family's integrity. Or perhaps there is a culture within the family that a man must commit crimes to prove his manhood.

To return to the analogy of the thermostat, suppose you find yourself in a rather cold house and, finding a small fireplace in the front room, decide to light a fire. Unfortunately, you fail to notice that the thermostat that controls the central heating is also in the front room. The warmth of the fire causes the thermostat to turn off the central heating for the rest of the house. So, though it gets warmer immediately in front of the fire, the house as a whole gets colder than ever. In order to heat up the house as a whole, you'd need to know about the thermostat and know how to adjust it. Just stoking up the fire without adjusting the thermostat will only generate a local heat, which is not enough to offset the loss of the central heating over all the rest of the house.

To give another analogy, if a group of people are playing poker and one player starts playing rummy, he won't get very far. The rest of the group will stop him from carrying on, or they will evict him from the game. If he wants to play rummy, he needs to persuade the rest of the group to play a different game.

Social workers, relationship counsellors and others who deal with family problems will often find that a particular member of a family – often a child – is identified as 'the problem'. But if they look at it more closely from a systems perspective, they may well find that the problem lies in the whole group, and that the person identified as the problem may actually be performing a *helpful* role for the group, either by providing some kind of safety valve or by attracting outside help. The other family members may complain about this person's behaviour, but it may still turn out that in some way the family *need* this behaviour to continue.

If you are not accustomed to thinking about systems, this can seem quite a puzzling idea. The following activity may help to clarify it:

Activity 9.1

Mr and Mrs Smith have three children, Mary (18), Ricky (13) and Betty (10). Mr Smith works in the oil industry and this requires him to work abroad much of the time. There have been serious marital problems over the years. Mr Smith has had several affairs and has talked on several occasions of leaving home for good.

Ricky has started getting into trouble. He stays out a lot. He has been involved in shoplifting. He is missing a lot of school, and is under threat of being excluded because of his disruptive, defiant behaviour in the classroom and outside of it.

Mrs Smith has been diagnosed with depression.

Mr Smith has recently taken unpaid leave from work to be at home to support Mrs Smith, resulting in loss of income for the family, and also jeopardising his chance of a promotion to a new post of global operations manager.

Mary had a place at a university 200 miles away, but has now deferred because she is so worried about what is happening at home. She is working in a local shop.

Everyone in the family is very angry with Ricky. Mr Smith is particularly angry, not only about the disruption of his work, but also angry on behalf of Mrs Smith (who, in Mr Smith's view, has been made ill by Ricky) and Mary (who, as Mr Smith sees it, has had to put her future on hold indefinitely because of Ricky's selfishness).

But looked at in systemic terms, what purpose might Ricky's behaviour serve for the family system as a whole? And what might the family need help with to move forward? Looking at this as a problem for the family as a whole, what kind of interventions might be helpful?

Comments on Activity 9.1

You probably noticed that one effect of Ricky's behaviour has been to bring his father home more. Children's problem behaviours frequently seem to serve some function for the relationship of their parents. Difficult behaviour can bring together parents who are drifting apart by giving them a task which they have to work on together. Or, by drawing their anger on to himself, a child can prevent them from taking it out on one another. If you have a partner and are a parent, you may well have noticed for yourself how one of your children becomes more demanding when you and your partner are not getting on.

Ricky's behaviour has also had the effect of preventing his sister from leaving home. With a frequently absent father and a depressed mother, he may well have become quite dependent on her for support and is now managing to keep her available to him, and to delay the beginnings of the 'empty nest' transition for the family, which his parents may also be finding difficult, as it will put more focus on their own conflicted relationship. Mary herself may also be finding it difficult to separate from her family; she may be anxious about how her mother will cope, and what will happen to her parents' marriage. She may secretly welcome the excuse to delay her departure.

Having his parents and sister so angry with him cannot be pleasant for Ricky, but it may well be less scary for him than having them angry and rejecting of each other. It may well be less scary for the parents and the rest of the family too.

From a family systems point of view, any intervention would need to shift the perspective away from a view of this as being just Ricky's problem, and towards looking at the operation of the family as a whole. Structural family therapists, for instance, might work on establishing clearer boundaries between, on the one hand, the parental system of the mother and father (they need, one way or another to do the parenting) and, on the other hand, the children, so that Mary and (in his own much less obvious way) Ricky will not have to feel so responsible for looking after everyone.

If you are involved in social work or health visiting or some other profession which involves working with families having problems, you will doubtless have noticed how preoccupied people often seem to get with the question of 'whose fault is it?' or 'who started it?' or 'who is to blame?' Indeed, you may have noticed this within your own family or your own personal relationships. You may also have noticed that arguing about this rarely, if ever, seems to result in a solution.

From a systems perspective, these are simply the wrong questions. They are *linear* questions, applied incorrectly to *circular* systems, which means that arguing about them is a bit like arguing about which came first: the chicken or the egg (or about whether the thermostat controls the room temperature or vice versa). It is the whole system that needs to be looked at if change is going to come about.

THE FAMILY LIFE CYCLE

If we look at family systems rather than at individuals, not only do we need to jettison linear explanations for behaviour in favour of circular ones, we must also set aside linear models of development in favour of *cyclical* ones. By linear models, we mean models such as that of Erikson which sets out life in ascending stages beginning with birth and ending with death. Individuals *are* born and grow older and die in that order but a family is not born and (except in catastrophic circumstances) does not die, and birth follows death within a family almost as surely as death follows birth.

Indeed, it is perfectly possible for a family to be dealing simultaneously with the death of one of its members and the birth of another, and it is a certainty that any family will be dealing with several of Erikson's stages all at the same time. As Monica McGoldrick, Nydia Garcia Preto and Betty Carter point out, a family is usually at least a three-generation system, and nowadays often a four- or even five-generation one (2016a: 1). It is not unusual for a family to be dealing with the transitions involved in adolescence, those involved in mid-life and those involved in the onset of old age, all at once, because parents are typically at the mid-life stage when their children reach adolescence, and grandparents are typically at or past retirement age. When we look at families as systems, growth and development are a cycle and not a line. But it is a cycle of a particularly complex kind, because events do not follow one another round and round in order like the cycle of the seasons. In a family, winter, spring, summer and autumn may all be happening at the same time.

McGoldrick et al. consciously offer their family life cycle model as an alternative to the linear and individual model of Erikson. While acknowledging that Erikson's model set out to 'to highlight the interaction of the developing child with the society' (2016a: 7), they suggest that it does not go far enough. Erikson's stages, they argue (echoing Carol Gilligan's critique discussed in Chapter 6, p. 121), 'actually emphasize not relational connectedness of the individual but the development of individual characteristics (mostly traits of autonomy) in response to the demands of social interaction' and, in so doing, 'they devalue by neglect most of the major tasks of adulthood: collaboration, interdependence, intimacy, caring, teamwork, mentoring, and sharing one's wisdom' (2016a: 7).

Stressors and system levels

For families, as for individuals, how they cope with these challenges will depend in part on their history. McGoldrick et al. (2016a: 16, 19–21) speak of 'horizontal stressors' and 'vertical stressors' (an idea we touched on in the previous chapter). 'Horizontal stressors' are challenges which are thrown up by the passing of time. They include both *predictable* events, like the birth of a child or the onset of adolescence, and *unpredictable* events, like illness, or redundancy, or divorce, or the discovery that a child has a disability. They also include events which will be absolutely central to some families' experience but completely alien to others. For example, in the modern world, millions of families are uprooted from their homeland, or broken up, or both, as a result of migration, whether this is for economic reasons or to escape tyranny or war. In other contexts, moving house within a single town may be the only physical move that a family ever has to deal with. 'Vertical stressors', on the other hand, are a sort of inheritance that is transmitted down through the generations of a family. For instance, some families have a history of mental health problems, some are unable to talk about sex, some are preoccupied with educational achievement, some have strong religious or political allegiances stretching back for many generations which individual family members cannot easily challenge, some have a pattern of absent fathers, or of powerful matriarchs, or of difficulties in coping with adolescence, or of drinking and violence. The possibilities are as numerous as families themselves.

You may remember from Chapter 2 that Erikson's model envisaged that different stages in life throw up new challenges ('crises'). These challenges are among the events that we are now calling 'horizontal stressors' but McGoldrick et al.'s term is much broader, since it covers, as we have seen, not only predictable life transitions but also unpredictable or unique events. Erikson also suggested that when we attempt to negotiate a new life challenge, we may have to revisit challenges from previous stages that have not yet been fully resolved. These pieces of unfinished business from earlier stages are what we are now referring to as 'vertical stressors'.

However, as we have seen, Erikson's model deals with individuals, albeit in a social context. The model we are now discussing looks at the horizontal stressors as challenges that are not just encountered by an individual but by a whole family. And it sees the issues from the past which make up the vertical stressors as coming, not just from an individual's own past, but from the history of the family as a whole, perhaps going back for many generations. Adolescence, for example, is not just a challenge for the individual concerned, but for her parents, and perhaps for siblings and grandparents as well. How well the family copes with it will depend not just on the history of the individual young person, but on the parents' own experience of adolescence, and perhaps their parents' before them.

But just as individuals belong to families, so do families belong to wider systems. Each family is part of a community, a social class, a culture, a society. … Each of these is a different 'system level', and each system level has its own horizontal and vertical stressors. Nations, for instance, have to deal with new events in the here and now (horizontal stressors) but they also have to deal with the legacy of history. If you look at recent events in parts of the world such as Israel/Palestine, you can see how whole societies have to deal not only with the day-to-day 'horizontal' issues that every nation faces, but also with the 'vertical' legacy of fears and aspirations that come from their particular history. (Thus, a huge vertical stressor for all Jewish people is of course the Holocaust, while for the Palestinian people, taken as a whole, the major vertical stressor is the mass flight from their historic homeland known as the Nakba.) Just as individual lives take place within, and are shaped by, their family contexts and family histories, so the lives of families are shaped in turn by their social and cultural contexts.

At any system level, difficulties are likely to occur when a horizontal stressor interacts with a vertical one. That is to say, the most challenging times are likely to be when something that is happening now touches on some painful and unresolved issue from the past. When this happens in a family, 'there tends to be a quantum leap in anxiety in the system' (McGoldrick et al., 2016a: 21), which may make it difficult to successfully complete the changes necessary to deal with the new horizontal event and move on from it. For example:

- If you come from a family with a history of difficulties with parenting, or loss of children, the birth of a child will produce heightened anxiety, far above the level of anxiety which this new event would produce in other families.

- If you come from a family where sexual abuse occurred, there are likely to be anxieties through the generations about physical contact and sex - even assuming that sexual abuse itself doesn't recur through the generations, which it frequently does.
- If you come from a family where great store was placed on intellectual achievement, then there will be high anxiety around exams and so on. The discovery that a child has learning difficulties might cause particular problems for such a family.

Often the same theme will emerge in different ways in different generations. A family with problems around the issue of *control* may in one generation be obsessively controlling, and in the next generation have problems with setting boundaries at all. Both these patterns, though apparently opposite, are problems with control. For example, one may sometimes encounter drug addicts who have had great difficulty in controlling their habit or any other aspect of their lives, whose parents are very highly controlled and controlling. While the drug-using child and the controlling parent may seem poles apart, they are both exhibiting difficulties around the question of control.

Probably the best way to look at this question of horizontal and vertical stressors is to consider some examples of how they might work in practice. The following activities may help with this.

Activity 9.2

Looking at your own family of origin, can you think of any examples of vertical stressors that seem to have been passed down the generations? You may be able to identify these stressors by looking at the kinds of events that your family seems to find particularly difficult, as these would be the occasions when horizontal and vertical stressors interact.

Or consider the following case example and ask yourself what horizontal and vertical stressors are interacting here:

Janice is 42. As a child, she was abused by her stepfather, sexually and physically. Her mother could not cope with her and at the age of 13, she entered the care system. She had several moves within the care system and suffered further abuse there at the hands of a male residential social worker.

She is now a single mother of three sons, each by a different father.

The two older sons are both teenagers and are now completely out of her control. They are not attending school. They are both offending regularly and using drugs. They come and go from the house as they please. They are aggressive and abusive to their mother if challenged.

Janice has asked for professional help with the two boys: she says she has lost it completely with them and she thinks they should be in care.

Comments on Activity 9.2

We don't know what vertical stressors you noticed in your own family but in Janice's case, we would suggest that there may be vertical stressors to do with:

- Adolescence – Janice's mother could not cope with her as an adolescent, and she has no confidence in her own ability to cope with her teenage sons. Further exploration might well reveal that a history of children being evicted from the family at adolescence goes back for several generations. It is not hard to imagine that the two boys in turn will find it hard to cope assertively with their own adolescent children when they themselves become parents.

- Male sexuality and aggression – Janice was abused by her stepfather and by a male worker in care. She has not had a stable relationship with a man. She is finding it hard to cope with her sons now they have reached the age of sexual maturity. Again, the history of abusive men might well turn out to have gone back further into the past. And again it is easy to imagine that the two boys will grow up to become men who are abusive to women and girls.

In the last chapter we looked at how disability affects the whole family system, and how the birth of a child with a disability is one of those moments when horizontal and vertical stressors are likely to intersect and react with each other (see p. 164). You may also have professional or personal experience of your own of how families cope with disability.

━━━ Activity 9.3 ━━━

Drawing on this, can you think of:

- horizontal stressors that might result from the presence of a child with a disability
- vertical stressors that might exist in particular families which might make successful family adaptation to having a child with a disability more difficult
- stressors that might exist at the system level of the wider society that might affect a family's ability to adapt.

Comments on Activity 9.3

A child with a disability may place extra stress on a family for the entirely practical reason that she requires more care than other children and therefore makes more demands and takes up more time. The need for care may also go on for longer than for other children. As well as demands on time, there may be additional demands on the family's money, its space and its capacity to ask for outside help.

Vertical stressors would include particular concerns, preoccupations or anxieties which might be triggered by the presence of a child with a disability. We earlier suggested that these might include a preoccupation with intellectual or sporting achievement, but many other issues might be brought to the fore. For example, issues about responsibilities for providing personal care might be highlighted. (Consider a family where, up to now, it has been accepted

(Continued)

(Continued)

in practice that personal care is a woman's job, although there has been some resentment about this on the part of the women in the family. What would be the impact of a child who requires enormous amounts of personal care?) Or, in some families where there are anxieties on the part of family members about getting enough care or attention, the arrival of a child with considerable needs for personal care might well increase anxieties and tensions. You will no doubt be able to think of many other instances such as these.

Some disabling conditions, like cystic fibrosis and Duchenne muscular dystrophy, can be inherited, as can some forms of visual and hearing impairment. This may lead to guilt on the part of the parents, combined with complicated feelings about their own genetic inheritance, and also to anxiety about future parenthood, making this both a vertical and a horizontal stressor.

Moving to other system levels, you might have considered the different social context that exists in societies such as some Scandinavian countries, where there is a high level of public provision for children with disabilities, as against societies where there is none, and where making provision is the financial and personal responsibility of the family concerned. You may also have considered the different beliefs, values and prejudices about disability that exist in different social contexts.

STAGES IN FAMILY LIFE

Taking a family as opposed to an individual view of human development, we see that each developmental stage – birth, adolescence, marriage, divorce, remarriage, retirement, death – affects the whole family, and not just individual members of it. And each stage sets tasks for the whole family. When your children become adolescents, for instance, this poses challenges for you as a parent, as well as for your children. And when you grow old and frail and cannot cope with daily life on your own, this poses challenges for your spouse and your children as well as for you. In both cases, there are not just practical problems to be solved, but adjustments to be made to the way the whole family operates. In family systems terminology, a successful transition into a new phase normally requires not only a 'first-order' change, but a 'second-order' change. Alan Carr distinguishes between first- and second-order change as follows:

> First-order change involves a change in the relationships among elements in a system without an alteration in the rules governing those relationships. An alteration in these relationship rules is entailed by second-order change. (2012: 78)

We earlier used the example of a card player who wishes to change from poker to rummy.

McGoldrick et al. offer a table (2016a: 26–7) of family life-cycle stages. We are purposely not showing such a chart here, partly because we want to emphasise that the way families grow and change is cyclical not linear (the process has no beginning and no end) and several transitions can be taking place at the same time. We also wish to acknowledge, as these authors themselves take pains to point out, that families do not necessarily all go through the same stages. Many families, for example, have to deal with separation, divorce and remarriage, but others do not. And some families may have to deal with challenges that other families do not have to contemplate at all: migration to other countries, for example, or the complete disruption of family life by warfare.

But we will now look at some of the transitions that families characteristically have to negotiate together.

Young single adults leaving home

When a young adult leaves the parental home, this involves a transition for the whole family. Not only does the young adult have to revise his or her role, but the parents and grandparents will need to redefine theirs in relation to the young adult and to the other parts of their lives. Many families find this hard. Some parents encourage the young person to remain dependent, and some young people do indeed remain dependent. Others do the opposite and try to break off contact with their family of origin, thus perhaps denying themselves the possibility of genuinely renegotiating the relationship (so that they remain stuck with a sort of adolescent attitude towards their parents).

Sometimes, young adults find it difficult to leave the parental home at all. It is important to acknowledge that there are some factors at work here that are not just to do with the family, like the difficulties, particularly for young people, in obtaining secure and affordable housing, which have increased greatly in the UK in recent years, leading them to continue living with their parents for longer than in the past. These are aspects of a wider system level than the family, the level of society as a whole, which we will discuss in the next chapter. But we also need to consider what might be going on for the other family members, as well as for the young person and the parents. It may be that there is a general anxiety throughout the system about what will happen to the parental marriage after the 'nest is empty'. If so, the young person staying at home may well be the system's attempt to shore this up. We might find, for instance, that there is pressure of various kinds which makes it difficult for the youngest to leave home.

Couples, marriage, separation and divorce

When people come together as a couple, this is usually seen as the joining of two individuals but if we look at families as systems, then the couple relationship involves changing two entire systems which overlap, to develop a third system. This is always challenging for the two individuals at the centre of it, who bring different expectations and preferences to the newly created couple, but it is also a challenge for the family systems which those two individuals have come from, and are still part of, and problems with renegotiating relationships within that wider system may often cause problems within the couple. For instance:

- The couple's parents may interfere too much and the couple may find it difficult to stop this. That is, they may find it difficult to create a sufficiently strong boundary around their own sub-system to allow it to become a genuine system in its own right (you may remember the analogy of the amoeba that would simply dissolve if it was not contained by a membrane). It might be, for instance, that a young man's mother finds it hard to relinquish the close relationship with her son that she had when he was living at home, and he is afraid to hurt her feelings by resisting, and this may create difficulties in his relationship with his partner. Solving the problem may involve not only the couple both changing their behaviour, but his mother accepting that she now has a different role.

- On the other hand, the new couple may go to the opposite extreme, and cut themselves off as an isolated twosome. This could come about as a reaction to the older generation being too intrusive and refusing to deal with the couple as autonomous adults. The couple's attempted solution may cut them off from support which they actually still need and may create difficulties between them. A more durable and helpful solution might involve not only the two of them but also the wider family making, or accepting, changes.

- Sometimes one or both of the members of the couple may still be too enmeshed in their family of origin to be able to invest in a real new system or to accept the implications of the new arrangement. For example, if a man continued to regard his mother as his first point of contact when he wanted to discuss problems and triumphs in his life, he might be effectively excluding his partner from feeling that they are really a couple. Suppose, for the sake of argument, that the couple's sexual relationship broke down as a result, you can see that it would probably be fruitless to try to deal with this in isolation as a purely sexual problem. The underlying problem would be to do with the son and his mother failing to make the adjustments necessary to allow the new couple system to get off the ground. The sexual difficulty is merely a symptom.

Just as becoming a couple requires adjustments of whole systems and not just of the individuals involved, so do separation and divorce, and the forming of new relationships and remarriage, when they occur. There are certain tasks which the members of the couple and the system as a whole need to complete in order to move on. Somehow, each partner needs to grieve for and move on from all the hopes and expectations, including 'future plans and fantasies' that were invested in the relationship (Ahrons, 2016: 383–4). Yet, at the same time, they cannot cut off completely because, particularly if there are children, the old couple relationship cannot completely cease to exist as a system, but must radically be renegotiated to take into account the new realities. And reconstituted family systems are likely to be even more complex, involving three or four, or even more, overlapping family systems rather than just two, and sometimes involving wide age differences which can cut across generations. For example, an older father with a new baby from a second or third relationship may have grandchildren the same age from a first relationship. Somehow new relationships need to be negotiated which allows the family's systems and subsystems to adapt to all of this.

Family members becoming parents

Again, this requires a change in the whole multigenerational system. The couple system must 'make space for children physically, psychologically, and spiritually' (McGoldrick et al., 2016b: 281), but members of the wider family, including the grandparents, must also make space for the couples to become parents. So, when parents experience serious difficulties in making the transition to this new role, it can reflect a problem with the whole system, and not just with the couple. Grandparents who have had difficulty in giving up their own role as parents can inadvertently prevent their adult children from feeling like parents themselves, and in some may even actively undermine them, while those who have struggled with aspects of their own parenting role may find it difficult to give the new parents the kind of support they need. And these patterns may well stretch back into earlier generations.

Adolescence

When children in a family reach adolescence, a new phase begins, in that fundamentally different boundaries need to be established. Adolescence is not just something that happens to an individual. Once again, it is relationships within the entire family that need to be renegotiated. In particular, parents at this stage need to change their attitude to control. It is no longer desirable or realistic to attempt to control every aspect of their child's life. Failure to make this shift might lead to the young person giving up on working her own way through to autonomous adulthood (perhaps resulting in 'identity foreclosure' or 'identity diffusion' as discussed in Chapter 6). Or it might result in the adolescent refusing to accept control, and parents getting frustrated at what (to them) feels like impotence.

This phase commonly coincides with the 'mid-life' of the parents, when they themselves will often be facing other new challenges of their own. For instance: 'parents may be called upon to be their own [ageing] parents' caretakers... [while] at the same time supporting their now often ornery adolescents' (Garcia Preto, 2016: 312). If there are marital problems at this stage, this is likely to exacerbate the young person's difficulties while also making it harder for the parents to work together to help resolve them. Not only can different stages of the family life cycle occur at the same time, but they impact on one another in complex ways.

Family members growing old

When members of a family reach old age, further adjustments are required in the family system for it to be able to cope with the new circumstances. Difficulties in making the adjustment may result from older family members refusing to give up the power they once had (trying to hang on to it through manipulation, for example), or alternatively opting for a passive, dependent role. Or they may result from younger family members, on the one hand, refusing to accept the lessening powers of the older ones and continuing to make the same demands on them as ever, or, on the other, treating them as completely incompetent and refusing to accept that they are capable of doing anything.

When parents become frail and dependent on others for care, the adjustment involved for the whole family system is very considerable, and is likely to churn up old difficulties from the past (vertical stressors). The adult children of the elderly person are confronted, perhaps, with their mixed feelings about their own childhood (when they were the ones who were dependent and the elderly parent was the one with the power). Siblings whose contact may have been limited to social gatherings, may now be forced to work closely together in arranging care for the elderly relative, and old sibling rivalries can often be reawakened.

This stage can often coincide with the previous stage discussed: as grandparents become old, grandchildren may be passing through adolescence.

The systems model of development: summing up

For a model of this kind, it is not necessary to insist that a particular sequence of steps is the only one possible (in different cultures, very different sequences may occur, and within a single culture, there will be many different patterns). What *is* central to a systems model, though, is the idea that, whatever the transitions to be gone through, their successful negotiation is a task for the whole system, not just the individual – and that problems that occur are problems for the whole system too.

Each family system negotiates or fails to negotiate these transitions partly as a result of the absence or presence of vertical stressors, some of which may be unique to that family, some of which may be pervasive in society generally. The implications for practical work with families are that it is important to be aware of the family as a whole, its culture, its vertical stressors and the pattern of relationships that exist within it. Successful transitions require the participation of the wider family system as much as possible.

It may be useful to measure these ideas about stages and transitions in family life against your own experience:

━━━━━━ Activity 9.4 ━━━━━━

Reflecting on your own experience of family transitions, either as an adult or as a child or adolescent, can you think of examples of how these were successfully negotiated, and of transitions which were more difficult? What were the factors in your family culture that contributed to this? Can you identify any vertical and/or horizontal stressors that were at work?

The transition that almost everyone reading this book will have experienced, or if not, will be contemplating, is the departure from the parental home. How did you yourself negotiate this? (If you are still living with your parents, ask yourself how you might deal with this transition in the future.)

How were you helped or hindered by your parents and other members of your family? Looking back on it, how easy did you make it for them to change their role in relation to you? Was there anything else going on at the same time (that is, a horizontal stressor) that made the process more difficult?

What 'vertical stressors' existed/exist in your family that might have added to the difficulties of this particular transition?

What aspects did you/will you/would you find difficult as a parent dealing with your own children making this transition?

Comments on Activity 9.4

Thinking about the transition of leaving the parental home, everyone's experience will of course be different, but the sort of vertical stressors that exist in some families might be:

- a history of parental marriages breaking down following the departure of children
- a history of depression on the part of one or both parents, following the departure of children

- a history of young adults entering into unhappy relationships soon after departure from home.

Horizontal stressors, as well as the transition itself, would be other difficult events occurring around the same time, such as:

- illness in the family
- separation or divorce
- a bereavement
- the family moving house
- a parent experiencing stress at work or losing a job.

Factors which would make this transition easier would be a family culture which encourages independence and self-reliance and parents who are able to let go of their hands-on parental role and move to a different kind of relationship with their adult children while still offering support and a secure base.

In terms of other family transitions, if you are older you may be in a position to see patterns of similarity and difference in vertical and horizontal stressors and in family culture across the generations as you compare, say, the way you were parented with your own experience of parenthood, or your own adolescence with that of your children.

LARGER SYSTEMS

As we have noted, the application of systems theory to families is something that is usually discussed in books on family therapy, rather than in textbooks on human development, and it has been tested in the therapy room rather than in the psychological laboratory. (The latter is true also of psychodynamic theory, incidentally, though psychodynamic theory has spawned a much larger theoretical literature and has found its way into most of the textbooks on psychological development.) However, it offers a developmental model which illuminates areas which might otherwise be neglected by the psychological models discussed so far in this book. No serious theory of human development ignores the context in which people grow and change, but the systemic model is unique in its emphasis on the pattern of relationships that form family systems.

It is important to remember though that, as McGoldrick et al. (2016a) repeatedly emphasise, the family (immediate and extended) is just one of a number of system levels, standing in between the individual on the one hand, and the community, culture and wider society on the other. One criticism that can be made of approaches to family therapy that focus too exclusively on the family system is that, by seemingly taking away responsibility from individuals and locating it in the group as a whole, it is in danger of ignoring the question of power. This is particularly apparent when the model is applied to abusive family situations where, as White et al. (1993: 58) point out, 'taking a supposedly "neutral" stance in therapy sessions tacitly supports the power imbalance which exists in the family resulting in the continued oppression of the victims'. McGoldrick et al.'s model (2016a) addresses this by including factors that exist not simply at the level of the family, but at societal and cultural system levels, such as sexism, homophobia and poverty.

Some members of the family have more power than others:

> People become drawn into habitual patterns that may not be to their individual liking, for reasons of economic survival [and/or] for protection of their young and their elderly dependants ... [and] choice will also be dependent on relative power related to age. (Barnes, 2004: 18)

And if we wish to understand *that*, we need to look outside of the family. Just as proponents of the family systems model can object to excessive focus on the individual as being too narrow, so could an excessive focus on the family system be criticised for failing to take into account larger systems, such as communities, cultures and societies. We noted in Chapter 5, when discussing the learning of gender roles, how difficult it was for one or two adults in isolation to change their child's perception of gender-appropriate behaviour, because of the pervasive influence of the wider society. This is an example of how a larger system, at a higher 'system level', can be more powerful than either the individual or the family. And these larger systems, like families, themselves grow and change and themselves have enormous importance to individual human development.

In the next chapter we will look further at this wider social context within which all human growth takes place, and consider our subject matter from more of a sociological point of view.

CHAPTER SUMMARY

- In this chapter, we introduced some basic concepts from systems theory and suggested that these ideas can be applied usefully to human groups, and particularly to families.
- We suggested that by looking at families in a systemic way, a new perspective is gained, which can be lost by more 'linear' and individually focused models.
- We then looked at a systemic approach to the family life cycle, contrasting it to earlier stage theories. In the systems model, development is part of a cycle. (From the point of view of a family, birth follows death just as much as death follows birth.)
- Finally, we suggested some limitations of a family systems perspective. We suggested that it was in danger of ignoring power differentials within a family. In addition, we argued that the family itself, just like a human individual, can be seen as a component of still larger systems.

Some aspects of these larger systems will be the subject of the next chapter, which looks at human growth and development from a sociological perspective.

Tangled Webs

The systemic perspective can be applied to any family or any group of people that comes together for any length of time, so it would be possible to apply it in some way or another to all of the Tangled Webs cases. We gave the following two examples at the beginning because the pressures and demands made on individuals by their families are particularly to the fore:

Maryam Begum's family (Case E). In this three-generation family, several transitions are occurring close together. Maryam, the oldest family member, has developed dementia, meaning that she has moved from being the one who looked after everyone, to the one that everyone has to look after. This happens in many families, of course, but dementia is particularly challenging because the individual ceases to be aware of what is happening. The middle generation, Jamal and Amina, are in their fifties, and are having to adjust both to becoming carers for the older generation (a burden which is falling particularly heavily on Amina), and to their three sons reaching or approaching adulthood. These transitions are all horizontal stressors, as is, in its own way, the ongoing hostility from their neighbours. The religious beliefs of the older two generations, and their history as immigrants who have experienced real poverty in their country of origin, add another layer of complication to all of this, which can be seen in this context as vertical stressors. The oldest son, 'Monty', has severed all contact with his family because he has found it impossible to make the transition to an autonomous adult in a way that seemed acceptable to his parents. (Or, to put it another way, the system was unable to adjust into a new form which everyone could live with.) What happened with Monty has in itself become a vertical stressor for the family, such that the second son, Kabir, aged 24 (who, it's important to note, is our sole source of information here), is finding it impossible to come out to his parents as gay, because he feels that it will be too much for them to bear, given what happened with Monty, and everything else that is going on. However, Kabir has managed to leave the family home, and embark on a career, while it would seem that the youngest son, Sajid, may find it difficult to break away from home (and the family business) at all. We might also consider the question of power differences, since it is possible to argue (on the basis of Kabir's account at least) that the family is organised very much around avoiding upsetting one individual (Jamal, the father), even if this means huge sacrifices by other family members.

The Dudley/Harris family (Case G). In the case of the Begum's neighbours the Dudley/Harris family, power differences are so acute that it seems very unlikely that an intervention based purely on working with the family as a system is likely to be successful or appropriate: the whole family seems to be organised around the needs of Lee Harris, father of Josh and partner of Lisa, who is the mother of Josh and the other three children. Why does Lisa put up with it? One way of looking at this is to look at the vertical stressors that may be present. Lisa, for instance, may bring to this family a history of abuse by men. At a different system level, the whole family lives within a culture which has historically accepted the domination of, and even physical abuse of, women by men. Lee, in turn, may well have a history which makes it seem to him essential to control and dominate, so that he has chosen a partner with whom he can do just that.

 You can access Tangled Webs by visiting **https://study.sagepub.com/tangledwebs**

Further reading

Barker, P. (2007) *Basic Family Therapy,* 5th edn. Oxford: Blackwell.

Barnes, G. (2004) *Family Therapy in Changing Times,* 2nd edn. Basingstoke: Palgrave.

Carr, A. (2012) *Family Therapy: Concepts, Processes and Practice.* Chichester: Wiley.

McGoldrick, M., Garcia Preto, N. and Carter, B. (eds) (2016c) *The Expanding Family Life Cycle: Individual, Family and Social Perspectives,* 5th edn. Boston: Pearson.

All of these books give clear accounts of the systemic model described in this chapter. McGoldrick et al. (2016c) is the one we have drawn upon most heavily in this chapter, because of its systemic focus on life-cycle transitions.

IT TAKES A VILLAGE

A SOCIOLOGICAL PERSPECTIVE

— TANGLED WEBS —

This chapter deals with the wider social context in which our lives unfold. If you want to look at some cases before reading this chapter, you could ask yourself, 'How do the circumstances in which this person or family is living their life (culture, social class, financial resources, ethnicity, religion, gender, sexuality, disability) make a difference to the options available to them as they grow up, become adults, become old?' Three cases you might like to look at are: **Max Sullivan and Gloria Johnson (Case F), Jenny Quinton and Gloria Johnson (Case C)** and **Mary Carpenter (Case D).**

 You can access Tangled Webs by visiting **https://study.sagepub.com/tangledwebs**

Let us return yet again to the scenario of the birth of a human being with which we started this book, and which we came back to in the previous chapter. But this time, let us pay more attention to the setting of the scene rather than the leading actors (the child, the mother, the father, the midwife, the doctor). In doing so, we will try to shed more light on some of the questions we asked right at the beginning of this book:

> *What will she become? Will she be the prime minister or an office cleaner? Will she be happy? Will she be healthy? Will she be loved? Will she win honours or commit crimes? Will she one day be in a place like this bringing her own baby into the world?*

Suppose that the birth is taking place in a hospital in a war zone, with the noise of shelling in the background, a shortage of medical supplies if anything goes wrong, and no safe place to take the baby home to. Or, in a hospital in South Africa serving a community struggling to cope with the ravages of AIDS, to a mother who is HIV positive. Or, in a society where the birth of a girl baby will be greeted with consternation, just because she is not a boy. Circumstances such as these will have a profound effect on the new-born infant and the family into which she is born.

The way we set the original scene made a lot of assumptions, reflecting what we accept as the norm in our culture and society. The mother will be there, of course, in any cultural context, but for all sorts of reasons, the father may not be. A crowd of other family members may fill the room, or the mother may be alone. The birth may not be taking place in a hospital at all, and this may be by choice or because that alternative is not available. The doctor and the midwife may not be available either, with the skills, resources and technology to deal with any complications that may arise during the labour or the birth. The chances of the happy outcome in our scenario are very different for different countries, and different social groups within each country.

Birth itself is a universal human experience, but the *way* it is experienced will vary hugely according to the social, cultural and economic context in which it takes place. What is true of birth is of course also true for the rest of our lives. How long we are likely to live, for instance, varies enormously depending on where we were born. The World Health Organisation Commission on Social Determinants of Health reported in 2008 on patterns of health inequality, and summarised its findings thus:

> Our children have dramatically different life chances depending on where they were born. In Japan or Sweden they can expect to live for more than 80 years; in Brazil, 72 years; India, 63 years; and in one of several African countries, fewer than 50 years. And within countries, the differences in life chances are dramatic and are seen worldwide. The poorest of the poor have high levels of illness and premature mortality. But poor health is not confined to those worst off. In countries at all levels of income, health and illness follow a social gradient: the lower the socioeconomic position, the worse the health. (CSDH, 2008: 1 [introduction])

In fact, the statistics from this report that made the news headlines in Britain were not those comparing different countries, but those from two different districts of Glasgow, close geographically but worlds apart in terms of wealth. Life expectancy in a poor inner-city district was 54, while in an affluent suburb it was 82 (CSDH, 2008: 32). While one can debate whether some of the factors in adult behaviour which contribute to this huge difference (for example poor diet, alcohol abuse and drug abuse) should be seen as lifestyle choices or socially determined factors, children have no choice about the circumstances into which they are born. Education, for instance, has a key role to play in children's life chances – not just their own education, but that of their mothers – and this is something that most children and parents have no choice about. The WHO report quotes evidence from several studies which show a strong relationship between the educational attainment of mothers and the survival, health and educational attainment of their children. It also reports that in 2008 an estimated 75 million children across the world of primary school age were not in school.

It is these wider social factors that we want to consider in this chapter.

A SOCIOLOGICAL PERSPECTIVE

'It takes a village to raise a child' is an African proverb (popularised by Hillary Clinton in the title of a book [Clinton, 1996]) which expresses the significance of the wider society in the course of individual development. Opinions vary about the degree to which it is a factor – those who take an individualist perspective would agree with Margaret Thatcher's famous dictum that 'there is no such thing as society' (Thatcher, interviewed by Keays, 1987), while another point of view is that the individual is defined by their relationship to others, and to the groups and communities which are formed by these networks of individual relationships.

What is this alternative view of the individual? Broadly, it is a sociological view. We can only touch briefly on a few relevant sociological concepts in this chapter, but sociological perspectives intersect with and relate to many aspects of what we have already discussed in previous chapters. For example, we have already looked at one model for thinking about the individual in relation to others in Chapter 9: family systems theory. In Chapter 8 we pointed out that 'disability' is not simply a matter of individual impairment but about the way that people with impairments are seen and responded to by the rest of society. And taking it further back, when we looked at object relations theory (including attachment theory) we were considering how our development is profoundly influenced by our earliest relationships with those around us. Donald Winnicott (discussed in Chapter 2) famously said, 'there is no such thing as a baby', meaning that it makes no sense to think of a baby in isolation; he can only function and be understood in relation to his mother as part of the mother–baby dyad (Winnicott, 1975 [1958]: 99). The sociologist Norbert Elias makes a similar point when he states that, 'The concept 'individual' refers to interdependent people in the singular, and the concept 'society' to interdependent people in the plural' (Elias, 1978: 125). The infant is socialised first by the mother or primary caregiver, then by the rest of the family – and then by the wider community of extended family, neighbours, friends and social institutions with which he comes into contact. And as he – or she – grows up, he will increasingly play his part in shaping the lives of others in a process of mutual influence and exchange.

Although there is a sense in which Margaret Thatcher was right to point out the danger of talking about society as if it were a concrete, objective entity (she went on to say that there are only individual men and women, and of course this is true), 'society' is a word that describes the way these individuals interact with and relate to each other, and the institutional structures through which those relationships are shaped, and within which they are contained. To fail to take account of the influence of society on the course of human growth and development is a bit like trying to describe learning to swim without mentioning water.

In Chapter 7 we looked at the lifespan approach to human development, and saw that one of the features of this approach is an understanding of the interaction between the individuals and their environment. Closely related to this is the more sociological life course perspective (Hunt, 2005), which takes account of the fact that, as we have seen throughout this book, the categories with which we understand the growth and change of human beings – ideas like childhood, adolescence, old age – are themselves uncertain and shifting all the time, as is the context within which human change takes place. This applies particularly to age and life stages, but also to social status, family, community and value systems. The term 'life course' is seen as one that 'does not assume a stable social system, but one that is constantly changing' (Hunt, 2005: 21). It emphasises the social construction of human experience, as opposed to the biological processes of growth, development and ageing.

In the rest of this chapter we will explore some aspects of the interface between sociology and psychology as it relates to human development. We will look at social construction and some of the social mechanisms which shape our understanding of ourselves and the developmental options open to us, and then we will consider some of the aspects of the social world which influence the direction of our development; class, gender and culture.

BRONFENBRENNER'S ECOLOGICAL SYSTEMS THEORY

The psychologist Urie Bronfenbrenner made an important contribution to the understanding of the relationship between individuals and their environment with the development of his ecological systems theory. Working on the frontiers of psychology and sociology, he based his ideas on the work of the sociologist Kurt Lewin, and was also influenced by Piaget. Lewin, writing in 1935, had begun to explore the way that personality and environment react together to influence an individual's behaviour. Bronfenbrenner pointed out that subsequently more attention had been paid by academic theorists and researchers to the individual, psychological perspective than to the environmental, social one (Bronfenbrenner, 1979: 16). This led him to develop his own model of the ecological environment, which he described as 'a set of nested structures, each inside the other, like a set of Russian dolls' (Bronfenbrenner, 1979: 3). You will see the obvious similarity with the notion of 'system levels' we discussed in Chapter 9.

The four structures/levels/settings he identified are:

1 microsystem - the immediate setting in which the individual finds themselves, for example home, school, work
2 mesosystem - the network of relationships between the different interacting microsystems which make up the individual's world

3   exosystem – those settings where the person is not present, but which nevertheless affect them, for example the effect on young children of factors relating to their parents' employment, or the effect of a planning decision taken by the local council on the street where you live
4   macrosystem – the wider cultural context in which the smaller systems are contained, and through which ideology and values are transmitted.

This model offers a way of understanding how individuals relate to the environment in which they find themselves, and how cultural norms and values are transmitted to individuals and played out in relationships. The interconnections and transitions between the different levels of the ecological system are as important as what happens within each level, and movement between them often involves a change of *role* for the individual – a concept to which we will return later. Incidentally, if you are a social work student, you will recognise Thompson's well-known PCS (personal, cultural and structural) model of anti-oppressive practice as a multi-level systemic model of this kind (Thompson, 2016).

SOCIAL CONSTRUCTION

Another influential perspective on the relationship between the individual and the social world is that of social construction, a term first used by Berger and Luckmann (1967). Like Bronfenbrenner's theory, it places the individual essentially in a social context. It sees the reality of the social world we experience as constructed out of the interactions between individuals and groups in society, and mediated through ideology and culture:

> …the developing human being not only interrelates with a particular natural environment, but with a specific cultural and social order, which is mediated to him by the significant others who have charge of him. (Berger and Luckmann, 1967: 66)

The social model of disability discussed in Chapter 8 is a good example of how social construction operates. The reality of a disabled person's experience is constructed by her interactions with the world around her. For someone who uses a wheelchair, the inability to walk is a physical, personal fact, real in any social context, but the degree to which this is experienced as a disability is dependent on the degree to which the society in which she lives makes it possible, or impossible, for her to interact with it. She will literally be excluded from buildings where there is no provision for wheelchair access, and she will also feel excluded in more subtle ways by a culture which does not reflect positive images of people like herself. If she never sees media images of wheelchair users taking part in mainstream activities alongside non-wheelchair users on an equal basis, and if those around her relate to her in a way that assumes she is unable to do things for herself, she will have a further obstacle to overcome as well as the weakness in her legs – her socially constructed lack of belief in her ability to play a full part in society.

Language is an important part of this process because it is a major medium of the social interaction between individuals and groups.

> Our sense of who we are depends on what meaning others make of us and how they convey that meaning back to us. This is an essential premise that underpins all of social constructionist thinking: the sense of who one is, the self, the I, are all constructed in the interaction between the individual and others. (Campbell, 2000: 16)

Language which has negative, patronising or stereotyping connotations is one of the ways in which disability is socially constructed, hence the importance attached to the language used in areas such as disability or ethnicity. So for example we now talk about 'people with disabilities' and not 'the handicapped'. However, the difficulty is that there is also a constant interaction between language and the people who use it. Finding the 'right' word does not make the prejudices and assumptions behind the original 'wrong' word go away, and in time these negative connotations attach themselves to the new words too. 'Handicapped' replaced the even more negative term 'cripple', and was seen as acceptable in its day. So long as the experience of these excluded groups is described in the language of the mainstream world, and the voices of those groups themselves are not heard in the words chosen to speak about them, language will continue to have a tendency to reinforce social exclusion and restrict the developmental pathways available. To some extent language shapes what is possible and what is not.

SOCIAL ROLES

One of the ways in which social construction operates is through social roles – the cluster of expectations which become attached to a particular position, status or job.

> Institutions are embodied in individual experience by means of roles ... By playing roles, the individual participates in a social world. By internalizing these roles, the same world becomes subjectively real to him. (Berger and Luckmann, 1967: 91)

In order to make sense of new information about the diverse world in which we find ourselves, we need some kind of map – so we look for a category or a label to tell us how to act in new situations, or what to expect of new people we encounter. Social roles help us to do this. For example, when we meet someone for the first time one of the first questions we are likely to ask is 'what do you do?' because the answer to that question will tell us a lot more than what their job is. We are trying to find out about their social status, what we have in common with them, and whether we want to get to know them better. Asking about their job role is a short cut to doing this, because we think we know the kind of person who is likely to be a teacher, a policeman or a demolition worker. (Of course, like all short cuts, this can sometimes lead us badly astray!)

The word 'role' comes from the world of the theatre and acting. As Shakespeare says in the well-known passage from *As You Like It* (2008 [1599]):

All the world's a stage

And all the men and women merely players:

They have their exits and their entrances;

And one man in his time plays many parts ... (Act II, Scene vii: 138)

Shakespeare goes on to describe the 'seven ages of man' – a sixteenth-century version of the stages of human development. We see one man passing through and being transformed by a series of roles, from the 'infant mewling and puking in the nurse's arms', and the schoolboy, growing up to become in turn lover, soldier and magistrate, before reaching old age and finally declining into 'second childishness'.

Roles are not just descriptive – they are prescriptive. Shakespeare's description above charts an orderly progression through the life cycle, in which the lover's role belongs only to youth, and it isn't possible to be both a lover and an old man. As we noted in Chapter 7, progress through life is not always as neat as this, but the 'social clock' which tells us what society thinks we ought to be doing at a certain age influences and constrains us. Social roles carry a heavy weight of expectation. And of course, in the terms of the life course perspective we discussed earlier, they also depend on the social context of the time. For instance the 'parts' Shakespeare enumerates, from schoolboy to magistrate, were only available in Elizabethan England to men, and indeed this was the case for several more centuries.

A famous psychology experiment by Zimbardo and colleagues (Haney et al., 1973) showed how powerful the influence of role expectations can be in determining how we act. Two groups of American university students were invited to take the roles of prisoners and guards in a simulated prison situation for a maximum of two weeks. The volunteers were all considered to be mature and well-adjusted. The guards' brief was simply to maintain order in the prison situation. In spite of the fact that there were no pre-existing differences or divisions within the group, within the first few days there was an extreme polarisation between the two groups assigned to the different roles, with the prisoners rebellious, violent and distressed, and the guards behaving towards the prisoners in a brutal and intimidating fashion. This extreme reaction was a surprise to the team conducting the experiment, which had to be concluded early because it was becoming dangerous.

This is a dramatic example of the influence of role expectations on behaviour, showing how frighteningly quickly we can 'grow into' the roles which are assigned to us. You can probably think of everyday examples from your own experience, such as a colleague at work being promoted to a managerial role, resulting in a change in your relationship with them. Some of the roles we play in the course of our lives become a significant and permanent part of our identity, such as parental or professional roles. Others are adopted only briefly, like becoming a member of the audience at the theatre. Some roles may or may not become permanent. For example, we become a patient when we visit our doctor, but if we become chronically ill, the role of patient will become a more central part of our identity. Some roles we choose (like applying for a particular job, or choosing to go to the theatre and become a member of the audience), while others are thrust upon us (like getting ill and becoming a patient). But the distinction between chosen roles and involuntary roles may not always be clear. All kinds of factors, both to do with our individual circumstances and with wider social forces, may limit the choices available to us as we progress through life, or steer our development in a particular direction. Think, for example, about the many steps in the process by which our baby might end up in the very different roles of prime minister or office cleaner, and the choices which might or might not be open to her along the way.

━━━━━━━━━━ **Activity 10.1** ━━━━━━━━━━

1 Thinking of yourself at this moment in your life, what roles do you play? Examples might be parent, partner, carer, manager, student, clown, listener, organiser - which are the most import-ant ones? Which ones are you most comfortable with? And which do you find difficult? Are there any roles from which you feel excluded because of your background or other factors? We are not always aware of the different roles we play, but if you have recently experienced a change of role, for example, if you have just become a student, or a new parent, it may be easier to start by thinking about this new role, and then of the other roles you play in your life (we often speak of 'wearing many hats').

2 You are probably reading this book because you have chosen a particular professional role involving caring for others. Have you always played this role in your life? And if so, has it been a chosen role or one you have felt you had to play?

Comments on Activity 10.1

You will probably have concluded that some roles feel more natural to you, while others sit less comfortably, and you may have considered the reasons for these differences. It may be that some roles are ones you feel you have chosen, while others have been forced on you. Sometimes we are uncomfortable because we feel that we are being asked to reverse roles - for instance, when a teacher signs up for an evening class, and becomes a student, with someone else in the teacher role, or when someone who is used to looking after others - such as a parent, carer, nurse or doctor - themselves needs to be looked after because of illness or incapacity. Often the discomfort comes from the fact that a more powerful role is being exchanged for a less powerful one. We may also be uncomfortable in a new role because we do not know what is expected of us, or are not confident that we can meet expectations. As we described above, social roles are all about what is expected of us by others - 'society' - in specific situations. You may remember that Erikson characterised the adolescent life crisis as identity versus role confusion (see p. 114), and the challenge of the transition to adult life presents us with many new roles all at once. If we are able to meet this challenge and make the right choices, playing these new roles successfully will contribute to our developing a sense of identity.

STEREOTYPING AND LABELLING THEORY

Stereotyping is what happens when unfounded generalisations such as expectations about roles become too rigid, and leads us to lose sight of the fact that those about whom we general-ise are individual human beings. So we will have a set of assumptions about a particular group of people – what they will be like, how they will act – which will colour our real-life experiences of them. Gender stereotyping is one example; racial stereotyping is another.

Labelling theory describes how those who are stereotyped may respond to the expectations by becoming what they are expected to become, and how, once a label is applied, it becomes very difficult to see beyond it. It was first proposed by Howard Becker (1963) in his work on deviance, and has also been applied to other areas such as mental illness and educational attainment. Rosenthal and Jacobson (1968) demonstrated the effects of teachers' expectations on their students' performance by selecting a group of students at random and telling their teachers that the students showed potential for developing their intelligence. IQ tests then showed that these students had progressed more rapidly than their peers. You may yourself have experienced the effects of being 'labelled' either positively or negatively in the past, per-haps by a teacher, or by some other powerful figure in your life, and be able to reflect on the effect this has had on you. Perhaps you were told you were good at sport, or that you could not sing, or that you were very caring?

━━━━ Activity 10.2 ━━━━

Jamie is just about to start a new school, having moved house with his mother after his parents' divorce. His new teacher meets his old teacher at a training day before the beginning of term, and they get talking about Jamie. His old teacher says that she found him very difficult and is glad that he has moved; he was disruptive in class and she doesn't think he is very bright. What effect is this likely to have on Jamie's subsequent progress in his new school?

Comments on Activity 10.2

It is likely that Jamie's behaviour in his old school was affected by the family's stress around the break-up of his parents' marriage, and he seems to have given his teacher a hard time. Now he has an opportunity to make a new start, so it is unfortunate that this informal encounter between his teachers took place when it did. Professional written reports would be more likely to confine themselves to factual information and to avoid general judgemental statements. Hopefully his new teacher will have read this book! He will have to work hard to set aside what he has heard and the sinking feeling that will go with the news of a potentially disruptive newcomer to his class, and to approach Jamie's arrival with an open mind. If he accepts the two 'labels' that his colleague has given Jamie – 'disruptive' and 'not very bright' – his behaviour is likely to communicate these expectations to Jamie, and this will have a negative effect on Jamie's ability to put the past behind him and reach his full potential.

When outsiders look at a particular group and make stereotyped assumptions about it, this in turn affects the self-perceptions of those who belong to that group, and what they are able to achieve. Stereotyping is an important aspect of the social model of disability, and it also powerfully affects people with mental health problems. The assumptions that are shared by outsiders and insiders are reflected in the way that society is organised, and the way in which its social institutions function. If you were a woman living in Britain in the nineteenth century, for example, you would have been unlikely to consider yourself capable of achieving a university degree because universities were not open to women. And they were not open to women because of the assumptions of the time about a woman's role, which, for middle class women, was exclusively concerned with marriage, homemaking and raising children, and was seen as a subordinate one to the role of the man who was active in the world outside the home. And if you were a working-class woman your very limited education and your economic position, as well as your gender, would have placed a university education beyond your reach or imagination.

While belonging to a particular group within society can make us the object of stereotyping and negative perceptions, it is also a highly significant aspect of our sense of identity. We 'identify with' other members of the same group, and the sense of belonging and solidarity which this gives can empower us and influence the development of our attitudes and opinions. We are members of a group from the first day of our lives, and that family group is held within a system of other groups, as we saw from Bronfenbrenner's model.

There is a difference between *primary groups*, where there is real interaction between group members (clubs, etc.), and *secondary groups,* where there is not. The term *primary group* was first used by the American sociologist Charles S. Cooley, who described it as a group which 'involves the sort of sympathy and mutual identification for which "we" is the natural expression' (Cooley, 1909, cited by Sprott, 1958: 16). In Bronfenbrenner's terms, primary groups are part of an individual's microsystem and secondary groups belong to the exosystem or the macrosystem. We have more choices about the primary groups we join (church, university class, football team), but the secondary groups we belong to (community, ethnic group, gender) are often those that are more visible to others.

We define ourselves, not only by the groups we belong to, but by those we don't belong to. The psychological defence mechanisms of splitting and projection, which we described in Chapter 2, operate powerfully in group situations and lead people to locate all the good in the group which they belong to, and all the bad in the 'other' group. Divisions and rivalries between different groups in society such as neighbourhoods, gangs, football teams and ethnic and religious groups are common everywhere in the world.

As we have seen, an individual will be part of many different groups, large and small, within society. The groups we belong to are a part of the identity which we recognise for ourselves, and also of the identity which others ascribe to us. Thus our membership of them will affect us in complex ways. These may be positive, adding to our sense of self and belonging, but there may also be a negative effect which undermines our confidence and limits our opportunities. We have considered in previous chapters the effect of the immediate family group on the course of our development, and in the first part of this chapter we have thought about how the development of our identity is also influenced by the wider social systems in our immediate environment: the groups we engage with and the roles we choose, or are assigned. In Bronfenbrenner's terms, we have been focusing on the microsystem and the mesosystem. We will now turn our attention to the exosystem and the macrosystem: those broader aspects of society with which we don't engage directly, and whose influence on us may be less immediately apparent. We will consider, very briefly and broadly, three of the most significant lines along which society divides: gender, class and ethnicity.

DIVISIONS IN SOCIETY

Gender

In Chapter 5 we explored the processes by which we learn gender roles as we grow up, and we acknowledged that these roles are, at least in large part, socially constructed. The social construction of gender in Britain, Europe and the USA has changed hugely in the last few generations. Women now take their place alongside men as equal players in the public sphere rather than being confined to the domestic world, although there are still factors which work against them, such as the so-called 'glass ceiling', the process whereby women are often prevented from reaching the top ranks of organisations by prejudices, assumptions and restrictive practices which, like glass, are not readily apparent to the outside observer, but nevertheless create an impenetrable barrier. And women's pay continues to be lower on average than that of men, in spite of equal pay laws. In 2018 in the UK, government legislation came into force requiring larger companies and organisations to report on their gender pay gap. This revealed that eight out of ten paid women less than men (Guardian, online). When it comes to parenthood, in spite of the fact that it is now the cultural norm for both parents to be involved in caring for their children, in practice it is still usually women who carry the majority of the domestic and childcare responsibility, and whose careers and earning potential suffer as a result. This is borne out by research on the gender pay gap showing that it increases as women get older (Dex et al., 2008).

Class

Social class is another factor which can strongly influence the course of individual development, both because of the part it plays in defining identity and because of the extent to which it creates or restricts life choices. Some have declared class to be dead (for example, Pakulski and Waters, 1996, in the *The Death of Class*. Others take a different view; for example, Westergaard (1995) maintains that class inequalities hardened in the late twentieth century, with the richest increasing their share of wealth and income at the expense of the poorest in society. To understand this debate it is important to distinguish between social inequality and a class system. Those who argue that class is no longer relevant do not deny the existence of social inequality, or of hierarchies of power and influence, but would argue that the differentiation is between individuals, and not organised along class lines, and that class no longer creates a barrier to the progress a talented person can make. Income, of course, is not the only factor which defines social class, although it is important, and it is linked with other factors such as education, power and prestige. The definitions of social class that are commonly used for research purposes are organised around the work people do, whether they are professionally qualified and how much responsibility they carry, and broadly speaking, the higher the social class, the higher the income.

This raises the issue of social mobility: how easy it is for an individual to move from one class to another in the course of his or her lifetime. Is equality of opportunity in modern society a reality or merely a slogan? Social mobility has been much studied and debated by sociologists in the last half century, beginning with John Goldthorpe's work in the 1960s (Goldthorpe et al., 1969). More recent research in Britain suggests that an individual's chances of moving from one social class to another have actually declined (Blanden et al., 2004). A press report on these findings summed them up thus:

> Britain is 'seizing up' and social mobility is declining. ... Today's middle classes, many of them the sons and daughters of people who climbed the social ladder in the 60s, are consolidating their hold on high status and highly paid jobs and blocking the ascent of children from lower class backgrounds. (Walker, 2002)

Putting these findings in an international context, a further study (Blanden et al., 2005) compared social mobility in eight Western countries and found that it was lowest in Britain, with the USA not far behind, though it was only in Britain that it had actually declined. A recent report from the international Organisation for Economic Co-operation and Development on income inequality focuses particularly on this issue, and is entitled *A Broken Social Elevator? How to Promote Social Mobility* (OECD, 2018: 4).

So in terms of opportunity, class remains an important factor in today's society. And it is still an important aspect of our identity. An analysis of interviews conducted with a cross-section of Manchester residents in 1997–9 concluded that people wanted to see themselves as 'ordinary' individuals rather than identifying strongly with a particular class, but that the context of social class was still important: 'Class does not determine identity, but it is not irrelevant either. It is a resource, a device, with which to construct identity' (Savage et al., 2001: 888). Class may be a changing phenomenon, but it continues to be a factor that influences our course through life, and helps to determine who we become.

Race and ethnicity

The concept of race is now generally seen as a social construct: 'it has no biological basis and is more to do with how people classify physical differences' (Hunt, 2005: 45). Ethnicity and nationality, however, are important aspects of identity, and of course they can be combined in many different ways. An ethnic African Caribbean person may for example be British or American by birth and nationality, and for each individual the relative importance and meaning which they attach to their ethnicity and their nationality will be different, for all sorts of complex reasons to do with family history and relationships and past and current social and cultural experience. Writing from the perspective of social anthropology, Thomas Hylland Eriksen defines ethnicity as concerned with 'aspects of relationships between groups which consider themselves, and are regarded by others, as being culturally distinctive' (2002: 4) though he acknowledges that in everyday usage it has become associated with minority issues in particular. His definition, because it is based on social construction – the way that the identities of self and others are perceived – allows for the possibility of flexibility and change over time. This seems essential in today's rapidly moving and often contradictory world, where globalisation brings us together one minute and drives us apart the next.

Belonging to an ethnic minority group in a society can also have a profound effect on life chances through the forces of stereotyping and social exclusion, as we will see in Activity 10.3 below. The Joseph Rowntree Foundation reported in 2017 that the UK poverty rate is twice as high for Black and Minority Ethnic (BME) groups as for the white population (Joseph Rowntree Foundation, online).

Poverty, inequality, power and social exclusion

In considering these divisions in society, poverty and inequality emerge as significant factors. These are huge and complex social issues which we can only touch on here. What do we mean by poverty? Definitions of poverty can be absolute or relative; that is, it can be defined in terms of basic human needs like food and shelter, or in relation to what is generally seen in society as an acceptable standard of living. But in fact there is always a social context; even what is considered adequate food and shelter will vary from one time and place to another. For example, in the UK and elsewhere in the first half of the twentieth century having no indoor toilet was quite common, whereas now it would be regarded as unacceptable. Relative definitions of poverty, however, place it firmly in the context of inequality and social exclusion. It means not having the resources and choices that are generally taken for granted, for example, access to the internet or the money for family holidays or school trips. The definition of poverty itself can be a political issue, as is the question of how governments should deal with it. The welfare state in the UK, which was part of the post-war reconstruction and supported consensually by all governments until the 1980s, has increasingly come under attack from the neo-liberal right, who believe that it is a factor contributing to poverty rather than a means of addressing it.

Inequality is increasing worldwide. Figures from the Organisation for Economic Co-operation and Development show that it is at its highest level for more than half a century (OECD, 2018). And a powerful argument can be made that poverty is an issue that has an effect on the development and life chances not just of those who are poor, but of those across the whole of society. In their book *The Spirit Level* Richard Wilkinson and Kate Pickett (2010) present evidence that inequality in a society affects the well-being of all its members. They found that health and social problems were more prevalent across the whole range of income in countries where inequality was greater.

Another recurring theme has been that of power and influence – who has it, where it comes from, how it is exercised in society and what it means to be without it. In our birth scenario we looked at the chances of the baby ending up as prime minister or an office cleaner (see Activity 1.2), and we thought in terms of nature and nurture. In this chapter we have been focusing on aspects of nurture that are beyond the immediate control of parents, and belong to the wider social context. For example, if our baby is the child of the Smiths, a long-term unemployed father and an office-cleaner mother, they will be unable to afford private education for their child, and are unlikely to be in a position to move to the catchment area of a 'good' school, or to provide the extras like music lessons, sports clubs and trips abroad that can supplement a basic education. Statistics show that the overwhelming majority of those going to university are from middle-class backgrounds, and that this is particularly true of the elite universities whose degrees are the passport to careers which command high salaries and a high degree of social influence (Reay et al., 2005). Life is rather like a Monopoly game in which the rules have been changed so that some players start with thousands and others start with almost nothing. Depending on your social class, your ethnic background, your gender and where you were born, there are huge variations in the options that are available to you, which will be affected by how you are seen, and 'labelled' by those around you. Racism, sexism and other assumptions based on stereotypes are powerful forces of social exclusion.

━━━━━ Activity 10.3 ━━━━━

Josh is an 18-year-old who likes to go drinking with his friends. When they have had a bit to drink, they sometimes shout and swear and damage property. How is this behaviour likely to affect his chances in life if he is:

- a white university student?
- unemployed and black?

Comments on Activity 10.3

If you concluded that a group of drunken unemployed black youths would be much more likely to attract the attention of the police than a group of drunken white university students, you would be right. And the evidence also shows that if Josh is arrested, he is more likely to be charged and convicted if he is black, thereby acquiring a criminal record which will damage his future prospects of employment. A study of data from 1999 to 2000 by Phillips and Bowling showed that African Caribbean people were significantly more likely to be arrested than white people, and if arrested, were more likely to be given a custodial sentence (Phillips and Bowling, 2002). There are different ways of interpreting the significance of these figures, but Phillips and Bowling conclude that there is evidence that racism is a factor. This kind of institutional racism was defined in the MacPherson Report into the police handling of the murder of the black teenage student Stephen Lawrence in London as:

> The collective failure of an organisation to provide an appropriate and professional service to people because of their colour, culture or ethnic origin. It can be seen or detected in processes, attitudes and behaviour which amount to discrimination through unwitting prejudice, ignorance, thoughtlessness and racist stereotyping which disadvantage minority ethnic people. (MacPherson, 1999)

The authors of this book are both white, so we do not have personal experience of institutional racism, but we have been struck by the fact that for black colleagues of a similar age to us, being stopped by the police is a fact of life. It is something that has never happened to either of us.

CULTURE AND HISTORY

The example above shows how the rowdy activities of unemployed black youths are more likely to attract police attention than those of white university students, so they will feature in media crime reports, affecting public perception of risk. The media and popular culture play a key role in the social construction of reality. News reporting gives us a window on the wider world in which we live, in local, national and international dimensions. Marshall McLuhan (1962) used the term 'global village' to describe the way that electronic media have transformed modern society to bring events beyond our own communities alive for us through the use of a combination of words, visual images and different points of view which have a far greater immediacy and intimacy than the written word alone. And, however true that was in 1962, the advent of the internet has brought us into even closer contact with what is happening worldwide on a minute-by-minute basis and the development of social media has given us a whole range of new ways to engage with this, and perhaps to become part of the story ourselves.

But if the media open a window on the world, it is often hard to keep in mind the limitations of the window's frame. There is much that we don't see because it isn't regarded as interesting or important by those who select the news, and news values are determined ultimately by the market – what will sell because people want to read about it or watch it. There has always been a reciprocal relationship between those who produce and those who consume the news, and this effect is intensified by social media. Popular culture becomes a kind of mirror. We talk about 'image' – which is a mirror word, and our image is part of our identity formation, reflected back from what we identify with in the wider cultural context. A major preoccupation of popular culture is lifestyle and fashion. It becomes particularly important in adolescence, when we are looking outside the immediate family for role models. It is often expressed through how we look – our haircuts, the clothes we wear, the music we listen to. The history of adolescence in Britain is inextricably linked with the history of popular culture, emerging in the 1950s with teddy boys, beatniks, mods and rockers in an unbroken but constantly changing line of fashions and groupings – to name any currently in vogue would be to risk with certainty their being out of date by the time this book is published.

It is not just in adolescence that image is important to us. Our identity is deeply entwined with popular culture all our lives – where we choose to live, which newspapers we read, where we go on holiday. Advertising of course has its part to play here; it constructs a narrative in which we want to place ourselves. The advertising industry has come a long way from the early days of simple exhortations to buy in bold capitals to become a sophisticated way of speaking to our aspirations and our conscious and unconscious desires for status, and of associating ourselves with particular groups by how we spend our money. And much thought is given to the location of advertising – to careful targeting of the message.

These patterns of cultural identifications and lifestyle preferences were described by the French sociologist Bourdieu (1984) as the 'habitus'. It is a useful concept which represents another way of thinking about social stratification which takes into account differences and distinctions that are more complex and elusive than those relating to occupation and social roles.

Our sense of identity is also bound up with history – both our own individual and family history, as we saw in Chapters 7 and 9, and the wider currents of national and international affairs and social and political change. And the interaction between culture and history is a powerful one. As an example of this, consider the way in which the history of the Second World War has been kept alive in Britain, although most of those who experienced it as adults are now dead. Watching *The Great Escape* on Christmas Day was for years as much part of the traditional British Christmas as turkey and tinsel. This kind of reworking of the past owes more to myth than to history. The narrative is one in which heroes are larger than life and good and bad are clearly delineated, with no room for moral ambiguity – a bit like the myth of the American West, as portrayed in countless films. It is the way in which the present tries to make a relationship with the past, and so construct a coherent narrative of identity. Often, there are competing narratives which contribute to this process. The Vietnam war, for example, has inspired a wide range of film interpretations over time, from the heroic, patriotic treatment of *The Green Berets* to the horrific and crazy fantasy world depicted in *Apocalypse Now*.

As well as the stories we are told, we have our own personal experience of history, which becomes a part of our identity. For example, the generation who can remember wartime and post-war rationing and shortages have a different attitude to consumption and waste from those generations who have grown up later, and those gay men who grew up when homosexual activities were still illegal are likely to find it much more difficult to be open about their sexuality than younger men. These differences in historical experience can make it difficult for different generations to understand each other, and living in a rapidly changing, post-modern society increases the difficulty of dialogue between the generations. It also affects the status of older people, as we will discuss in the next chapter. In cultures where the process of change is slower, the life experience of the older generation is a valuable resource to be drawn on, while in societies like our own, their knowledge and experience is more likely to be dismissed as outdated and irrelevant.

Life course theory, discussed earlier, emphasises the importance of the time and place of the individual's experience:

> Age cohorts are likely to have been influenced by the same economic and cultural trends so that members typically display comparable attitudes and values and can claim similar experiences. (Hunt, 2005: 23)

This is recognised in the way different generations are popularly labelled – baby boomers, millennials, generation X, for example. Within generations many of the formative experiences of different life stages, for example adolescence or parenthood, will be shared, and these will be very different across different generations.

This perspective of a constantly changing society has a long history; the Greek philosopher Heraclitus said that 'everything flows' and 'you cannot step twice into the same river' (as quoted by Plato, [5th – 4th century BCE] 1998). The following activity gives you an opportunity to consider how social change can affect the experience of individuals.

▄▄▄▄▄▄▄▄▄ Activity 10.4 ▄▄▄▄▄▄▄▄▄

Sally is an 18-year-old who has been going out with her boyfriend for six months when she discovers that she is pregnant. Think about the differences in her experience if this happened in 1958, 1968, 1988 or 2018. What choices would she have? What effect will this have on the rest of her life, her boyfriend's and her baby's? How will she be seen by her family, friends and neighbours? And what might her experience be in 2025?

Comments on Activity 10.4

You will probably have identified many differences. In terms of choices, in Britain, abortion was not legal until 1967. Before 1970, when the age of majority was lowered from 21 to 18, Sally would not have been legally adult. In 1958 Sally's choices would have been marriage (with her parents' consent), illegal abortion, leaving home to have her baby in secret in an institution and having it adopted, or social disgrace. Her family might also have taken the option of passing the child off as her mother's – a not uncommon solution to the dilemma for that generation. By 1968 abortion would have been a legal option, though one which would have been more readily available if she had the money to pay for it privately than if she had to rely on the NHS. And it was just beginning to be socially acceptable to bring up a child alone, or to live with a partner outside marriage, though this still varied hugely between individual families and communities. The stigma attached to unmarried motherhood continued to decrease, and by 1988 terminating the pregnancy, being a single parent, living with a partner and marriage would all have been seen as possible options in this situation. Today, marriage would be much less likely to be chosen as an option; in 2016 under half of births (47.6 per cent) occurred within marriage or civil partnership as opposed to just under 80 per cent in 1986 and over 90 per cent in 1963 (ONS, 2017). There will still be consequences for the young parent – such as the interruption of education and career plans or the foreclosure of adolescent identity formation which we discussed in Chapter 6 – but an unplanned pregnancy is unlikely to lead to the kind of social exclusion that was common in the past. Yet the experiences of the past can still be a factor in the present; the Sallys of previous generations are the grandmothers of today's young parents, and can offer support, or not, to those young people and their parents.

In speculating about how attitudes and choices might change in the future, we might expect the trend towards greater choice and less stigma to continue, and perhaps for advances in medical science to play a part in it. But other factors may work against this. Objections and challenges to legal abortion are regularly raised, and, particularly in the USA, this has led to changes of the law to reverse previous steps towards liberalisation. And the world we live in today is full of political and economic uncertainty which seems likely to continue; young people who have been unable to get educational qualifications and are less flexible because of parental responsibilities will be particularly disadvantaged by limited job opportunities and decreasing social support.

In this chapter we have tried to put individual human development into a social context. In the terms of Bronfenbrenner's ecological systems theory, discussed earlier, we have focused here on the exosystem and the macrosystem rather than on the microsystem and the mesosystem which are the focus of the rest of this book. We have only been able to outline a few sociological concepts, and to touch on some complex ideas which make links with history, philosophy, politics and cultural studies. We hope that you will be inspired to read more. The developing human being is always a figure in a landscape, and to study the one without some awareness of the other is to miss an essential dimension.

CHAPTER SUMMARY

- In this chapter we have been looking at the wider social factors which influence human growth and development.
- We explored what it means to look at the individual from a sociological point of view, and saw the importance of the framework of social structures and relationships within which we live.
- We looked at Bronfenbrenner's ecological systems theory as a way of understanding how social systems influence the individual.
- We considered the idea of social construction; that the way we see ourselves and our lives is strongly influenced by the individuals and institutions around us and our interactions with them.
- We discussed social roles, stereotyping and labelling theory and explored how they influence the development of our identity and our life chances. We looked at the ways in which the groups we belong to contribute to defining our identity.
- We considered some of the lines along which society is divided, and looked at aspects of gender, class and ethnicity which relate to our identity formation and our life chances, in the context of power and social exclusion.
- We explored the significance of the cultural and historical setting in which an individual grows up, and how this can affect intergenerational relationships.

Tangled Webs

Of course all the characters in our case studies are influenced, as we all are, by the kinds of social forces we have been discussing in this chapter. The three case studies we mention here are perhaps those where the sociological dimension is most apparent.

Max Sullivan and Gloria Johnson (Case F). Gloria's task of supporting her family and parenting her children is made more difficult by the pressures of poverty and racism. She is doing her best to avoid social exclusion, but the personal cost is high. We learn about these struggles from the perspective of estate agent Max, who is from a very different social background and class, and thus sees Gloria's life in sharp contrast to his own. If Gloria herself was talking about her situation, she would probably describe it as normal, nothing out of the ordinary. Max's professional role also makes him very aware of the changes and pressures in the housing market, which is a key aspect of the structure of society. In Bronfenbrenner's terms, it is part of the exosystem, and is influenced in its turn by the ideological values of the macrosystem which determine whether access to appropriate and affordable housing is regarded as a right, and a priority for a fair society, or something to be left to market forces.

Jenny Quinton and Gloria Johnson (Case C). We meet Gloria again in her role as carer for Jenny, a young woman with physical disabilities. This time we hear Gloria's voice, but not that of Jenny. Both she and Jenny's mother Libby share a commonly held view of disability – a well-meaning, protective attitude, but one which can contribute to the social construction of disability when it treats disabled people as not fully adult, and has difficulty recognising their right to self-determination.

Mary Carpenter (Case D). Mary is ageing and recently bereaved, and the case study gives us a perspective on the formative events, changes and losses over her life course. She has always lived in the same area, but in her lifetime she has seen its social structure (exosystem) change in ways that are now affecting her and adding to her sense of loss through loss of local shops, social facilities and general social cohesion. She is also affected by other social trends; her daughter, like many other younger people, has moved a long way away from the area where she grew up, so that Mary no longer sees her grandchildren regularly. Developments in information technology and social media can help to mitigate the effects of geographical separation by making a different kind of connection, but Mary has not so far been able to keep pace with these changes in ways of communication, and risks increasing social isolation as a result.

 You can access Tangled Webs by visiting **https://study.sagepub.com/tangledwebs**

Further reading

Berger, P. and Luckmann, T. (1967) *The Social Construction of Reality.* London: Penguin.
Hunt, J. (2005) *The Life Course: A Sociological Introduction.* London: Palgrave Macmillan.
Haralambos, M. and Holborn, M. (2013) *Sociology Themes and Perspectives*, 3rd edn. London: HarperCollins.

This basic textbook gives a good general overview of sociology, including the topics we have touched on in this chapter.

COMING TO A CONCLUSION

DIMENSIONS OF OLD AGE

— **TANGLED WEBS** —

If you would like to look at some cases before reading this chapter, we suggest you look at **Maryam Begum (Case E: Maryam Begum's family)** and **Mary Carpenter (Case D)**, two elderly women quite close in age, but in very different circumstances.

 You can access Tangled Webs by visiting **https://study.sagepub.com/tangledwebs**

We concluded the previous chapter by observing that the developing human being is always a figure in a landscape, and certainly it would make no sense to describe the experience of 'growing old' without reference to the landscape in which it occurs, for the role and status of old people varies enormously from one society to another, as does the age at which a person is seen as being 'old'. It is, as Pat Thane points out in her survey of social histories of old age and ageing,

> the stage of life which encompasses greater variety than any other. It can be seen, in any time period, as including people aged from their fifties to past one hundred; those possessing the greatest wealth and power, and the least; those at a peak of physical fitness and the most frail. In consequence of this variety many different histories and fragments of histories of old age are emerging. (2003: 93)

There are, of course, biological factors in ageing which are general to all societies, and there are also existential issues which seem likely to come to the fore in later life in whatever culture. (As we grow older, we are increasingly faced with the fact of our mortality, just as in early childhood we must come to terms with finding ourselves in a strange new world.) But how society manages these biological changes and existential questions – and the ways that are open to us to deal with them as individuals – varies from one social context to another.

In the UK and other industrialised and post-industrial countries, for instance, retirement from work is an important transition point in the process of growing old. But retirement is not a universal human phenomenon. It is an entirely culture-specific event.

> Until the development of public welfare schemes in the second half of the twentieth century, older people seldom had a chance to retire from work, and in most cases that meant being dependent on family support or individual savings ... It was only in the second half of the twentieth century that retirement became such a general phenomenon but nowadays it is a key part of the modern life-course and widely taken for granted. (Künemund and Kolland, 2007: 167)

These authors go on to observe that retirement is an example of what Kohli (1986) called 'the institutionalisation of the life course' – 'the evolution of a chronologically standardised sequence of life phases and life events ... arranged according to the labour force needs of the economies of industrialised societies' (Künemund and Kolland, 2007: 167). Another example would be the phenomenon of adolescence which, we suggested in Chapter 6, has come to be seen as a distinct stage of life partly as a result of the advent of compulsory secondary schooling. And as with adolescence, retirement is not only a modern phenomenon but a phenomenon of industrialised countries. In much of the non-industrialised world there is no compulsory retirement and no state pension, just as there is no compulsory secondary schooling. Even within the industrialised world, there are large variations in the age at which retirement occurs, as Künemund and Kolland discuss (2007: 168). In the UK legislation governing compulsory retirement and payment of state pensions has changed considerably over the last decade. The default retirement age of 65 was abolished in 2011, and from 2010 the age at which the state pension is paid is gradually being increased. This means that people will have to carry on working for longer in order to provide an income for themselves. This may be good news for those who enjoy their jobs and want to continue working beyond the age of 65, but not for others, particularly those working in physically demanding or stressful jobs, who will struggle to cope and maintain their effectiveness into their late sixties.

In broad terms, it makes sense to distinguish between the earlier and later stages of old age, and such a distinction is not new. In the England of several hundred years ago a distinction was drawn between 'green' old age and later old age (Thane, 2003: 98). Peter Laslett's book *A Fresh Map of Life* (1989) popularised the term 'third age' to describe the post-retirement phase of life, when people have the time and energy for learning and contributing to society, as distinct from the 'fourth age' of failing health and intellectual powers which may come towards the end of life. The term developed in the context of the University of the Third Age, a voluntary educational organisation in which older people share their skills and knowledge with each other.

We will now look in more detail at the changes involved in old age, but you might first like to consider the case example in the following activity. We should add that this example is not meant to represent a *typical* old person, but is intended to give an instance of the kind of issue that can arise for professionals working with old people.

Activity 11.1

Consider the following case study and ask yourself what position you might take, if you were a professional involved in the situation it describes – the general practitioner, a social worker, a community nurse, a member of the hospital staff ...

Miss Kipling (aged 82) lives in a house on her own with a large number of cats. She is very isolated, venturing out once a week for her shopping, but avoiding almost all social interaction with her neighbours. A niece, Mrs Yeats, who lives some way away, visits her a few times a year. Miss Kipling is physically quite frail. On several occasions, neighbours have had to call out the police on hearing her shouting, to find her lying on the floor where she has fallen and been unable to get up. On these occasions the police and neighbours have always been concerned about the dirty condition of the house, and its poor state of repair.

A recent fall resulted in a broken leg, and Miss Kipling is now in hospital. Mrs Yeats has been summoned as next of kin, and there is a strong feeling on the part of Mrs Yeats and the neighbours that Miss Kipling should not return to her own house, but should be found a place in a residential care home. The arguments given for this are that:

- Miss Kipling is clearly not safe, and could fall and lie for a long time without being found. It would be irresponsible to allow her to return, since it could easily result in a fatal accident.
- Miss Kipling's house and her cats are now a health hazard.
- Miss Kipling would be happier with company and others around her.
- It is not fair on Mrs Yeats or the neighbours to have the worry of her – and it is difficult for Mrs Yeats to keep coming at short notice.
- Miss Kipling is increasingly confused. According to Mrs Yeats, Miss Kipling showed no sign of recognition at first when she visited her in hospital, and seemed unsure as to where she was. Her neighbours suggest that she is becoming demented.

(Continued)

(Continued)

Having considered this case, and decided what stance you would take on it, ask yourself whether your thoughts would have been different if Miss Kipling had been aged 32.

Comments on Activity 11.1

You may have noticed that Miss Kipling's physical safety was assumed by the neighbours not to be Miss Kipling's own responsibility, but a responsibility that is being placed, unreasonably, on themselves. It seems to us that with younger people, we are more ready to accept that the taking of risks is a matter of personal choice.

It may have struck you too that, if Miss Kipling had been a young woman, the health hazard allegedly posed by her cats and living conditions might be a matter that neighbours would deal with by complaining

to Miss Kipling herself, or by taking the matter up legally. They would be less likely to suggest that Miss Kipling is not fit to have a home of her own.

Finally, it may have struck you that the neighbours are very quick to assume that Miss Kipling is growing demented. A younger person might well be confused in similar circumstances – a fall resulting in a broken bone, a long wait to be discovered, and then a hospital admission – but this would not, anything like so readily, be considered to be evidence of permanent mental decline.

PHYSICAL CHANGES

Physical decrepitude and poor health are not inevitable in old age. As Christina Victor observes, describing British data:

> The popular stereotype of old age as a time of universal and inevitable chronic health [problems] and impaired activity, is somewhat inaccurate. While the reported prevalence of a longstanding limiting illness increases with age, it is not a universal characteristic of later life. A little over half of men and women aged 85 and over living in the community report that they do not have a longstanding disability or illness that impairs their activity levels. (Victor, 2005: 141)

Victor goes on to note that the extent of chronic health problems in old age is linked to other factors such as class, gender, ethnicity and former occupation, which further undermines the notion that steep physical decline and ageing are necessarily linked. Citing Meltzer et al. (2000), she notes that people who had manual occupations are 20 per cent more likely to have a disability than people who had non-manual occupations. This finding is in line with the statistics from the World Health Organisation Commission on the Social Determinants of Health previously quoted in Chapter 10 (p. 194).

It is important to avoid having an expectation of inevitable poor health in old age, because such an expectation can be a self-fulfilling prophecy. If we receive negative messages when we are old such as 'Well, what do you expect at your age?' this is likely to actually discourage us from remaining active, resulting in a deterioration in our fitness. Nevertheless, some physical decline is of course a normal part of ageing, and the incidence of disability, physical and sensory, becomes higher as later life progresses, so that managing it becomes for many part of the challenge of this stage of life:

> I did think about moving because I wanted a walk-in shower, because I cannot get ... I mean before my husband died I couldn't get in the bath ... well, I could but I couldn't get out. But when he died I thought I couldn't have a bath, so my son fixed a shower up over the bath. But now since I have done this, and my back again, I can't get in to have a bath. And I have put in to the council to see whether I could have a walk-in shower, but oh no that was it, I am not disabled enough. ... ('Nancy', quoted by Peace et al., 2006: 143)

As the quotation also illustrates, another challenge of old age is the loss of others. Here the speaker is focusing on the loss of practical support when her husband was no longer there to help her get out of the bath, and this is an important aspect of bereavement for many older people with disabilities, adding to the difficulties they face with the activities of daily living. But, of course, the emotional impact of bereavement is also huge, as we will discuss in the next chapter, and the longer people live the more often they are likely to have to face this as they outlive their partner, siblings, relatives and friends.

COGNITIVE CHANGES

Some old people suffer severe short-term memory loss as a result of specific forms of dementia such as Alzheimer's disease or vascular dementia. It is sometimes assumed that such problems are a natural consequence of ageing, but in fact as Ian Stuart-Hamilton observes, 'dementia is not totally a condition that occurs in old age – it is simply far more *probable* that if a person develops dementia it will be in late rather than early adulthood' (2012: 219, his emphasis). He also notes, drawing on research carried out for the Alzheimer's Society, that severe dementia becomes more common as people live to an older age, rising from around 6 per cent in 65–69-year-olds to around 23 per cent for those aged 95 or older (2012: 220). However, psychological research confirms what most old people report: there is generally some deterioration in memory in old age, even in the majority of old people who do not suffer from any form of dementia. The problem seems to lie particularly in the area of retrieving items from memory. That is to say, the memories are still there, but are harder to locate, so that old people are more prone than younger people to the experience 'I know I know it, but I can't put my finger on it'. This is demonstrated by the fact that old people fare less well – in comparison to younger people – on tests of recall than they do on tests of recognition (Marcoen et al., 2007: 50).

This difficulty with retrieval may reflect a more general slowing down of some cognitive processes linked to changes in the brain. It is known that there is a loss of brain volume associated with ageing, but it is not clear exactly how this relates to psychological functioning (Stuart-Hamilton, 2012: 83–4). Old people do less well on tests of 'fluid intelligence', which are tests involving finding solutions to problems not previously encountered, as opposed to tests of 'crystallised intelligence' (Cattell, 1971), which involve problems that draw on accumulated knowledge (Marcoen et al., 2007: 51).

One type of intelligence that is traditionally associated with old age is the kind that is known as 'wisdom'. (Our guess is that if you were asked to call to mind an image of a 'wise man' or a 'wise woman', then that image would be of an older person.) Wisdom is a hard quality to define, however, with the result that it doesn't lend itself very readily to psychological tests, with their characteristic multiple-choice questions and puzzles. Nevertheless, some researchers have attempted to do so, by posing problems to subjects involving long-term issues and complex and ambiguous situations open to more than one interpretation. Interestingly, while not all old people did better on these tests, old people were more highly represented than other age groups among those who did do well (Baltes et al., 1992).

While there is a biological basis for some cognitive decline, external pressures also have a major effect on old people's cognitive functioning. Most professionals who work with elderly people will probably have noticed how old people can become dramatically more 'confused' (like 'Miss Kipling' in Activity 11.1) as the result of an admission to residential care or hospital – a form of psychological defence at a time of frightening loss of control over one's own life. This question of loss of control is a topic that we'll return to below.

TASKS AND CHALLENGES

Late adulthood – old age – is the last of Erikson's eight stages (see Table 2.2, p. 41) and he assigns to it a sort of summing-up task. You may recall that Erikson's model envisages that to understand a person at any stage of life you need to understand the challenges that they have had to confront at earlier stages, and the extent to which they have successfully or unsuccessfully resolved them. What is different about old age is that if we fail to negotiate *this* stage successfully, there will not be further opportunities later. Hence *integrity versus despair* is what Erikson (1995 [1951]) identified as the 'crisis' of this particular stage. A successful outcome would include: acceptance of one's life for what it has been, freedom from the burden of regret that it had not been different, and acceptance that one's life is one's own responsibility. Erikson referred to this as the achievement of 'ego integration'. An acceptance of one's own small place in the scheme of things could be said to be part of what is commonly referred to as 'wisdom', a quality which, as we noted above, is commonly associated with old age. So perhaps Erikson's 'ego integration' could be seen as the achievement of a kind of wisdom.

This statement from the British politician Lord (Denis) Healey at the age of 83, seems to us to illustrate what might be entailed in achieving 'ego integration':

> Personally, I did not notice much change until I was 75. From that age on, I have found my memory deteriorating and my senses getting less acute. ... I can distinguish between different vowels, but all consonant sounds are the same to me. I can fail to see something I am looking at when it is staring me in the face.

There is a saying that when you are old, you either widen or wizen. ... Physically I have wizened; I lost two stones in weight between the ages of 75 and 77. I can no longer run upstairs as I used to do. I find travel very tiring. Psychologically I have widened. I am much more interested in people as human beings and can imagine them at every age from childhood onwards when I see them.

I have lost all interest in power and position and no longer worry about making money. I still enjoy my work, but only what I want to do. ...

I am much more sensitive to colours, shapes and sounds. My eye will automatically compose a clump of flowers or a corner of a landscape into a picture. ... I get greater pleasure out of the sound of different instruments.

I have become exceptionally sensitive to sunlight, which immediately moves me to pleasure. ... I love my wife, my children and my grandchildren more than ever. ... (Healey, 2000: 3)

But Lord Healey had many advantages. He was no doubt comfortably off financially, he clearly had a caring family around him. He could look back on a distinguished career, which included serving as Chancellor of the Exchequer and deputy leader of the Labour party, in which he had many interesting experiences, met many interesting people and had ample opportunity to develop and use his talents. Not everyone adjusts so contentedly to the final stage of life. And for those who do not reach the state of 'ego integration', Erikson suggests, there can be despair, a sense that life has not been as it should have been and that it is now too late to change it.

This despair may be expressed as a contempt for people, institutions or the world in general, or as a retreat into a passive, helpless role. Successful ageing depends on the satisfactory resolution of issues raised earlier in life, but it also depends on external factors: the opportunities and encouragement available in a person's environment. And one of the aims of those who work with older people must surely be to maximise those opportunities, and to recognise the scale of the task that is involved in growing old.

The challenges of growing old require adaptation not just from old people themselves but from those around them. From a systems perspective (as discussed in Chapter 9), a successful transition into old age requires adjustments from the entire family system. Elderly couples, for instance, may need to renegotiate their relationship, and not just their individual lives, if they are to cope comfortably with the changing roles and more time together that result from retirement. The couple relationship may not always survive this transition, and separation and divorce in later life are becoming more common. Statistics in the UK show that the number of people over 60 getting divorced has increased since the 1990s, although it has fallen for the population as a whole (ONS, 2013). This is partly due to a higher proportion of older people in the general population and increased life expectancy, and also because divorce has become more socially acceptable, and women are less likely to be economically dependent on their husbands, and therefore have more choices open to them.

The wider family also needs to make changes. An ideal adjustment would perhaps be one in which the members of the extended family were sensitive to the possibility that it might be necessary to reduce their demands on ageing family members (for help in looking after grandchildren, for example), and to offer them additional support when necessary, yet without at the same time characterising them as more helpless or incapable than they really are. But how easily the family is able to make this adjustment will depend on family history (vertical stressors) and on the other challenges now facing the family as a whole (horizontal stressors).

The following activity looks at a fictional instance of a family struggling to cope with some of the challenges of old age.

Activity 11.2

What horizontal and vertical stressors can you identify in the family described in the following case example? (See p. 180 for a reminder about these terms.)

Mr and Mrs Patel (aged 80 and 75) came to Britain in the 1970s as refugees from Uganda, where Mr Patel ran a chain of grocery shops. When they arrived, they had no money, because their home and property in Uganda had been confiscated during the Idi Amin era. However, they were able to set up a new business (a convenience store), which is now run by their two daughters. Mr and Mrs Patel have no sons.

Mr Patel has always been reliant on his wife to provide for him in the home, and she is no longer really able to do this as she suffers from severe arthritis and is in fact physically much frailer than Mr Patel.

He is suffering from mild dementia as a result of arteriosclerotic illness, with the result that he forgets things after even a few minutes and is often muddled about who he is talking to. He sometimes imagines that he is back in Uganda, or even in India where he was born. He constantly imagines that his wife and daughters are plotting against him. He also requires pretty constant supervision from a safety point of view. He has turned a gas fire on without lighting it and has been picked up wandering in the street, not knowing where he is.

Mr and Mrs Patel have never had a very happy marriage. Both of them are rather 'highly strung', volatile people, and Mr Patel in particular can be domineering and 'bullying'. He has always found it difficult to come to terms with what happened in Uganda.

Mrs Patel's daughters say that she is being made ill by the worry and stress of trying to cope with Mr Patel and she is now on anti-depressant medication. Neither of the daughters is willing to have Mr Patel living with them, though they do try to provide support to Mrs Patel. Both daughters insist that for his own safety and his wife's health, Mr Patel should now be in residential care.

However, confused as he is, Mr Patel is still able to state, absolutely adamantly, and tearfully, that he does not want to have to leave his home. His one supporter in the family is his son-in-law Sanjay (now separated from Mr and Mrs Patel's older daughter), who says that Mr Patel has worked hard all his life to provide for the family, has had to cope with the constant nagging and attempts to undermine him of his wife and daughters – and does not deserve to be pushed out.

Comments on Activity 11.2

Among the possible vertical stressors you may have noticed are marital problems and a possible tendency for the family to polarise into male and female camps. The family's expulsion from Uganda, associated with a loss of property and prestige, is likely to make the suggestion of giving up his family home especially distressing for Mr Patel.

Among the horizontal stressors you might have included: Mrs Patel's arthritis, Mr Patel's arteriosclerotic illness, the current marital difficulties between the daughter and son-in-law, and perhaps the demands of running the family business.

Professionals providing services to older people (for example care coordinators, GPs or community nurses) really need to have some understanding of these family dynamics if they are to accurately assess the needs of old people and their carers in any given situation. It is not simply a question of gathering the 'facts'.

OLD AGE AND SOCIETY

As we have already observed, old age is, like adolescence (or adulthood, or childhood) as much a social construction as a biological fact. So what old age means to an individual will depend not only on factors like physical health and level of cognitive functioning, but on the messages they receive from those around them and from society at large. Even physical health and cognitive functioning are themselves directly affected by external circumstances and messages received from others (see the discussion in the previous chapter on 'labelling'). It is important not to assume that, because old people happen to behave in a certain way in certain circumstances, that behaviour is in some way inevitable. The debate about 'disengagement', which we'll describe shortly, illustrates this point very well.

Having noted that the way old people perceive themselves will be shaped by the world around them, one must bear in mind that the world is also changing. For instance:

- Demographic changes resulting from a declining birth rate and longer lifespans mean that old people are a larger proportion of the population than in most other periods of history, particularly in the industrialised world, where an estimated 29.9 per cent of the population of Europe will be over 65 by the year 2050 (Peace et al., 2007: 2). This is likely to have huge consequences for the status of older people in society and their relationship with the rest of the population.
- Differences in the average lifespan of men and women also mean that there are more elderly women than men.
- Rapid social and technological change in society generally, as well as longer lifespans, means that the world in which old people find themselves is vastly different from the one in which they grew up. This would not have been true to anything like the same extent in many pre-industrial cultures, where technology and social mores might remain relatively unchanged for generations.
- Social expectations about the participation of older people in the economy change over time (for example, retirement age) as do welfare provisions for old people (pensions, social care).
- The political 'clout' of older people may increase. People over 65 could constitute well over a third of the European electorate by 2050.

Disengagement

The term 'disengagement' was coined in the 1960s by Cumming and Henry (1961) to describe the generally reduced involvement of old people in the outer world. Models of ageing tended at that time to be *medical* models expressed in terms of deteriorating functioning, and the term 'disengagement' was supposed to provide a more positive way of describing – and thinking about – the process of letting go of external involvement that is typical of many older people.

Cumming and Henry suggested that this disengagement from external interests – along with other personality changes such as a preference for simple and familiar situations – does not represent any sort of reduced functioning, but rather a way of preserving energy for other tasks which have become more important. These tasks, in their view, were really of the kind envisaged by Erikson, to do with reflecting on, reviewing and coming to terms with one's life as a whole.

One obvious criticism of disengagement is that not all old people conform to that pattern. We can probably all think of elderly people who are just as engaged with the world around them as they would have been when young. Other critics of the idea, such as Estes et al. (1982), have pointed out that disengagement is often forced upon old people, for example by compulsory retirement or by institutional care. Old people do not necessarily *want* to give up their involvement in the world. The theory of disengagement, according to this view, simply lends legitimacy to a process by which society chooses to marginalise its elderly people and, so to speak, to tidy them away out of sight.

There is no reason, incidentally, why both Cumming and Henry *and* Estes should not be right. Disengagement could indeed be a normal and necessary psychological characteristic of old age, and yet also be exploited as a concept for political ends. You may remember from Chapter 3 that Bowlby's attachment theory may likewise have been taken on board by those wishing for political reasons to get women out of the industrial workforce, but this does not invalidate the theory itself.

Control

In Chapter 5, we discussed the idea that passivity and helplessness can itself be a form of behaviour that is learned in situations where we have no control. Many old people do experience a sense of reduced control over their environment for a variety of reasons, and this can lead to anxiety, depression and low self-esteem, and even to reduced physical health.

One study (Langer, 1983) demonstrated the importance of a feeling of control in a residential home setting. A group of residents was addressed by the home administrator with speeches that placed an emphasis on their responsibility for their own lives. The speaker encouraged them to make decisions and gave them actual decisions to make as well as asking them to take responsibility for things in the home environment other than themselves. Another group of residents was addressed by the same person with speeches that emphasised the responsibility of the staff of the establishment to provide care for them and meet their needs. Of the latter group, 71 per cent were found to become more debilitated in a period as short as three weeks, while in the former group, 93 per cent showed overall improvement.

The fear of losing control of one's own life is common in old age, but it is not necessarily an inevitable feature of old age. After all, some of the most powerful people have been old people. (For instance, Donald Trump was elected president of the United States at the age of 70, and Pope Francis was 76 when he became pope.) Just as disability is not only a result of impairments but also of society's attitude to people with impairments, so the feeling of losing control is in part a product of society's attitude to old people. Langer's experiment illustrates how a feeling of losing control – even if the feeling is as a result of no more than different *words* – can have a very dramatic effect on general well-being. Old people experience many difficulties which can lead to a feeling of loss of control. They may have limited financial resources, compared to people in work, and limited life choices as a result. Some, though not all, have to deal with physical impairments. All will be aware of at least some loss of their physical power, and be aware that younger people around them are physically more capable (old people may feel more vulnerable to crime, for example). And even if they are mentally and physically in very good shape, old people may have to deal with the *assumption* that this is not the case.

Indeed, in some contexts old people are treated as if they are not adults at all (infantilised) and spoken to as if they were dependent children ('Have we been to the toilet yet, Mrs Jones?'). Sachweh (1998, cited by Westerhof and Tulle, 2007: 246) found in a study of German nursing homes that 'baby talk', the high pitch and exaggerated intonation that is used in talking to small children, was used by staff in over half of the interactions with residents, and that 'we' as opposed to 'you' (as in 'have we been to the toilet?') was used in nearly two thirds of interactions.

Ageism

'Ageism' is a word coined by analogy with 'sexism' and 'racism' to mean the unwarranted application of negative stereotypes to old people. We've just mentioned the example of old people being patronised and infantilised, as if by being old they had ceased to be adult. The assumptions that are made about old people can be like the assumptions that are made by racists or sexists in that they result in judgements being made about old people which are not the same as those that would be made about younger people in the same situation.

We do not wish to portray all old people as necessarily victims of oppression and injustice. Many old people would not see themselves in such a light at all, and, as we have seen, there are positive as well as negative stereotypes of old age, and powerful old people as well as powerless ones. But negative stereotypes do exist and they do have an effect on people. If old people are labelled as 'bad-tempered', 'inflexible', 'senile' or whatever else, then they are likely to live up to the expectations created. Westerhof and Tulle (2007: 249), discussing the evidence for the effects of expectations on performance and self-perceptions, note that there is an extra twist when we impose negative labels on old people, since most of us eventually become old people ourselves. 'It has been argued,' they write, 'that as individuals age, the stereotypes they previously held about older people are turned towards themselves.' Ageism rebounds on the ageist! Like all stereotypes, stereotypes of old age are a 'short-cut' to try and make sense of something of which we have no direct experience, or to avoid thinking about it. Old age will always remain unknown territory until we reach it ourselves.

Certainly there *are* numerous negative images of old people. There are far more demeaning terms for old people than there are for other age groups. Think of 'wrinkly', 'fuddy-duddy', 'old dear', 'old fart', 'old crow' or 'old bat'. Indeed, only children seem to be comparable with the elderly in having derogatory terms (like 'brat') which are specific to their age group. A number of unwarranted generalisations are also made about old people's health and mental capacity, though the majority of old people are *not* sick or demented and there is no medical condition that is exclusive to old age. For example, as mentioned earlier, developing dementia tends to be associated with old age and is sometimes talked about as if it was an inevitable part of the ageing process (with terms such as 'going gaga' and 'losing her marbles' being used), though in fact it happens to only a minority of elderly people and can happen, albeit more rarely, to younger people also.

Another common assumption is that old people are no longer sexually active. Given that sexual activity is generally seen as one of the prerogatives of adulthood, this is perhaps an instance of the way that old people are 'infantilised' as a result of ageism. The fact is that old people tend to remain sexually active well into 'old age'. An American survey found for instance that, among the over-seventies, 79 per cent of men and 65 per cent of women reported that they were sexually active (Brecher, 1984).

In the political arena, old people are also sometimes negatively characterised as an unsustainable burden on the public purse, a 'burden' (to use a word which some old people seem to use about themselves) because of the cost of pensions, social security benefits, health and social care (see Westerhof and Tulle, 2007: 239). In the UK in recent years, as benefits and other financial support for younger people have been cut, a potential for intergenerational conflict is emerging as the so-called 'baby boomer' generation (those born in the years following the Second World War) reach old age and are perceived to have 'had it all' as beneficiaries of the welfare state in the course of their lives – student grants, affordable mortgages and now earlier retirement, and good pensions and associated benefits.

If we contrast the active, positive attitude of famous and successful elderly people – such as Lord Healey quoted earlier – with that of those who seem to have accepted, or felt forced into, a passive, dependent, childlike role, we can perhaps get some sense of the impact of ageism on old people who do not have the same advantages. Social attitudes to old people, however, are not fixed, and this is evidenced by the fact that in different societies, old people are viewed in different ways.

CULTURAL DIFFERENCES

Old people are traditionally seen as repositories of wisdom, but Western industrialised society does not place the value on the wisdom of old age that is, or was, given to it in other cultures. David Gutmann (1987), an anthropologist who compared attitudes to ageing in industrialised societies with attitudes in the Middle East and Central America, suggested that old age flourishes in a stable, coherent culture with well-defined traditions. In such a culture, women become more powerful in the extended family as they enter old age. Older men tend to disengage from day-to-day decision making and action, but become custodians for the values of their culture. In less industrialised societies, there is also likely to be more interdependency between generations as land is farmed together, and inherited by the next generation, while 'modern societies in contrast have pursued change and innovation, and moved away from intergenerational dependency' (Gilleard and Higgs, 2000: 43).

The constantly changing circumstances of modern society make these authoritative roles much harder to play because old people are a bit like time travellers. As discussed at the end of the previous chapter, old people at the beginning of the twenty-first century were brought up in a society vastly different from the one in which they now find themselves, with very different values and social mores. Though they will of course have adjusted to new developments over the years, the values they were brought up with were the product of a very different context. In a rapidly changing world, we may seem to have somewhat less to offer as we grow old than would have been the case if we lived in a society which did not change so very quickly, for the lessons we have learnt will quite often come from experiences which are no longer relevant to present-day experience.

This book is intended for those working in or studying for the caring professions, so we will end this chapter with an activity in which we invite you to reflect on how such professionals work with old people. It is worth remembering that our attitudes to older people are really our attitudes to our own future selves.

Activity 11.3

Erikson described the central task of old age as resolving the 'crisis' of integrity versus despair. Think of old people you've known or worked with, and try to think of instances of people who have managed to achieve some sense of integrity in old age - and others who have not. (The latter might be evident either as a resigned passivity or as a general hostility.) Can you see any common factors among those who manage to achieve integrity, and those who do not?

What role can professionals and others play in helping old people accomplish this task?

Comments on Activity 11.3

You have probably been able to think of some examples, though of course many old people will fall somewhere in between the two extremes. Resolving any 'crisis' (in Erikson's sense) is ultimately something that a person can do only for themselves, but it may have occurred to you that the modern welfare system is full of attitudes which can hardly help old people to feel positive about the last stage in their lives. Perhaps you felt that if we treated old people as (a) human beings (rather than merely logistical problems), and (b) adults (rather than quasi-children), this might help. One of the things that seems to be important in achieving integrity is to be able to look back on one's life with a sense of achievement and not too many regrets. But too often, interactions with older people by care workers (who may be the only social contacts they have) allow little time for anything but their present-day care needs, and so there is no opportunity to talk about and share the lives they have led, or the roles and relationships that have made up their past.

CHAPTER SUMMARY

- In this chapter, we looked at the changes that occur in old age, including physical and cognitive changes. While some common changes may be biological in origin, we should be careful not to assume that they apply equally to all old people. An assumption that all old people have poor health, for instance, would not only be unwarranted by the facts, but could also have the effect of being a self-fulfilling prophecy.
- We then looked at the particular tasks and challenges in old age, using Erikson's idea of old age as a time when our principal task is to come to terms with, or reconcile ourselves to, our lives as a whole. We also looked briefly at the challenges that old age poses not only to individuals but to families.
- We then looked at old age in a social context. We looked at the idea of 'disengagement', relating it to Erikson's model, but also asking the question as to what extent an old person's disengagement from the world is a psychological necessity, and to what extent it is actually imposed by society.
- We also discussed the diminished control over the rest of the world that commonly occurs in old age and its impact on the individual.
- We considered the impact of prejudice against old people: ageism.
- Finally, we briefly considered cultural differences and the consequences of living to old age in a very rapidly changing society.

In the next and final chapter, we will consider dying and death.

Tangled Webs

Two old people are included in the Tangled Webs case studies, though you may like to look at people in other cases and think about what old age may be like for them when they reach it.

Maryam Begum (Case E: Maryam Begum's family). In this chapter, we have discussed the idea of old people being like 'time travellers' who have arrived in the present from a very different time. For Maryam Begum, this is especially true. This is because firstly, in addition to having been born 81 years ago, she was born in a different continent, and in a society which is very different from the London borough where she now lives. (As her grandson Kabir observes, his grandparents were peasants, they were barely literate, and they were brought up with very traditional Muslim beliefs.) And secondly, Maryam has developed Alzheimer's disease, meaning that she is confused about where she is, and imagines herself to be back in the Bangladesh of her youth. (Actually when she was born, what is now Bangladesh was part of British India, becoming East Pakistan when she was about 12, and only becoming a separate country in its own right when she was in her thirties: Maryam has seen a lot of change in her life!) Because of her dementia, she has to be prevented from leaving the house for her own safety (something that might not have been necessary, possibly, had she still been living in a Bangladeshi village with little traffic and neighbours who knew her). The basic autonomy we associate with adulthood, in other words, has had to be taken from her, and she is supervised in the way that a small child is supervised, though she was once (by Kabir's account) a source of support and encouragement for all the family. If she can no longer understand where she is, or why this is happening, one can understand why she might feel angry and afraid, and lash out at those who are trying to look after her. While she must feel powerless, perhaps terrifyingly so, her impact on the family is huge.

Mary Carpenter (Case D). Mary is 77. Her GP has decided that she is suffering depression, and has prescribed antidepressants. Like many her age, she has some health problems (osteoarthritis and high blood pressure) but she appears particularly anxious about them. A nasty fall seems to have contributed to this. In fact she seems lacking in confidence and anxious about life in general. She doesn't like to go out alone, and has become socially isolated, as well as physically unfit, gaining a lot of weight, which aggravates her health problems. She lost her husband Ken two years ago, and in the case study she is being visited by a bereavement volunteer. At a superficial level, her withdrawal into her home could be described as a form of disengagement, but it does not feel like a choice she had made happily or willingly. A number of factors seem to be preventing her from reaching the kind of 'integrity' that Erikson identified as a positive outcome for this stage of life. She has not worked through the bereavement, and is still having difficulty seeing herself as a person in her own right, rather than part of a couple of which half is now missing; she can no longer perform the challenging role as a foster-carer which gave her life meaning; her grandchildren are far away in Australia, so that it is difficult for her to take on an active role as grandmother, to which, with all her experience and skills, she would probably have been particularly well suited. If her bereavement volunteer can help her move on from some of her losses, she may be able to feel more positively about this stage in her life. She still has things to offer, after all. We know that two of her former foster-children (Zak Renton and Tracey Green) are still in the area, and have greatly valued her support in the past. Perhaps she still has a role she can play in their lives?

 You can access Tangled Webs by visiting **https://study.sagepub.com/tangledwebs**

Further reading

Bond, J., Peace, S., Dittman-Kohli, F. and Westerhof, G. (eds) (2007) *Ageing in Society*, 3rd edn. London: Sage.

A particularly comprehensive collection of writings on many different aspects of the psychology and sociology of old age.

Stuart-Hamilton, I. (2012) *The Psychology of Ageing: An Introduction*, 5th edn. London: Jessica Kingsley.

THAT GOOD NIGHT

DEATH, DYING AND BEREAVEMENT

— TANGLED WEBS —

This chapter deals with death and bereavement. If you'd like to look at some cases before going further, you could look at **Mary Carpenter (Case D)**, who lost her husband Ken two years ago, or at **Tracey Green (Case J)**, who also lost Ken, but as a foster-father.

 You can access Tangled Webs by visiting **https://study.sagepub.com/tangledwebs**

We have put this chapter on death after the chapter on old age, so we should start by acknowledging that of course death is not the exclusive property of the old. Though death is the end of life, as birth, with which we started this book, is the beginning, we can die at any age. We may have to cope with the death of others at any age too, although as Sidell (1993: 151) observes, 'death has become increasingly unfamiliar to young people' in modern industrialised and post-industrial society. Most people live to old age and most people die in the relatively segregated environment of the hospital with the result that many people, for much of their lives, have little direct exposure to death. Many adults, for example, have lived through their lives without ever actually seeing a dead person.

It is certainly the case that in the UK, most people who die are old, and most die away from home. Of those who died in England and Wales in 2016, 84 per cent were 65 or older, and 68 per cent had passed their 75th birthday. Out of all deaths (at whatever age) in England and Wales during that year, just 23 per cent took place at home (figures derived from ONS, 2017b).

As with other events which we have discussed, death is both a biological event and a social one. Death occurs when the body ceases to function as a biological entity, but the meanings attached to it, both by the individual concerned and by those around her, are dependent on the complex web of personal and social circumstances in which the death occurs, as well as on the way of dying itself. Indeed, Clive Seale (1998: 34) makes the point that biological death and social death need not necessarily coincide:

> The material end of the body is only roughly congruent with the death of the social self. In extreme old age, or in diseases where mind and personality disintegrate, social death may precede biological death. Ghosts, memories and ancestor worship are examples of the opposite: a social presence outlasting the body.

Caroline Currer adds that there is actually quite a widespread fear of social death prematurely preceding actual death: 'There is evidence in certain cemeteries ... of mausolea with bell-towers with a connecting wire through into the coffin to enable the allegedly deceased person to ring the bell in the event of waking' (Currer, 2001: 25).

Here, we are going to look at death at three 'system levels' (to use a term which we discussed in Chapter 9, and also in Chapter 10). We will consider first death in the context of society as a whole, then (under the heading 'Death and others') death at the level of family and community, and finally death as an individual experience. But, as ever, dividing the subject up in this way is in the end an artificial device. All the topics under these headings could in fact be discussed with reference to each of these three levels. Religious belief, for example, can have a very direct impact on the individual experience of death, but religions are something developed and maintained at the level of society as a whole. Death itself is not just an event, but an existential question, one with which we struggle at every level and in every culture and social context.

DEATH AND SOCIETY

Dying takes place in a social context and how we deal with it is shaped in part by the society in which we live. Among the many areas of difference between different cultures and different epochs, are the following:

- The extent to which death and dying or dead people are a matter of everyday experience.
- Beliefs as to the existence and nature of an afterlife: All the world's major religions include some conception of an afterlife, but its components vary greatly. Consider, for instance, the ideas of heaven, hell, purgatory and limbo in Roman Catholic theology, the widespread belief in ghosts, or the Buddhist idea of a soul being reborn again and again on earth in different human and animal forms. In modern secular industrial cultures, many people do not believe in any kind of continuation of personal existence after death, but many still do.
- Cultural beliefs regarding acceptable and appropriate expressions of grieving: In some cultures an extravagant display of grief is encouraged, while in others restraint and containment of emotion are admired and seen as decorous.
- Funeral rituals and the treatment of human remains: The different practices that exist for the latter include cremation, burial, mummification and even 'sky burial', as practised in some Native American cultures, where human remains are placed on a platform to be consumed by birds.
- The extent to which dying people are made aware of the fact that they are dying: Cartwright et al. (2007), report considerable variations among doctors from different countries as to whether they would, in principle, always discuss with a terminally ill patient, topics such as the diagnosis, the incurability of the disease or life expectancy. For instance, only 11 per cent of Italian doctors surveyed said they would always discuss the incurability of the disease, with 64 per cent saying they would do so if asked, and 25 per cent saying they would not do so at all. By contrast, 98 per cent of Dutch doctors said they would always discuss this, 2 per cent said they would if asked, and less than 1 per cent said they would not do so at all.

We shall not attempt to cover all these topics in this chapter. What we will do now is look at two themes in current thinking about death.

The denial of death

According to one view of contemporary attitudes to death, we live in a society that denies death – and death is now a taboo subject in the way that sex once was.

According to this view, death is hidden in hospitals or institutions and we no longer know how to talk about death, or to help the bereaved, or to mourn properly for the dead.

A leading exponent of this perspective has been Ariès (1976), a French historian, who argued that in medieval times people were much more at home with death, which was visible all around them. He argues that in modern times medical science has led to the idea of controlling illness and controlling nature. Instead of believing in an afterlife, we comfort ourselves with the illusion that *this* life can be prolonged indefinitely by defeating death. So death becomes something to be battled against, as illustrated by the media cliché: 'X finally lost her courageous battle against cancer.' In modern times, it is argued, the doctor fighting disease has replaced the priest fighting for the salvation of the soul. Writing about how society copes with anxiety about death at an organisational level, Anton Obholzer also draws a parallel between the role of doctors and that of priests in the past:

> I believe that many of the organisational difficulties that occur in hospital settings arise
> from a neglect of the unconscious psychological impact of death or near-death on patients,

their relatives and staff. Hospitals are as much an embodiment of a social system that exists to defend society and its citizens against anxieties about death as are churches; from a psychic point of view, doctors occupy a similar niche to priests. (Obholzer, 1994: 171)

He also suggests that 'our health service might more accurately be called a "keep-death-at-bay" service'.

But, as doctors ultimately cannot abolish death, death has become segregated, hidden away. People avoid others who are bereaved or dying. Dying people are isolated as a result and deprived of support which they might otherwise receive.

This idea can be extended also to our treatment of old people. In the previous chapter, we discussed the concept of 'disengagement' (Cumming and Henry, 1961), and the debate as to whether disengagement in old age reflected a psychological need on the part of old people, or merely a need on the part of the rest of society to justify the marginalisation of old people. Kearl (1989) takes the latter argument further by suggesting that the purpose of disengagement is to remove from society those who are likely to die, so that the rest of us need not be confronted by the fact of death. There are two views on disengagement, and it is also possible to argue, as does Kalish (1985) that disengagement is a useful psychological preparation for dying, on the part of the individuals concerned. Kalish argues that disengagement is one reason that old people tend to find it easier to accept their own imminent death than do younger people: they have already begun the work of letting go.

This difference of view on disengagement reflects a difference of view on the whole 'denial of death' thesis. Many commentators would dispute whether the 'denial of death' in modern times is really as extreme as Ariès (1976) argued, or whether there has been such a fundamental change as he suggests in comparison with previous periods of history. Some degree of denial of death is surely inevitable to allow us to get on with our own lives, and probably always has been at any stage in history. Indeed, Seale (1998: 211) argues that our whole social and cultural life – the stories we tell ourselves about the nature and meaning of life – can be seen as defences against death:

> Social institutions which are reflected in the minutiae of conversational exchanges, are based on a successful but continuing active defence against disorder and decay, the root cause of which is the temporal nature of bodily existence.

Some psychoanalytic thinkers would argue that we battle not only against the fact of death but against our own 'death instinct', an innate drive towards annihilation:

> Besides the instinct to preserve living substance and to join it into ever larger units, there must exist another, contrary instinct to dissolve those units and to bring them back to their primeval, organic state. (Freud, 1961 [1930]: 118–19)

Melanie Klein in particular draws heavily on this concept and speaks of two instincts at war with each other. The ego is 'faced at the very beginning of its development with the task of mobilising libido [life-instinct] against its death instinct' (Klein, 1975 [1933]: 250). If we look at it this way, death becomes, not just an external enemy to be kept at bay, but a drive within ourselves to be managed, as we have to manage our other drives and longings.

'Revivalist death'

Since the mid-twentieth century something of a reaction has occurred to the medicalised model of death so that we now also have what Walter (1994) calls a 'revivalist' model, in which death is seen as an important stage of life to be, if not celebrated, at any rate experienced to the full. There would seem to be a close parallel here with changes of attitude to childbirth where, during the same period, there was a similar reaction against an excessively medicalised approach and towards a more personal one in which the individual concerned, rather than the professionals, is placed at centre stage. This changing view of death was reflected in the growth of the hospice movement.

In the 'revivalist' view the dying person herself is seen as choosing her own way of dealing with her own death, rather than subjecting herself to the control of doctors, and death is seen as a psychological process, rather than just a medical event – something to be worked through, rather than blotted out. Dying, in this model, is a process of coming to terms with the end of one's life, the final culmination of the process of integration which we discussed in the previous chapter. We should note, however, that the logical consequence of giving more choice to dying people about the manner of their dying means that some might actually *choose* the more medicalised model. The 'revivalist' approach is itself only one way of looking at things.

Society's attitudes to dying seem to fluctuate between several different perspectives. The practical implications of this for those working with dying or bereaved people would seem to be that it is important to be aware that there is no one 'right' approach, and that people may have very different views about the social context of death. It is also essential to have thought through one's own attitude on these matters, and to be aware of one's feelings about death in general. The Buddhist writer and teacher Soygal Rinpoche puts it like this:

> You cannot help the dying until you have acknowledged how their fear of dying disturbs you and brings up your most uncomfortable fears. Working with the dying is like facing a polished and fierce mirror of your own reality ... Looking at your fears honestly will also help you in your own journey to maturity. Sometimes I think there could be no more effective way of speeding up our growth as human beings than working with the dying. (Soygal, 2008: 183)

You may like to use the following activity to consider your own thoughts on this:

Activity 12.1

Should dying people always be informed that they are dying? And if not, in what circumstances should they not be informed, and who should take the decision not to inform them?

(Continued)

(Continued)

Suppose you are a doctor and your patient Mr J is dying of cancer. His daughter, who is his only sur-
viving relative, has been told that the disease is terminal and untreatable. She insists that Mr J should
not be informed of this, saying that it would be cruel and would cause him quite unnecessary distress.

On the other hand, Nurse B who is also caring for Mr J, feels very strongly that Mr J should be
informed. She says that, if it was her, she would certainly wish to be informed and would be very
angry if she was not informed, and was therefore deprived of the opportunity to say her goodbyes to
life. Nurse B does not consider that her daughter, or anyone else, would have any right to deny her
this information. To deny Mr J this information, she says, would be to deny him his right to be treated
as an adult.

What would you do? Would it make any difference to you if Mr J came from another country, and if
his daughter informed you that in their country dying people were not normally told the nature of
their illness?

Comments on Activity 12.1

The question of whether or not to tell
dying people that they are dying is not one
that has a final definitive answer, because
in different societies at different times,
there have been different views about
what is appropriate, and because different
individuals have different needs and different
ways of handling things. Your decision might
be simpler if you were able to establish what
Mr J's own views on this matter had been
in the past, or if you were able to find out
what was the norm in the country from which
he had come. (If Mr J came from a country
where dying people were not normally told, it
is likely that he himself would be aware that
this was the norm, and would not himself
expect to be told.) But, ultimately, you would
need to try to find some way of exploring
what Mr J's own wishes were. Does he really
want frankness, or does he cope better by
keeping his distance from the facts? If you
could take time to encourage him to talk
about his situation in an open-ended way,
with you or with another trusted person, you
might well pick up some clues to help you
decide how best to deal with the issue.

DEATH AND OTHERS

In Chapter 6, we discussed the psychological stages that are involved in transitions, moving
from initial shock and incredulity through depression and self-doubt to eventual letting go.
In Chapter 9, when we looked at the family life cycle from a systems perspective, we presented
the idea that every transition that occurs is not just a challenge for the individual but also for
every other member of their family network. This is true of marriage or the formation of a couple
relationship, the birth of a child, puberty, retirement, and the onset of old age. All of these events
require, to a greater or lesser extent, that a whole group of people have to find a way of letting
go of an old and familiar order of things, and (whether they wish it or not) to re-establish themselves as best they can in new and unfamiliar territory. And this is also true of death.

There are a few very isolated people whose death has little significant impact on anyone else, and some unloved people whose death is not mourned. There are also some people who are loved but whose death is felt more as a welcome release by all concerned than as a cause for sadness. But generally, for family and friends, the corollary of a death is bereavement and grief. In the case of deaths which are predictable, that grief does not just follow on from the death, but includes the 'anticipatory grieving' which can also be experienced by the dying person herself.

Grief is a reaction to what can be a massive disruption in one's social world. When we grieve for someone we loved, we are also grieving for the part of ourselves that we invested in that person. Freud noted the apparent similarity between mourning and melancholia (depression), but suggested that in melancholia this investment in the other is complicated by unconscious feelings, so that the person who has suffered the loss 'knows *whom* he has lost but not *what* he has lost in him' (Freud, 1957 [1917]: 245). This relates to the difficulties experienced by those with insecure attachment patterns which we discuss below. More generally, Seale (1998: 211) suggests that grief

> is in fact an extreme version of an everyday experience of 'grief' which is routinely worked upon in order to turn the psyche away from awareness of mortality and towards continuation in life.

In other words, Seale is suggesting that it is in the nature of life that we are constantly struggling with the possibility of death and loss. An actual bereavement simply brings our worst fears to the fore. We might use the analogy of a flood occurring in a landscape, such as the Cambridgeshire Fens, which is normally kept dry by constant pumping. The flood itself is an exceptional event but the possibility of it has never been far away.

The nature and extent of grief, and the ability of the bereaved person to come to terms with their loss, will depend of course on a whole range of factors, including the personal history of the grieving person, the nature of the relationship and the manner and timing of the death (see the discussion below, on timely and untimely deaths).

Attachment and loss

In thinking about bereavement, it is useful to go back to attachment theory. You may remember that John Bowlby's major works were entitled *Attachment*, *Separation* and *Loss* (1997, 1998a, 1998b), and it is of course sadly the case that the risk of loss is the inevitable price to be paid for the many benefits of forming an attachment. Colin Murray Parkes, in his study of bereavement, puts it like this:

> The pain of grief is just as much a part of life as the joy of love; it is, perhaps, the price we pay for love, the cost of commitment. (Murray Parkes and Prigerson, 2010: 6)

Murray Parkes worked closely with Bowlby, coming at the attachment theory from the perspective of studying bereavement, which has been his lifetime's work. Insights from his research and writing have been hugely influential in developing ways of working with those who have been bereaved, for example, through the charity Cruse in the UK (Cruse, online). The major aspects of bereavement reactions he identifies are:

1 an alarm reaction of anxiety and restlessness which feels physiologically like fear
2 anger and self-reproaches
3 post-traumatic stress reactions
4 pining and searching for the lost person
5 finding a continuing bond with the lost person
6 excessive, prolonged or distorted grief
7 a sense of dislocation between the world that is and the world that should be
8 a process of realisation, moving towards acceptance of the loss
9 helplessness and hopelessness; depression.

(Murray Parkes and Prigerson, 2010: 253)

Clearly, not all of these features will be present in every case. Every bereavement is different, as every individual and their history is different. It is not a stage model, though the earlier features on the list relate more to the initial, traumatic stages of loss, moving through the process of grieving to an adjustment, or not, as the case may be. You will notice echoes here of the model of transition described in Chapter 6 and summarised below. It also connects with Kübler-Ross's description of how people react to the news of their own impending death, which we will discuss shortly. There are also, of course, links with the stages that young children go through in separation from their parents, which we described in Chapter 3 (p. 50).

According to attachment theory, people who as children had a secure attachment with their carers are able to internalise the security that came from that relationship (the 'secure base') and this will not only help them to form satisfactory adult relationships, but will help them to withstand the pain of loss in the future. Sable (1989) undertook a study of widows who had lost their husbands in the previous one to three years. She found that women whose early attachment histories had been relatively secure coped better with their bereavement than women with histories of insecure attachment, experiencing less distress and less depression.

Writers on attachment theory suggest that we can identify characteristic grieving patterns for the avoidant attachment style and for the ambivalent attachment style. Avoidant individuals, who try to be self-reliant, often display delayed grief reactions.

> The typical attempts to be emotionally self-reliant and wary about forming intimate relationships means that the loss of someone close … triggers the usual defence mechanisms of emotional shut-down and distancing. In the short term at least the person suffering the loss may not cry or appear to be unduly upset. Those who fail to grieve remain vulnerable to future losses. Seemingly exaggerated grief reactions to a loss experience … can sometimes be accounted for when it is realised that the individual never really acknowledged or adjusted to the earlier loss of a significant attachment relationship. (Howe, 1995: 136)

On the other hand, ambivalently attached people seem to be more than averagely vulnerable to 'severe protracted grief' (Murray Parkes, 2006: 79). Howe suggests that people who have internalised anxious/ambivalent patterns tend to experience relationships in which there are 'equal measures of desperate clinging and resentful anger'. As a result, if the other partner dies, the bereaved person may experience 'guilt and self-blame (because anger and hostility had been a constant feature of the relationship) and acute pain (because there is now no one emotionally available)' (Howe, 1995: 136). In cases of *chronic grief*:

> individuals cannot seem to escape their feelings of despair and depression. It may be that their relationship with the lost other was characterised by deep feelings of ambivalence. ... The simmering resentment that may have lurked beneath the surface of the relationship is still difficult to acknowledge and so the true range of feelings associated with the grief fail to receive proper expression and therefore remain unresolved. (Howe, 1995: 137)

Narratives of grief

From a sociological perspective, Seale (1998), as we have already mentioned, sees society constructing various discourses or narratives with which somehow to contain or combat the fact of death. This takes place at the system level of society as a whole. He suggests that 'in late modern society medicine and psychiatry offer one of a number of discourses that people have constructed as a sheltering canopy against the adverse consequences of embodiment' (Seale, 1998: 211). ('Embodiment' refers to the fact that we are physical, biological entities, the consequence of which is that we cannot avoid dying.) But he also describes ways in which individuals construct their own narratives to deal with their own feelings in particular circumstances. Each of us when bereaved has to deal with the fact that a loved or familiar person is no longer available, and to make some sense perhaps of the suffering and indignities that person may have suffered at the end. Often there is also guilt or regret about not having been there, or not having done more to help, or of having left things unsaid or unresolved until it was too late.

Coming to terms with a death may in part be seen as the construction of a narrative which in some ways lays these distressing feelings to rest. You may remember from the discussion of transitions in Chapter 6 that the latter stages in the model we presented were:

- *Letting go* of the old order of things as they existed prior to the new event (which have been clung onto up to now in defiance of the new circumstances).
- *Testing and exploring* the new circumstances, trying out new identities and starting to form new attachments.
- *Searching* for meaning by looking back at the past from the new viewpoint of it being in the past, reappraising it and trying to make sense of it.
- *Integration*, when the transition process is complete and we feel 'at home' in the new reality. New behaviours and new ideas about ourselves have become part of our sense of our own identity.

Many people who have lost someone to whom they have been very close would say that they never 'feel at home' in the new reality. But constructing a narrative, an explanation to oneself about what has occurred and how it makes sense in the scheme of things, would seem to be part of the work involved in being able to find a way into a future life of which the lost other person will no longer be a part, except in memory.

A very simple and rudimentary example of this process, perhaps, is the common custom in Britain in recent times of laying flowers at the site of fatal accidents and murders. The people who do this do not necessarily know the deceased person personally, but it is as if they are seeking to cover up the image of tragedy and violence associated with a particular spot, with a new image of beauty and growth. Their actions may also sometimes resonate with more personal losses, and help them to come to terms with them. Bereaved people in Western societies by and large no longer follow the fixed rituals of grief which in the past helped to give a framework for this process of transition, albeit often a rigid one, like the Victorian customs which precisely described mourning dress and how long it should be worn. Now it is much more up to each individual and family to choose or devise their own rites of passage. Most of these decisions must be made when family members are still in the first shock of loss, and it is easy to see how having an accepted ritual to follow can ease this pressure. Such rituals are a part of many spiritual traditions, such as the Jewish practice of 'sitting shiva', where family members remain at home for seven days after the funeral while they are visited and comforted by relatives and friends. The Caribbean 'nine-nights' tradition brings family and friends together to grieve, share memories and celebrate a life, and is also believed to help the spirit of the person who has died to depart peacefully (Gordon, 2018). Buddhist rituals around death, described in *The Tibetan Book of Living and Dying* (Soygal, 2008), similarly aim to ease the spirit's passing from life.

The rituals associated with spiritual traditions are an important part of the narrative of grief for those who follow them. They focus both on the person who has died and on those who mourn their death, and offer a container for the potentially overwhelming feelings stirred up by death and bereavement.

Loss and restoration

Another account of the process of coping with bereavement is offered by a 'dual process model' (Stroebe and Schut, 2001). Its authors suggest that two types of coping are involved in bereavement, which they call respectively 'loss-orientated' and 'restoration-orientated' (see Figure 12.1).

While other models imply a chronological sequence in which coming to terms with loss is followed by 'building a new life', these authors suggest that a 'waxing and waning' occurs and that grieving people typically oscillate between grieving and getting on with life. They point out that in reality bereaved people do take 'time off from grieving' (Stroebe and Schut, 1999: 212), and have to address themselves to the practical adjustments that are required in the wake of a death (financial arrangements, for example) and indeed to other matters.

Loss-orientation and restoration-orientation, then, are two separate kinds of work that bereaved people face, though the former is what is conventionally seen as grieving, and has received much more attention. It is interesting that the model illustrated in Figure 12.1 envisages that to get on with *either* of these tasks requires a degree of denial. Loss work involves turning away from the here and now, while restoration work involves turning away from the pain of grief. This is a reminder that while denial (or 'defensive exclusion') can be harmful and counter-productive in its effects, it is also a very necessary psychological mechanism.

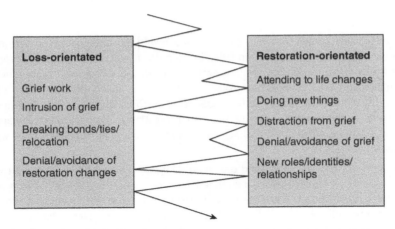

Figure 12.1 Bereavement: Oscillation between loss-orientated and restoration-orientated tasks (from Stroebe and Schut, 2001: 396)

Stroebe and Schut (2001) suggest that there are individual differences as to how people allocate their time between loss-orientation and restoration-orientation, and that this can lead to conflict between survivors. For example, following the death of a child, the parent who focuses more on restoration may be seen by the other parent as not grieving, whereas in fact this person simply has a different *way* of grieving. These authors also suggest that typically men are more restoration-orientated when bereaved, while women are more loss-orientated. Female grief has, it seems, historically been studied more than male grief, in contrast to other areas that we have discussed in this book where generalisations have sometimes been made from a mainly male perspective.

Stroebe and Schut postulate that oscillation between loss-orientation and restoration-orientation is likely to be psychologically more healthy than going to either extreme. In one study (Schut et al., 1997), they tried out different kinds of grief counselling with widows and widowers. What they found was that:

> 'Teaching' bereaved men and women to cope in the way that the opposite sex usually adopts (teaching men to be more emotion-orientated and women to be more problem-orientated) was associated with a lowering of distress. (Stroebe and Schut, 1999: 219)

━━━━━━━━━━ **Activity 12.2** ━━━━━━━━━━

Tony lost his partner Michael a year ago to cancer, when Michael was 75 and Tony was 63. They'd been together as a couple for more than 30 years, but it had always been a fractious and difficult relationship, and Tony had always felt a little in Michael's shadow. Friends invariably referred to them as 'Michael and Tony', for instance, never the other way round. Michael, 12 years older than Tony, was the more flamboyant and confident one of the two. They'd moved across the country twice in order to

(Continued)

(Continued)

accommodate Michael's career, with Tony simply falling in with this and finding the best job he could in the new area. And somehow they'd both fallen into a pattern whereby Tony took responsibility for almost all of the domestic tasks. Tony was resentful about this, but had never quite found a way of effectively challenging it. Sometimes he'd asked himself why he stayed with Michael at all, and wondered if this reflected his own lack of self-confidence as much as anything else, his own doubt that he would ever again find someone as attractive and interesting as Michael to be his partner. There were times too, when he sensed that Michael was disappointed in him, and would have wished for a partner more like himself.

In the latter stages of Michael's long and drawn-out illness, Tony had been faced with a choice of either taking retirement earlier than he'd intended in order to care for Michael, or allowing Michael to enter a nursing home. It had been a hard decision. He was in a job that he enjoyed and one where, after a somewhat unsatisfying career, he felt that he'd finally found his niche. But he felt he couldn't just abandon Michael in his time of need, and he gave up his job and became a full-time carer to Michael, who, after a busy, active and productive life, hated the sick role, and proved an awkward and cantankerous person to care for. Tony resented the fact that his sacrifice hadn't been appreciated, coming as it did after a lifetime of playing second fiddle, but he contained his resentment. It didn't seem fair to be angry with Michael when he was so obviously desperate and frail.

After Michael's death, Tony grieved horribly. His former employers would have been willing to take him back, but even a year on, he simply doesn't emotionally feel up to it. Friends who were supportive are starting to fall away, and some of them have spoken quite sharply to Tony about the need to move on, but he simply doesn't know how to do this. Tony visits his GP who refers him to a counsellor attached to the GP practice.

What kinds of things might the counsellor need to think about, and what reasons might there be for Tony's difficulties in coming to terms with his loss?

Comments on Activity 12.2

Part of Tony's difficulty is likely to be bound up with the complicated and ambiguous feelings he always had about the relationship. He is aware that he sometimes wanted to get out of the relationship completely. He knows he only cared for Michael at the end with reservations and with resentful feelings that, yet again, he was having to take second place to Michael's needs. He perhaps worries now that he didn't love Michael enough, or that he did love him very much, but never really let Michael know it. If 'grief is the price we pay for love' perhaps Tony feels that he must carry on grieving to prove that he really did love Michael, or to recompense Michael for not having loved him

enough. Or perhaps part of the grief that is pushing up to the surface is a long-standing grief for the happier relationship that he'd always hoped for, and which it may now be too late to find. This may well be connected not just with his experience of relationships as an adult, but with his childhood attachment relationships; the history of his relationship with Michael suggests the pattern of ambivalent attachment which we have described above and in Chapter 3.

The popular expression 'moving on' in relation to grief can be unhelpful, with its implications that the loss can somehow be left behind and forgotten. Mourning actually involves a slow process of integrating the experience of loss into one's life, and finding a new direction, not just carrying on as before after a brief interruption. Tony is not unusual in still grieving at the end of the first year, though, as we have seen, there are good reasons why the process may be a more difficult one for him than it is for some. It will be hard for his friends to witness this, as they will feel powerless to help, and being too close to Tony's grief may remind them of the fragility of their own lives and happiness.

Counselling would offer Tony a space to express his grief without having to worry about it being too much for the counsellor to hear. It would also give him the opportunity to talk about his relationship with Michael and to try to make sense of his conflicting feelings through constructing a narrative. A counsellor could give him permission to express the anger he feels with Michael, which he has struggled to repress for so long, rather than turning it in on himself in the form of the depression from which he now seems to be suffering.

Hopefully, this will free him to also access the loving feelings he had for Michael, and his sense of loss will become more about the loss of his partner rather than of the part of himself that had confidence, competence and a sense of agency. At present, these feelings of low self-worth are preventing him from feeling he can return to work, and, in terms of Stroebe and Schut's model, keeping him firmly on the loss-orientated side of the balance, and preventing him from engaging with the restoration-orientated tasks of building a future for himself. The counsellor might also explore whether there are prototypes of Tony's ambivalent relationship with Michael in his early attachment history (maybe a parent who made it difficult for him to express what he needed, or whose own needs often took priority, or who often seemed disappointed in him). If this is the case, working with Tony on these earlier relationships may help him to disentangle his feelings about the more distant past from his response to his present loss.

THE INDIVIDUAL EXPERIENCE OF DEATH

People deal with the fact of their own death in many different ways, depending on their own personality, their culture and the actual circumstances.

Predictable and unpredictable deaths

Some deaths – such as death from cancer – can be predicted in advance by the person who is dying as well as by others. It is these deaths which the 'revivalist' model and the hospice movement, which we discussed above, really address. In such circumstances, the dying person herself can go through a grieving process for her *own* life.

Kübler-Ross (1970), a psychiatrist who worked extensively with terminally ill patients, has described the reaction to news of a terminal illness as going through several stages:

1 *denial* ('It can't be true. You've made a mistake ...')
2 *anger* (against doctors, family members, God ... someone must be blamed)

3 *bargaining* (the dying person attempts to make some kind of deal with fate: 'just let me live to see my grandchild …')
4 *depression* (feelings of guilt, fear of dying, loosening of relationships, preoccupation with a sense of loss)
5 *acceptance* (letting go, the end of the struggle …).

You can see that although not divided up in exactly the same way, this is very much the same pattern as the transition model which we discussed in Chapter 6.

Not all deaths can be predicted in this way. There are many sudden, unexpected deaths. Many deaths occur as a result of heart disease, often involving a sudden heart attack. Fatal accidents are another kind of sudden unexpected death. There are also chosen deaths, not only suicides, but also less clear-cut choices to let go of life, perhaps after a long illness. (There is currently an ethical debate in the UK about whether the law should be changed to legalise assisted dying in some of these circumstances; at present people suffering from terminal and disabling conditions who choose to die must travel to countries like Switzerland, where assisted dying is legal, to obtain medical assistance to die in dignity with the support of family and friends at a time and in a manner of their choosing.) And, though 'old age' per se is not a cause of death, many old people die as a result of a series of health problems, so that the actual cause of death is quite hard to define. In such cases there may not be a moment at which the dying person is clearly faced with the knowledge that she is dying. There are cases too where others may know that a person is dying but the knowledge has been withheld from the dying person herself. As we noted earlier, this may be more common in some cultures than others.

Timely and untimely deaths

The way we experience death – and the way also that it is experienced by others – may be greatly influenced by whether we see the death as timely or premature. In the case of old people, death is often accepted as inevitable and even as 'fair'. In England, when a person dies at quite an old age, it is commonplace for others to remark: 'Well, he had a good innings.' (For readers who do not come from the cricket-playing part of the world, we should explain that the reference is to the game of cricket and a batsman's 'innings' is the time he lasts on the pitch.) We also speak of a 'ripe old age', where the connotations of the word 'ripe' are of fruit or corn that has reached the time where it is ready to be gathered or reaped. Death itself, of course, is traditionally the 'grim reaper'.

And dying does seem, in general terms, to be a rather different experience for the old person than it is for younger people. Young people who learn that they are dying may feel cheated of life, just as their friends and relatives may feel that they have been stolen prematurely from them. One study of attitudes to dying among old people found that older people most often personified death as 'gentle, well-meaning' (Kastenbaum and Alsenburg, 1976). 'Speaking generally, one of the many benefits … of living well into old age,' write Young and Cullen (1996: 27), who interviewed dying people and their relatives in the East End of London, 'was that death was easier to accept.' As an 80-year-old interviewee of theirs remarked:

When I was your age … I'd have been terrified of dying but not now. As you grow older
it becomes inevitable. I'm not afraid of dying, no, nor the manner of dying. I just don't
think about it. It doesn't trouble me at all. (Young and Cullen, 1996: 25–6)

One reason for this resignation seems to be that in old age, most people will increasingly have
experienced the death of friends and loved ones. 'I do my book at Christmas and it's crossing out
such a lot', said one old person (quoted in Sidell, 1993).

We do not wish to suggest that this degree of acceptance is characteristic of *all* old people. But, as
Sidell puts it (1993: 155), many old people do not seem to follow the famous advice of the poet
Dylan Thomas to his father:

Do not go gentle into that good night,

Old age should burn and rave at close of day;

Rage, rage against the dying of the light.

(Thomas, 1973: 474)

On the contrary, many seem to yield to the 'good night' of death without a fight. The implication
of this is that old people tend to reach Kübler-Ross's stage of *acceptance* in relation to their own
death more easily than younger people, if 'easily' can ever be an appropriate word when talking
about this most fundamental of tasks.

People dying at a younger age seem to spend more time at the earlier of Kübler-Ross's stages
(denial, anger, bargaining and *depression*). For the younger people in Young and Cullen's study,
'their general inclination … was to struggle against the onset of death (or the unseemly accelera-
tion of ageing that death implies) with all the vigour they could muster' (1996: 27).

Whether a fighting spirit makes final death any easier or more difficult we do not know,
and even those who are very close to the end can do no more than guess. But during the
period which leads up to it, such a spirit certainly does give something to live for. (Young
and Cullen, 1996: 36)

But we should be careful not to overgeneralise about younger people, any more than about older ones.
Even for those who die before old age, the approach of death may be accepted, even if not welcomed.

'Things are both more trivial than they ever were, and more important than they ever were', said
the playwright Denis Potter, dying at 59, in an interview with Melvyn Bragg, 'and the difference
between the trivial and the important doesn't seem to matter – but the *nowness* of everything is
absolutely wondrous' (Channel 4, 1994 cited by Seale, 1998: 129).

Death and the afterlife

Death, many people believe, is not the end. We would guess that the vast majority of the population of the world still subscribes to belief systems which include the idea of an afterlife. Carl Jung

was quite open to the idea of an afterlife and he considered that the idea was a useful one for many people. Acknowledging that some 'feel no craving for immortality, and ... shudder at the thought of sitting on a cloud and playing the harp for ten thousand years', he nevertheless thought that:

> for most people it means a great deal to assume that their lives will have an indefinite continuity beyond their present existence. They live more sensibly, feel better and are more at peace. (Jung, 1995 [1961]: 332)

Freud by contrast saw religious beliefs in general in a very negative light:

> The whole thing is so patently infantile, so foreign to reality, that to anyone with a friendly attitude to humanity it is painful to think that the great majority of mortals will never be able to rise above this view of life. (Freud, 1961 [1930]: 261)

Researchers have looked into the question of whether a belief in an afterlife helps us to face death and found, not surprisingly, that a simple 'yes' or 'no' answer is not forthcoming. Kalish and Reynolds (1976) found that people with strong religious convictions showed the least anxiety about death, though people with confused religious beliefs, interestingly, showed *more anxiety* than did atheists. Wink and Scott (2005: 212) found that 'moderately religious individuals feared death more than individuals for whom religion played either a central or a marginal role in life'. They observe that:

> individuals who do not have a definite (either religious or secular) view of mortality as suggested by a moderate or lukewarm religious engagement or a disjunction between religious beliefs and practices are particularly vulnerable to fear of death in late adulthood. (2005: 212)

Whether or not a belief in an afterlife is helpful to the dying is of course a very different question than that of whether an afterlife actually exists, but this is a question that we will not attempt to address.

THE END

We began this book with the image of a baby's birth, and so it seems appropriate to conclude it like this:

> *In a bed in a side room on a hospital ward, an elderly woman is drawing close to death. It is some hours since she last spoke and it is not clear whether she is entirely conscious. There are four other people in the room: a son, a daughter, a daughter-in-law and a nurse. They can all see that the end is very near. The son and the daughter are holding their mother's hands. The daughter is murmuring 'Dear mum, dear, dear mum ...'*
>
> *And then she stops. 'She's gone', she says, and they all know it is so. There were five people in the room a moment ago, but now there are only four.*

CHAPTER SUMMARY

- In this chapter we looked at the social context of death, drawing attention to the many cultural differences that exist in relation to death. We have drawn attention in particular to two approaches within secular industrialised society: the medicalised approach (which some suggest represents a 'denial of death') and the 'revivalist' approach which places an emphasis on dying as a part of life to be experienced by the individual concerned.
- We then looked at the impact of death on those around the dying person, discussing the nature of grief and bereavement.
- Finally, we looked at the ways that death is experienced by the dying person, looking at different factors and focusing in particular on the differences between deaths that could be predicted in advance and those that could not, and between deaths in old age and deaths at other ages. Finally, we mentioned the impact of different beliefs in the possibility of an afterlife.

— Tangled Webs —

In two of the cases in Tangled Webs, bereavement is a particular issue, although you could consider bereavement in relation to other cases (for instance: how would the Begum family cope with the death of Maryam?).

Mary Carpenter (Case D). Mary lost her husband, Ken, two years ago. In our experience this is a long enough time that many people will have stopped talking to her about her loss, and may assume that she is past the grieving stage. However, it is apparent from the case study that Mary is still very much grieving, and some of her behaviour is characteristic of bereaved people, and this is not in fact unusual in such a timescale. She and Ken were a couple since school days (they even went to the same primary school) and throughout Mary's entire adult life up to the age of 75. We have noted that, when we grieve, it is not just for the deceased, but also for the part of ourselves that we have invested in that person. In Mary's case, the part of herself that she invested in Ken, and in the idea of herself and Ken as a couple, must surely go very deep into her conception of who she is.

Tracey Green (Case J). Tracey also lost Ken, who was her foster-carer, and father figure ('They were my parents really,' she says of Ken and Mary) from the age of eight. In Tracey's case, however, the loss of Ken is one of a series of traumatic losses, some through death, some for other reasons. She lost her father along with her two brothers at an early age, when he walked out of the family home. There was also a baby sister who she never met, who was adopted, and another small sister who was fostered separately from her when they came into care, a grandmother who died, and a mother who moved away and lost contact. It was worth thinking about how all that previous experience of loss may have affected her response to the death of Ken.

 You can access Tangled Webs by visiting **https://study.sagepub.com/tangledwebs**

Further reading

Currer, C. (2001) *Responding to Grief: Dying, Bereavement and Social Care.* Basingstoke: Palgrave. A book aimed specifically at social care workers with dying and bereaved people.

Murray Parkes, C. and Prigerson, H.G. (2010) *Bereavement: Studies of Grief in Adult Life.* London: Penguin.

APPENDIX 1

TANGLED WEBS: LIST OF CASES

A. Caitlin Smart (Dudley). Caitlin is an 8-year-old child from the **Dudley/Harris family.** Her teacher **Penny Sullivan** is discussing her with the head teacher, as she is worried about her progress and withdrawn behaviour.

B. Rob Thomas and Derek Harrow. Rob is a supported housing worker, and also partner of **Tracey Green.** He is concerned about Derek, a young man who has recently been asked to leave the supported housing accommodation because of aggression towards other residents.

C. Jenny Quinton and Gloria Johnson. Jenny is a young woman with physical disabilities. Gloria is one of her carers, and is voicing her concerns about Jenny's relationship with an older man to Jenny's mother Libby.

D. Mary Carpenter. Mary, former foster carer of **Tracey Green**, lost her husband Ken two years ago and is experiencing health problems as she grows older. She is receiving bereavement support from Richard, a volunteer.

E. Maryam Begum's family. Maryam is suffering from Alzheimer's disease, and is being cared for at home by her family. The **Dudley/Harris** family are neighbours. One of her grandsons, Kabir, describes the situation in a conversation with his partner Gary as they discuss whether Kabir should tell his family about their relationship.

F. Max Sullivan and Gloria Johnson. Max, an estate agent, is about to give Gloria notice to leave her privately rented accommodation. He has become friendly with Gloria and her children, and expresses his fears for the family's future.

G. Dudley/Harris family. The family's social worker **Tracey Green** writes a case summary in preparation for a meeting of professionals who are concerned about several of the children in this complex family.

H. Sullivan family. Penny Sullivan has been asked by her head teacher to consider a full-time teaching post, and in an email exchange she explains that she is unable to do this because of the demands of caring for her autistic son Jack and her concerns about the strain that this is putting on her relationship with her husband **Max.**

I. Veloso family. Estrela Veloso suffers from serious depression, and social worker **Tracey Green** is concerned about her and her much younger husband Pedro's ability to care adequately for 6-year-old Xenia. Community psychiatric nurse **Deanna Whitworth** is expressing a very different view, and Tracey is considering her response to this.

J. Tracey Green. Tracey came into social work after growing up in care. She was fostered by **Mary Carpenter** and her husband Ken. She is seeing a counsellor because she is finding her work stressful at present. Working with the **Dudley/Harris family** makes her particularly anxious. She is also reflecting on her relationship with her partner **Rob Thomas**, which is in some difficulty.

K. Zak Renton. Zak is a 16-year-old resident of the supported housing project where **Rob Thomas** works, and **Derek Harrow** was a resident until recently. His mother has had mental health problems throughout his childhood, with periodic hospital admissions. He was previously fostered by **Mary Carpenter**, but this is no longer possible. Rob and his co-worker Jade are struggling to build a relationship with Zak, and are discussing this with community psychiatric nurse **Deanna Whitworth**, who knows the family well.

L. Deanna Whitworth and Zoe Scott. Deanna meets up with a colleague from her psychiatric nurse training and talks about her concerns about her partner Zoe's drinking problem.

APPENDIX 2

TANGLED WEBS: TOPICS AND CASE STUDIES

Table A2.1 Tangled Webs: Topics and case studies

Topic	Most relevant chapters (key chapter in bold)	Key case studies
Attachment	**3**, 7, 12	A. Caitlin Smart (Dudley)
		G. Dudley/Harris family
		I. Veloso family
		J. Tracey Green
		L. Deanna Whitworth and Zoe Scott
		D. Mary Carpenter
		K. Zak Renton
Cognitive changes	**4**, 8, 11	A. Caitlin Smart (Dudley)
		H. Sullivan family (Jack)
		E. Maryam Begum's family
Cultural expectations/ differences	1, 6, **10**	B. Rob Thomas and Derek Harrow
		E. Maryam Begum's family
		I. Veloso family
Identity formation	2, **6**, 7	B. Rob Thomas and Derek Harrow
		E. Maryam Begum's family
		F. Max Sullivan and Gloria Johnson
		G. Dudley/Harris family
		H. Sullivan family (Sarah)
		K. Zak Renton
		L. Deanna Whitworth and Zoe Scott
		C. Jenny Quinton and Gloria Johnson
		D. Mary Carpenter
Learning theory	**5**	A. Caitlin Smart (Dudley)
		G. Dudley/Harris family
		F. Max Sullivan and Gloria Johnson
		K. Zak Renton

(Continued)

Table A2.1 (Continued)

Topic	Most relevant chapters (key chapter in bold)	Key case studies
Loss and transitions	2, 3, **6**, 7, 8, 9, 11, **12**	C. Jenny Quinton and Gloria Johnson H. Sullivan family J. Tracey Green D. Mary Carpenter E. Maryam Begum's family K. Zak Renton
Mirroring	2	G. Dudley/Harris family I. Veloso family K. Zak Renton
Resilience	**1**, 3, **6**, 12	D. Mary Carpenter F. Max Sullivan and Gloria Johnson J. Tracey Green C. Jenny Quinton and Gloria Johnson
Social construction	**8, 10**	C. Jenny Quinton and Gloria Johnson F. Max Sullivan and Gloria Johnson H. Sullivan family D. Mary Carpenter
Stereotypes/prejudice/discrimination	8, **10**, 11	D. Mary Carpenter F. Max Sullivan and Gloria Johnson H. Sullivan family L. Deanna Whitworth and Zoe Scott C. Jenny Quinton and Gloria Johnson
Systemic theories	**9, 10**	A. Caitlin Smart (Dudley) B. Rob Thomas and Derek Harrow E. Maryam Begum's family F. Max Sullivan and Gloria Johnson G. Dudley/Harris family H. Sullivan family I. Veloso family J. Tracey Green K. Zak Renton L. Deanna Whitworth and Zoe Scott
Unconscious processes	2	B. Rob Thomas and Derek Harrow I. Veloso family K. Zak Renton H. Sullivan family J. Tracey Green L. Deanna Whitworth and Zoe Scott

REFERENCES

A Two Year Old Goes to Hospital 1952, film, Robertson Films, London. Available on DVD from Concord Media, Ipswich.

Agnew, R. (2009) *Juvenile Delinquency Causes and Control*. 3rd edn. Oxford: OUP.

Ahrons, C. (2016) 'Divorce: An unscheduled family transition', in M. McGoldrick, N. Garcia Preto and B. Carter (eds), *The Expanding Family Life Cycle: Individual, Family and Social Perspectives*, 5th edn. Boston: Pearson, pp. 376–93.

Ainsworth, M. (1967) *Infancy in Uganda: Infant Care and the Growth of Love*. Baltimore, MD: Johns Hopkins University Press.

Ainsworth, M., Blehar, M., Aters, E. and Wall, S. (1978) *Patterns of Attachment: A Psychological Study of the Strange Situation*. Hillsdale, NJ: Lawrence Erlbaum.

Alcoholics Anonymous (2018) *The Twelve Steps of Alcoholics Anonymous*. Accessed May 2018 at www.alcoholics-anonymous.org.uk/About-AA/The-12-Steps-of-AA

Allen, D. and Adams, P. (2013) *Social Work with Gypsy, Roma and Traveller Children*. London: BAAF.

Anderson, E.S., Dunlea, A. and Kekelis, L. (1993) 'The impact of input: language acquisition in the visually impaired', *First Language 13*: 23–49.

Appleyard, K., Egeland, B., Van Dulmen, M. and Sroufe, A. (2005) 'When more is not better: the role of cumulative risk in child behaviour outcomes', *Journal of Child Psychology and Psychiatry 46*: 235–45.

Ariès, P. (1976) *Western Attitudes Towards Death*. London: Marion Boyars.

Arnett, J.J. (2004) *Emerging Adulthood: The Winding Road from the Late Teens through the Twenties*. New York: Oxford University Press.

Azrin, N.H. (1959) 'Punishment and recovery during fixed ratio performance', *Journal of the Experimental Analysis of Behavior 2*: 303–5.

Baillargeon, R. (1987) 'Object permanence in 3.5- and 4.5-month-old infants', *Developmental Psychology 23*: 655–64.

Baillargeon, R., Li, J., Gertner, Y. and Wu, D. (2011) 'How do infants reason about physical events?' in U. Goswami (ed.), *The Wiley-Blackwell Handbook of Childhood Cognitive Development*, 2nd edn. Chichester: Wiley-Blackwell, pp. 11–48.

Balbernie, R. (2001) 'Circuits and circumstances: the neurobiological consequences of early relationship experiences and how they shape later behaviour', *Journal of Child Psychotherapy 27* (3): 237–55.

Baltes, P.B. (1987) 'Theoretical propositions of lifespan developmental psychology', *Developmental Psychology 23*: 611–28.

Baltes, P.B., Smith, J. and Staudinger, U.M. (1992) 'Wisdom and successful ageing', in T.B. Sonderegger (ed.), *Nebraska Symposium on Motivation 39*. Lincoln, NE: University of Nebraska Press, pp. 123–67.

Bandura, A. (1977) *Social Learning Theory*. Englewood Cliffs, NJ: Prentice-Hall.

Barber, B. (1992) 'Family, personality and adolescent problem behaviours', *Journal of Marriage and the Family 56*: 375–86.

Barker, P. (2007) *Basic Family Therapy*, 5th edn. Oxford: Blackwell.

Barnes, C. (2012) 'Understanding the social model of disability: past, present and future', in N. Watson, A. Roulstone and C. Thomas (eds), *Routledge Handbook of Disability Studies*. Abingdon: Routledge, pp. 12–29.

Barnes, G. (2004) *Family Therapy in Changing Times*, 2nd edn. Basingstoke: Palgrave.

Baron-Cohen, S. (1989) 'The autistic child's theory of mind: a case of specific developmental delay', *Journal of Child Psychology and Psychiatry 30* (2): 285–97.

Baron-Cohen, S. (1997) *Mindblindness: An Essay on Autism and Theory of Mind*. Cambridge, MA: MIT Press.

Barone, L. and Guiducci, V. (2009) 'Mental representations of attachment in eating disorders: a pilot study using the Adult Attachment Interview', *Attachment and Human Development 11* (4): 405–17.

Bateson, G. (1973) *Steps to an Ecology of Mind*. St Albans: Paladin.

Baum, W. (2005) *Understanding Behaviorism: Behavior, Culture and Evolution*. Oxford: Blackwell.

Baumrind, D. (1991) 'The influence of early parenting style on adolescent competence and substance abuse', *Journal of Early Adolescence 11*: 56–95.

Beardslee, W. and Podorefsky, D. (1988) 'Resilient adolescents whose parents have serious affective and other psychiatric disorders: importance of self-understanding and relationships', *American Journal of Psychiatry 145* (1): 63–9.

Beattie, M. (1992) *Codependent No More: How to Stop Controlling Others and Start Caring for Yourself*. 2nd edn. Center City, MN: Hazelden.

Beck, A.T. (1963) 'Thinking and depression. 1: Idiosyncratic content and cognitive distortions', *Archives of General Psychiatry 9*: 324–33.

Beck, A.T. (1964) 'Thinking and depression. 2: Theory and Therapy', *Archives of General Psychiatry 10*: 561–71.

Becker, H.S. (1963) *Outsiders*. New York: Free Press.

Berenbaum, S.A. and Hines, M. (1992) 'Early androgens are related to sex-related toy preferences', *Psychological Science 3*: 202–6.

Berger, P. and Luckmann, T. (1967) *The Social Construction of Reality*. London: Penguin.

Berlin, L., Ziv, Y., Amaya-Jackson, L. and Greenberg, M.T. (eds) (2005) *Enhancing Early Attachments: Theory, Research, Intervention and Policy*. New York: Guilford Press.

Bernstein, D., Atance, C., Meltzoff, A. and Loftus, G. (2007) 'Hindsight bias and developing theories of mind', *Child Development 78* (4): 1374–94.

Berthoud, R. (2006) *The Employment Rates of Disabled People* (research report 298). London: Department for Work and Pensions. Accessed online July 2018 at www.researchgate.net/publication/247867179_The_Employment_Rates_of_Disabled_People

Blakemore, J.E.O. (2003) 'Children's beliefs about violating gender norms: boys shouldn't look like girls and girls shouldn't act like boys', *Sex Roles 48*: 411–19.

Blakemore, J., Berenbaum, S. and Liben, L. (2009) *Gender Development*. Hove: Psychology Press.

Blanden, J., Goodman, A., Gregg, P. and Machin, S. (2004) 'Changes in intergenerational mobility in Britain', in M. Corak (ed.), *Generational Income Inequality*. Cambridge: Cambridge University Press.

Blanden, J., Gregg, P. and Machin, S. (2005) *Intergenerational Mobility in Europe and North America*. London: Centre for Economic Performance.

Boden, M. (1994) *Piaget*. London: Fontana.

Bond, J., Peace, S., Dittman-Kohli, F. and Westerhof, G. (eds) (2007) *Ageing in Society*, 3rd edn. London: Sage.

Boswell, J. (1996) *The Marriage of Likeness: Same-Sex Unions in Pre-Modern Europe*. London: Fontana.

Boucher, J. (2017) *Autistic Spectrum Disorder: Characteristics, Causes and Practical Issues*, 2nd edn. London: Sage.

Bourdieu, P. (1984) *Distinction: A Social Critique of the Judgement of Taste*. London: Routledge and Kegan Paul.

Bowlby, J. (1940) 'The influence of early environment in the development of neurosis and neurotic character', *International Journal of Psychoanalysis 21*: 154–78.

Bowlby, J. (1951) *Maternal Care and Mental Health*. Geneva: World Health Organisation.

Bowlby, J. (1990 [1953]) *Childcare and the Growth of Love*. Harmondsworth: Penguin.

Bowlby, J. (1997 [1969]) *Attachment*. London: Pimlico.

Bowlby, J. (1998a [1973]) *Separation*. London: Pimlico.

Bowlby, J. (1998b [1980]) *Loss*. London: Pimlico.

Brambring, M. (2007) 'Divergent development of manual skills in children who are blind or sighted', *Journal of Visual Impairment & Blindness 101* (4): 212–14.

Brecher, E.M. (1984) *Love, Sex and Aging: A Consumers' Union Report*. Boston: Little, Brown.

Brei, N., Schwarz, G.N. and Klein-Tasman, B. (2015) 'Predictors of Parenting Stress in Children Referred for an Autism Spectrum Disorder Diagnostic Evaluation', *Journal of Developmental and Physical Disabilities 27* (5): 617–35.

Bronfenbrenner, U. (1979) *The Ecology of Human Development*. Cambridge, MA: Harvard University Press.

Bronstein, P., Fitzgerald, M., Briones, M., Pienadz, J. and D'Ari, A. (1993) 'Family emotional expressiveness as a predictor of early adolescent social and psychological adjustment', *Journal of Early Adolescence 13*: 448–71.

Brooks-Gunn, J. and Paikoff, R. (1997) 'Sexuality and developmental transitions during adolescence', in J. Schulenberg, J. Maggs and K. Hurrelmann (eds), *Health Risks and Developmental Transitions during Adolescence*. Cambridge: Cambridge University Press, pp. 190–219.

Burman, E. (1994) *Deconstructing Developmental Psychology*. London: Routledge.

Burke, P. (2004) *Brothers and Sisters of Disabled Children*. London: Jessica Kingsley.

Burke, P. (2008). *Disability and Impairment: working with children and families*. London: Jessica Kingsley.

Bussey, K. (2011) 'Gender Identity Development', in S.J. Schwartz, K. Luyckx and V.L. Vignoles (eds), *Handbook of Identity Theory and Research*. London: Springer, pp. 603–28.

Butler, J. (1990) *Gender Trouble: Feminism and the Subversion of Identity*. New York: Routledge.

Calderwood, K.A. and Rajesparam, A. (2018) 'A critique of the codependency concept considering the best interests of the child', *Families in Society 95* (3): 171–8.

Campbell, D. (2000) *The Socially Constructed Organisation*. London: Karnac Books.

Carers UK (2014) *Policy Briefing – Facts about Carers*. Accessed online June 2018 at www.carersuk. org/for-professionals/policy/policy-library/facts-about-carers-2014

Carey, N. (2012) *The Epigenetics Revolution: How Modern Biology is Rewriting our Understanding of Genetics, Disease and Inheritance*. London: Icon Books.

Carmichael, P. and Davidson, S. (2009) 'A gender identity development service', *The Psychologist 22* (11): 916–17.

Carr, A. (1989) 'Countertransference to families where child abuse has occurred', *Journal of Family Therapy*. *11*(1), pp. 87–97. Available online at https://onlinelibrary.wiley.com/doi/pdf/10.1046/j..1989.00335.x (Accessed July 2018).

Carr, A. (2012) *Family Therapy: Concepts, Processes and Practice*, 3rd edn. Chichester: Wiley-Blackwell.

Carskadon, M. and Acebo, C. (2002) 'Regulation of sleepiness in adolescence: updates, insights and speculation', *Sleep 25*: 606–16.

Cartwright, C., Onwuteaka-Philipsen, B., Williams, G., Faisst, K., Mortier, F., Nilstun, T., Morup, M., van der Heide, A. and Miccinesi, G. (2007) 'Physician discussions with terminally ill patients: a cross-national comparison', *Palliative Medicine 21* (4): 295–303.

Casey, B., Galvan, A. and Hare, T. (2005) 'Changes in cerebral functional organization during cognitive development', *Current Opinion in Neurobiology 15* (2): 239–44.

Cattell, R. (1971) *Abilities, Their Structure, Growth and Action*. New York: Houghton Mifflin.

Channel 4 (1994) *An Interview with Dennis Potter*. London: Channel 4 TV.

Chappell, A.L. (1998) 'Still out in the cold: people with learning difficulties and the social model of disability', in T. Shakespeare (ed.), *The Disability Reader*. London: Cassell, pp. 211–20.

Chassin, L., Hussong, A. and Beltran, I. (2009) 'Adolescent substance use', in R.M Lerner and L. Steinberg (eds), *Handbook of Adolescent Psychology*. Hoboken, NJ: Wiley, pp. 723–63.

Chen, Z., Sanchez, R.P. and Campbell, T. (1997) 'From beyond to within their grasp: analogical problem solving in 10- and 13-month-old infants', *Developmental Psychology 33*: 790–801.

Chisholm, J. and Sieff, D. (2015) 'Live Fast, Die Young: an evolved response to hostile environments', in D. Sieff (ed.), *Understanding and Healing Emotional Trauma: Conversations with Pioneering Clinicians and Researchers*. London: Routledge, pp. 163–81.

Chodorow, N. (1978) *The Reproduction of Mother*. Berkeley: University of California Press.

Cione, G., Paolicelli, P.B., Sordi, C. and Vinter, A. (1993) 'Sensorimotor development in cerebral palsied infants assessed with the Uzgiris-Hunt scales', *Developmental Medicine and Child Neurology 35*: 1055–66.

Clinton, H. (1996) *It Takes a Village*. New York: Simon & Schuster.

Clulow, C. and Mattinson, J. (1989) *Marriage Inside Out*. Harmondsworth: Penguin.

Cobb, N. (1995) *Adolescence: Continuity, Change and Diversity*, 2nd edn. Mountain View, CA: Mayfield.

Colby, A., Kohlberg, L., Gibbs, J. and Lieberman, M. (1983) 'A longitudinal study of moral judgement', *Monographs of the Society for Research in Child Development 48*: 1–24.

Coleman, J. (2011) *The Nature of Adolescence*, 4th edn. London: Routledge.

Coleman, P. and O'Hanlon, A. (2017) *Ageing and Development*, 2nd edn. London: Routledge.

Compas, B. (1995) 'Promoting successful coping during adolescence', in M. Rutter (ed.), *Psychosocial Disturbances in Young People: Challenges for Prevention*. Cambridge: Cambridge University Press, pp. 247–73.

Compas, B. and Reeslund, K. (2009) 'Processes of risk and resilience during adolescence', in R.M. Lerner and L. Steinberg (eds), *Handbook of Adolescent Psychology*. Hoboken, NJ: Wiley, pp. 561–617.

Cooley, C.S. (1909) *Social Organisation*. New York: Scribner.

Cox, M.V. (1991) *The Child's Point of View*, 2nd edn. Hemel Hempstead: Harvester.

Cramer, P. (2006) *Protecting the Self-defense Mechanisms in Action*. New York: Guilford Press.

Crawford, M. and Popp, D. (2003) 'Sexual double standards: a review and methodological critique of two decades of research', *The Journal of Sex Research 40* (1): 13–26.

Crawley, A.C. (ed.) (1992) *Geoffrey Chaucer: The Canterbury Tales*. London: David Campbell Publishing.

Crews, F., He, J. and Hodge, C. (2007) 'Adolescent cortical development: a critical period of vulnerability for addiction', *Pharmacology, Biochemistry and Behavior 86* (2): 189–99.

Crittenden, P.M. (2008) *Raising Parents: Attachment, Parenting and Child Safety*. Cullompton: Willan Press.

Crittenden, P.M. and Newman, L. (2010) 'Comparing models of borderline personality disorder: mothers' experience, self-protective strategies and dispositional representations', *Clinical Child Psychology and Psychiatry 15* (3): 433–51.

Crockett, L., Bingham, C., Chopak, J. and Vicary, J. (1996) 'Timing of first sexual intercourse: the role of social control, social learning and problem behaviour', *Journal of Youth and Adolescence 25* (1): 89–111.

Cruse. Accessed online May 2018 at www.cruse.org.uk

CSDH (Commission on the Social Determinants of Health) (2008) Closing the Gap in a Generation: Health Equity through Action on the Social Determinants of Health. *Final Report of the Commission on the Social Determinants of Health*. Geneva: World Health Organisation.

Cumming, E. and Henry, W. (1961) *Growing Old: The Process of Disengagement*. New York: Basic Books.

Currer, C. (2001) *Responding to Grief: Dying, Bereavement and Social Care*. Basingstoke: Palgrave.

Currie, C., Zanotti, C., Morgan, A., Currie, D., de Looze, M., Roberts, C., Samdal, O., Smith, O.R.F. and Barnekow, V. (eds) (2012) *Social Determinants of Health and Well-being among Young People. Health Behaviour in School-aged Children (HBSC) Study: International Report from the 2009/2010 Survey*. Copenhagen: WHO Regional Office for Europe (Health Policy for Children and Adolescents, No. 6).

Dale, N. and Salt, A. (2007) 'Early support developmental journal for children with visual impairment: the case for a new developmental framework for early intervention', *Childcare, Health and Development 33* (6): 684–90.

Daniels, H. (ed.) (2017) *An Introduction to Vygotsky*, 3rd ed. Hove: Routledge.

Dennison, C. and Coleman, J. (1998) *Adolescent Motherhood: The Relation between a Young Mother and her Mother*. Research report. Brighton: Trust for the Study of Adolescence.

Dex, S., Ward, K. and Joshi, H. (2008) 'Gender differences in occupational wage mobility in the 1958 cohort', *Work, Employment and Society 22*: 263–80.

Diamond, L.M. and Savin-Williams, R.C. (2009) 'Adolescent sexuality', in R.M. Lerner and L. Steinberg (eds), *Handbook of Adolescent Psychology*. Hoboken, NJ: Wiley, pp. 479–523.

Dillenburger, K. and Keenan, M. (1997) 'Human development: a question of structure and function', in K. Dillenburger, M. O'Reilly and M. Keenan (eds), *Advances in Behaviour Analysis*. Dublin: University College Dublin Press.

Dillon, F.R., Worthington, R.L. and Moradi, B. (2011) 'Sexual identity as a universal process', in S.J. Schwartz, K. Luyckx, and V.L. Vignoles (eds), *Handbook of Identity Theory and Research*. London: Springer, pp. 649–70.

Dinnerstein, D. (1987) *The Rocking of the Cradle and the Ruling of the World*. London: The Women's Press.

Docherty, D., Hughes, R., Phillips, P., Corbett, D., Regan, B., Barber, A., Adams, M., Boxall, K., Kaplan, I. and Izzidien, S. (2010) 'This is what we think', in L.J. Davis (ed.), *The Disability Studies Reader*, 3rd edn. Abingdon: Routledge, pp. 432–40.

Doidge, N. (2007) *The Brain that Changes itself: Stories of Personal Triumph from the Frontiers of Brain Science*. London: Penguin.

Donne, J. (1962 [1624]) 'Meditation XVII (from Devotions Upon Emergent Occasions)', in G.R. Potter and E.M. Simpson (eds), *Sermons of John Donne*, Vol. 7. Berkeley: University of California Press, p. 369.

Durkin, K. (1995) *Developmental Social Psychology*. Oxford: Blackwell.

Elbert, T., Pantev, C., Wienbruch, C., Rockstroh, B. and Taub, E. (1995) 'Increased cortical representation of the fingers of the left hand in string players', *Science 270* (5234): 305–7.

Elias, N. (1978) *What is Sociology?* London: Hutchinson.

Eliot, L. (2001) *Early Intelligence: How the Brain and Mind Develop in the First Years*. London: Penguin.

Elliot, A. (2002) *Psychoanalytic Theory: An Introduction*. Oxford: Oxford University Press.

Emerson, E. and Hatton, C. (2007) 'The socioeconomic circumstances of children at risk of disability in Britain', *Disability & Society 22* (6): 563–80.

England, M. and Sim, L. (2009) *Depression in Parents, Parenting, and Children: Opportunities to Improve Identification, Treatment, and Prevention*. Washington: National Academies Press. Available online at https://www.ncbi.nlm.nih.gov/books/NBK215116/ (Accessed July 2018).

Epstein, C.F. (1997) 'The multiple realities of sameness and difference: ideology and practice', *Journal of Social Issues 53*: 259–78.

Erikson, E. (1980 [1959]) *Identity and the Life Cycle*. New York: W.W. Norton.

Erikson, E. (1994 [1968]) *Identity, Youth and Crisis*. New York: W.W. Norton.

Erikson, E. (1995 [1951]) *Childhood and Society*. London: Vintage.

Eriksen, T.H. (2002) *Ethnicity and Nationalism: Anthropological Perspectives (Anthropology, Culture and Society)*, 2nd edn. London: Pluto Press.

Ernst, M. and Spear, L.P. (2009) 'Reward systems', in M. de Haan and M.R. Gunnar (eds), *Handbook of Developmental Social Neuroscience*. New York: Guilford Press.

Estes, C.C., Swan, J.S. and Gerard, L.E. (1982) 'Dominant and competing paradigms in gerontology', *Ageing and Society 2*: 151–64.

Family Relations Institute (2011–2018). Accessed online July 2018 at https://www.patcrittenden.com/include/dmm_model.htm

Farrell, M.P. and Rosenberg, S.D. (1981) *Men at Mid-life*. Boston, MA: Auburn House.

Fiske, S. and Taylor, S. (2017) *Social Cognition: from Brains to Culture*, 3rd edn. London; Sage.

Flores, P.J. (2004) *Addiction as an Attachment Disorder*. Lanham, MD: Jason Aronson.

Fodor, J. (1983) *The Modularity of Mind*. Cambridge, MA: MIT Press.

Fonagy, P. and Target, M. (2005) 'Bridging the transmission gap: An end to an important mystery of attachment research?', *Attachment & Human Development 7* (3): 333–43.

Fonagy, P., Gergely, G., Jurist, E. and Target, M. (2002) *Affect Regulation, Mentalisation and the Development of the Self*. New York: Other Press.

Foucault, M. (1980) *Power/Knowledge*. London: Harvester Wheatsheaf.

Franklin, C. and Warren, K. (1999) 'Advances in systems theory', in C. Franklin and C. Jordan (eds), *Family Practice*. Pacific Grove, CA: Brooks/Cole, pp. 397–425.

Freud, A. (1968 [1937]) *The Ego and the Mechanisms of Defence*. London: Hogarth Press.

Freud, S. (1957 [1917]) *Mourning and Melancholia*, standard edn, Vol. *14*. London: Hogarth Press.

Freud, S. (1959 [1926]) *The Question of Lay Analysis*, standard edn, Vol. *20*. London: Hogarth Press.

Freud, S. (1961 [1923]) *The Ego and the Id*, standard edn, Vol. *19*. London: Hogarth Press.

Freud, S. (1961 [1930]) *Civilization and its Discontents*, standard edn, Vol. *21*. London: Hogarth Press.

Freud, S. (1963 [1916–17]) *Introductory Lectures on Psychoanalysis*, standard edn, Vol. *16*. London: Hogarth Press.

Freud, S. (1964 [1933]) *New Introductory Lectures in Psychoanalysis*, standard edn, Vol. *22*. London: Hogarth Press.

Freud, S. (2003 [1949]) *An Outline of Psychoanalysis*. London: Penguin.

Freud, S. and Breuer, J. (1955 [1895]) *Studies on Hysteria*, standard edn, Vol. *2*. London: Hogarth Press.

Frith, U. (2003) *Autism: Explaining the Enigma*, 2nd edn. Oxford: Blackwell.

Frith, U. (2008) *Autism: A Very Short Introduction*. Oxford: Oxford University Press.

Frosh, S. (1997) *For and Against Psychoanalysis*. London: Routledge.

Frydenberg, E. (2008) *Adolescent Coping: Advances in Theory, Research and Practice*. Hove: Routledge.

Gallagher, H. and Frith, C. (2003) 'Functional imaging of "theory of mind"', *Trends in Cognitive Science 7* (2): 77–83.

Galpin, J., Barratt, P., Ashcroft, E., Greathead, S., Kenny, L. and Pellicano, E. (2017) '"The dots just don't join up": Understanding the support needs of family of children on the autistic spectrum', *Autism 22* (5): 571–84.

Garcia Preto, N. (2016) 'The transformation of the family system during adolescence', in M. McGoldrick, N. Garcia Preto, and B. Carter (eds), *The Expanding Family Life Cycle: Individual, Family and Social Perspectives*, 5th edn. Boston: Pearson, pp. 304–20.

Garmezy, N. and Rutter, M. (eds) (1983) *Stress, Coping and Development in Children*. New York: McGraw Hill.

Gath, A. (1977) 'The impact of an abnormal child upon the parents', *British Journal of Psychiatry 130*: 405–10.

Gay, P. (1988) *Freud: A Life for our Time*. London: Macmillan.

Gender Identity Development Service. *Referral Figures for 2016–17*. Accessed online April 2018 at http://gids.nhs.uk/number-referrals

Gerhardt, S. (2004) *Why Love Matters: How Affection Shapes a Baby's Brain*. Hove: Routledge.

Giedd, J.N. (2008) 'The teen brain: insights from neuroimaging', *Journal of Adolescent Health 42*: 335–43.

Gielen, N., Havermans, R.C., Tekelenburg, M. and Jansen, A. (2012) 'Prevalence of post-traumatic stress disorder among patients with substance use disorder: It is higher than clinicians think it is', *European Journal of Psychotraumatology 3* (17734): 1–9.

Gilleard, C.J. and Higgs, P. (2000) *Cultures of Ageing: Self, Citizen and the Body*. Harlow: Prentice Hall.

Gilligan, C. (1982) *In a Different Voice: Psychological Theory and Women's Development*. Cambridge, MA: Harvard University Press.

Golding, K. (2008) *Nurturing Attachments: Supporting Children who are Fostered or Adopted*. London: Jessica Kingsley.

Goldthorpe, J.H., Lockwood, D., Bechofer, F. and Platt, J. (1969) *The Affluent Worker in the Class Structure.* Cambridge: Cambridge University Press.

Golombok, S. and Fivush, R. (1994) *Gender Development.* Cambridge: Cambridge University Press.

Gordon, N. (2018) Accessed online May 2018 at www.theguardian.com/lifeandstyle/2018/may/05/grandmas-traditional-jamaican-wake-brought-me-closer-to-the-windrush-generation

Goswami, U. (2011a) 'Inductive and Deductive Reasoning', in U. Goswami (ed.), *The Wiley-Blackwell Handbook of Childhood Cognitive Development*, 2nd edn. Chichester: Wiley-Blackwell, pp. 399–419.

Goswami, U. (ed.) (2011b) *The Wiley-Blackwell Handbook of Childhood Cognitive Development*, 2nd edn. Chichester: Wiley-Blackwell.

Graber, T. and Brooks-Gunn, T. (1996) 'Transitions and turning points: managing the passage from childhood through adolescence', *Developmental Psychology 32*: 768–76.

Green, J. and Goldwyn, R. (2002) 'Annotation: attachment disorganisation and psychopathology: new findings in attachment research and their potential implications for developmental psychopathology in childhood', *Journal of Child Psychology and Psychiatry 43* (7): 835–46.

Greenberg, M.T. and Kushe, C. (1989) 'Cognitive, personal and social development of deaf children and adolescents', in M. Wang, M. Reynolds and H. Walberg (eds), *The Handbook of Special Education: Research and Practice*, Vol. 3. New York: Pergamon, pp. 95–129.

Grossman, F.K. (1972) *Brothers and Sisters of Retarded Children.* Syracuse, NY: Syracuse University Press.

Guardian (2018) 'Gender pay gap figures reveal eight in 10 firms pay men more'. Accessed online July 2018 at https://www.theguardian.com/money/2018/apr/04/gender-pay-gap-figures-reveal-eight-in-10-uk-firms-pay-men-more

Gullotta, T., Adams, G. and Markstrom, C. (2000) *The Adolescent Experience*, 4th edn. San Diego: Academic Press.

Guo, G. (2005) 'Twin Studies: What can they tell us about Nature and Nurture?' *Contexts 4* (3): 43–7.

Gullotta, T., Adams, G. and Markstrom, C. (2000) *The Adolescent Experience*, 4th edn. San Diego: Academic Press.

Gutmann, D.L. (1987) *Reclaimed Powers: Towards a New Psychology of Men and Women in Later Life.* New York: Basic Books.

Haddon, M. (2014) *The Curious Incident of the Dog in the Night-time.* London: Penguin Random House.

Halberstam, J. (2018) *Trans*: A Quick and Quirky Account of Gender Variability.* Oakland: University of California Press.

Halford, G.S. and Andrews, G. (2011) 'Information-processing models of cognitive development', in U. Goswami (ed.), *The Wiley-Blackwell Handbook of Childhood Cognitive Development*, 2nd edn. Chichester: Wiley-Blackwell, pp. 697–722.

Haney, C., Banks, C. and Zimbardo, P. (1973) 'Interpersonal dynamics in a simulated prison', *International Journal of Criminology and Penology 1*: 69–97.

Haralambos, M. and Holborn, M. (2013) *Sociology Themes and Perspectives*, 3rd edn. London: HarperCollins.

Hare, T.A., Tottenham, N., Galvan, A., Voss, H.U., Glover, G.H. and Casey, B.J. (2008) 'Biological substrates of emotional reactivity and regulation in adolescence during an emotional go-nogo task', *Biological Psychiatry 63* (10): 927–34.

Harlow, H. (1963) 'The maternal affectional system', in B.M. Foss (ed.), *Determinants of Human Behaviour*. London: Methuen, pp. 3–29.

Hassett, J., Siebert, E. and Wallen, K. (2008) 'Sex differences in rhesus monkey toy preferences parallel those of children', *Hormones and Behavior 54* (3): 359–64.

Healey, Lord, D. (2000) 'Golden oldies', *The Guardian* (*'Society'* supplement), 27 September, p. 3. Accessed online July 2018 at www.theguardian.com/society/2000/sep/27/guardiansocietysupplement

Heard, D.H. and Lake, B. (1986) 'The attachment dynamic in adult life', *British Journal of Psychiatry 149* (4): 430–38.

Herrnstein, R.L., Loveland, D. and Cable, C. (1976) 'Natural concepts in pigeons', *Journal of Experimental Psychology: Animal Behaviour Processes 2*: 285–302.

Higashida, N., Mitchell, D. and Yoshida, K. (2014) *The Reason I Jump*. London: Hodder and Stoughton.

Higgins, D., Bailey, S. and Pearce, J. (2005) 'Factors associated with functioning style and coping strategies of families with a child of autistic spectrum disorder', *Autism 9* (2): 125–37.

Hodapp, R.M. (1998) *Development and Disabilities: Intellectual, Sensory and Motor Impairments*. Cambridge: Cambridge University Press.

Hodapp, R.M. and Krasner, D.V. (1995) 'Families of children with disabilities: findings from a national sample of eighth-grade students', *Exceptionality 5*: 71–81.

Holmes, J. (2014) *John Bowlby and Attachment Theory*, 2nd edn. London: Routledge.

Holmes, T.H. and Rahe, R.H. (1967) 'The social readjustment rating scale', *Journal of Psychosomatic Research 11*: 213–18.

Holt, S., Buckley, H. and Whelan, S. (2008) 'The impact of exposure to domestic violence on children and young people: a review of the literature', *Child Abuse & Neglect 32* (8): 797–810.

Hopson, B. (1981) 'Response to the papers by Schlossberg, Bramner and Abrego', *Counselling Psychologist 9* (2): 36 ff.

Howe, D. (1995) *Attachment Theory for Social Work Practice*. London: Macmillan.

Howe, D. (2005) *Child Abuse and Neglect: Attachment, Development and Intervention*. Basingstoke: Palgrave Macmillan.

Howe, D. (2011) *Attachment Across the Lifecourse*. Basingstoke: Palgrave Macmillan.

Howe, D., Brandon, M., Hinings, D. and Schofield, G. (1999) *Attachment Theory, Child Maltreatment and Family Support*. London: Macmillan.

Howells, G. (1997) 'A general practice perspective', in J. O'Hara and A. Sperlinger (eds), *Adults with Learning Disabilities*. Chichester: Wiley, pp. 61–79.

Hunt, S.J. (2005) *The Life Course: A Sociological Introduction*. Basingstoke: Palgrave Macmillan.

Huxley, A. (2014 [1932]) *Brave New World*. London: Vintage Classics.

Iwaniec, D. (2004) *Children who Fail to Thrive: A Practice Guide*. Chichester: Wiley.

Jacobs, M. (2003) *Sigmund Freud*. London: Sage.

Jaques, E. (1965) 'Death and the mid-life crisis', *International Journal of Psychoanalysis 46*: 502–14.

Jensen, G.D. and Tolman, C.W. (1962) 'Mother–infant relationship in the monkey, *Macaca Nemestrina*: the effect of brief separation and mother–infant specificity', *Journal of Comparative Physiological Psychology 55*: 131–6.

Joseph Rowntree Foundation (2017), *Poverty and Ethnicity in the Labour Market*. Accessed online July 2018 at https://www.jrf.org.uk/report/poverty-ethnicity-labour-market

Juffer, F. and Bakermans-Kranenberg, M.J. (2008) *Promoting Positive Parenting: An Attachment-based Intervention*. London: Psychology Press.

Jung, C. (1995 [1961]) *Memories, Dreams, Reflections*. London: Fontana.

Kahn, S., Zimmerman, G., Csikszentmihalyi, M. and Getzels, J.W. (1985) 'Relations between identity in young adulthood and intimacy at mid-life', *Journal of Personality and Social Psychology 9*: 117–26.

Kail, R. (2004) 'Cognitive development includes global and domain-specific processes', *Merrill-Palmer Quarterly 50* (4): 445–55.

Kalish, R.A. (1985) 'The social context of death and dying', in R.H. Binstock and E. Shanas (eds), *Handbook of Ageing and the Social Sciences*. New York: Van Nostrand Reinhold, pp. 149–70.

Kalish, R.A. and Reynolds, D.K. (1976) *Death and Ethnicity: A Psychocultural Study*. Los Angeles: University of Southern California Press.

Karmiloff-Smith, A. (1995) *Beyond Modularity*. Cambridge, MA: MIT Press.

Kastenbaum, R. and Alsenburg, R. (1976) *The Psychology of Death*. New York: Springer.

Kearl, M. (1989) *Endings: A Sociology of Death and Dying*. Oxford: Oxford University Press.

Kielhofner, G. (2008) *Model of Human Occupation: Theory and Application*. Baltimore, MD: Lippincott Williams and Wilkins.

Kierkegaard, S. (2001 [1843]) *The Kierkegaard Reader*. Edited by J. Chamberlain and J. Rée. Oxford: Blackwell.

Klein, M. (1975 [1933]) 'The early development of conscience in the child', in M. Klein, *Love, Guilt and Reparation and Other Works*. London: The Hogarth Press, pp. 248–57.

Klein, M. (1986 [1946]) *The Selected Melanie Klein*. Edited by J. Mitchell. Harmondsworth: Penguin.

Kobak, R., Cassidy, J. and Ziv, Y. (2004) 'Attachment related trauma and Post-traumatic Stress Disorder', in W.S. Rholes and J.A. Simpson (eds), *Adult Attachment: Theory, Research and Clinical Implications*. New York: Guilford Press, pp. 388–407.

Kohlberg, L. (1980) 'Stages of moral development as a basis for education', in B. Munsey (ed.), *Moral Development, Moral Education and Kohlberg*. Birmingham, AL: Religious Education Press.

Kohli, M. (1986) 'The world we forgot: a historical review of the life course', in V. Marshall (ed.), *Later Life: The Social Psychology of Aging*. London: Sage, pp. 271–303.

Kroger, J. (2000) *Identity Development: Adolescence Through Adulthood*. London: Sage.

Kroger, J. (2004) *Identity in Adolescence: The Balance Between Self and Other*, 3rd edn. London: Routledge.

Kroger, J. and Marcia, J. (2011) 'The identity statuses: origins, meanings and interpretations', in S.J. Schwartz, K. Luyckx and V.L. Vignoles (eds), *Handbook of Identity Theory and Research*. London: Springer, pp. 603–28.

Kübler-Ross, E. (1970) *On Death and Dying*. London: Tavistock.

Künemund, H. and Kolland, F. (2007) 'Work and retirement', in J. Bond, S. Peace, F. Dittman-Kohli and G. Westerhof (eds), *Ageing in Society*, 3rd edn. London: Sage, pp. 167–85.

Kuster, A. (2010) 'Deaf utopias? Reviewing the sociocultural literature on the world's "Martha's Vineyard Situations",' *Journal of Deaf Studies and Deaf Education 15* (1): 3–16.

L'Engle, K., Brown, J. and Kenneavy, K. (2006) 'The mass media are an important context for adolescents' sexual behavior', *Journal of Adolescent Health 38* (3): 186–92.

Laflin, M., Wang, J. and Barry, M. (2008) 'A longitudinal study of adolescent transition from virgin to nonvirgin status', *Journal of Adolescent Health 42* (3): 228–36.

Langer, E. (1983) *The Psychology of Control*. London: Sage.

Langlois, J.H. and Downs, A.C. (1980) 'Mothers, fathers and peers as socialization agents of sex-typed play behaviors in young children', *Child Development 51*: 1237–47.

Laslett, P. (1989) *A Fresh Map of Life*. London: Weidenfeld & Nicolson.

Lazarus, R.S. (1993) 'Coping theory and research: past, present and future', *Psychosomatic Medicine 55*: 234–47.

Lazarus, R.S. and Folkman, S. (1984) *Stress, Appraisal and Coping*. New York: Springer.

Leaper, C. and Friedman, C.K. (2007) 'The socialisation of gender', in J.E. Grusec and P.D. Hastings (eds), *Handbook of Socialisation: Theory and Research*. New York: Guilford Press, pp. 561–87.

Lerner, J.V., Phelps, E., Forman, Y. and Bowers, P. (2009) 'Positive youth development', in R.M. Lerner and L. Steinberg (eds), *Handbook of Adolescent Psychology*. Hoboken, NJ: Wiley, pp. 524–58.

Levinson, D. (1978) *The Seasons of a Man's Life*. New York: Ballantine.

Levinson, D. and Levinson, J. (1996) *The Seasons of a Woman's Life*. New York: Knopf.

Lewin, K. (1935) *A Dynamic Theory of Personality*. New York: McGraw-Hill.

Lewis, V. (2003) *Development and Disability*, 2nd edn. Oxford: Blackwell.

Lollar, D.J. (1994) *Social Development and the Person with Spina Bifida*. Washington, DC: Spina Bifida Association of America.

Lowenthal, M., Thurnher, M. and Chiriboga, D. (1975) *Four Stages of Life: A Comparative Study of Women and Men Facing Transitions*. San Francisco: Jossey-Bass.

Maccoby, E. and Martin, J. (1983) 'Socialisation in the context of the family: parent–child interaction', in E. Hetherington (ed.), *Handbook of Child Psychology: Socialization, Personality and Social Development Vol IV*, 4th edn. New York: Wiley.

MacPherson, Sir W. (1999) *The Stephen Lawrence Inquiry*. London: Stationery Office.

Main, M. and Goldwyn, R. (1994) 'Adult attachment rating and classification systems', version 6.0, unpublished manuscript, University of California at Berkeley.

Main, M. and Hesse, E. (1990) 'Parents' unresolved traumatic experiences are related to infant disorganised attachment status: is frightened and/or frightening parental behaviour the linking mechanism?', in M.T. Greenberg, D. Cicchetti and E.M. Cummings (eds), *Attachment in the Pre-school Years: Theory, Research and Intervention*. Chicago: University of Chicago Press, pp. 161–84.

Mallory, M. (1984) 'Longitudinal analysis of ego identity status', unpublished doctoral dissertation, University of California, Davis.

Marcia, J. (1966) 'Development and validation of ego identity status', *Journal of Personality and Social Psychology 3*: 551–8.

Marcoen, A., Coleman, P. and O'Hanlon, A. (2007) 'Psychological ageing', in J. Bond, S. Peace, F. Dittman-Kohli and G. Westerhof (eds), *Ageing in Society*, 3rd edn. London: Sage, pp. 38–67.

Mareschal, D., Johnson, M.H., Sirois, S., Spratling, M.W., Thomas, M.D.C. and Westermann, G. (2007). *Neuroconstructivism: How the Brain Constructs Cognition*. Oxford: Oxford University Press.

Marx, K. (1986 [1845]) Extract from *The German Ideology*, in J. Elster (ed.), *Karl Marx: A Reader*. Cambridge: Cambridge University Press.

Masson, J. (2003) *The Assault on Truth: Freud's Suppression of the Seduction Theory*. New York: Ballantine Books.

McAdams, D. (1997) *Stories We Live By: Personal Myths and the Making of the Self*. New York: Guilford Press.

McAdams, D. (2005) *Redemptive Self: Stories Americans Live by*. Cary, NC: Oxford University Press.

McAdams, D. (2010) 'Personality development: continuity and change over the life course', *Annual Review of Psychology 61* (1): 517–42.

McCrae, R.R. and Costa, P.T. (2003) *Personality in Adulthood: A Five-Factor Theory Perspective*, 2nd edn. New York: Guilford Press.

McGoldrick, M., Garcia Preto, N. and Carter, B. (2016a) 'The life cycle in its changing context: individual, family and social perspectives', in M. McGoldrick, N. Garcia Preto and B. Carter (eds), *The Expanding Family Life Cycle: Individual, Family and Social Perspectives*, 5th edn. Boston: Pearson, pp. 1–62.

McGoldrick, M., Petkov, B. and Carter, B. (2016b) 'Becoming parents: the family with children', in M. McGoldrick, N. Garcia Preto and B. Carter (eds), *The Expanding Family Life Cycle: Individual, Family and Social Perspectives*, 5th edn. Boston: Pearson, pp. 280–303.

McGoldrick, M., Garcia Preto, N. and Carter, B. (eds) (2016c) *The Expanding Family Life Cycle: Individual, Family and Social Perspectives*, 5th edn. Boston: Pearson.

McLuhan, M. (1962) *The Gutenberg Galaxy: The Making of Typographic Man*. Toronto: University of Toronto Press.

Meltzer, D., McWilliams, B., Brayne, C. and Johnson, T. (2000) 'Profile of disability in elderly people: estimates from a longitudinal study', *British Medical Journal 318*: 1108–11.

Meristo, M., Falkman, K., Hjelmquist, E., Tedoldi, M., Surian, L. and Siegal, M. (2007) 'Language access and theory of mind reasoning: evidence from deaf children in bilingual and oralist environments', *Developmental Psychology 43* (5): 1156–69.

Mind (2013) 'Postnatal depression'. Accessed online July 2018 at www.mind.org.uk/ information-support/types-of-mental-health-problems/postnatal-depression

Minnes, P. (1988) 'Family stress associated with a developmentally handicapped child', *International Review of Research on Mental Retardation 15*: 195–226.

Mitchell, J. (2003) *Siblings*. Cambridge: Polity Press.

Moore, S. and Rosenthal, D. (2006) *Sexuality in Adolescence: Current Trends*, 2nd edn. Hove: Routledge.

Murray Parkes, C. (2006) *Love and Loss*. London: Routledge.

Murray Parkes, C. and Prigerson, H.G. (2010) *Bereavement: Studies of Grief in Adult Life*. London: Penguin.

Music, G. (2011) *Nurturing Natures: Attachment and Children's Emotional, Sociocultural and Brain Development*. Hove: Psychology Press.

National Autistic Society. Accessed online July 2018 at http://www.autism.org.uk/

National Scientific Council on the Developing Child (2010). Working paper 10: Early experiences can alter gene expression and affect long-term development, at http:// developingchild.harvard.edu/wp-content/uploads/2010/05/Early-Experiences-Can-Alter-Gene-Expression-and-Affect-Long-Term-Development.pdf (Accessed online July, 2018).

Neugarten, B.L., Moore, J.W. and Lowe, J.C. (1965) 'Age norms, age constraints and adult socialisation', *American Journal of Sociology 70*: 710–17.

Neugarten, B.L., Wood, V., Kraines, R.J. and Loomis, B. (1963) 'Women's attitudes towards the menopause', *Vita Humana 6*: 140–51.

Obholzer, A. (1994) *The Unconscious at Work*. London: Routledge.

OECD (2018) *A Broken Social Elevator? How to Promote Social Mobility*. Paris: OECD. Accessed online July 2018 at http://www.oecd.org/social/soc/Social-mobility-2018-Overview-MainFindings.pdf

ONS (Office of National Statistics) (2013) *Older People Divorcing, 2011*. Accessed online July 2018 at www.ons.gov.uk/ons/rel/family-demography/older-people-divorcing/2011/index.html

ONS (Office of National Statistics) (2017a) *Statistical Bulletin: Births in England and Wales: 2016*. Accessed online, April 2018, at https://www.ons.gov.uk/peoplepopulationandcommunity/birthsdeathsandmarriages/livebirths/bulletins/birthsummarytablesenglandandwales/2016ONS (Office of National Statistics)

ONS (2017b) *Deaths Registered in England and Wales (Series DR)* [Dataset], 2016. Accessed online April 2018, at https://www.ons.gov.uk/peoplepopulationandcommunity/birthsdeathsandmarriages/deaths/bulletins/deathsregistrationsummarytables/2016

Pakulski, J. and Waters, M. (1996) *The Death of Class*. London: Sage.

Pantev, C., Roberts, L.E., Schultz, M., Engelien, A. and Ross, B. (2001) 'Timbre-specific enhancement of auditory cortical representations in musicians', *NeuroReport 12* (1): 169–74.

Peace, S., Dittman-Kholi, F., Westerhof, G. and Bond, J. (2007) 'The ageing world', in J. Bond, S. Peace, F. Dittman-Kohli and G. Westerhof (eds), *Ageing in Society*, 3rd edn. London: Sage, pp. 1–14.

Peace, S., Holland, C. and Kellaher, L. (2006) *Environment and Identity in Later Life*. Maidenhead: Open University Press.

Perosa, L.M., Perosa, S.L. and Tam, H.P. (1996) 'The contribution of family structure and differentiation to identity development in females', *Journal of Youth and Adolescence 25*: 817–37.

Perry, D. and Bussey, K. (1979) 'The social learning theory of sex difference: imitation is alive and well', *Journal of Personality and Social Psychology 37*: 1699–712.

Petitto, L. and Marentette, P.F. (1991) 'Babbling in the manual mode: evidence for the ontogeny of language', *Science 251*: 1493–6.

Phillips, C. and Bowling, B. (2002) 'Racism, ethnicity, crime and criminal justice', in M. Maguire, R. Morgan and R. Reiner (eds), *The Oxford Handbook of Criminology*, 3rd edn. Oxford: Oxford University Press.

Phinney, J.S. (1989) 'Stages of ethnic identity development in minority group adolescents', *Journal of Early Adolescence 9*: 34–49.

Phinney, J.S. (1993) 'A three-stage model of ethnic identity development', in G.P. Knight and M.E. Bernal (eds), *Ethnic Identity, Formation and Transmission Among Hispanics and Other Minorities*. Albany, NY: State University of New York Press, pp. 61–79.

Phinney, J.S. and Alipuria, L.L. (1990) 'Ethnic identity in college students from four ethnic groups', *Journal of Adolescence 13*: 171–83.

Piaget, J. (1930) *The Child's Conception of Physical Causality*. London: Routledge.

Piaget, J., Montangero, J. and Billeter, J. (1977) 'Les correlats', in *L'Abstraction réfléchissante*. Paris: Presses Universitaires de France.

Pierce, W.D. and Cheney, C.D. (2004) *Behavior Analysis and Learning*, 3rd edn. Mahwah, NJ: Lawrence Erlbaum Associates.

Pinker, S. (2007) *The Language Instinct*. New York: HarperCollins.

Pinkstinks (2008) Accessed online April 2018 at www.pinkstinks.org.uk

Plato (1973) *Phaedrus and Letters VII and VIII* (trans. Walter Hamilton). Harmondsworth: Penguin.

Plato (1998) *Cratylus* (trans. C.D.C. Reeve). Cambridge: Hackett.

Polivy, J., Herman, C.P., Mills, J. and Wheeler, H. (2003) 'Eating disorders in adolescence', in G. Adams and M. Berzonsky (eds), *Blackwell Handbook of Adolescence*. Oxford: Blackwell, pp. 523–49.

Powell, R., Symbaluk, D. and Macdonald, S. (2002) *Introduction to Learning and Behaviour*. Belmont, CA: Wadsworth.

Quinn, P. (1998) *Understanding Disability – A Lifespan Approach*. London: Sage.

Reay, D., David, M.E. and Ball, S. (2005) *Degrees of Choice: Class, Race, Gender and Higher Education*. Stoke-on-Trent: Trentham Books.

Reber, R. (2004) 'Availability', in R. Pohl (ed.), *Cognitive Illusions*. New York: Psychology Press, pp. 147–64.

Ridley, M. (2004) *Nature via Nurture: Genes, Experience and What Makes us Human*. London: Harper Perennial.

Riesz, E. (2004) 'Loss and transitions: a 30-year perspective on life with a child who has Down Syndrome', *Journal of Loss and Trauma 9* (4): 371–82.

Robertson, J. and Bowlby, J. (1952) 'Responses of young children to separation from their mothers', *Courier of the International Children's Centre 2*: 131–42.

Rosenbaum, J.E. (2006) 'Reborn a virgin: adolescents' retracting of virginity pledges and sexual histories', *American Journal of Public Health 96*: 1078–103.

Rosenthal, R. and Jacobson, L. (1968) *Pygmalion in the Classroom*. New York: Holt, Rinehart and Winston.

Rutter, M. (1981) *Maternal Deprivation Reassessed*, 2nd edn. Harmondsworth: Penguin.

Rutter, M. and the English and Romanian Adoptees Study Team (1998) 'Developmental catch-up, and deficit, following adoption after severe global early privation', *Journal of Child Psychology and Psychiatry 39* (4): 465–76.

Ryan, R.M. and Lynch, J.H. (1989) 'Emotional autonomy versus detachment: revisiting the vicissitudes of adolescence and young adulthood', *Child Development 60*: 340–56.

Rycroft, C. (1995) *A Critical Dictionary of Psychoanalysis*, 2nd edn. London: Penguin.

Sabatier, C. (2008) 'Ethnic and national identity among second-generation immigrant adolescents in France: the role of social context and family', *Journal of Adolescence 31*: 185–205.

Sable, P. (1989) 'Attachment, anxiety and loss of husband', *American Journal of Orthopsychiatry 59* (4): 550–56.

Sachweh, S. (1998) 'Granny darling's puppies: secondary babytalk in German nursing homes for the aged', *Journal of Applied Communication Research 26*: 52–65.

Santrock, J.W. (2012) *Adolescence*, 14th edn. New York: McGraw Hill.

Sartre, J.-P. (2001 [1943]) *Basic Writings* (edited by Stephen Priest). London: Routledge.

Savage, M., Bagnall, G. and Longhurst, B. (2001) 'Ordinary, ambivalent and defensive: class identities in the northwest of England', *Sociology 35* (4): 875–92.

Savin-Williams, R.C. (2011) 'Identity development among sexual minority youth', in S.J. Schwartz, K. Luyckx and V.L. Vignoles (eds), *Handbook of Identity Theory and Research*. London: Springer, pp. 671–89.

Savin-Williams, R.C. and Ream, G.L. (2007) 'Prevalence and stability of sexual orientation components during adolescence and young adulthood', *Archives of Sexual Behavior 36*: 385–94.

Sayers, J. (1998) *Boy Crazy*. London: Routledge.

Schindler, A., Thomasius, R., Sack, P.-M., Gemeinhardt, B., Küstner, U. and Eckert, J. (2005) 'Attachment and substance abuse disorders', *Attachment and Human Development 7* (3): 207–28.

Schofield, G. and Beek, M. (2006) *Attachment Handbook for Foster Care and Adoption*. London: BAAF.

Schore, A. (2000) 'Attachment and the regulation of the right brain', *Attachment and Human Development 2* (1): 23–47.

Schore, A. (2001) 'Effects of a secure attachment relationship on right brain development, affect regulation and infant mental health', *Infant Mental Health Journal 22* (1–2): 7–66.

Schore, J.R. and Schore, A.N. (2008) 'Modern attachment theory: the central role of affect regulation in development and treatment', *Clinical Social Work Journal 36*: 9–20.

Schut, H., Stroebe, M., de Keijser, J. and van den Brout, J. (1997) 'Intervention for the bereaved: gender differences in the efficacy of grief counselling', *British Journal of Clinical Psychology 36*: 63–72.

Seale, C. (1998) *Constructing Death: The Sociology of Dying and Bereavement*. Cambridge: Cambridge University Press.

Segal, J. (2004) *Melanie Klein*, 2nd edn. London: Sage.

Seigal, D.J. (1999) *The Developing Mind: Towards a Neurobiology of Interpersonal Experience*. New York: Guilford Press.

Seligman, M. (1975) *Helplessness: On Depression, Development and Death*. San Francisco: Freeman.

Sempik, J., Ward, H. and Darker, I. (2008) 'Emotional and behavioural difficulties of children and young people at entry into care', *Clinical Child Psychology and Psychiatry 13* (2): 221–33.

Seroczynski, A., Jacquez, F. and Cole, D. (2003) 'Depression and suicide during adolescence', in G. Adams and M. Berzonsky (eds), *Blackwell Handbook of Adolescence*. Oxford: Blackwell, pp. 550–72.

Shakespeare, T. (2014) *Disability Rights and Wrongs Revisited*, 2nd edn. Abingdon: Routledge.

Shakespeare, W. (2008 [1599]) 'As you like it', in S. Greenblatt, W. Cohen, J. Howard and K. Maus (eds), *The Norton Shakespeare*, 2nd edn. New York: Norton.

Sidell, M. (1993) 'Death, dying and bereavement', in J. Bond, P. Coleman and S. Peace (eds), *Ageing in Society*, 2nd edn. London: Sage, pp. 151–79.

Skinner, B.F. (1953) *Science and Human Behaviour*. New York: Macmillan.

Skinner, B.F. (1960) 'Pigeons in a pelican', *American Psychologist 15*: 28–37.

Skinner, B.F. (1974) *About Behaviorism*. London: Jonathan Cape.

Solnit, A. and Stark, M. (1961) 'Mourning and the birth of a defective child', *Psychoanalytic Study of the Child 16*: 523–37.

Sophocles (1984) *The Theban Plays* (trans. Robert Fagles). Harmondsworth: Penguin.

Soygal, R. (2008) *The Tibetan Book of Living and Dying*. London: Rider.

Spear, L. (2000) 'The adolescent brain and age-related behavioral manifestations', *Neuroscience and Biobehavioral Reviews 24* (4): 417–63.

Sperlinger, A. (1997) 'Introduction', in J. O'Hara and A. Sperlinger (eds), *Adults With Learning Disabilities*. Chichester: Wiley, pp. 3–16.

Sprott, W.J.H. (1958) *Human Groups*. Harmondsworth: Penguin.

Steinberg, L. and Silverberg, S.B. (1986) 'The vicissitudes of autonomy in early adolescence', *Child Development 57*: 841–51.

Storr, A. (1973) *Jung*. London: Fontana.

Stroebe, M. and Schut, H. (1999) 'The dual process model of coping with bereavement', *Death Studies 23*: 197–224.

Stroebe, M. and Schut, H. (2001) 'Models of coping with bereavement: a review', in M.S. Stroebe, R.O. Hansson, W. Stroebe and H. Schut (eds), *Handbook of Bereavement Research*. Washington: American Psychological Association.

Stuart-Hamilton, I. (2012) *The Psychology of Ageing: An Introduction*, 5th edn. London: Jessica Kingsley.

Sugarman, L. (2001) *Life-Span Development: Frameworks, Accounts and Strategies*, 2nd edn. Hove: Psychology Press.

Sullivan, P. and Knutson, J. (2000) 'Maltreatment and disabilities: a population-based epidemiological study', *Child Abuse & Neglect 24* (10): 1257–73.

Svanberg, J. (2018) *The Psychology of Addiction*. Abingdon: Routledge.

Taylor, L. (2005) *Introducing Cognitive Development*. Hove: Psychology Press.

Thane, P. (2003) 'Social histories of old age and aging', *Journal of Social History 37* (1): 93–111.

Thatcher, M., interviewed by Douglas Keays (1987) 'Aids, education and the year 2000!', *Woman's Own*, 31 October, pp. 8–10.

Thomas, D. (1973) 'Do not go gentle into that good night', in P. Larkin (ed.), *The Oxford Book of Twentieth Century English Verse*. Oxford: Clarendon Press, p. 474.

Thompson, N. (2016) *Anti-discriminatory Practice*, 6th edn. London: Palgrave.

Tupuola, A.M. (1993) 'Critical analysis of adolescent development – a Samoan woman's perspective', unpublished masters thesis, cited by Kroger (2004).

Umaña-Taylor, A.J. (2011) 'Ethnic identity', in S.J. Schwartz, K. Luyckx and V.L. Vignoles (eds), *Handbook of Identity Theory and Research*. London: Springer, pp. 791–809.

UN (2006) *Convention on the Rights of Persons with Disabilities*. Accessed online 1 July 2018 at http://www.un.org/disabilities/documents/convention/convoptprot-e.pdf

UPIAS (1976) *Fundamental Principles of Disability*. London: Union of the Physically Impaired Against Segregation.

Victor, C. (2005) *The Social Context of Ageing: A Textbook of Gerontology*. London: Routledge.

von Bertalanffy, L. (1971) *General System Theory: Foundations, Development, Application*. London: Allen Lane.

Vygotsky, L.S. (1962) *Thought and Language*. New York: Wiley.

Vygotsky, L.S. (1978) *Mind in Society*. Cambridge, MA: Harvard University Press.

Walker, D. (2002) 'New breed of middle class closes ranks: social mobility suffers as poorer children kept off ladder', *Guardian*, 18 May. Accessed online, July 2015 at www.theguardian.com/uk/2002/may/18/britishidentity.socialsciences

Walker, S. (1984) *Learning Theory and Behaviour Modification*. London: Methuen.

Walter, T. (1994) *The Revival of Death*. London: Routledge.

Warren, D.H. (1994) *Blindness and Children: An Individual Differences Approach*. Cambridge: Cambridge University Press.

Watson, J.B. (1931) *Behaviourism*, 2nd edn. London: Kegan Paul, Trench and Trubner.

Watson, L. (2010) 'Enuresis', *InnovAit 3* (2): 91–4.

Webster, R. (2005) *Why Freud Was Wrong: Sin, Science and Psychoanalysis*, 3rd edn. Oxford: Orwell Press.

Westbrook, D., Kennerley, H. and Kirk, J. (2011) *An Introduction to Cognitive Behaviour Therapy*, 2nd edn. London: Sage.

Westergaard, J. (1995) *Who Gets What? The Hardening of Class Inequality on the Late Twentieth Century*. Cambridge: Polity Press.

Westerhof, G. and Tulle, E. (2007) 'Meanings of ageing and old age: discursive contexts, social attitudes and personal identities', in J. Bond, S. Peace, F. Dittman-Kohli and G. Westerhof (eds), *Ageing in Society*, 3rd edn. London: Sage, pp. 235–54.

Westermann, G., Thomas, M.S.C. and Karmiloff-Smith, A. (2011) 'Neuroconstructivism', in U. Goswami (ed.), *The Wiley-Blackwell Handbook of Childhood Cognitive Development*, 2nd edn. Chichester: Wiley-Blackwell, pp. 723–48.

Whitaker, D.J. and Miller, K.S. (2000) 'Parent–adolescent discussions about sex and condoms: impact on peer influences of sexual risk behaviour', *Journal of Adolescent Research 15* (2): 251–73.

Whitbourne, S.K. (1996) *The Aging Individual: Physical and Psychological Perspectives*. New York: Springer-Verlag.

White, J., Essex, S. and O'Reilly, P. (1993) 'Family therapy, systemic thinking and child protection', in J. Carpenter and A. Treacher (eds), *Using Family Therapy in the 90s*. Oxford: Blackwell, pp. 57–86.

WHO (2011) *World Report on Disability*. Accessed online June 2018 at whqlibdoc.who.int/publications/2011/9789240685215_eng.pdf?ua=1

Wilkinson, R.G. and Pickett, K. (2010) *The Spirit Level*. London: Penguin.

Willemsen, E.W. and Waterman, K.K. (1991) 'Ego identity status and family environment: a correlational study', *Psychological Reports 69*: 1203–12.

Windle, M., Miller-Tutzauer, C. and Domenico, D. (2000) 'Adolescence, suicidal behaviour and risky activities among adolescents', in G. Adams (ed.), *Adolescent Development: The Essential Readings*. Oxford: Blackwell, pp. 261–74.

Wink, P. and Scott, J. (2005) 'Does religiousness buffer against the fear of death and dying in late adulthood? Findings from a longitudinal study', *Journal of Gerontology 60B* (4): 207–14.

Winnicott, D. (1975 [1958]) *Through Paediatrics to Psychoanalysis*. London: Karnac.

Winnicott, D.W. (2005 [1971]) *Playing and Reality*, 2nd edn. London: Tavistock/Routledge.

Wiseman, M. and Davidson, S. (2012) 'Problems with binary gender discourse: Using context to promote flexibility and connection in gender identity', *Clinical Child Psychology and Psychiatry 17* (4): 528–37.

Wolfensberger, W. (1998) *A Brief Introduction to Social Role Valorization*. Syracuse, NY: Training Institute for Human Services, Syracuse University.

Wood, D., Bruner, J. and Ross, G. (1976) 'The role of tutoring in problem solving', *Journal of Child Psychology and Psychiatry 17*: 89–100.

Wren, B. (2014) 'Thinking postmodern and practising in the enlightenment: Managing uncertainty in the treatment of children and adolescents', *Feminism and Psychology 24* (2): 271–91.

Young Children in Brief Separation 1967–71, film, Robertson Films, London. Available on DVD from Concord Media, Ipswich.

Young, M. and Cullen, L. (1996) *A Good Death: Conversations with East Londoners*. London: Routledge.

INDEX